HELL-BENT

HELL-BENT

THE CRAZY TRUTH ABOUT THE "WIN OR ELSE" DALLAS COWBOYS

SKIP BAYLESS

HarperCollinsPublishers

HarperCollins books may be purchased for educational, business, or sales promotional use. For information please write: Special Markets Department, HarperCollins Publishers, Inc., 10 East 53rd Street, New York, NY 10022.

Designed by Alma Hochhauser Orenstein

Library of Congress Cataloging-in-Publication Data

Bayless, Skip.
    Hell-bent : the crazy truth about the "win or else" Dallas Cowboys / Skip Bayless.
      p.   cm.
    ISBN 0-06-018648-8
    1. Dallas Cowboys (Football Team) I. Title.
GV956.D3B394   1996
796.332'64'097642812—dc20   96-24456

96 97 98 99 00 ❖/HC 10 9 8 7 6 5 4 3

To Amy, who never fails on fourth-and-one

CONTENTS

Acknowledgments ix
The Blind Men xi

1 Tortured Soul 1
2 Of Sons and Moonshine 13
3 Tragic Magic 29
4 The Man Who Fired Tom Landry 45
5 Betrayal 55
6 Super Ego 66
7 Enemy Territory 82
8 Battle Lines 99
9 Dehydration 116
10 Cancer 132
11 Planet Jerry 147
12 Break Love 165
13 Family Secrets 183
14 Earthquake 203
15 The N-Word 220
16 Bozo 234
17 The Luckiest SOB Ever 248
18 Relief 267
19 Masters of the Universe 283

Photographs follow page 146.

ACKNOWLEDGMENTS

I can only imagine how difficult it is to be the mother of three children under five years old. I don't care to imagine how difficult it is to deal with me on a daily basis while I'm writing a book. For about three months Shari Wenk deftly juggled four children, including me. Calling Shari my agent doesn't begin to describe how much she has done for me. She is also a talented editor, and without her talent I would have been lost.

Everything about *Hell-bent* was highly unusual, from the subject matter to the editing. My one disappointment was that I didn't get a chance to work with Rick Horgan, the project's original editor. But fate blessed me with Adrian Zackheim, who edited Barry Switzer's bestselling *Bootlegger's Boy*. What were the odds? Though thrown into the game with the clock running out, Adrian did a phenomenal job of running the two-minute offense that was our production schedule. Thanks also to copy editor Joe McKeown for the thoughtful, thorough job he did. Joe often saved me from myself—as did HarperCollins attorney Matthew Martin, who (if possible) made a legal review enjoyable.

But this book, start to finish, was also edited by Shari Wenk. Without her hours of suggestions, I wouldn't be nearly as proud of the final product. Thanks especially to her husband, Keith, for allowing the many interruptions.

Thanks to Tony Barnard for letting me borrow his computer

and stay on schedule after my ex-computer couldn't take the pressure and quit on me.

Thanks to *The Insider*'s David Vaughn for his friendship and to *The Insider*'s Mickey Spagnola for his insight.

Thanks to Layne Murdoch for his spectacular photography. Thanks to Paul Schoonover for his legal expertise and integrity. Thanks to Larry North, for sharing the workouts that saved my sanity.

Special relationships: Joe Valerio, Jeff Neuman, Bruce Scott, Grant Burget, Craig Humphreys, Skip Hollandsworth, Nancy Nichols Murphy, Dextor Clinkscale, and Pat Toomay.

Thanks to Natalie Merchant and 10,000 Maniacs for "These Are Days," which I listened to at least 10,000 times as I wrote. These were days.

And thanks to Michael Chabon for *The Mysteries of Pittsburgh* and *Wonder Boys,* which inspired and humbled me each night at about 3 A.M. I too suffer from the Midnight Disease, Michael—a glorious affliction.

THE BLIND MEN

I t's crazy now, as I'm trying to write this book. One side calls, then the other. Troy Aikman calls, then Barry Switzer. Back and forth. Troy's Boys call, then members of Switzer's "Oklahoma Mafia."

I call Jerry Jones.

He calls me.

Troy says that Barry says that Troy said that Jerry said that Barry said . . .

Very crazy.

And to think, just after the 1995 Dallas Cowboys season ended, I wondered if Aikman, Switzer, or Jones would talk about the issues in this book. Now everyone has talked and talked until the lines blur between truth and fiction, right and wrong, sanity and insanity.

As I've told them all, I'm interested only in the truth as best I can know and understand it. As much as I like Aikman, Switzer, and Jones, I've tried to get to know them without becoming too close. I'm trying—and perhaps failing—to write objectively about three of the most complex, fascinating humans I've had the privilege of knowing.

These three are at the epicenter of the most intriguing period of the most intriguing team in sports history. I've followed the Cowboys since I was a kid growing up in Oklahoma City. My parents took me to a Cowboys game at the Cotton Bowl soon after the team was born in 1960, and I was hooked. So many great players, great characters, great stories. I didn't write books on the Cowboys called *God's Coach* and *The Boys*; they wrote themselves.

Now *Hell-bent* has hold of my soul and it won't let go. Some days, I think I'm the one who has gone a little crazy. Some days . . .

Don Beck is calling, and I'm calling Beck, the author, newspaper columnist, and psychologist who has studied the Cowboys and their coaches. The more I'm caught in the Aikman-Switzer cross fire, the more Beck advises I "jettison" myself. "Just go and write your book," says Beck. "Right now, you're dealing with three fragile, undependable systems."

Aikman's. Switzer's. Jones's.

I have met with Aikman, at his request. He has opened the conversation by telling me that (1) he did not call receiver Kevin Williams the n-word and (2) he is not gay.

Completely crazy.

I've asked Troy Aikman if he took dives in two losses to Washington, coached by his big-brother figure, Norv Turner.

Insane.

Michael Irvin has been indicted. Why am I not surprised? Larry Brown has been signed by the Oakland Raiders for $2.5 million a year. Why am I shocked? Headline in the April 8 issue of *Sports Illustrated:* "If This Is America's Team, Woe Is America." Why am I rolling my eyes?

At Jones's request, I've met with him at his new mansion in Highland Park. As in the Pizza Hut commercial he did with Deion Sanders, Jones says he wants "both"—a happy coach and a happy quarterback.

I tell him that's just not possible.

Now another insider is calling and suggesting he might name a future child after me. He also asks that I leave him out of this book.

Now the coach is calling. He's mad at me, and he should be. The quarterback has told the coach that I told the quarterback that the coach told me some things the coach did not tell me. Did the quarterback misunderstand me? Hear only what he wanted to hear?

I feel for the quarterback.

I feel for the coach.

"Go write your book," says Beck.

I am writing about how—somehow—the Dallas Cowboys are in a position to become the "Team of the Nineties." I'm writing about talent and luck, loyalty and betrayal, denial and paranoia, love and money, genius and naiveté, image and reality, Jerry and Jimmy,

Jimmy and Troy, Troy and Norv, Troy and Barry, Barry and Larry, Larry and Jerry and Barry . . .

I am writing about the most unbelievable story I've run across in twenty-five years of journalism.

I apologize in advance for the foul language. Above all, I want this to be real. The Dallas Cowboys are not cartoon superheroes flashing across your TV screen. Their achievements are even more unbelievable because the players, coaches, and owner are all so painfully human.

I apologize, too, if I occasionally get in the way of the story. Too often, I was part of it. Several of Switzer's close friends are friends of mine. Leigh Steinberg, Aikman's agent, is a close friend of mine. Perhaps I let myself get too close to Larry Lacewell, John Blake, Norv Turner, and several others. These relationships allowed me unusual insights and caused highly unusual complications. This story is a "pickup sticks" of crossed paths and coincidences dating back to rural Arkansas in the early fifties. Sometimes I was entangled.

That's why, as I write, I keep remembering an ancient allegory suggested to me by Don Beck. It's about six blind men who heard that the prince had a new elephant at his palace. They had never been around an elephant and wanted to experience one, so they went to the palace, where the guards allowed them to touch the elephant. One blind man touched the elephant's side, which reminded him of a wall. The second took hold of the trunk, which was like a snake. The third grabbed an ivory tusk, which felt like a spear. The fourth held on to a leg and compared it with a tree. The fifth ran his hands over an ear, which felt like a fan. The sixth found the tail and concluded an elephant is like a rope. No, said the first blind man, an elephant is like a wall. No, said the second, an elephant is like a snake. No, a spear, said the third. A fan, said the fifth. They argued so loudly that they woke the prince from his nap.

Out he came and explained to the blind men that an elephant is a very large animal with parts that are like a wall, a snake, a spear, a tree, a fan, and a rope. The prince told them they all were right— and all wrong, because each had touched only a part of the elephant. But what the blind men could not know is that the total elephant can easily transport six men. "And now," said the prince, "you will ride on it all the way home."

Finally, in January of 1996, the Cowboys, their coach, and their owner rode their elephant all the way home. It's a magnificent elephant, though perhaps no single member of the organization was able to stand back and view it in all its grandeur. Perhaps Aikman and Switzer and the blindly loyal supporters of each clung so intensely to their parts of the elephant that they lost sight of the whole. Perhaps I'm in the best position to see the elephant.

The phone is ringing again, but I'm not answering.

I am writing everything I know.

1

TORTURED SOUL

Really, I'm not sure what it is he does as a
head coach.
—Troy Aikman on Barry Switzer

Troy Aikman stood alone facing his Texas Stadium locker. He
was dressed for the civilized world now, his hair combed but
still wet from the shower. He was wearing blue jeans and cowboy
boots with a tan sport coat over an open-collared white shirt.

At a glance, he looked nothing like a time bomb.

He was leaning into his cubicle, packing his athletic bag with
the same meticulous concentration with which he had just operated
the Dallas Cowboys offense. Just an hour or so earlier, the Cowboys
had disposed of the NFL team with the best record, Kansas City.
Now Aikman's team had pulled even with the Chiefs at 10–2. The
Cowboys had ten days to rest and recover for four fairly easy
December games against division rivals Washington, Philadelphia,
New York, and Arizona. The tension had been cut like the discarded
tape that littered the locker-room floor. It was Thursday evening,
November 23. I naively believed everyone in the organization was
about to celebrate a bountiful Thanksgiving.

I was very wrong about the quarterback.

For nearly two seasons, something had "eaten" at him, as he
told me much later—drained him, taken the fun out of playing professional football. That something was about to explode into what
must be the most bizarre, paranoia-plagued conflict in sports his-

tory. Soon, the coach would be led to believe the quarterback was a gay game-tanking racist out to get him fired and Norv Turner hired, while the quarterback would view the coach as the owner's half-crazy puppet who had gone out of control and directed certain media members to criticize and expose the quarterback. Only in Dallas. These plots and subplots, vicious rumors and dangerous truths, would make the TV show *Dallas* look like the sitcom *Alice*.

The locker room was nearly empty now, save for three or four roving reporters, two or three players, and an ESPN crew that waited anxiously by the door for Aikman. As I approached his locker, I should have known. His back-to-the-room body language said, "Do not disturb." I had no idea he was ticking. I was dangerously unaware I had been labeled "the enemy."

I had been told Aikman was upset with me, probably over something I'd written in a column for *The Insider*, a newsletter delivered electronically to subscribers in every state. I had been told several players were upset that Aikman, who left the November 12 San Francisco game with a knee injury in the first quarter and didn't return to the game or even the sideline. The injury turned out to be no more than a bad bruise, and Aikman played—and played exceptionally well—the following Sunday in Oakland. An injury-wracked San Francisco had beaten Barry Switzer's Cowboys for a third straight time—had humiliated Dallas 38–20 at Texas Stadium with an unknown Elvis named Grbac at quarterback. In all three losses, Aikman had thrown costly, uncharacteristic interceptions. This time, Aikman hadn't even stayed to face the postgame media interrogation alongside his teammates.

So at the bottom of my column, after criticizing Switzer and defensive coordinator Dave Campo, I asked, "Do the 49ers now have Aikman's number the way the Cowboys had [49er quarterback] Steve Young's for three straight games [when Jimmy Johnson was coach]? Is that why Aikman was hesitant to return to Sunday's game with nothing more than a bruised knee?"

I thought that was a fair and reasonable question. I didn't launch into any anonymous mudslinging from frustrated teammates. I didn't suggest Aikman wimped out physically, but that he was stung psychologically. With San Francisco up 24–0 barely into the second quarter, Aikman understandably could have been so devastated that he decided not to return. Why not preserve what was left of his dignity and prevent serious injury? He and his teammates had fought back from a 21–0 deficit in the previous season's NFC championship game in San Francisco—yet still had fallen short, 38–28. So, said Jerry Jones, "it was just so hard for them to keep fighting this time."

I decided that if the Cowboys won on Thanksgiving, I'd catch Aikman after the game and give him the opportunity to tell me I was wrong. I figured he'd be in a good enough mood that he might even say, "I can't even remember why I was upset."

But he remembered.

In my newspaper columns, I was occasionally tough on Aikman during his first two seasons with the Cowboys. Occasionally, he was tough on me. But our disagreements had been expressed with respect and without profanity. Really, from about 1992 until that night, I thought our working relationship had been pretty good. Hadn't he been a willing and responsive guest on my radio show several times in 1994 and 1995? Hadn't he done a long interview with me for an *Inside Sports* cover story I did on him in the spring of '95? Hadn't he called to thank me for the way I handled the material?

I had never experienced the Aikman who was about to declare war on me—or at least on me by association.

Ironically, over the previous year or so, I feared I had grown too sympathetic to Aikman. There was so much to like and pity about him. What the world expected of him had escalated to the sick stage. Compared to Aikman, former Cowboy coach Tom Landry and former quarterback Roger Staubach had it easy: They appealed mostly to Americans who believe in God and country. But millions more couldn't identify with Landry because he looked and acted too much like the Pope, or with Staubach because he could be such a goody two-cleats. Maybe each had his closet groupies, but to me neither exactly oozed sex appeal.

Surveys done for the Cowboy marketing department indicate that Troy Aikman, twenty-nine and single, is America's number one heartthrob—and, to boot, one of the country's top five most popular sports stars. Unlike Staubach, Aikman has some Hollywood and some Nashville in him. He has had highly publicized flings or at least flirtations with country singer Lorrie Morgan and actresses Janine Turner and Sandra Bullock. Aikman knows lots of country-music stars and shows up at lots of concerts. Even during some TV interviews, Aikman keeps that ever-present bulge of snuff in his lower lip. Aikman has some bite to him, some edge. Aikman is still idolized by the Landry and Staubach worshipers, but he also attracts the Garth Brooks crowd, lots of Richard Petty lovers, and Clint Eastwood fans—male and female. Aikman is *big*.

In fact, he looks much bigger in person than he looks on the field. He is a big 6'4", 230 pounds. It's almost as if his forearms, shoulders, and thighs were intended for a man 6'6", 250 pounds.

Aikman, who spent part of his childhood on a farm outside Henryetta, Oklahoma, is farm-boy big. Raw-boned, L'il Abner big. Even his eyes, nose, and lips seem a little too big for his face. But the total package—especially with streaks of black warpaint under the big blue eyes and the golden highlights in his hair catching the Sunday afternoon sun—is ruggedly handsome. Aikman was made to be a Cowboy: He looks like he could have ridden in with Gus and Call from *Lonesome Dove*. He could be Gary Cooper's son. He has an NFL reputation for being as tough as Eastwood was in any of his "man with no name" Westerns. Aikman, the strong, silent type, usually lets the bullets he throws do his talking.

Especially to white fans, who have a dwindling number of white stars with whom to identify, Aikman has become the Last Gunfighter, the Last American Hero, an NFL version of Mickey Mantle from rural Oklahoma, minus the tragically bad knees and thirst for strong drink. Troy Kenneth Aikman: great white sports god.

So how can any human live up to that myth? Sometimes Aikman tries. But he is not L'il Abner or even a young Terry Bradshaw. Aikman sometimes is too intelligent and introspective for his own good. If only Aikman could shut down his brain after games. But he locks in so intensely for four quarters that sometimes he can't quit thinking. His brainpower runs amok, turns on him, eats at his psyche, makes him crazy. He can't help asking himself: Why? Why was I put in this body? Why do so many people worship me because I can throw a football? Why are my interests so different from most guys who play this insanely violent game?

Many sports stars live in a world of blissful ignorance: They basically eat, drink, have sex, and star. Their athletic greatness is mostly inborn and instinctive. It never dawns on them to pause and, from their mountaintops, look down—to ask why. Of course, this thinking with the body can lead to some long falls.

Yet Aikman's stardom is based on his mental as well as physical abilities. His exceptional natural talent lies in his ability to throw quickly with velocity and, more important, accuracy. For such a big man, his delivery is confined, tight, precise, efficient—a reflection of the way he wants his life to operate. If his throwing motion were a golf swing, it would be Hogan's. It's not that Aikman can throw the hardest or the farthest; it's that, once he locks on an open receiver, he can cock and fire unusually fast while still generating exceptional velocity and maintaining the most consistent aim in the game. Over the last four seasons, it's doubtful any quarterback has correctly chosen more open receivers and hit them with more catchable passes than Aikman has.

Yet Aikman's talent is wired tightly to the motherboard that is his brain. In truth, the Last Gunfighter is no gunslinger or gambler or scrambler. He is robo-quarterback: part robot, part computer. He isn't fueled by adrenaline; he operates on muscle memory. Unlike an Elway or a Marino or a Favre, his strength is not spontaneous creativity. (Yet, significantly, despite their one-man-show talent, Elway, Marino, and Favre have not one Super Bowl championship among them, while Aikman has three.) Though Aikman runs well, he is no Steve Young, prone to bolting from the pocket for a game-turning run. Aikman does not "make things happen." He executes plays to perfection. Elway, Marino, and Favre are thesauruses; Aikman is the dictionary.

While Staubach desperately wanted to call his own plays—that was Landry's hallowed domain—Aikman doesn't even call many audibles. Too much instinctive guesswork, broken concentration. Just tell him the play and he will execute it precisely the way he has thousands of times in training camp and practice, reading the safety and his "progressions"—options 1–2–3. If his blockers protect him long enough, one of his receivers invariably will break open. The split second Aikman finds him, *bang*, the ball is gone.

That's one reason he has never been a last-minute magician, an Elway or Marino. He has always been so dominantly efficient for four quarters that he rarely has been in need of a last-ditch drive. Don't ask him to make up a play in the huddle, duck and dodge rushers while scrambling in circles, then throw a 70-yard wobbler that Michael Irvin rises to rip away from three defenders in the end zone. That was Staubach to Drew Pearson.

Aikman is a quarterback who takes his job as seriously—while feeling as much stress—as an air-traffic controller. During the season he cannot abide distractions or disruptions. His game—his life—is built on intense preparation and focus. On tiny details, perfect order, total control. Shirts arranged in the closet by style and color. Appointments kept to the second. Routes run by receivers to the inch and millisecond.

And then the game ends, and he must leave the protective confines of his armor and offense and venture back into an unreal world he cannot control. He must live amid the idol-worshiping chaos his brilliant execution has wrought.

No wonder Aikman is fascinated by Elvis. Not the 49er, the King. In the spring of 1995, Aikman made his first trip to Graceland, Elvis Presley's shrine. Aikman says, "There has never been anybody, not just in music, who has captured the nation the way he did." He scoffs at the comparison, but especially around Dallas-Fort Worth, Aikman has become an Elvis. He can't even stop by a

7-Eleven for a tin of snuff without causing an autograph riot. Girls climb over his back fence and sit on his back porch, fantasizing he'll come out and propose—or perhaps offer to show them his bedroom. Aikman constantly complains about the inestimable price he pays for being the Dallas Cowboys' $50 million man. A newspaper printed a map showing the location of the new spread he lives on outside Dallas, and Aikman's reaction was somewhere between outrage and disbelief. *Why is this happening to me?* Aikman's friends referred to Verna Riddles, who until recently served as his guard-dog secretary and deal-making advisor, as Troy's "Colonel Parker."

On Aikman's first trip to Graceland, he was so mobbed by autograph seekers that the day was ruined. Imagine: Aikman was being treated like Elvis on the King's sacred ground. A few days later, he returned in disguise to tour Graceland without distraction. Aikman views Elvis as a rare talent who died prematurely and sadly. Aikman's favorite Elvis song is a poignant one, "In the Ghetto." Several people close to Aikman say he has a private fear of dying young and lonely. Pondering Elvis's tragic end, Aikman surely wonders: How, at the height of your popularity, can you maintain any perspective when people treat you like such a god? How do you know who truly cares about you anymore? Would your friends and family pay as much attention to you if you were Troy Smith?

The real Aikman struggles to be happy. The world won't let him. The Cowboys' owner and coach won't let him. The quick-tempered perfectionist in him won't let him. Several members of the Cowboy organization wish he had a safety valve, an escape, an outlet for his frustrations. He has no woman in his life and won't consider marriage, he says, until he's through with football. He plays some golf. He plays around on his computer. He plays with his tropical fish, his favorite hobby. "Quirky" is a word Aikman uses to describe himself. He's also "very complex," he says. Yet as much as he might disagree with or detest this view, his life for now is basically defined by Cowboy wins and losses. For Jerry Jones, that can be extremely beneficial or dangerous.

Says a Cowboy source: "Troy can be as unpredictably crazy in his way as Charles Haley can be." Aikman fans will be shocked and offended by that comparison. Defensive end Haley is a well-known time bomb capable of going off on the coaching staff and "retiring" after a win as well as a loss. Dennis Rodman probably would call Haley crazy. But in Aikman's way, he can be just as hair-trigger sensitive. Some days, Gary Cooper Jr. whines to the media about what seem like the littlest things. Some days, John Wayne II can act babyish about some minor injury that most pro football players would ignore. Sometimes the little things affect him worse than the big things: It's the spots on the mirror that distract and upset him. But faced with a major career decision or major injury, "Troy is a stud," says agent Leigh Steinberg.

Aikman is a sometimes confused and confusing mix of his father's distant toughness and his mom's loving tenderness; of suburban L.A., where he lived until he was twelve, and rural Oklahoma; of the Internet and smokeless tobacco; of stoic confidence and raging insecurity. Yes, insecurity. How would you like to be the human most responsible for preserving the weekly bragging rights of millions of followers of America's Team? How would you like to carry the burden of a Dallas, Texas, that hitches its self-image to the Cowboy star? Cowboy losses are followed by Blue Mondays, when production falls dramatically in the Dallas-Fort Worth workplace. It's difficult enough to play quarterback for any NFL team, let alone for the Cowboys. Aikman is the Atlas expected to hold up the Cowboy world.

All of which is why several Cowboy sources have referred to Aikman as a "tortured soul."

Yet if Aikman is reading this, his rage perhaps just flashed to the surface like a cold sweat. He will suppose he knows who my sources are, and in his mind, perhaps, their plot against him will sicken.

That, in retrospect, is what happened Thanksgiving night.

I eased up beside Aikman's locker. After wins or losses, he can be unpredictably friendly or withdrawn, depending on microscopic mistakes that have been made by the offense. This time I couldn't read him. So I got right to it, saying, "I understand you're upset over something I wrote."

He identified me only out of the corner of his eye. He did not look up. He kept packing his bag as he said, "Anymore, anything you write is a fucking joke. I just sit back and laugh at it."

I was stunned. I wasn't prepared for an insult.

Now he was throwing things in his bag as if they were third-down passes. His voice rose. I could hear some hurt little boy in Aikman's profane anger. Usually, Aikman hides his emotions behind an intimidating dead-eye gaze. But now, as he swung his head toward me, his eyes were wild. He said, "Two years ago at camp, you told me you had to keep an arm's length from people you write about. You said you couldn't become friends with them so you could stay objective. That's bullshit."

I'm ashamed to admit I thought Aikman was upset because I had avoided becoming friends with *him*. Was I ever missing the point. Stumbling ahead, I said, "Troy, I have pretty good sources"—which actually were very good—"who questioned why you left the San Francisco game." Several NFL coaches outside Dallas had asked me why Aikman hadn't returned—not to mention his disillusioned teammates and several concerned team officials. But I was sparring with one hand tied behind my back. I couldn't divulge any names, and I was hoping he wouldn't demand any.

Instead, he said, "Your sources are a fucking joke."

It would be a few days until I realized Aikman was referring to Switzer and the one assistant coach Switzer trusted, John Blake. Perhaps Aikman also had in mind Cowboy scouting director Larry Lacewell—maybe even Jerry Jones. But in general he meant any of the Switzer backers that the Aikman supporters called the "Oklahoma Mafia."

Backers? Supporters? Incredibly and perhaps predictably, the battle lines officially were being drawn between the Switzer camp and the Aikman camp, and war would be waged for the rest of the season and into the off-season. Battle lines? War? Weren't the Cowboys 10–2?

Not for long.

Even now, my head aches with the unimaginable details: Aikman still hasn't quite forgiven Jones for firing Jimmy Johnson, a coach Aikman once despised but suddenly bonded with because of their shared passion for tropical fish and perfect practices . . .

Switzer, forced to inherit Johnson's staff, wrongly assumed he would have one ally among his new players—the quarterback who played two years for him at the University of Oklahoma . . .

Aikman watched in horror as the same lack of discipline that helped get Switzer fired at Oklahoma began turning the Cowboys into the OU Sooners, with players late to practice and laughing at curfews . . .

Switzer was wounded and infuriated when Aikman began "demeaning me on national TV," as Switzer says . . .

Aikman realized Switzer was becoming the buddy to and even puppet for Jones that Jones always wanted Johnson to be . . .

Aikman's perfect football existence under Johnson—one that had produced two straight Super Bowl championships—was turning into one big Super Bowl mansion with cigarette butts on the carpet, spoiled milk in the refrigerator, and filthy bathrooms. Where was the commitment, the passion from Switzer? Leigh Steinberg told me, "Switzer came in with this attitude of, 'Hey, I don't need this. I've won my championships [three national titles at Oklahoma]. If this doesn't work out, I'll go back to my couch in Norman [where the University of Oklahoma is located].' But the players desperately wanted to win a third straight Super Bowl [in 1994, Switzer's first Cowboy season], and they wanted Barry the coach, the father figure, to share that goal. I mean, these guys are still kids at heart. It was almost like parental abandonment."

At least for Aikman it was—especially after the Cowboys failed to win their unprecedented third straight Super Bowl.

Yet Switzer was stunned to discover that Aikman maintained phone friendships with Johnson and former Cowboy offensive coordinator Norv Turner, now coach of the rival Washington Redskins. *What?* There was Jimmy Johnson, sitting in the catbird seat as a Fox and HBO commentator, armed with inside info from Aikman! There was the ex-coach who most wanted to see Switzer and Jones fail! There was Turner, Aikman's soul mate and guru, tinkering weekly by phone with Aikman's delicate psyche! There was Aikman, trying to figure a way to get Switzer fired and Turner hired!

At least, that's what Switzer began to suspect.

These things do not happen every day in the NFL. By the way, I neglected to mention that for sixteen years while he was at Oklahoma, Switzer was Public Enemy No. 1 among Texas fans in Dallas. I wish I could write fiction this good.

Just when Switzer, surrounded by Johnson's assistants and Johnson's players, thought his new world couldn't get any lonelier, he figured out that—*What?*—two of Aikman's best friends were the two most powerful media voices in Dallas-Fort Worth. *No wonder they're trying to get me fired!* Did Aikman really like or need Dale Hansen and Randy Galloway? Hansen is the color analyst on the Cowboy radio network, as well as a radio talk-show host (KLIF) and top-rated sportscaster (WFAA-TV Channel 8). Galloway is a top-rated radio talk-show host (WBAP) as well as the lead sports columnist for the *Dallas Morning News*.

The "Oklahoma Mafia" referred to Hansen and Galloway as "Troy's Boys." Also considered by Switzer backers to be in the Aikman camp were Johnson-hired assistants Joe Avezzano, Joe Brodsky, and Hubbard Alexander, who were close to the quarterback.

"Mafia" members included John Blake, Danny Bradley, and Dean Blevins. Each played for Switzer. Blake and Bradley are like sons to Switzer; Blevins is more like a brother. Blake, hired by Johnson, coached the Cowboy defensive line. Bradley, the Cowboys' "director of programs," counseled young players. Blevins, the most powerful media voice in Oklahoma, hosted Jerry Jones's TV show and Switzer's radio show in Dallas-Fort Worth, besides doing college football games for ABC.

A Cowboy staffer says, "By themselves, John and Danny and Dean are very nice guys with good hearts. But they get enmeshed in the dysfunction that is Barry Switzer. Barry is a great guy who carries so much baggage from his childhood."

By the end of the 1995 season, the Cowboys were one big happy dysfunctional family. At times Switzer and Aikman, no matter how many loyal supporters they have around them, perhaps have one thing in common: They feel lonely.

In December it got really wild.

Allegations flew back and forth. Very little of this stuff hit the papers or airwaves. But as you'll see, the charges were very real.

And unreal.

Did Aikman take a dive in the two Washington games to make Norv Turner look like a genius and Switzer look like a buffoon? Twice the Cowboys lost to the Redskins, who finished 6–10. Was Aikman trying to "get" Switzer? Was he afraid to play too well, because his Super Bowl "reward" might be several more seasons of Switzer?

Was the "Oklahoma Mafia" trying to get even with Aikman or protect him from himself? Was he in denial about his racism? Was he taking his tongue-lashing of black teammates too far?

Did Switzer direct Dave Garrett, his new hand-picked play-by-play Cowboy-network radio announcer, to be hypercritical of Aikman? That's what the Aikman camp believed.

But that was nothing compared to this: The Switzer camp wondered if the Hansens and Galloways were protecting Aikman's image because of the rampant rumor that he's gay. Troy Aikman, Bachelor No. 1? As I'll explain later, I felt pressure from Switzer supporters to "write the truth" about Aikman, who is well aware of the rumors and insists they're nothing but rumors.

For me, a hell-bent 1995 season had come to this: chasing gay rumors.

When Cowboy PR director Rich Dalrymple says, "There's never been a season like it, and there never will be," he is not exaggerating.

Aikman soon lost all respect for Switzer. Now, he says, "I don't give Barry any credit for any of our wins, nor do I blame him for any of our losses. Really, I'm not sure what it is he does as a head coach."

But in early December, the Aikman camp thought Switzer was doing everything in his power to undermine the one player he most needed to save his job. Ten days after Aikman unleashed his frustration on me, he let Kevin Williams have it for running a bad route during the Washington game at Texas Stadium. The following day, influenced by his supporters, Switzer called Aikman into his office and confronted the quarterback about what he had yelled at Williams. Had he come across as racist? Lunacy ensued. Aikman quit speaking to Switzer. Aikman went through "one of the worst weeks of my life," which culminated in a Cowboy loss in Philadelphia, which culminated in Switzer's infamous fourth-and-a-foot decision, which earned him the *New York Post* nickname "Bozo the Coach."

Throughout the season commentators had referred to Switzer and Jones as "Dumb and Dumber." Aikman was increasingly irritated and embarrassed by the behavior of the coach *and* the owner. To Aikman and other owners, Jones, the wildcatting oil man, was treating the NFL like his private drilling lease. Jones had defied NFL Properties laws by signing with Nike and Pepsi. Jones had been sued by the NFL for $300 million. Jones had countersued for $750 million. Jones had beaten the salary cap system by signing Deion Sanders with a record $13 million bonus. To Aikman, "Neon Deion" had influenced many Cowboys to drift even further beyond the confines of class and sportsmanship with their choreographed touchdown celebrations. In-season drug suspensions of Cowboys Leon Lett and Clayton Holmes were followed by Michael Irvin's postseason drug possession charge.

"The shine is off the star," Aikman told me. "When I first put on the helmet in '89, I was very proud to wear it. I'd like to think that whoever takes over for me would feel the same way, but we're headed in the wrong direction."

All that after Jones, upon signing Deion, told the world that anything short of winning the Super Bowl was "unacceptable." Unheard of. You almost could hear Aikman's sigh all the way to Tempe, Arizona, the Super Bowl site.

So it was that two weeks after the Super Bowl, Troy Aikman summed up the 1995 season with a statement that might sound like an egotistical exaggeration to some outsiders and that did sound self-serving to some insiders (including Switzer). Aikman was more relaxed now, as he sat with a snuff cup in a meeting room at the Cowboy practice facility. But he remained bitterly proud. Quite earnestly, Aikman told me, "From what I know about sports, and what I know about what went on inside this team, what we accomplished this year was the greatest achievement in sports."

I said, "You mean, in sports this year?"

He shook his head no. "Ever," he said.

The greatest accomplishment of any team ever? Greater than, say, Joe Namath's upstart AFL New York Jets shocking the big bad Baltimore Colts of the NFL in Super Bowl III? Greater than the

New York Knicks, inspired by an injured Willis Reed's valiant effort, beating the Lakers in the seventh game of the 1970 NBA Finals? Greater than the Los Angeles Dodgers, lifted by an injured Kirk Gibson's pinch-hit home run, stunning the favored Oakland A's in the 1988 World Series? Greater than the NCAA titles won by underdogs North Carolina State in 1983 and Villanova in 1985?

Ever, said Aikman.

Did the Cowboys suffer major late-season injuries? Only one, to defensive end Charles Haley, who was able to play in the Super Bowl. Were the Cowboys a bunch of undertalented overachievers? No, they were the NFL's most talented team. Did they play as dominantly and flawlessly in the playoffs as Cowboy Super Bowl winners did following the 1992 and 1993 seasons, when they beat San Francisco in NFC championship games? No, the '95 Cowboys beat three pretty good teams (Philadelphia, Green Bay, and Pittsburgh) by playing three pretty good games.

Yet Aikman believes what he and in turn his teammates overcame—much of it caused by the Switzer camp—qualified the Cowboys for the greatest achievement ever. As one high-placed team source says, "Troy's just saying that what *he* did was the greatest achievement ever."

Maybe it was.

Or maybe Aikman can feel only one part of the elephant.

You decide.

During the season, I tried to remain detached and impartial. But Aikman, prompted by his supporters, concluded that I was "Barry's boy," as he told Dale Hansen. To me, this was one more half-truth that grew into a fabrication. Though I'm friendly with several people close to Switzer, I've never been close to Switzer. Not once have I socialized with him. I've always liked him—if you're around him much, how can you not? Publicly, I did say from the day he was hired that his style would be an effective complement to Jimmy Johnson's and that the Cowboys could win a Super Bowl with Switzer as their coach. But Barry's boy?

You decide.

That Thanksgiving night, one person left in the locker room had even less of an idea of what was going on than I did. Bonnie Bernstein of ESPN waited by the door as Aikman stormed away from me. "Troy?" she said, trying to stop him for a quick word on camera.

He didn't slow down as he snapped, "I'm not doing any more goddamn interviews."

And into the night he went.

2

OF SONS AND MOONSHINE

Charles Dickens couldn't make up Barry Switzer.
—Daily Oklahoman *columnist Berry Tramel*

One morning in late March of 1994, caller after caller to my radio show expressed shock or rage. From a distance, many fans and media observers were astonished that Jerry Jones had fired Jimmy Johnson. Hadn't Jimmy just won back-to-back Super Bowls for Jerry? Yes, but even during the first Jimmy-Jerry Super Bowl run, assistant coaches and front-office lieutenants had privately predicted the two wouldn't last through '93. Frankly, I was surprised Jones hadn't fired Johnson earlier.

But Jones's next move shocked me.

A caller said to me, "Jerry mentioned something [to newspaper reporters] about how he should have fired Johnson and hired Barry Switzer a long time ago. Was he kidding?"

"He had to be," I said off the top of my head. "He'd sooner hire *me* than Barry Switzer."

The following day, I sat in a packed press conference as Jerry Jones introduced Barry Switzer as the Dallas Cowboys' third head coach. As I watched, I very slowly shook my head and thought, "This cannot be happening." I knew too much about the improbably crisscrossed, star-crossed paths of Jones, Switzer, Troy Aikman, Jimmy Johnson, and Larry Lacewell, the Cowboy scouting director and Jones's chief advisor.

To comprehend this incomprehensible story, you must retravel these sometimes twisted paths through Arkansas and Oklahoma. You must understand why Aikman once chose to attend Barry Switzer's football camp and to play for him at the University of Oklahoma . . . why Switzer and Johnson and their families once vacationed together . . . why Jones idolized the Switzer who coached him at the University of Arkansas . . . why Johnson felt betrayed by Lacewell, who gave Johnson his start in college coaching and taught him much of what he knows . . . why Switzer once betrayed his best friend Lacewell and why, if Switzer has his way, Lacewell will be the Cowboys' fourth head coach, as early as the 1997 season.

Larry Lacewell? Switzer owes him in so many ways.

They were born about eight months and ninety miles apart in 1937 in southern Arkansas. Switzer lived outside Crossett; Lacewell up in Fordyce, the hometown of college football's biggest legend, former Alabama coach Paul "Bear" Bryant. Switzer and Lacewell first sized each other up at a junior high swim meet. Switzer remembers Lacewell, who even now stands no taller than 5'5", as a "brash little kid." Lacewell remembers Switzer being "like a man even when he was a teenager. He knew everything."

Today, Lacewell always refers to Switzer as "Switzer," even to his face. And while friends always call Lacewell "Lace," Switzer calls him "Lacew'll," condensing the second syllable.

A Mutt-and-Jeff friendship grew in their college years. Switzer loves telling stories about "what a helluva athlete Lacewell was," a scatback in football, a waterbug gunner in basketball—"and always funny as hell, just like he is now." Switzer was even in the stands the night a tackler's finger caught Lacewell in the eye, which had to be removed. "He was down for so long [on the field], I knew it was trouble," Switzer says.

Lacewell was in awe of Switzer's bullish man-child physique and nature. As a high school senior, Switzer stood about 6'1" and weighed around 190 pounds—big enough to play in the offensive line in those days. Switzer's natural strength and quickness—he was the state shot-put champ—brought him scholarship offers from several schools, including LSU and Arkansas. Switzer had grown up wanting to be an Arkansas Razorback, so he headed for Fayetteville.

Lacewell wasn't quite good enough to make it at Arkansas and wound up playing football at Arkansas State in Jonesboro. But Switzer sometimes hitchhiked the three hours to Jonesboro for a weekend with Lacewell and some of their down-home buddies. Lacewell says, "Going to school in Fayetteville at the University was kind of like being in the big city, and for a while Switzer didn't really feel comfortable there. He just had so much insecurity because of his background. Let me tell you, in those days, if you were a bastard or a bootlegger's son, you were treated like an outcast, and you had to be tough."

To explain some of Barry Switzer's seemingly inexplicable behavior, you must understand his upbringing. His father—whose brothers became a judge and a lawyer—had a fairly high IQ and a generous heart. Frank Mays Switzer despised hypocrisy; his word was his bond. He made lots of money. Yet he and his wife and two sons lived four miles west of Crossett in a house without electricity, running water, indoor toilet, or telephone. The west side of Crossett was all black, and the closest "houses" to the Switzers were a dozen or so shanties whose residents were black.

That's because Frank Switzer was a bootlegger and loan shark whose clients mostly were black.

Barry Switzer fondly remembers, "He was the black sheep of his family—a rounder, a womanizer, Rhett Butler . . . But genetically, the family is smart. My mom was valedictorian of her high school class. She read all the time." Switzer received an appointment to the Naval Academy but would have been required to spend a year at Columbia Prep School in Washington, D.C., to improve his math grades. Younger brother Donnie graduated from Dartmouth and Vanderbilt Law School and wants to become a novelist. Switzer's oldest son, Greg, is studying to be a concert pianist.

Says Lacewell, "One thing Switzer, Jimmy, and Jerry have in common is that they're all highly intelligent."

Yet Barry Switzer's father taught him an unconventional sense of right and wrong.

When World War II ended, the Switzer family moved back to Arkansas from Long Beach, California, where Frank had found work in a shipyard. Barry had just finished the third grade. Back in Crossett, Frank tried to go into business for himself—tried and failed at several ventures such as selling used cars and running a fishing camp. "But," Switzer writes in his autobiography, *Bootlegger's Boy*, "he did discover a way to make a living for his family."

Barry Switzer was taught that providing for family and friends is life's highest priority, even if it requires bending or breaking a silly rule or hypocritical law. His father began making runs down into Louisiana, just a few miles south, bringing cases of whiskey back into dry, Bible-Belt Ashley County and selling it by the pint and half-pint. Barry's enduring childhood memory: car after car pulling up in front of the house driven by a customer signaling with one finger for a pint or with thumb flicked across index finger for a half-pint.

Occasionally, some of Crossett's most respected citizens—even prominent church leaders—would visit the Switzers under the cover of darkness and purchase moonshine. That reinforced Barry's belief that his father was providing a public service. Hell, everybody drank, Barry reasoned. Life was tough and alcohol loosened people up, made 'em forget about their problems for a while. Blacks, whites, everybody. Didn't his own dad drink a fifth of whiskey every night? So what if he was breaking a dumb law? So he didn't pay any taxes. At least he wasn't robbing banks and shooting innocent people.

That perhaps was the way Barry Switzer would approach some of the right-vs.-wrong decisions he would face as a head coach. He was taught to consider every situation as unique, to weigh the codes or rules or laws or ethics or morals in question and ask, "Is anyone really being hurt here?" And just as important, "Can any good come out of this?" Damn the hypocrisy, the "right" image. Do it your way. Hell with your critics. Switzer's bootlegged version of the golden rule: "I was taught to be a no-bullshit guy who treated everybody, rich or poor, famous or unknown, the way I would want them to treat me."

So his dad sold whiskey. Barry Switzer has consumed as much alcohol as most (if not all) fifty-eight-year-olds still alive. Yet Switzer looks forty-eight. While then-and-now pictures of Jerry Jones show he has aged markedly since buying the Cowboys seven years ago— this franchise will suck the life out of those who run it—Switzer at times appears even younger than the day he was named Cowboy coach. Switzer still smokes cigarettes, chews tobacco, and drinks alcohol just about every night. A bottle of wine drowns his demons; so far, his body has been able to withstand the side effects. "It's all genes," Switzer says. "My daddy gave me great plumbing. He was a powerfully built man who was in great shape till the day he died."

Frank Switzer often took young Barry with him in the car as he made his rounds through Colored Town. "I saw how he interacted with black people—he taught me well. People would come running to borrow money from him. 'Mr. Frank! Mr. Frank!' I saw the compassion he had for those people. I saw what he did for them."

Switzer says his father put "many" blacks through college, giving them the $600 to attend Arkansas AM&N (now Arkansas Pine
Bluff, where Switzer's son Doug played quarterback in 1995 for an
all-black team). "All Daddy asked for was their grades," Switzer
says. "One kid lied to him because he wanted to attend the school of
theology and go into the ministry, and he knew Daddy was a devout
atheist." Switzer laughs. "The kid was scared to death."

Even now, says Switzer, he's stopped in public by a black man
or woman who says, "You're Mr. Frank's son. He put me through
school." One man told Switzer he went on to become a warden of a
federal penitentiary. Only in Switzer's upside-down world—in which
two wrongs sometimes do make a right—could a bootlegger pay for
the education of a warden.

Is it possible Barry Switzer was the only white boy ever to pick
cotton for a black man? He did, as a fourth-grader. Most of his
friends were black, and a black woman named Irma Reynolds
helped raise him. "My black 'grandmother.' She was a tough son of
a bitch," Switzer says, chuckling. "Guys would pull up and try to get
Irma to give 'em a pint on credit. She'd say, 'You goddamn nigger, I
know Mr. Frank wouldn't do that for you.'"

Frank Switzer, whose great-grandfather was a Baptist preacher,
taught Barry that many town leaders, who said they believed in
God, were "goddamned hypocrites" because they wouldn't sit on the
same bench with a black person. Switzer also says his respect for
blacks helped him see something that changed his entire outlook on
sports—and perhaps helped make him millions of dollars in the
long run. Switzer never felt threatened by or superior to the black
race. So by the eighth grade, it was easy for him to grin, shake his
head, and readily acknowledge that most blacks were more gifted
athletically than most whites.

"I knew they were better by just playing basketball against
them," he says. "I was a pretty good athlete, but it didn't take a
fuckin' physiologist to see I wasn't quite as quick and I couldn't
jump as high as they could."

In his 1990 *Bootlegger's Boy*, Switzer writes, ". . . I believe there
are a lot of 'knee-jerk' liberal types out there who are going to try to
label me as a racist. I am, in fact, the world's leading nonracist. Ask
any of my black friends or players. And also recognize that I have
been in the business of coaching superior athletes of all colors for
over thirty years . . . and my recognition that, *in general*, blacks were
better athletes than whites, particularly in certain areas, led me to be
one of the leaders of integration in intercollegiate athletics . . .

"In general there is no question but that the black athlete has

superior physical skills in all games that involve running and jumping and catching. In fact, I personally believe that it was probably
the black athlete who drove the whites into inventing the weight
room and also into taking steroids . . . Just think about it. How
many *great* college or pro running backs and receivers in the last
twenty-five years or so have been white? A few. But just a very few.
And we've only been talking about football! We haven't even gotten
into basketball! Enough said."

Barry Switzer owes many of his liberal views to his father. Yet not all
of the Frank Switzer in Barry is healthy. Frank would do crazy things
when he was drunk, such as pulling the pistol he always wore and
shooting at household objects. Like father, like son? Says a chuckling
Lacewell, "I've seen Barry Switzer do some crazy, crazy things."
Drunk or sober. Once, upset that so many of his backs were fumbling
during an Oklahoma practice, Switzer ducked into the huddle with a
.357 magnum he had borrowed from a sheriff visiting the workout.
Switzer told his players, "If one more of you sumbitches fumbles, I'm
going to use this on you." And, he says, he fired it right there inside
Owen Field. "They thought I was crazier than hell. And I was."

Given Switzer's pistols-and-whiskey home life and the tragic
fates of his father and mother, Lacewell sometimes wondered how
Switzer could keep from being a little crazy. The people of Crossett
treated star athlete Switzer like such an outcast—you might say he
was the scarlet letterman—that he had to send friends up to the
doors of girls he dated. If their parents had known the bootlegger's
boy was hiding in the car, no way would the girls have been allowed
to go. And no way could Switzer have taken a girlfriend home to
meet Mom and Dad. Mary Louise Switzer was so miserable living
with her bootlegger husband that, according to Barry, she constantly anesthetized herself with barbiturates and alcohol. Not only
was Frank breaking the law—he eventually did time in prison—but
he constantly cheated on her and she knew it. Frank made little
secret of his black mistresses.

If Mary Louise confronted Frank about his womanizing, he
would sometimes beat her, especially if he was drunk. "That's the
part that makes me ashamed about him," Barry says, tears welling.

Barry Switzer says he's more like his mother than his father.
"I'm much more open and touching, loving. I'm always grabbing my
kids and hugging them. I knew Daddy loved me. But he damn sure
didn't express it."

On the night of August 29, 1959, when Barry was twenty-one
years old, his mother came in to say good night to him. In his book,

he writes, "I didn't totally understand the hell she was living through. I was too young to know how really desperate her every-day life was . . . She loved me and she needed my love so much, but as I looked at her sitting there on the bed kind of glassy and smil-ing, loaded on prescription drugs and booze, something broke inside me and I said things to her I will always regret. I said, 'Mother, I would rather not ever see you again, and know you are safe and well taken care of, than to see you like this all the time.'

"She leaned over to kiss me.

"I turned my head away."

Mary Louise Switzer got up, took a pistol from the closet, walked out on the back porch, and shot herself.

Years later, when Larry Lacewell accidentally cut himself, Switzer tried to make a "you'll live" joke by saying, "Hell, I've seen more blood at one time than you've seen your whole life." Lacewell says, "Obviously, what happened was devastating to him. But what surprised me was that he never talked about it. Something like that I'd have to talk about. But it was like he kept it all bottled up inside. That side of Switzer has always concerned me."

That side has concerned several people close to Switzer, who have wondered if he would take his own life. One close friend of Switzer's told me, "I just pray I don't hear one day that he put a gun in his mouth."

For about twenty years, Switzer kept a monstrous guilt caged inside: He thought he had caused his mother's suicide. Only when he and brother, Donnie, finally talked about the tragedy did Switzer discover his mother had left a suicide note. She had planned to take her life before her oldest son had refused her good-night kiss.

The note said, "Dear Frank . . . you can't imagine . . . how much courage it takes to do this. My one request is please don't let Jewel see me."

Jewel was Frank's girlfriend at the time.

One too many girlfriends finally cost Frank Switzer his life.

It happened in 1972. One black girlfriend caught Frank with another and shot him in the chest. Then, as she rushed him to the hospital in town over a gravel road at dusk, she lost control on a curve and hit a power pole, the car exploding into flames. She and Frank burned to death. Doctors said Frank was in such good health he probably would have survived the gunshot.

Two months later, Barry Switzer was named head coach at the University of Oklahoma, chosen over Larry Lacewell and Jimmy Johnson.

*   *   *

She was a freshman from Stuttgart, Arkansas, the duck-calling capital of the world. He was a senior captain on the Arkansas football team, a starter at linebacker and guard, and a big man on campus. He walked the Arkansas campus as if he ran it—a benevolent bully speaking to everyone, taking guff from no one. His "animal magnetism," she says, made him even more handsome than he was. He had the appeal of a young Marlon Brando in *The Wild One*, an intoxicating mix of good boy and bad boy.

She stopped him to ask directions to the journalism building.

Barry Switzer has blamed many of his problems on "the damn media." He should have known: Any relationship that began with directions to the journalism building was ill-fated.

In *Bootlegger's Boy*, he writes, "There was something about her that shined like a light, something electric in her personality." Kay McCollom, a math major and all-state cornet player in the high school band, became Arkansas's featured twirler. She also became Mrs. Barry Switzer, for eighteen years.

Now the ex–Mrs. Switzer says with a sarcastic laugh, "The real reason he liked me was because my daddy [Slick McCollom] owned this big reservoir that Barry loved to catch bass in."

They were married in 1963, Switzer's second year as an assistant coach at Arkansas. Switzer was a favorite of highly respected Arkansas head coach Frank Broyles, whose endorsement one day would make Switzer head coach of the Cowboys. Not only did Switzer earn Broyles's respect with his football IQ, but, Broyles said, "He's the best motivator I've ever been around." In '64 the Razorbacks went 11–0, beat Nebraska in the Cotton Bowl, and won the only national championship in Arkansas football history. On the same sideline that day in Dallas were assistant coach Switzer, an offensive lineman named Jerry Jones from North Little Rock, and a defensive lineman named Jimmy Johnson from Port Arthur, Texas.

What were the odds against those three eventually having such a dramatic impact on the 1990s history of a sorry expansion team called the Cowboys that played at the Cotton Bowl back then?

By the way, Larry Lacewell was recreation director at the camp Kay McCollom Switzer attended each summer during high school, and Lacewell once casually dated Johnson's future wife, Linda Kay, who's from Marked Tree, Arkansas, and remains (as the ex–Mrs. Johnson) one of the ex–Mrs. Switzer's closest friends. What were the odds?

Kay Switzer remembers Jerry Jones as "one football player everyone thought of as smart, because he made such good grades."

Jones probably played football not so much because he loved to play the game—like it was his calling, his religion—but because he realized football was the quickest way for a young man to be popular and powerful in life. At 200 pounds, soaking wet with sweat, Jones willed himself into a starting right guard his senior year through torturous conditioning and his willingness during practices to take and give punishment. Once his football career ended, Jones did not channel any athletic frustration into, say, playing lots of golf for lots of money, the way so many ex-athletes do. He has played some recreational tennis, but does not exercise. He still has a maniacal desire to compete, but not in participation sports. In college he played because football players got the most respect and the prettiest girls. Jones even used his Razorback status to make a little spending money. Vintage Jones: He started a one-man business taking fans to the airport as soon as he could shower and dress. Who better to chauffeur them than a player who could share the inside story of the game they had just seen? Knowing Jones, the fare was steep and customers got their money's worth.

But at that point, Jones apparently didn't have enough cash to repair the damage he did to Switzer's 1955 Ford Fairlane, which Switzer had parked in an athletic-dorm parking lot on the hill above the stadium. Vintage 100-mph Jones: With permission to borrow someone else's car, Jones jumped into Switzer's by mistake, released the emergency brake, and realized the key wouldn't fit in the ignition. Jones climbed out of Switzer's car for a moment to look for the right car. Switzer's began to roll down the hill. Before Jones could catch it and leap back into the driver's seat, it picked up speed and went careening into the one tree between the parking lot and the end zone.

Switzer didn't know who had wrecked his precious Ford Fairlane until years later, when Jones confessed. One day, Jones would more than make it up to him.

In 1966 Switzer received a promotion (but took a pay cut from $12,000 to $10,500) to follow Arkansas assistant Jim McKenzie to the University of Oklahoma, where McKenzie had replaced head coach Gomer Jones after a 3–7 season. Of the Switzers' drive from Fayetteville to Norman, Oklahoma, just outside Oklahoma City, Kay Switzer says, "I wasn't too well traveled. I actually thought we'd see Indians with headdresses."

When his playing career ended at Arkansas State, Larry Lacewell thought about going to law school. But his mother knew Bear Bryant, and Bryant had kept up with little Larry, the "Fordyce

Flash." Alabama coach Bryant hired Lacewell as a graduate assistant, until he began law school.

Lacewell would experience many trials, but none in the courtroom. He coached two years at Alabama, then began an odyssey that eventually took him to Wichita State, where he was defensive coordinator. In need of an assistant, Lacewell called Barry Switzer for a recommendation. "What about Jimmy Johnson?" said Switzer. Johnson had won Switzer's respect as a crafty defensive lineman whose brain was his quickest body part. A coaching position at Florida State had fallen through, so Johnson was stuck in an assistant's job at Picayune High School in Mississippi. Neither Lacewell nor Switzer knew Picayune hadn't won a game that season.

Lacewell hired Johnson over the phone. "I told him we couldn't afford to move him and couldn't afford to pay him much. I said, 'You better talk to your wife.' But before I could hang up, he said, 'I'm comin'.' I knew right from the start that Jimmy was different. When he didn't have a penny to his name, he was driving a Corvette. When people didn't drive motorcycles, he had a motorcycle. Took me frog-giggin' on the back of it . . . "

At Wichita, Lacewell met Criss. They were married the following year—with Johnson as best man—after Lacewell and Johnson had joined Johnny Majors's Iowa State staff. Majors had taken the Iowa State job after Oklahoma assistant Switzer turned it down.

Small world.

In 1969 Lacewell returned to Oklahoma, where he had coached in '66, to be defensive coordinator. The following season, Johnson joined the OU staff as defensive line coach. The offensive coordinator was Switzer.

Imagine.

Switzer, his wife, and their kids used to take vacations with Johnson, his wife, and their kids in Galveston, Texas. This happened during the years that Tom Landry's Cowboys were losing, then winning their first Super Bowls. And there, sipping beer on a South Texas beach, were the two coaches who would follow Landry while carrying on a bitter personal rivalry.

To follow this, you need a family tree with many branches.

Lacewell and Johnson "used to go at it like cats and dogs," says Lacewell. "Jimmy was so damn headstrong, but he was smart as hell. He'd drive me crazy in meetings because he'd never take a note and he'd never forget a detail. We'd talk defense for hours, and we'd be at each other's throats [over philosophy] then come back the next morning and be like brothers again. We'd lose a game and he'd say,

'That's it. I'm getting out of coaching.' And I'd take him seriously. But that was just Jimmy."

Much later, when Johnson became the second head coach of the Cowboys in 1989, he said, "Larry Lacewell knows more about the technical aspects of football than anyone I've been around. Larry knows the Xs and Os. I'd never tell him this, because our egos would get in the way, but I probably learned more pure football from Larry Lacewell than anyone I ever worked with."

Switzer says simply, "I trust Larry Lacewell's football judgment more than anyone I've ever been around."

On January 26, 1973, Oklahoma head coach Chuck Fairbanks made a stunning announcement: He was leaving for the NFL, to coach the New England Patriots. Switzer, the likely successor, was stunned because he knew Oklahoma had amassed enough talent to make Fairbanks a living legend. Revolutionary, evolutionary talent. In fact, the Sooners were about to go thirty-seven games over four seasons before losing again. How often has a first-time collegiate head coach inherited one of the all-time greatest collections of speed and athleticism?

About as often as a coach with no NFL experience inherits a Dallas Cowboys team that has won back-to-back Super Bowls.

"The Switzer Luck," Lacewell calls it with a mix of amusement and amazement. Many of Switzer's friends and family members call him "the luckiest son of a bitch who ever lived." No matter how he has abused his body—or sometimes his relationships with friends and family—Switzer keeps "hitting the lottery," as he calls being given the Cowboy job. No matter how undisciplined his personal (and sometimes professional) life has been, great things consistently have happened to him and his football teams.

"Maybe," says former OU quarterback Dean Blevins, now a close friend of Switzer's, "that's because good things happen to people with good hearts."

For sure, pure luck wasn't the reason the '73 Sooners were loaded like a .357 magnum. Switzer had been responsible for acquiring many of the Texas-bred bullets he soon would fire at the University of Texas. As offensive coordinator, Switzer had convinced the OU staff to go south of the Red River that divides Oklahoma and Texas and to bring back black stars almost the way his daddy once transported whiskey. By then, says Switzer, the days of a Bear Bryant or Bud Wilkinson outcoaching everybody were over. Too many Frank Broyleses had produced too many Barry Switzers—bright young coaches with a solid grasp of the Xs and Os, the tricks and solutions.

"By 1970," says Switzer, "it was mostly about who had the best talent."

From *Bootlegger's Boy*: "Every time Oklahoma would sign a Joe Washington, a Greg Pruitt, a Billy Brooks, a David Overstreet, a Thomas Lott, a Billy Simms [all great black skill-position players from Texas] . . . the official line that came back from Austin [home of the University of Texas] was: 'Well, you know why those black kids go to the University of Oklahoma, don't you? The kids are poor and need money. Oklahoma buys them, simple as that.' Bullshit. They came to us for the same reason the whites did—to be winners, to be champions. And more important, to be part of our family."

That was the key. Switzer, whose childhood had been a horrifying joyride through flying bullets, broken whiskey bottles, and the snakes that lurked by the outhouse, began creating a more "stable" family in his OU locker room. Children of alcoholics will tell you how traumatic it is when, as a small child, you can't quite trust the impaired faculties of the two parents upon whom you are completely dependent. Now, at OU, Switzer was re-creating life outside Crossett, with Barry Switzer as Frank Switzer. Now, he had dozens of sons for whom he would express his love the way Frank never did for Barry.

I've known many blacks and many whites who have played or coached for Switzer, and invariably their fondest memories were the times—usually after he's had a few victory drinks—when he wrapped an arm around their neck and said into their ear, "I love you, motherfucker."

It was Switzer, even as an OU assistant, who began to generate an unbeatable force field based on the Switzer code: Play hard, party hard. Switzer showed his players that the quickest route to women and professional wealth was through the end zone. He encouraged them to have as much legal fun as they wanted—hell, *he* did—as long as they were ready to "play your ass off" on Saturdays. He let them grow their hair, wear bandannas, dance after touchdowns, trash-talk—as long as they busted their butts. Word spread among potential black and white recruits that OU was the place to win and, as Switzer likes to say, "win the party"—to have fun. How many coaches outpartied his players and bragged to them about it the next day? Switzer was shattering the molds—and, perhaps, the myths—of the Bryants, the Woody Hayeses, the Joe Paternos. Switzer operated with a sort of brazen naiveté. Why couldn't he do it that way? Damn the hypocrisy. Why play along with the rusty old "white man's" myth that every great football player is supposed to drink only milk, save themselves for marriage, and be in bed by nine, after at least three hours of homework per night?

Yet this isn't to stereotype Switzer's teams as marauding bands of beer-swilling, sex-crazed animals. Switzer attracted as many talented, book-smart players as the legendary coaches did. (Significantly, Switzer's three children turned out to be bright, conservative, and clean-living.) Switzer encouraged each of his players to be themselves, whether they wanted to study anatomy in class or at Norman's nightspots. If they were good in school, he was quick to brag on them and tell them how proud he was of them. If you couldn't have paid them to attend classes at OU if not for football, Switzer didn't harp on them to do their homework.

Switzer's teams always had as much never-quit character as they had hell-raising characters. Switzer always surrounded himself with sharp assistants who made sure his teams were well prepared tactically and fundamentally. Offensive strategy came easily for Switzer, who is a good chess player. Says Lacewell, "People forget what a fine football coach he is."

The constant always was—and still is—that football players love playing for Barry Switzer. Playing *hard* for him. "No matter how tough the circumstances," says Lacewell, "his teams have always played hard for him. I've never seen a team quit on him." Switzer appeals to the animal in every kid—Christian or lion—who chooses to play such a brutal game. As Jerry Jones says, "Barry Switzer is the guy I want at my back in the dark alley."

At OU, Switzer was creating something unique. His Sooners drank together, studied together, fought together, won together, and forged a lifetime bond. Once a Sooner, always a Sooner. Today, one of his biggest problems is finding enough time to return calls from ex-Sooners. He's constantly helping them find jobs or even helping to financially support some who can't find work.

Sooner loyalty is blind loyalty. That's why Barry Switzer was so blindsided by what eventually happened with one-time Sooner Troy Aikman.

For a time, Darrell Royal was probably bigger in Texas than Tom Landry. Or Lyndon Johnson. Or Davy Crockett. Remember the Alamo? Many University of Texas football fans probably believed Royal fought there alongside Crockett and Bowie and Travis. Royal was a great ol' boy who relaxed by "pickin' gittar" with Willie Nelson. But what Royal did best was coach hard-nosed, straight-ahead, throwback, crewcut football, just the way Bubba loved it. Royal almost always beat the hell out of Oklahoma in the annual border-war game in Dallas.

Royal grew up in Hollis, Oklahoma, and played at OU back in its crewcut days. What a kick Texas fans got out of a former Okie coaching their Longhorns to victory after victory over Oklahoma. What a kick in the stomach it was for Royal when this rogue Switzer stole his wishbone and started stealing recruits from Texas. In 1969 Royal won his last national championship with a low-risk, low-speed wishbone that featured mostly straight-ahead handoffs to rugged pluggers. "Last all-white team that ever will win a national championship," says Switzer, who borrowed the wishbone concept, souped it up, and turned it loose on Texas in 1971. In '71, '72, and '73, OU threw a party at Texas by an astounding average score of 42–17.

Switzer, loading his backfield mostly with high-speed blacks, turned the wishbone into a high-risk, high-reward option attack featuring a halfback of a quarterback who constantly attempted daredevil perimeter pitches. This wishbone, like its inventor, lived on the edge. Switzer's backs either fumbled or went 80 yards for a touchdown—which pretty much mirrored his life. Switzer didn't sweat the details—the bobbles, the miscues. All he cared about was the final score. Typically, Switzer's Sooners might fumble twelve times, lose six, and win 72–14.

Not exactly Troy Aikman's idea of a perfect game.

Switzer's wishbone, his rapport with the black athletes, and his ethics perhaps contributed to Royal's taking what probably was an early retirement after the 1976 season. Before that year's OU-Texas game, a friend of Lacewell's named Lonnie Williams, who lived in Texas, slipped into a Longhorn practice in Austin and reported what he saw to Lacewell. Royal found out about it and went to the media with it. Switzer denied Oklahoma had "spied" on Royal's practice, though he later admitted it did happen, mostly because he found there was no NCAA rule against spying.

Many University of Texas fans still hold Switzer responsible for driving Darrell Royal out of coaching.

So why did the seven-member Oklahoma board of regents take several days to decide Switzer would succeed Chuck Fairbanks? Years later, says Jerry Jones, Fairbanks told him he definitely recommended Switzer to the regents and athletic department officials over Jimmy Johnson. Yet several regents told Lacewell they had one reservation about Switzer: his lifestyle. Even as an assistant, Switzer's legend had grown as a drinker and carouser. He wasn't particularly discreet. You might call it the Norman (Oklahoma) Conquest. The man-child from Arkansas had become a child-man: a coach who still acted like a player.

Even today, some of his ex-players refer to him as "the world's greatest cocksman."

At fifty-eight, Switzer hasn't changed much. Psychologist Don Beck, who worked with Switzer for a period at Oklahoma, describes Switzer's base nature as "express self now; hell with others." Beck says Switzer basically quit maturing as his Sooners went on their winning rampage from 1973 to 1975. There is "nothing abstract or conceptual" in his approach to coaching or life, says Beck. "It's all in the moment. Brash. Gutsy. It's hedonism. In the flesh. Reptilian. Guttural. His players are warriors, and he's one of 'em. That's why he's so good one-on-one [with football players]."

He was one of 'em: See girl, get girl. That's just the way it was with most football players. The difference: Switzer, perhaps, was in constant need of some fresh sexual salve for his childhood wounds.

"I fear," says Beck, "that Barry's destined to be a lonely soul."

The regents knew of young Switzer's "romantic" reputation. They also knew he was married with three young children. Could the program withstand a scandal in the head coach's personal life? If Switzer won, yes. If not . . .

It's possible Larry Lacewell's strong recommendation of Switzer finally convinced the regents. Lacewell interviewed for the job. "But honestly, I told them Switzer would be a great choice. Our whole staff was very supportive of him getting the job. After all, he had saved our jobs [by reinventing the wishbone]."

And after all, Switzer had the imposing physical stature and the leading-man looks and magnetism. "Believe me, that matters," says Lacewell, who was charming in his own sawed-off, cotton-topped, country-clever way. But he wasn't Switzer.

Finally, Switzer was named head coach and Lacewell assistant head coach. The two did a TV show together, *The Barry and Larry Show*. At first Lacewell was the funny one. "But Switzer started taking a cue from me and coming out of his shell. He was liable to say anything."

Kay Switzer was surprised it took the regents so long to name her husband head coach. She says he lied and told her "the problem was that the board of regents thought he didn't have a classy enough wife. That nearly killed me."

Many nights, Kay and Lacewell's wife, Criss, kept each other company, sometimes sharing a fifth of scotch into the wee hours. "I really just thought Barry was out drinking," Kay says. "How stupid I was. He was out doing the world. When he needs to be, he can be the world's greatest liar."

Today, she lives by herself in Little Rock. She's still, as daughter Kathy says, "a spitfire." But Kay Switzer says she still loves Barry.

"A person could not dislike him, no matter what he had done." Kay says he still calls "when he needs a mom."

But Kay Switzer tires of reading stories about how rough Barry's childhood was. "He uses that as an excuse. Just because his father was a fuckaround doesn't mean he has to be. I mean, I was beaten [as a child] and put in the closet. But I didn't do that to my kids."

By the mid-seventies, Barry was the king of "Switzerland"—and Lacewell's fame nearly matched the head coach's. "It was funny," says Lacewell. "He never had the kind of ego head coaches usually had. He always gave all the credit to the assistants—I guess because he really didn't think the head coach was all that important, and he couldn't face his assistants if he turned into an actor and started telling the media how great he was. He definitely wanted us to share in the glory . . . Here I was a short little shit-ass country boy, and I had my own TV show. I was famous."

Once, while Switzer and Lacewell waited for a flight in an Oklahoma City airport bar, some guy made fun of his little buddy's white shoes. *Boom!* Switzer backhanded the guy. When the guy tried to fight back, Switzer dropped him with one punch as the airport police came running.

But there was a limit to Switzer's respect for Lacewell.

Times were wild. Nobody had heard of AIDS. Lots of Bobs and Carols were swapping with Teds and Alices. The OU coaching staff—still a bunch of kids themselves—was often fueled by alcohol. Affairs resulted like wishbone fumbles.

In the spring of 1978, Lacewell discovered that Switzer had been having an affair with Criss. How could he do that to his best friend? Perhaps *because* Lacewell was his best friend. The higher the risk, the greater the rush—the better the painkiller?

On a staff trip to Hawaii, Lacewell stormed into the Switzers' bungalow in the middle of the night, yanked his best friend out of bed by the foot, and confronted him. Kay Switzer, who had suspected Barry and Criss for some time, rolled over and tried to go back to sleep.

Lacewell left Oklahoma in a rage. Three years later, Kay divorced Barry. Kay says, "I gave him a chance to quit [cheating on her] and of course he didn't. He said, 'Kay, I just didn't think you'd do it [file for divorce].' I didn't come out of it too well financially [though without legal obligation Barry still sends her about $2,000 a month]. But I still have my pride."

Lacewell was left with one question. "As big as Switzer's heart is," he said, "the one thing I've never quite understood is why he sometimes breaks the hearts of those who love him the most."

3

TRAGIC MAGIC

And when I die I'll be Sooner dead . . .
—*From the Oklahoma fight song*
"Boomer Sooner"

Troy Aikman spent his childhood in Cerritos, California, very near Long Beach, where Barry Switzer spent his formative years. Year-round sunshine, the nearby beach, Disneyland, the Hollywood influence—Southern California gave Aikman and Switzer a jarring beach-boy background for soon-to-be-country boys. California kids forced to retrace the *Grapes of Wrath* trail to rural Oklahoma or Arkansas can have it rough. They know this fairy-tale world exists out there by the Pacific—"Great place to grow up," says Switzer—yet they're stuck in the backwoods among kids who wouldn't know Knott's Berry Farm from the one up the road.

Maybe it isn't coincidence that Aikman and Switzer describe themselves as loners.

After Aikman's seventh-grade year, his parents decided to move the family to a 172-acre ranch seven miles from Henryetta, Oklahoma, a glass-factory town of about 6,500 some two hours by pickup from the University of Oklahoma. "I just knew my life was over," says Aikman, whose dream had been to play baseball for the traditionally powerful University of Southern California before advancing to the big leagues. Henryetta is a long way from the big leagues.

The move was so traumatic for Aikman that, when he became

famous, the first book he chose to do wasn't an "I'm the greatest" autobiography; it was an advice-for-kids book called *Things Change*. And how: Now Aikman was ordered to slop the hogs every morning. But he didn't dare complain. Aikman, an only son, did not argue with his father, who didn't say much and didn't have to. Troy was taught to keep his mouth shut and work his fingers to the bone— almost literally. Once, while he and his father were herding bulls into a chute for vaccination, Aikman noticed Ken Aikman stifle pain when he bumped a bandaged finger. His dad worked pipeline construction jobs in California and often banged up his hands without complaint. But Troy knew this was no scratch.

It took several tries, but he finally convinced his father to show him the wound. Troy was shocked to see the tip of his father's finger had been cut off, exposing the bone. It took several more tries to convince him he needed to get it cleaned and stitched. The doctor warned Ken Aikman not to work for a month. He immediately flew back to California and was back to work in a couple of days.

Troy Aikman was taught men don't cry.

Barry Switzer says, "I'm a weenie. I cry easy."

Troy Aikman was taught that men don't show emotion, especially around strangers.

Barry Switzer, any time or place, can be a raw nerve of unpredictable tirades or painfully honest revelations or childlike silliness or high jinks.

Aikman and Switzer longed at times for their fathers to express their love for them. Yet Switzer never felt the pressure to please his father. "I knew how proud he was of me," Switzer says. Aikman never was quite sure about his father. Only after he was named MVP in the Cowboys' first new-era Super Bowl victory did his sister provide the highlight: She told Troy that their father had told her he was "as proud as he had been in his life." Even that secondhand hug "was incredible to me," said Troy, "knowing my dad."

Aikman attributes part of his success in pro football's no-pain, no-fame world to showing his dad that he, too, can play with a sliced-off finger if necessary (or a concussion or a busted shoulder or a torn-up knee or a pulled hamstring or a split chin or a sprained thumb or any of the many injuries Troy Ache-man has endured playing quarterback for the Dallas Cowboys). He also credits Ken Aikman with teaching him the value of getting up early, being on time, and working hard, even for the common wages his father always earned. Even if Troy played football for free, he would be the same demanding perfectionist his father was of him.

Unless, that is, his mom calmed him down. "She's as sweet as apple pie," Aikman says. Not only are Aikman's Cerritos and Henryetta streaks often at odds, but so are his conflicting mom and dad sides. Aikman has told me, "One side of my personality is exactly like my father: very intense, driven, and focused. Then there are other sides from my mother: very sensitive and compassionate toward others. Sometimes those two personalities conflict."

So do Southern California and Oklahoma. "What I don't like is people stereotyping me. On one hand I like down-home things; on the other hand, I like elaborate things. I can relate to a wide spectrum of people because I've been on both ends. When I went to UCLA I didn't wear cowboy boots. I wore what I have on now [print beach-type button-down shirt, shorts, and deck shoes]. When I get to Oklahoma or Texas, I wear my boots. That's me, too . . . When we got ready to go to the first Super Bowl, Leigh [Steinberg] said we needed to talk about how I was going to deal with the media on press day, because it's extremely important how you come off. I said, 'I'm just going to be myself.' He said, 'What is yourself?'"

His mom side is a clotheshorse. The dad side is the neat freak who wants his clothes arranged perfectly by style and color in his closet and drawers. The mom side prompts him to change his hairstyle often: wet look, dry look; reverse-curl bangs, combed back; parted down the middle, parted on the side; long in back, short all over. Aikman says he was the first in his new eighth-grade class in Henryetta to wear his hair over his ears. For a new kid, that took nerve (from his dad) and creative flair (from his mom).

Perhaps the mom side was most responsible for the high school typing contest Aikman won against an all-girl field at Okmulgee State Tech (75 words per minute). The dad side triggered his urge to play football, and it was his dad who told Troy that quitting at midseason wasn't allowed. That happened during Troy's first year in Henryetta, when he decided he was tired of football. Two years later, as a high school sophomore, Aikman started at quarterback for the Henryetta Fighting Hens.

Just about every Fighting Hen dreamed of being a Sooner. Just about every kid in Oklahoma did. The Dallas Cowboys were big in Oklahoma; perched atop Texas, Oklahoma is something of a Texas wannabe. But the Cowboys weren't quite as magical as the OU Sooners. In Oklahoma, the Sooners were at least as important as oil.

Before Oklahomans discovered the wonders of college football, the only bowl they knew was the dust bowl depicted in John Steinbeck's bleak, tragic *The Grapes of Wrath*. Prairie dust storms darkened the sky and made farming nearly impossible and state pride as scarce as rain. Thousands of Oklahomans migrated to California looking for steady work tending the promised land, and often found the grass no greener.

So when Dr. George Cross took over as University of Oklahoma president in 1944, the state was in search of a new identity. Cross is credited with creating and feeding what became known as the "Oklahoma Football Monster" to help Oklahomans overcome their inferiority complex. Cross once told the Oklahoma legislature, "I want to build a university of which the football team can be proud."

Thanks to Cross and coach Bud Wilkinson, whose teams captured the country's imagination with a record forty-seven-game winning streak, many Oklahomans began making frequent trips to a tropical bowl, Miami's Orange Bowl, annual New Year's home of the Big Eight champion. Oklahoma football put the state on the national map. Growing up in Oklahoma City, attending lots of OU games, I personally experienced the phenomenon. By the sixties, when my family went on out-of-state vacations, telling people we were from Oklahoma invariably prompted, "Ah, the Sooners." Incredibly, just because we were Sooner fans gave us a sort of celebrity status. Talented athletes who probably wouldn't have chosen OU if not for its football team were winning out-of-state bragging rights for me and my family.

Only in America.

But you have to understand what it meant to someone from such a downtrodden state to watch the Oklahoma Sooners knock off national powers and wind up number one in the country, as Barry Switzer's Sooners were voted in 1974 and 1975. The crimson-and-cream jerseys . . . the student spirit leaders called Rufnex shooting shotguns in the air as overflowing Owen Field erupted after touchdowns . . . the incessant fight song "Boomer Sooner" . . . the horse-pulled Sooner Schooner racing up and down the field at wishbone speed . . .

By Aikman's junior year at Henryetta, Barry Switzer's stature in Oklahoma had eclipsed Will Rogers's. Then again, Switzer had become Will Rogers with a dark side: a charming rogue, the man many hated to love. It wasn't that Switzer never met a fan he didn't like, but that he never met one who wouldn't grudgingly like him if his Sooners won.

Switzer's father would have gotten a chuckle out of the nickname Sooners. It refers to the Oklahoma settlers who jumped the gun before the Land Run of 1889. Sooners staked out their plots the night before. Sooners were cheaters. To some, Barry Switzer was born to be a Sooner.

Yet he so spoiled Oklahomans with eight straight Big Eight championships and an average of 10.4 wins and 1.1 losses that sportswriters were again calling fans "Chinamen." The nickname was born one 1950s Saturday during the forty-seven-game winning streak when Oklahoma had beaten Kansas State by "only" 13. *Daily Oklahoman* sports editor Jay Simon fielded call after call from fans wanting to know the score—then what the hell was wrong with OU. Simon finally turned to other staffers and said, "I wonder how much rice a Chinaman can eat?"

Switzer had become a bull in a Chinaman's closet. Many writers from Oklahoma City and Tulsa who covered the seventies Sooners have told me it was nearly impossible to ask Switzer anything but a "positive" question during group interviews. He was king, above cross-examination. With profane explosions, he mostly bullied scribes who dared question why, for instance, he had chosen to go for it on fourth-and-one. Like many old-school coaches, Switzer believed the media who "got to" cover his team should stick to writing about the good things.

By 1980, in part because the bootlegger's boy flaunted his drinking and partying and womanizing, Switzer constantly was being accused of—and angrily denying—everything from buying players to point-shaving to profiting from insider stock tips. Most of it, he said, came from what he calls "fiction writers"—newspaper and magazine writers in search of dirt-filled stories based on misleading half-truths or outright lies that sell more newspapers and magazines. But the most outlandish rumor had to be the "Switzer-Lacewell Orange Bowl Conspiracy" rumor that swept the state after Switzer's most humiliating loss ever, 31–6, as an 18-point favorite over his alma mater, Arkansas, in the '78 Orange Bowl. A win that night would have given Switzer another national championship.

My mother was more upset and confused by that loss than any OU loss ever. Many OU fans had to have a reason for it, other than the Razorbacks were better prepared and outplayed the Sooners. Talk spread like an oil-field fire that Switzer and Lacewell threw the game to pay off Las Vegas gambling debts. Yes, Switzer loves going to Vegas. But strategically sabotaging your team to throw a national championship game?

That game, by the way, was the last Switzer and Lacewell would coach together.

But beginning in 1981, three straight four-loss seasons made Switzer more and more vulnerable. By then, the "Chinamen" considered 8–4 a losing season. Switzer says an athletic department "conspiracy" was afoot to get him fired. Switzer says the bury-Barry movement was led by a regent named Mickey Imel. Switzer probably hadn't endeared himself to Imel by telling a joke about him at a stag party. In *Bootlegger's Boy*, Switzer writes of playing golf with Imel and telling a group of OU supporters: "Watching Mickey play golf is kind of like watching somebody masturbate. Everybody watching gets sick. Mickey's the only one that gets any enjoyment out of it."

As Kay Switzer says, "Sometimes Barry would try to be funny and just embarrass me to death."

Switzer says he buried the "conspiracy" with help from many in the athletic department who remained loyal to him. But living on the edge for so long has made Switzer susceptible to paranoia. For years his father was on the lookout for lawmen and robbers. For years Switzer was on the lookout for NCAA investigators armed with false accusations . . . for righteous hypocrites trying to undermine him . . . for "fiction writers" plotting to set him up for a fall. Several times during the 1995 Cowboy season, Switzer mentioned to me "my paranoia about the damn media." By then, he was battling what he and his loyalists considered the most vicious and powerful bury-Barry conspiracy Switzer has faced: the one orchestrated by Troy Aikman's friends.

The summer before his senior year, Aikman actually attended the Barry Switzer Football Camp. Now, Aikman would sooner attend Barry Manilow's football camp. Even more unlikely, young Aikman was primarily a passer attending a camp run by OU staffers who taught mostly the option running attack. Oh, well, it was 1983, and Aikman was just a shy, naive kid from a ranch some 100 miles east on I–40.

For Aikman it was worth it just to play on the same artificial turf the Sooners roamed.

One of Switzer's assistants mentioned to the head coach that he should take a look at this quarterback from Henryetta. Switzer's first question: "Is he black?" Today, that kind of question might irritate a proud Aikman, who might consider it reverse-racist bias. But OU coach Switzer knew that, usually, the superior quickness and agility of blacks better suited them for running the tightrope that is the wishbone. Switzer was informed that Aikman was a white kid with enough speed (4.7 in the 40-yard dash) and athletic ability to run the option, but that he could throw the hell out of the ball. Hmmm, thought Switzer, and walked out into the July heat to watch this Troy Aikman throw.

"I saw a tall blond, 6'3", 185," Switzer says, "and after two or three throws, I thought, This guy doesn't know how good he is." *Hmmm.* Memories of his '74 and '75 national championships were beginning to fade. He was beginning to take some heat in the papers.

And Jimmy Johnson was courting Aikman. Since Johnson had become head coach at Oklahoma State, in Stillwater, Switzer had dusted him three straight seasons. But one thing the OU coach cannot survive is losing to OSU, still derisively called the "Aggies" by Sooner fans. (Oklahoma State was once Oklahoma Agricultural and Mechanical.) The OU coach could get away with losing an occasional game to Texas or Nebraska, but forcing Sooner fans to live for a year with gloating "Aggies" was not acceptable.

Hmmm, thought Switzer, if Johnson is shrewd enough to put this kid in a pro-style offense and turn him loose . . . It wasn't that Aikman was being recruited nationally by passing programs like Stanford or BYU or Miami. His senior team would miss the playoffs with a 6–4 record. Aikman was not all-everything.

Yet why risk watching Aikman mature into some golden-armed Switzer killer? Switzer walked straight across the Owen Field turf and did something he says he never had before with a quarterback: He offered him a scholarship on first glance. In those days, the NCAA allowed each school's football program about twenty more total scholarships, and Switzer could afford to use one on a player who might not help OU—but might hurt OU at OSU. Of course, Switzer did have to convince Aikman that ground-bound Oklahoma would throw the ball more—and friends of Switzer's laugh that the only passes he knew how to throw were after hours. Yet the previous season, Switzer *had* resorted to showcasing the talent of freshman back Marcus Dupree in the I formation—a two-back set that allowed for two split receivers (instead of the wishbone's one) and more passing options.

Says Aikman, "I was told they would use a lot more I."

Johnson warned Aikman that wouldn't happen, but Aikman wanted to be a Sooner. Switzer didn't lose any sleep over how he had sold Aikman. What the hell, Switzer thought, if Aikman turned out to be pretty good, OU would throw more.

In "Switzerland," Barry was afraid of no player. He was the Franchise, undefeated when challenged by the greatest of Sooners. There was a limit to his leniency. Says Lacewell, "One thing about Switzer: Don't push him into a corner or he will come out swinging with both fists." Just as Aikman signed, Marcus Dupree left Oklahoma after a nationally publicized who's-the-boss clash with Switzer. Dupree, who turned pro after his sophomore season, "could have been the best who ever played the game, if he'd wanted," says Switzer.

Switzer calls Brian Bosworth the best linebacker he ever coached. Yet Bosworth's "The Boz" image—he turned himself into a Stallone/Schwarzenegger superhero—soon outgrew even Switzer's loose boundaries. When Bosworth pushed Switzer into a corner with negative remarks about the "out of control" program, Switzer ran him off before his senior season.

But Switzer kept winning because there was always another potential all-American out there somewhere on the Oklahoma or Texas prairie. One day, Switzer would find that things are very different in pro football. Dallas is not in "Switzerland." Troy Aikman is not Dupree or "The Boz." But in early 1984, the name Aikman didn't mean much to OU fans, or even probably to Switzer. Aikman would start off about fifth on the quarterback depth chart.

If Aikman's mom had heard some of the legendary night-before-game stories about Switzer, she might have been horrified. Lots of mamas and some daddies probably would have been. Lots of Mrs. Aikmans might not have sent their precious Troys off to this surrogate father.

Before several Oklahoma-Texas games, I was told by ex-players, assistant coaches, athletic department officials, and media people that Switzer had done it again: He had closed the motel bar and had a rip-roaring hangover that might kill lesser men. Those who loved him were worried about him. Yet they usually grinned and said, "Oh, well. That's 'Switz.'" Always had been. Always would be. The guy seemed indestructible. By kickoff, he had shaken off the hangover as if it were a hangnail. No one ever said Switzer's drinking impaired his ability to coach.

Before his divorce, the Orange Bowl joke was always, "Switzer needs three hotel rooms: One for his wife, one for his girlfriend, and one if he gets lucky."

But the all-timer involved an old running buddy (and University of Arkansas running back) named Dale Boutwell, who probably would have given Switzer a good fistfight when they were teammates. Switzer was comfortable around Boutwell because he, too, was from a small town in Arkansas—Cotton Plant. Boutwell often was down on his luck, and when he showed up in Norman, he could be a bad influence on even Switzer.

One Friday night the team stayed at a hotel in Oklahoma City before busing to Stillwater for a game against Oklahoma State. Switzer and Boutwell partied most of the night—booze, broads, the works—and Switzer failed to make it to the team breakfast. In fact, the buses were about to leave when an assistant called Switzer's room from the lobby, to see if he was running late. Boutwell answered, obviously awakened from a deep sleep. When the assistant asked for Switzer, Boutwell said, "What do you want with him?"

"Well," said the assistant, "I think there's a game today in Stillwater."

So the buses were a few minutes late leaving? Don't sweat the details. Switzer made it. OU won. Somehow, Boutwell and Switzer didn't drink each other to death. In fact, one day they would be roommates in Dallas.

Switzer had recruited option quarterback Danny Bradley out of Pine Bluff, home of Arkansas Pine Bluff, to which his father had sent several of Crossett's blacks. "I basically raised Danny Bradley," says Switzer. "He's like a son to me."

Bradley, who is black, started at quarterback for the '84 Sooners. He was backed up by Mike Clopton, a junior-college transfer who was ruled ineligible early in the season. Troy Aikman had proven to be a little better than second-year quarterback Kyle Irvin, who also was white and had been redshirted as a freshman. But neither young quarterback dazzled the coaching staff, and freshman Aikman had been redshirted, meaning he could add a fifth year of eligibility if he didn't play in a game his first season. You can just hear Switzer saying, "Damnit, that's the last time I recruit two white quarterbacks."

In fact, the Sooners were recruiting one of the most elusive little option wizards OU assistants had ever seen, from Banning High School, south of Los Angeles. Most schools wanted Jamelle Holieway, who was black, to play defensive back in college. Not OU, one program that kept its options open. Clearly, Switzer wasn't planning to junk the wishbone for Aikman.

Certainly not in '84, with senior cocaptain Bradley at the controls. Bradley would be named Big Eight offensive player of the year. As a starter, Bradley would be 9–0–1 that regular season. But Bradley would miss one game, against Kansas in Lawrence, with thumb and ankle injuries. The staff thought he could be ready to play in a week, but not that Saturday.

Switzer had no choice but to waste Aikman's redshirt year by playing him at Kansas. "I wasn't ready," Aikman says. According to several staff members, they worried about the kid from Henryetta because he sometimes failed to grasp the simplest offensive concepts. "He always had that faraway look in his eyes," one Switzer staffer says. "We wondered if we were reaching him. We had our doubts about how football-smart he was."

Meanwhile, Aikman had his doubts about Danny Bradley. Says a Cowboy source, "Troy felt like, when he was a freshman, Danny really 'big-timed' him—you know, acted too cool for him and didn't really give him the time of day."

Twelve years later in Dallas, Bradley would plead with Aikman to help him get a job with the Cowboy organization.

In 1984 the ex–Henryetta Fighting Hen also was struggling to adjust to Switzer's athletic dorms, which seemed like a nonstop combination of Mardi Gras and New Year's Eve. "Pretty wild," Aikman understates, one corner of his mouth lifting into a grin. "Of course, you have to remember that I didn't drink in high school and thought that no athlete should drink." Aikman would get angry when he'd hear about other high school athletes drinking beer. (Things change: Once, in the spring after his first Super Bowl triumph, Aikman was so hung over after the Troy Aikman charity gala that he overslept and missed the start of his own golf tournament.) But in '84, Ken Aikman's boy believed athletes should be more exemplary than Eagle Scouts. Even today, there remains an eighteen-year-old in Aikman who was a victim of the "role model myth" in sports. He arrived at OU prepared to look up to some of his heroes, including the coach. He was in for the same shock many fans experience when they put most Dallas Cowboys—or most pro athletes—on pedestals.

After a while Aikman wouldn't let his girlfriend come by herself to his dorm room; he made her meet him in the parking lot. Once, a freshman girl knocked on his door selling magazine subscriptions. He warned her to try selling in a safer dorm. She didn't take him seriously. She made it three or four doors in Bud Wilkinson Hall before she was surrounded by football players explaining how she could sell them lots of subscriptions.

In October of '84, Aikman was a wide-eyed Tom Sawyer as he started at Kansas for an OU team ranked number two in the country. Members of that Switzer staff still wish they had limited the game plan to take some pressure off young Aikman. Instead, the coaches attempted to let him do some of what he did best—and what they understood least. They let him pass. He threw three interceptions in the first half. For the game, he completed two passes— two shovel passes. Aikman went 2 of 14 as OU was shocked, 28–11, by lowly Kansas. *Toto, I've a feeling we're not in Henryetta anymore.* Around Oklahoma that night, Troy Aikman probably was cussed more than Barry Switzer.

"That's the kind of game that can ruin a young quarterback," Aikman says. It was an early tribute to his character that he rebuilt his confidence through many lonely jock-dorm nights as he waited for Danny Bradley to graduate.

But no, says Aikman, he does not hold any sort of subconscious grudge against Switzer for throwing him into that Kansas game.

The first I heard of it was in a motel bar in Columbus, Ohio, on Friday night, September 23, 1977. I don't believe Gary Gibbs used the term Sooner Magic, but he certainly described it. Gibbs, a good friend of mine who later succeeded Switzer as head coach, was a defensive assistant under coordinator Lacewell.

The following afternoon, before about 90,000 people, Oklahoma would play Ohio State in what Switzer called "one of the greatest games I ever saw or participated in." But that night, Gibbs predicted that if the game were close late in the fourth quarter, "We'll win because we just believe we'll win every close game. 'Lace' and [offensive coordinator] Gaylon Hall are better than [Ohio State's] coordinators, and when you play for Barry Switzer, you just think you're going to win."

That was it. Switzer's swagger inspired confidence the way perhaps no college coach ever had. Outwardly, anyway, he was just so damn sure of himself. The way he moved, smoked cigarettes, and cussed was just so commandingly cool. Switzer's body language was especially comforting to young men aged eighteen to twenty-two preparing to play before a vast sea of hostile Buckeye fans.

Cowboy radio analyst Dale Hansen remembers covering one of Switzer's Orange Bowl weeks and watching legendary Miami Dolphin coach Don Shula walk onto the field during an Oklahoma practice to say hello to Switzer. "It was amazing," Hansen says. "Shula can be very intimidating, but it was like Shula's body language changed, and all of a sudden *he* was being granted an audience by Barry Switzer. I mean, Switzer was just larger than life when he moved around the field during those practices."

Switzer's Sooners reflected the spectacular survival that had been his life: When you least expected it, he pulled off some great escape. A reward for all his good deeds? A pact with the devil? Pure luck? When I've pushed him for explanation, Switzer seems genuinely at a loss, saying, "I honestly don't know why a lot of things have broken right for me." As intelligent as he is in some areas, he isn't given to much introspection or analysis. He prefers to just react. That's his strength.

Perhaps that brazen belief in himself generated what came to be known as Sooner Magic.

Against Ohio State, Oklahoma jumped ahead 20–0. But the Buckeyes rallied furiously to take a 28–20 lead. The Sooners scored with 1:29 left in the game to cut the lead to 28–26, but the option was stuffed on a 2-point try. The Sooners tried the obvious onside kick—and magically recovered! With three seconds left, OU had positioned itself for a 41-yard field goal.

Ohio State coach Woody Hayes called time-out. He wanted to force the visiting kicker, Uwe von Schamann, to ponder the magnitude of the moment. But as the fans chanted, "Block that kick! Block that kick!" von Schamann began making like an orchestra leader, conducting their chant with his index fingers. Only Barry Switzer's kicker would conduct himself in such an outrageous manner. Of course, von Schamann then nailed a field goal from 41 yards that probably would have been good from 61. Suddenly, the only noise in that enormous stadium was made by the Sooners dogpiling von Schamann. Oklahoma 29, Ohio State 28.

Switzer calls it the most famous field goal in Oklahoma history.

Sooner Magic.

Late in the '83 season, after Switzer had dismissed Marcus Dupree from the team, the Sooners did the unthinkable, falling behind Jimmy Johnson's Oklahoma State "Aggies" 20–3 at halftime. Late in the game, Derrick Shepard turned a short pass into a near-miraculous 73-yard run with five broken tackles. OSU 20, OU 18. Johnson, expecting an onside kick, sent out his "good hands" team. Instead, Switzer ordered to kick deep. Ten members of the Sooner kickoff team heard the call—except freshman kicker Tim Lashar, who went ahead and onside kicked as his teammates raced downfield to cover a regular kickoff. But incredibly, the ball ricocheted off an OSU player's helmet right into the hands of OU's Scott Case, running full speed. Lashar kicked the winning field goal with 1:57 left, and Switzer was 5–0 against Johnson. Imagine Johnson's torment.

Sooner Magic.

It often was tragic for Nebraska. In Oklahoma's biggest game of the year—the one that nearly always decided the Orange Bowl berth, if not the national title—Switzer was 12–5 against Nebraska. Eight times Switzer's Sooners came from behind some impossible way to shock the Cornhuskers. Says Dale Hansen, a devout Nebraska fan, "All anybody in Nebraska thinks of Switzer is that he always pulled some rabbit out of the hat—some hook-and-lateral trick play—and beat poor old Tom Osborne. He really had Tom's number."

In 1984, after his humiliating debut, Troy Aikman watched as

Bradley returned to guide Oklahoma toward another Orange Bowl. That road again went through Lincoln, where Nebraska was a 6-point favorite. Late in the '95 Cowboy season, Cowboy staffer Bradley remembered the '84 game this way: "Our defense had just held them with a great goal-line stand at the 1-foot line. The score was tied, 10–10. With about 36 seconds left we had the ball fourth and about two at the 50. Switzer called time-out and called me over. He said, 'Thomas Lott did it in 1976. J. C. Watts did it in 1978. This is what you were recruited to do—to make a big play to beat Nebraska. Now go do it!' I said, 'What do you want me to run?' He said, 'I don't know what the hell to call. That's what you're supposed to do.' I went with our old faithful, 16 lead, the option off tackle to the short side of the field. [Tight end] Keith Jackson blocked down on the end. [Halfback] Steve Sewell got the linebacker. I cut upfield and outran the safety 50 yards for the touchdown. We won, 17–10."

Sooner Magic.

Actually, though, OU led 10–7 at the time of the goal-line stand. Bradley's late TD run—from 29 yards—merely iced the victory cake, 17–7.

Bradley is known to exaggerate slightly. Late in the 1995 Cowboy season, several Cowboy staffers and assistant coaches would wonder if Bradley had gotten a little carried away with Cowboy player complaints about Aikman. Bradley was passing them along to Switzer, the father figure he still strived to please.

In 1985 Aikman and Switzer faced an identity crisis: Are we a passing team that runs or a running team that passes? "To be honest," Aikman told me, "I never felt comfortable there, like I belonged."

Switzer says, "Our wishbone never quite got untracked with Troy at quarterback."

Jerry Jones says, "Troy is a very structured person—he wants to know school is out at 3:30, versus any ambiguous flow—which allows you to be a good option quarterback."

Aikman, of course, would one day turn into a fanatically precise and accurate dropback passer. Sticking him in an instinctive, extemporaneous running offense was unfair to him and the team. It was like dropping a methodical Henryetta farmboy in the middle of a New York City rush hour.

Aikman says, "They put in some things [new pass plays], but it wasn't what I thought it would be. I guess it was unrealistic to think things would change dramatically."

Some things don't change.

Switzer says, "Maybe things worked out best for everybody."

Though Aikman's offense had struggled, the Sooners were 3–0 when the University of Miami visited Norman. Hurricane warning: Miami had a new coach, Jimmy Johnson. This game would be a bizarre turning point in the careers of Johnson, Switzer, and Aikman.

Johnson, who finally had some OU-style talent, in effect did to Switzer what Switzer had done to Darrell Royal. During warm-ups and the coin toss, the Hurricanes did an OU on OU, taunting and trash-talking the Sooners in their own backyard. Johnson encouraged it, hoping to turn the psychological tables on a Switzer outfit that loved to intimidate visitors.

The Hurricanes quickly backed it up. Early on, Vinny Testaverde hit a sophomore receiver named Michael Irvin for a 56-yard touchdown. But Aikman responded by playing the game of his young life. He hit six of his first seven passes, including a 14-yarder for a TD. His 49-yard option run for a TD was nullified by a penalty. OU trailed 14–7 with nine minutes left in the second quarter when Aikman was creamed from either side just as he threw. His ankle was broken; he was gone for the season. If a similar fate befell Aikman the Cowboy, Super Bowl hopes would be shattered. But . . .

Sooner Magic?

Aikman was replaced by 5'9" freshman Jamelle Holieway, Aikman's flip (and hip) side. Jammin' Jamelle, who had no future in pro football, wore lots of jewelry and a cocky grin. He also wore out defenses with the quickest feet and mind Switzer ever saw in a wishbone quarterback. He wasn't quite ready to turn around the Miami game, which the Hurricanes won 27–14, but beginning the next Saturday, Holieway's Sooners won eight in a row, including the Orange Bowl, 25–10, over Penn State. Favored to win the Sugar Bowl, Johnson's Hurricanes self-destructed and were routed by Tennessee.

Switzer won another national championship.

It's doubtful his offense would have been nearly as dominant with Aikman at quarterback—or won its last eight without Holieway pulling the trigger. That would be Aikman's first bloody taste of the Switzer Luck. Aikman would experience it again in December of 1995.

Though Switzer would go 11–1 in '85, '86 and '87, each loss would be to Johnson. An irritated Switzer says, "It's as simple as this: When I had the better players, I beat Jimmy [at Oklahoma State]. When he had better players [at Miami], he beat me."

Yet many coaches have asked me this question about Switzer's "talent wins" theory: Who wins when the talent is equal? Arguably, the talent was equal when Oklahoma played Miami. Had Johnson and staff outcoached Switzer and staff? By then, had Switzer lost some of his drive and edge?

Whatever, that no longer was Aikman's problem. In the spring, he told Switzer he wanted to transfer, "and as a parent myself," says Switzer, "I knew it was the best thing." Yet it's significant that Switzer didn't merely tell Aikman "good luck." He asked where Aikman wanted to go. Aikman said Stanford, Arizona State, or UCLA. Switzer began calling those coaches to arrange visits. Once a Sooner, always a Sooner.

Aikman chose UCLA. That summer, when Aikman returned to Henryetta, Switzer called and asked if he wanted a job with a beer distributor in Tulsa. Sure, said Aikman. "We parted on very good terms," Aikman says. "Later [when Aikman was playing for Johnson in Dallas] Barry called to see if I'd help Doug [Switzer's youngest son, who played quarterback]. Jimmy didn't want me to, but I did it anyway, on an off day. No, Barry and I were fine."

Had Aikman stayed and been a fifth-year senior at Oklahoma in 1988, he probably wouldn't have been too pleased with Switzer's leadership. When Switzer wasn't late for practice, he sometimes missed it altogether. More and more, he lost touch by letting his assistants do just about all the coaching and recruiting. The boot-legger's boy, who still fought financial insecurity, constantly invested in various ventures that made and lost lots of money, according to his friends. He spent more and more time on his business interests and on his three children "who have always meant a helluva lot more to me than football . . . I want to make sure my kids never have to worry about money the way I had to." Some OU insiders considered him almost semi-retired. After all, after twelve Big Eight titles, how much rice can a Switzer eat?

In 1988 Oklahoma went "only" 9–3, including a Citrus Bowl loss and an NCAA probation. Switzer termed many of the violations "piss-ant"—and proof the NCAA was laying for Oklahoma.

Then, in a four-week period in early '89, one football player wounded another (his best friend) by shooting him in the chest with a pistol in the athletic dorm, quarterback Charles Thompson was busted for selling cocaine and eventually sent to prison, and a twenty-year-old white girl who went with a girlfriend to the athletic dorm for a blind date wound up getting raped repeatedly. Two black football players were convicted and given ten-year sentences.

From the cover of *Sports Illustrated* to *Nightline*, Switzer was strung up for running an "outlaw" program. Switzer counters that during his sixteen seasons as head coach, his program had been relatively free of such incidents—that these three crimes, as bad as they were, seemed even worse because they happened so close together. In fairness, while winning back-to-back national championships, the 1994–1995 Nebraska football program suffered six police-blotter incidents. But image-wise, "nice guy" Nebraska coach Osborne always was a four-touchdown favorite over Switzer.

One thing Switzer never quite accepted: His lifestyle was a lightning rod for criticism and rumor. He was a highly visible college coach—a "maker of men"—who wasn't exactly discreet about his boyish behavior.

Then, Switzer says in *Bootlegger's Boy,* he was told the FBI was trying to "get him" on allegations that he had been in a Las Vegas hotel room with people who had cocaine, that he had manipulated drug tests to protect his players, and that he had bet on college football games with a Vegas bookie and paid losses by interstate wire. All completely untrue, says Switzer. He wasn't charged with any crime.

But on June 19, 1989, Switzer was forced to resign.

School officials indicated that removing Switzer saved the school from further scandal—that "more things would have come out" if he had remained. Beyond that, athletic department sources blamed Switzer for paying less and less attention to recruiting and allowing too many obvious "bad apples" to be signed. In the end, there were just too many negatives, magnified by too much resentment and jealousy. The king had to be deposed.

Even Switzer finally admitted sixteen years probably was enough.

Yet with his reputation, Switzer knew no college president in America would hire him to coach. The NFL? He had no experience. He was fifty-one. Who would take a chance on him?

Jerry Jones.

He had kept in touch with Jones since their days at Arkansas, seeing him socially every couple of years. Four months earlier, Jones had bought the Dallas Cowboys. But Jones had hired the hottest coach in college football.

He had hired Jimmy Johnson.

As the small world turns.

4

THE MAN WHO FIRED TOM LANDRY

If I had known what I know now, I wouldn't
have hired Jimmy in '89.

—*Jerry Jones*

In early September of 1988, one of the worst hangovers Jerry
Jones ever had helped change his life in a way few lives have been
changed. The day before, he and son Stephen had left an oil-and-
gas convention in San Diego and flown their Learjet south to Cabo
San Lucas for a little getaway. Fatefully, Jones stuck the sports section of a San Diego newspaper in his suitcase.

One name Jerry Jones never read in the sports section was Jerry
Jones.

He had become something of a legend in the oil-and-gas fields
of Arkansas and especially Oklahoma, where he had struck it rich
by, in effect, going for it every time on fourth and one. He had
become something of a puppet master in Arkansas politics, funding
this candidate, pulling his plug on that one, perhaps winning favors
in high places. Former Arkansas Congressman Tommy Robinson, a
childhood friend of Jones, once accused Jones of shifting his financial backing to Robinson's gubernatorial rival in return for preferen-

tial treatment in a controversial gas deal. What became known as the Arkla deal gouged ratepayers, said Robinson, and made Jones enough money to buy the Cowboys. Investigations proved nothing. Jones's candidate, Sheffield Nelson, beat Robinson in the Republican primary but was whipped soundly by Bill Clinton.

"All that Tommy Robinson stuff was ridiculous," says Jones, who claims he had made enough before the Arkla payoff to buy a pro football team.

By 1988, Jones was getting bored with making money, playing politics, being the man behind the men. At forty-six, Jones was ready to see *his* face on TV. He was ready for a life change, a new challenge, something *fun*, damnit. Man, he missed being around football. Those were the days, playing for the University of Arkansas. Now, he wouldn't even be able to go to Fayetteville to watch Stephen play. His twenty-three-year-old son had just graduated and joined him in the oil-and-gas business.

But father and son had kicked around the idea of trying to buy an NFL team. In fact, while visiting daughter Charlotte at Stanford, Jones had talked the San Francisco 49er folks into letting him drop by, look around, and see how a franchise is run.

Now, in Cabo, Jones just needed to "let my hair down a little," as he says. Keeping up with the Joneses after hours wasn't easy. The first night, they wound up at a place called the Giggling Marlin, where *turistas* are strung up by their feet, like a prize catch, and allowed to drink as many free margaritas as they can drink while upside-down.

Jones no longer was giggling when Stephen awakened him early the next morning. Their charter boat awaited to take them out on the high seas to catch some real marlin. The mere thought of stinking fish and a rocking boat made Jones even queasier. "You go on," he told his son. For Jones, who prides himself on being able to out-"honky-tonk" the youngest bull and still pop out of bed early, this was a rare *no mas*. No doubt Stephen kidded him about getting too old to take the pounding. No, said Jerry. Go on.

Lying there, wasting away in Margaritaville, Jones scanned the San Diego sports section through one open eye. Man, he missed football. But he was too smart to be a coach. Coaches don't make enough money or ultimately have enough control. Coaches always work for somebody. Jones wanted to be that somebody. Several of the guys he played with at Arkansas—foremost Jimmy Johnson— had taken the long dirt road through places like Picayune, Mississippi, toward head-coaching jobs. "I started paying my coaching dues," says Johnson, adding sarcastically, "Jerry went off to make his million dollars."

At one point in his twenties, Jones was so deep in debt that a woman behind the car-rental counter at Dallas's Love Field cut his credit card in two, right in front of him and other customers. Jones says, "I was broke. I didn't know it, but I was dead broke." But he kept borrowing and guaranteeing family and friends he would hit the big one. As he says, "Unlike Jimmy, I've always had a high tolerance for ambiguity. I can live with getting that phone call [that it's a dry hole] without cutting my throat." Control-freak Johnson, on the other hand, needed to know "exactly who was on his team and that practice started at two o'clock sharp," said Jones. Johnson has been known to bet (and win) large sums at the blackjack table, but his card-counting prowess allows him to maintain control of his odds.

Jones is best when defying odds. Jones is an unsinkable, undeniable, two-fisted optimist. He thrives on being told he can't. He doesn't like to be called a cockeyed optimist; that infers dumb luck. Jones believes his guts and instincts (cockeyed as they may appear) will prevail. He's a tough-to-figure contradiction: He dearly wants everyone to love him, but he doesn't give a dry hole what anyone thinks about what he chooses to do. Criticism torments him but doesn't slow or deter him.

Jerral Wayne Jones smiles more than anyone I know. He steroid-smiles so hard that his head seems stretched sideways— Steve McQueen in a funhouse mirror, eyeteeth glinting, veins bulging from a short, thick neck, cleft prizefighter's nose flattened by the many figurative blows it has endured. But Jones is a dangerous adversary because he has thrown so many knockout punches while being pummeled against the ropes. His strength is that so many adversaries have underestimated him. He's prone to exuberant exaggeration that sometimes makes him sound goofy. Yet though he comes across like a somewhat naive country boy, he grew up on the rough side of the city, the Dogtown section of North Little Rock. He's almost always in a coat and tie only because that's the uniform of the business world. Status-symbol clothes and cars aren't important to him. Winning is.

Jones is almost always in the same upbeat, let's-go-get-'em mood. You sometimes want to stop him and say, "Jerry, isn't anything ever just a little bit wrong?" He's always walking as fast as most people jog. His toes point almost sideways as he moves, as if half of him wants to go one way and accomplish one thing while the other half wants to go another way and achieve something else.

It's as if he keeps checking his watch, thinking, "Man, I might only live until I'm 100. I've still got so much left to *do*." He says he rarely sleeps more than five hours a night. He'll listen to what could go wrong, then tell you what will go right. If you listen to him long enough, you'll find yourself believing things you *know* are not true.

Jones has a history of making what, at the time, seem to be incredibly stupid decisions that turn to gold. It's almost as if Jones is so dad-gummed sure he will succeed that he *wills* success. It's not that he merely wants to succeed, but that he must.

What if he hadn't taken the newspaper to Cabo? What if he hadn't had too much to drink? Jones scanned page four of the sports section . . . then page five . . . then he saw it. Both eyes opened. A little note in "transactions" said Dallas Cowboy owner H. R. "Bum" Bright had retained Salomon Brothers, an investment firm, to find a buyer for the team. *What? The Cowboys?* It couldn't be.

Jones threw on some clothes and took off for the lobby, where he was led to a room with a single telephone. The international operator said she'd call him back when she reached Salomon Brothers. Jones paced. The phone finally rang. The connection was terrible. Jones fairly yelled, "You don't know me but my name is Jerry Jones and I'm going to buy the Dallas Cowboys."

After he was deposed, the king didn't leave "Switzerland." Barry Switzer remained as visible as ever around Norman. In fact, he kept going to Oklahoma football games.

"Hell, I was happy," he says. "I was able to do all the things I do in business without having to follow a rigid schedule. I finally had time to travel with my kids and do some things I always wanted to do."

His daughter, a girlfriend, and many friends have a different view of the five years Switzer spent out of coaching. They saw a man who flirted with depression the way he did pretty girls. They saw a king who still lived in his kingdom while facing the reality he would never rule again. No matter how many companies and investments he involved himself in, he still wasn't in the headlines and the football arena, leading and competing. He could go on and on about the "over eighty companies I've invested in," about his insurance agency and the diagnostic clinics he and his doctor buddies were putting in all over the country. But his eyes had lost their spark. The manic emotions were strangely subdued.

Daughter Kathy, now twenty-six, says she "never left his side" during his exile from football and still argues with him about what a "good life" it was. "I say, 'Dad, I watched you for those five years.'

We'd go to football games and he was treated as a has-been. It was a bad feeling. It was not a nice five years.

"He slept late every day. He was wealthy. Things [in business] were skyrocketing for him. But he was not full of life, the way he had been. It was like he was in a slump. I said, 'Dad, you're only fifty-two. You're too young to act this way.' He kept telling me he was tired of college football. But he wasn't tired of coaching."

Girlfriend Becky Buwick, gymnastics coach at Oklahoma, calls it a "death without crying." She says Switzer didn't suffer "clinical depression," but that he sometimes was depressed. She says he was in search of a new purpose and that he definitely didn't find it at OU football games, where he sat in athletic director Donnie Duncan's box. "It was the saddest thing I've ever seen," she says. "It felt so divorced." Yet, walking back and forth from his car to the stadium, the ex-king was still mobbed for autographs.

A similar fate was suffered by former Cowboy president and general manager Tex Schramm, who helped design Texas Stadium—or Tex's Stadium—and create the metallic-blue image that propelled the Cowboys into becoming America's Team. As he was forced out by new owner Jerry Jones, Schramm surprisingly negotiated for one of Texas Stadium's most coveted luxury boxes. Schramm wanted to become a guest at a party he once threw? A fan who once was Caesar? He did. Or so he thought. In his first season as a spectator, he said of his Sunday torture, "Everybody says, 'Gee, great, now you can retire.' Well, when you retire, you're supposed to do something you want. This is what I want. My life is being in this arena."

The only arena left for Switzer was the restaurant Othello's. Nearly every night, Switzer and his daughter and friends gathered at Othello's, owned by a dapper, dedicated little gentleman from Italy named Pasquale Benso, affectionately known as Patsy. He and his daughter, Camille, are part of the Switzer family. Night after night, just as he'd done in the old days, Switzer held court around what's called the "Table of Truth," where no lies can be told. Yet in a way they all felt as if they were living a lie. It was almost as if they all were has-beens.

Several of Switzer's friends told me they worried he was drinking too much nightly wine at Othello's. Too many grapes of wrath? Kathy shrugs and says, "Drinking and partying is about all he had to do."

A year or so after he left OU, it became clear to Barry Switzer that he would never coach again.

*   *   *

Right away, Jerry Jones told Bum Bright he would bid for the Cowboys only if Bright would let him bring in a new coach. *Let him?* thought Bright, who felt more like hugging Jones. While others were interested in buying the team *because* Tom Landry always had been and would be coach, Bright was no Landry worshiper. In fact, because Landry had never made any attempt at getting to know Bright—hadn't even given the owner the time of night at team Christmas parties—Bright preferred selling to someone who wanted another coach.

Of a dozen or so bidders, the only someone was Jones. In effect, by taking Jones's offer, Bright fired Landry. A few months after the sale, Bright proudly admitted to me that he chose Jones in part to get even with Landry.

But few if any Cowboy fans wanted to hear that the evening Jones closed the deal—February 25, 1989, now known as "the Saturday Night Massacre." Jones, who had almost no experience dealing with the media, enthusiastically stumbled into a public-relations disaster. In trying to observe his "do-right rule," Jones decided to accompany Tex Schramm to tell Landry of the coaching change. Jones and Schramm took Jones's jet to Austin, where they found Landry just as he was coming off the golf course. Sketchy descriptions in the Dallas-Fort Worth media fed the imaginations of outraged Landry lovers. Most people envisioned Jones interrupting Landry's round to tell him, "Sorry, pops, you're history."

A shrewd PR advisor would have told Jones to let Schramm go alone, then to make Saturday night's press conference a Landry wake instead of a Christmas-morning celebration by the Jones family. Jones was branded "Jethro" Jones, the insensitive hick from the Arkansas sticks, "The Man Who Fired Tom Landry."

Privately, Jones probably savors being the man who fired Tom Landry. Jones knows he made history. Jones knows that many smart NFL people quietly thought it was time for Landry to step down after an incomprehensible twenty-nine years. Now, Jones knows he and the new coach quickly made fans forget their bitterness by building a team that won a Super Bowl in its fourth season.

Yet the night he "fired" Landry, he did slightly soften the blow for Landry fans by explaining he wanted to work with his teammate and roommate from Arkansas, Jimmy Johnson. In retrospect, though, by stressing how much Johnson meant to him—"He'll be worth five first-round draft choices and five Heisman Trophy winners"—Jones helped create one of the biggest myths in Cowboy mythology.

Just as the masses believed Jones assassinated Landry, fans everywhere accepted that Jerry and Jimmy were best buddies from Arkansas. They were not. Certainly not as far as Johnson was concerned. In early 1993, Johnson told me he played along with the "buddy" stories only because he didn't want to hurt Jones's feelings. He said the two never saw each other socially during their years at Arkansas. Johnson even dropped these two little bombs on me (and Jones): Johnson said (1) they roomed together on the road only because their names fell in alphabetical order and (2) they were cocaptains because every senior was a co-captain.

Recently, Jones dropped this little bomb on me (and Johnson): Jones says he leaned toward hiring Switzer over Johnson in 1989. Switzer hadn't yet been forced out at Oklahoma. Yes, the program had just been rocked by the shooting, the rape, and the arrest of its quarterback for selling cocaine. Yet Jones says Frank Broyles, whose advice he values most, gave Switzer the edge over Johnson. "And coach Broyles," says Jones, "is uniquely qualified to comment on both." Switzer and Johnson played and coached for Broyles.

Jones says, "From a standpoint of winning and coaching and motivating, Barry probably had the edge. Barry had the more distinguished record [his .837 college winning percentage is the fourth highest ever behind only Notre Dame's Knute Rockne at .881, Frank Leahy at .864, and Carlisle's George Woodruff at .846], but Jimmy had had more success on a contemporary basis. The swing for me was Jimmy's background in Texas [he grew up in Port Arthur]. I just thought he'd be a little more palatable for Cowboy fans."

Imagine this PR nightmare for some unknown from Arkansas who had just bought the Dallas Cowboys: "Firing" Landry and replacing him with "The Outlaw Who Ran Darrell Royal Out of Coaching." Barry Switzer was the Antichrist to many fans in Texas. That was too much even for a Jerry Jones. In February of 1989, with accusations mounting against Switzer at the University of Oklahoma, Jones made the wise choice. "I guess we had enough problems as it was, huh?" he says, chuckling. If Jones had hired Switzer, many OU insiders quietly would have said, "Thank you, Jerry," for saving them the negative publicity of having to fire Switzer.

In a weird irony, in late 1995 some Cowboy insiders would say, "Thank you, Oklahoma," for hiring a new head coach—Cowboy assistant John Blake—whose job security in Dallas was being threatened by mounting accusations from other assistants and from Troy Aikman.

Only in Dallas—and Norman.

After Switzer's Cowboys won Super Bowl XXX, in an interview for this book, Jones added some potent perspective to his original decision to hire Johnson over Switzer: "If I had known what I know now, I wouldn't have hired Jimmy in '89. The key word is undermine." Johnson, says Jones, tried to undermine him and assume complete control of the franchise. Johnson, he says, tried to undermine his credibility with the media, with assistant coaches, with front-office members, with players. With rising emotion, Jones expresses the essence of his "ideal" relationship with Switzer: "There's not an undermining bone in Barry Switzer's body. He's the antithesis."

If only Jones's quarterback agreed.

One night at a speaking engagement in Oklahoma City, Barry Switzer told his audience, "Man, I wish I had a best friend from college who would give me a ten-year contract to coach a pro team." When the remark got back to Johnson, he was insulted and vowed to end any relationship he had with Switzer. Yet Switzer wasn't trying to belittle Johnson. Switzer was speaking the sad truth.

Bum Bright didn't choose to sell the Cowboys to Jerry Jones only to undermine Landry. No, Bright also was pleasantly surprised by Jones's financial offer. Jones had scraped up enough cash—$140 million—to compete with big-boy bidders such as Jerry Buss, owner of the Los Angeles Lakers, and with a Japanese group said to be "price insensitive." A source close to the sale said, "The Japanese were ready to make an offer with no real sense of how much the Dallas Cowboys were worth. To them it was like, 'Oh, Dallas Cowboys! How much? Two hundred million? Three hundred?'" Bright, a World War II veteran, wasn't interested in doing business with the Japanese.

Today, Jones sighs and says, "People just don't want to hear this." But, he says, what he bought in '89 was "a piece of shit." Simply put, Tex Schramm was spending a whole lot more money than a 3–13 America's Team was generating. Ticket sales had become an embarrassment. Texas Stadium was no longer the place to see and be seen. Bum's bright idea—a new upper level of crown suites ringing the stadium—had become his crowning blow. Many sat unsold.

Schramm did Jones a career-making favor by telling him, "You will not make money owning this football team."

Jones jumped in with both "bare" feet and slowly turned a rich boy's toy into a fat-free, money-making monster. Jones refused to keep treating the Cowboys like some nonprofit religious institution. He took a media flogging for staff cuts, for raising ticket prices and downgrading the seat locations of longtime season-ticket holders, for prohibiting carry-in alcohol and forcing patrons to buy booze from Jones—for trying to make a buck off anything that had to do with the Cowboys.

Today, the Japanese group wouldn't be overpaying if it offered $300 million for the Cowboys.

Jones brought in a trusted old friend from Little Rock, investment banker George Hays, to be his vice president of marketing. Hays, silver of hair and tongue, breezed in with an attitude of, "Don't tell me what didn't work in the past."

Hays says, "They [Schramm's front office] created a great image of America's Team. But they were not marketing people from a business standpoint. They were losing $4 million a year, and nobody could figure out how to sell 108 [empty] suites."

Hays, with Jones's help, began superselling suites. They gambled that bigger suites would be more marketable to corporations and organizations, so they knocked out walls between smaller ten-seat suites and made them twenty-seaters. And they began knocking on doors, selling Jones's "guarantee" that the Cowboys would return quickly to status-symbol glory. Buy now, they said, and ex–Cowboy stars will drop by your new suite! Buy now and Cowboy scouts will visit you before games and let you in on game plans! Buy now and get to visit the field before games! Says Hays, "A CEO can be the toughest SOB out there and he will melt when he stands next to a Troy Aikman."

Right away Arkansas food king Don Tyson bought a big suite for $1 million. "That set the market value," says Hays. How suite it was. In all, Jones has made about $90 million off suite sales, says Hays. Texas Stadium now has 373 suites, the highest of any stadium in any sport.

"The suites were Jerry's cornerstone," Hays says. "They gave him liquidity. They knocked the debt down. They gave Jerry peace of mind."

The day Jones closed the deal with Bright, he called his father to tell him he had bought the damn Dallas Cowboys. Pat Jones didn't pay much attention but said, "I sold three signs today. Made good deals on 'em, too." Pat Jones has hustled all his life, selling everything from insurance to groceries to billboard space. He didn't know much about the Cowboys, until the next day's newspapers . . .

and the next day's . . . and the next. Only then did the impact of his son's purchase hit him.

Pat Jones called his son back and said, "I don't care if you have to do it with mirrors, smoke, whatever. You better be a success or you'll be ruined around the country. Your credibility is on the line."

5

BETRAYAL

If you have two starting quarterbacks, you have none.

—*Old football axiom*

The "piece of shit" franchise for which Jerry Jones paid $140 million had three assets: (1) The Dallas Cowboys' invaluable intangibles package (winning tradition, mystique, dormant national appeal); (2) star running back Herschel Walker; and (3) the first pick in the upcoming draft. Soon, Jones would have to rustle up enough cash to make the draft's best player the "highest paid rookie ever." The consensus pick by draft experts: UCLA quarterback Troy Aikman.

Finally, Johnson wouldn't have to compete for the right to sign Aikman.

Yet times and circumstances had changed. No longer was Johnson trying to shock the world by going 7–4 at Oklahoma State. Johnson and Jones shared one upstart goal: knocking all their NFL critics on their pompous asses by winning a Super Bowl, soon. As Johnson told me early in '89: You win championships with a dominant front four on defense and with a franchise quarterback. Back then, Johnson wasn't completely sold on Aikman as a cornerstone.

At UCLA, Aikman's Bruins twice had lost to crosstown rival USC and failed to make it to the Rose Bowl. Several Pac-10 coaches I talked to were in awe of his "measurables"—size, arm strength, release, foot speed—but they were leery of his intangibles. Was he a leader? Could he inspire a team, bring it from behind, make things happen when you most needed big plays? At the time, Joe Montana was establishing himself as the NFL's greatest winner ever. Montana was a former third-round draft choice oozing intangibles. Montana didn't have young Aikman's physical gifts. But Johnson wondered if Aikman had the gift of winning.

Then again, how could Johnson and Jones not take everybody's consensus number one pick? They'd be laughingstocks if they didn't take Aikman. Still, Johnson had a backup plan, though he certainly wasn't going to let Aikman in on it when they met at a Dallas-Fort Worth Airport hotel that spring.

Dimples flashing, Johnson can be a charmer "when he feels like it," says Jones. Says Larry Lacewell, "I've had more fun with Jimmy Johnson than I've ever had with anybody. He can be genuinely funny and charming." Especially when he has a motive. And with young Aikman, he had a strong one.

Aikman wasn't convinced he wanted to play for Johnson, either. Johnson and Jones had some selling to do.

During my first year at the *Los Angeles Times* in 1976, I was assigned a story on former Cal-Berkeley quarterback Steve Bartkowski, who had been the first player picked (by Atlanta) in the 1975 draft. Bartkowski had gone just ahead of Randy White, the initial member of the most famous draft haul ever, the "Dirty Dozen" rookies who revitalized and rocketed the Cowboys into Super Bowl X on January 18, 1976—a 21–17 loss to Pittsburgh. Atlanta fans were hoping "Peachtree Bart," as the golden-maned, golden-armed Bartkowski was being called, would likewise lift the star-crossed Falcons to January glory. Because the L.A. Rams were about to play the Falcons, their PR department arranged for me to call him in his Atlanta condo.

The guy who answered the phone said Bartkowski wouldn't be back for a few minutes. The guy said his name was Leigh Steinberg and that he was Bartkowski's agent. Steinberg and I began to chat and discovered we lived only a couple of blocks away from each other in West Los Angeles, near the Santa Monica Freeway and Overland. Small world.

Steinberg was trying to break into his business just as I was trying to rise in mine. At that point, I was a little further along: Bartkowski was Steinberg's lone client, mostly because they had known each other at Cal, where Leigh went to law school. When Steinberg returned to West L.A., where he still lived on a Pinto budget in the modest home of his parents (a high school principal and a librarian), we began to pal around. That Christmas Eve at my apartment, we debated Leigh's dubious future as a sports agent. (He called my complex "Death Valley Days" because it was so difficult to get to through the constant construction on Overland.) Steinberg was so discouraged about his lack of clients that he was prepared on January 2 to give up and join a downtown law firm. The day after Christmas, I was scheduled to interview University of Michigan players for stories I would be writing on the Rose Bowl, and though it was a borderline conflict of interest for me, I volunteered to mention Leigh's name to one of Michigan's senior stars. Linebacker John Anderson seemed like Leigh's type of guy—an all-American on and off the field—and though he was being hounded by agents, Anderson told me he would at least give Leigh a call.

They clicked. Anderson became a Pro Bowl fixture at linebacker for Green Bay. Within two years, Leigh Steinberg became the NFL's most powerful agent—and I took a job as a sports columnist in Dallas. Over the years, we joked about how odd it was that the draft never dealt him a star Cowboy client. He did have first-round pick Mike Sherrard in 1986, but injuries kept Sherrard from turning into a star.

Then fate struck.

Leigh called to tell me he had a chance to sign Troy Aikman. "It was so weird," Leigh said. "I went to talk to him at his apartment, and he lived in 'Death Valley Days.'" Yes, Aikman lived in the same complex I had. Very small world. And where had Aikman played his final college football game? In Dallas's Cotton Bowl. Against? Arkansas.

But we digress.

Soon, Steinberg and his new client were flying to Dallas to check out the new Cowboy coach and owner. Steinberg was apprehensive about Aikman's future in Dallas because of what had happened to Bartkowski in Atlanta. Behind porous offensive lines, "Peachtree Bart" had been torn limb from limb. "He took such a beating in his first couple of years," said Steinberg, "that it cut his career short. I don't want to see that repeated with Troy." Steinberg and I knew Paul Hackett from his coaching days at the University of Southern California, and Hackett had been Landry's offensive coordinator the previous three years. Hackett said, "The offensive line needs to be completely rebuilt. You cannot win at this level with [left tackle] Mark Tuinei and [left guard] Nate Newton."

Steinberg had considered trying to force Johnson and Jones to trade Aikman. But right away, Steinberg liked the two—especially

Jones. "I've never met anyone like this guy," Steinberg told me. The
red-line rpm, the conquer-the-world ambition, the creative thinking,
the obvious but irresistible salesmanship. Steinberg soon got to
know two of Jones's children, Stephen and Charlotte, who had
begun working for the Cowboys. "I don't care what has been written
about these 'rubes from Arkansas,'" Steinberg said. "Do not underestimate these people. The kids are smart as whips. Stephen was a
chemical engineering major, and Charlotte was an honors student
at Stanford and she's done some modeling. I'm very impressed."
Jones and Johnson "wined and dined us like you can't believe," said
Steinberg, who had come a long way from "Death Valley Days."

Aikman, a tough sell, was sold. Steinberg said, "He's convinced
he's going to be 'the Franchise' and that they're going to build a winner around him."

That June, as I was writing a baseball column on Nolan Ryan, a
frantic call from my office changed my plans. Stop the presses:
With the second pick in the supplemental draft, the Cowboys had
drafted Steve Walsh. *What? Why?*

Having completed a degree in international finance, Walsh had
decided to leave the University of Miami with a year of eligibility
remaining. What was left for him to accomplish? Under Johnson,
Walsh had gone 23–1 as a two-year starter, including a 12–0
national championship season in '87. With Walsh, Johnson had won
in some of the most hostile college towns—Ann Arbor, South Bend,
Tallahassee, and Baton Rouge. Walsh was a Joe Montana Junior.
Walsh dazzled scouts more with results than arm strength. Johnson
said, "He does so many things you can't coach. He's something special. He's a bottom-line quarterback. He knows how to win."

Walsh had precisely what Johnson wasn't sure about in Aikman:
proven prime-time intangibles. With Walsh, Johnson had beaten
Jamelle Holieway's Oklahoma in the Orange Bowl. If nothing else,
Walsh would be a very valuable insurance policy and trade asset.
But Johnson made it very clear, on and off the record, that Aikman
and Walsh would compete equally in training camp. Equal practice
repetitions. Equal playing time in preseason games.

Two top-of-the-draft, same-age rookie QBs competing against
each other? Unheard of. Several NFL executives suggested to me
that, in effect, Johnson belonged in a supplemental institution.

Steinberg said "the Franchise" was devastated by the maneuver.
"Troy just feels betrayed. Here they promise him he's going to be the
guy, and they turn around and do this." Johnson and Jones did not

spend any time wining and dining and reassuring Aikman.

As camp opened in Thousand Oaks, California, Steinberg drove out from L.A. (about an hour away) to discuss a potential trade demand with Aikman. But Aikman decided to hang in and see what happened. "Troy is such a stud," Steinberg told me that night. "You tell him his options, he listens, and says, 'Okay, then we have to do *this*.' Troy's amazing: If you win his trust, he will be completely loyal to you. But that trust is hard to win, and I'm afraid Jimmy has broken that trust with this 'used-car dealer' act. I mean, imagine how Troy feels. Now he's competing against Jimmy's guy: a guy Jimmy has been to war with and won with, a guy Jimmy likes personally, a guy this entire staff [seven of whom had coached at Miami] loves. It's really not fair."

It was somewhat the same feeling Barry Switzer would experience when he took over the Cowboys and realized Aikman was close friends with Johnson, Norv Turner, and several members of a Johnson staff inherited by Switzer.

For the first time in my career, I found myself in a can't-win position. I had made no secret of my friendship with Steinberg. If I kept writing about how great Troy Aikman would become, I would look to some as if I were selling out to my buddy Leigh. If I wrote about Aikman's obvious growing pains, I might offend or even alienate Leigh. In hindsight, I probably went out of my way to be critically objective about Aikman.

But what Aikman never quite seemed to understand or believe was that I wasn't acting alone. In evaluating young talent, I'm always influenced by the opinions of coaches or general managers. Because I had so much respect for Johnson's football instincts, I was heavily influenced by his doubts about Aikman. By the way, in '89 I was perhaps Johnson's lone media supporter. While he was being ridiculed by my colleagues and by veteran Cowboys (Everson Walls in particular) for being a brash college coach with no grasp of how the pro game works, I was writing column after column about Johnson's intangibles. My constant message: He's simply a winner. He'll soon figure a way to get it done.

The more I listened to Johnson and his assistants, the more I thought he would try to get it done with Walsh. While Aikman soon displayed unusual toughness and mid-range riflery, Walsh showed an uncoachable feel for the game. Yet accurate readings were difficult. The rookie QBs were surrounded by one of the worst supporting casts in league history. Showing no respect, Johnson had run off fading stars such as Danny and Randy White. Showing no regard for PR, Johnson decided to shop the Cowboys' lone gate attraction, Herschel Walker.

By October, Johnson had concluded that Walker had taken such a beating under Paul Hackett that he had lost some stomach for contact, along with some quickness. Johnson could see Walker was "tippin'," standing straight up and tiptoeing when he hit heavy traffic. Apparently, though, Minnesota president Mike Lynn could see only stars. Herschel Himself was available? Lynn decided to take Johnson and Jones to NFL school. Instead, the only one who got taken was Lynn, who made just the kind of catastrophic blunder that people kept waiting for Jones to make. For Walker and four draft picks, not only did Dallas get five pretty good players—Issiac Holt, Darrin Nelson, Jesse Solomon, David Howard, and Alex Stewart—but also three first-round picks, three seconds, and two thirds. Staggering. Nearly as amazing: Johnson and Jones were ripped for trading their lone star.

Though Johnson squandered some of the picks, the Cowboys eventually used the rest to take Emmitt Smith, Russell Maryland, Kevin Smith, and Darren Woodson—all for an over-the-hill running back.

But for the rest of the '89 season, Johnson's team became a revolving door of journeymen players. Garbage in, garbage out. The lone highlight came against the defending Super Bowl champions in a nationally televised Sunday-night game at Washington's RFK Stadium. Steve Walsh started and finished the game and didn't throw an interception. Walsh's offense didn't commit a turnover. Dallas 13, Washington 3 was the NFL upset of the year.

With Aikman starting eleven games, the Cowboys finished that season 1–15.

Again and again I heard from assistants, front-office members, and even from Jones: "Jimmy's not sold on Troy." Several times Johnson indicated his uncertainty to me with negative asides about some aspect of Aikman's game. I didn't quote Johnson on any of this, so many fans were unaware he had anything but respect for both young quarterbacks. But, armed with Johnson's private thoughts, I wrote and said on ESPN that Walsh was the better quarterback.

Obviously, I turned out to be very wrong. I'm not sure Aikman has ever quite forgiven me.

That off-season was one long cold war between Johnson and Aikman. The following September, with Aikman as starter, the Cowboys fell to 1–2. Both quarterbacks began to make public noise about how unhappy they were. Something had to be done. Along came New Orleans offering a first-, second-, and third-round draft choice for Walsh. Johnson took it, later admitting it was the toughest personnel decision he had ever made. Johnson soon began having second thoughts. The Cowboys lost four of the next six games, hitting bottom on November 4 during a 24–6 loss to the New York Jets at the Meadowlands. Aikman seemed to be getting worse. He made several poor decisions and often seemed lost. As a college or pro quarterback, Aikman had yet to play one complete game that made Johnson think he could be a big-timer.

One night the following week, Johnson spiraled down his personal black hole, and in front of several media members admitted he thought he had traded the wrong quarterback. Sick of losing, Johnson said, "Troy Aikman was a loser in college and he'll always be a loser in the pros."

Johnson's remark soon got back to Aikman.

The following Saturday night, I was supposed to hook up for dinner with Steinberg in Anaheim, California, where the Cowboys were to play the L.A. Rams on Sunday. I waited in my room at the team hotel for the call that never came. Steinberg apologized the next day at the game, saying, "Troy and I just had an awful lot to talk about. He doesn't want to play for Dallas next year. The situation has really gotten ugly. Troy feels ostracized by the coaches. He just doesn't think they've given him any support publicly or privately. Remember, he's just in his second year, and sometimes he needs someone to put an arm around him and tell him everything's okay. I know a lot of people see Troy as this macho stud, but he can be very sensitive.

"The situation with Johnson is bad enough, but Troy just doesn't have any respect for [thirty-year-old offensive coordinator] David Shula, and he's not alone. Troy thinks he's a nice guy, but nobody has much respect for him. Troy says he learned more at UCLA than he has from Shula. I mean, Troy calls a play in the huddle, and as they break to go to the line of scrimmage, he hears guys say, 'Oh, shit, that'll never work.' Troy's the first to admit he suffers brain-lock during games, but can you blame him?"

David Shula's attitudes vacillated between (1) the gentle, sensitive kid haunted by the pressure to live up to father Don's name and (2) the haughty know-it-all whose body language said, "Don't dare question me. I'm a Shula." That attitude is fingernails on Aikman's chalkboard. He was not impressed.

That Sunday at Anaheim Stadium, Johnson made an attempt to walk to the end of the bench and console Aikman after he threw an early interception. Afterward, Aikman didn't seem too impressed by the gesture. But the Cowboys had won, 24–21. He and Emmitt Smith had flashed some star qualities against a decent team on the road. Yes, the day after Aikman told Steinberg he wanted to be traded, the Cowboys played what became the turnaround game for Johnson and Jones. As they won the next four games, the coach and owner/GM began to see this team was about to shut up a lot of critics. Only an injury to Aikman in the second-to-last game of the season kept the Cowboys out of the playoffs. Probably to Aikman's surprise, Jimmy Johnson was the first coach to be named NFL coach of the year with a sub-.500 record. The Cowboys finished 7–9.

Partly as a concession to Aikman, and partly because the Cowboys finished twenty-eighth and last in NFL offense, Johnson demoted David Shula soon after the season. Shula left to take an assistant's job in Cincinnati, where he would become head coach, much to the amazement of many Cowboy coaches. Johnson went on a highly publicized search for a new coordinator, and for various reasons, failed or opted not to hire Gary Stevens, Ted Tollner, Joe Pendry, Bob Schnelker, Richard Williamson, and Dick Coury. It was beginning to look like nobody wanted the job.

That's when I got a call from Paul Hackett, who was head coach at Pitt. He said, "Jimmy Johnson's about to make the best hire he's ever made. He's going to hire my man Norv." *Who?* "Norv Turner." *Who?* I'd never heard of Norv Turner, who wasn't even a coordinator. Turner, I learned, coached receivers under Ernie Zampese and Dick Coury with the Rams. He and Hackett had coached together at USC. While boy-wonder Hackett had been hand-picked in 1986 by Schramm to be Landry's successor, Turner had been content to pay nine years of dues at USC and six more with the Rams. "Trust me," said Hackett, "he's going to be a star."

The first time I met Turner that spring, I had to squint to see star quality. He was a low-key, unassuming guy who had a day's growth of beard and uncombed hair. Turner looked as if he hadn't slept much. He often didn't, settling back into his office chair by five each morning to study more tape. Turner was pretty boring—until kickoff when he started calling plays from his pressbox perch. Coaches around the NFL will tell you no one has a better instinctive feel for game-planning, play-calling, and quarterback-making than Turner. A former quarterback at Oregon, Turner has an invaluable knack for talking a QB's language, winning his trust, easing into the kid's mind until it's his.

Turner took one look at Aikman and said just what Switzer first said: "This guy has no idea how good he is." But Turner was able to convince Aikman of his greatness. That one accomplishment eventually made Jimmy Johnson a "genius" and allowed Jerry Jones to rule the NFL world.

What if Johnson had hired any of the first five or so candidates? "Obviously," says Aikman, "I owe an awful lot to Norv." Turner took him out of Shula's downfield passing scheme and put him in the comfort zone of a highly structured West Coast ball-control offense based on shorter drops and quicker throws. Aikman eventually became an almost robotic extension of Turner's ingenuity. Aikman provided what Turner calls "probably the most uncanny accuracy in NFL history"; Turner matched it with Staubachian improvisation.

More important, Troy Aikman finally had the big brother he'd always wanted. Turner talked straight. No song and dance. No used cars to sell. No macho ego, like Johnson. Turner was a guy's guy without the constant need to prove his manhood by one-upping or belittling. Aikman said, "I knew the moment I met him [in Johnson's office] I could trust him."

Aikman and Turner would need a season before I would begin calling their offense Aikman-Turner Overdrive. In 1991, their first season together, the Cowboys were 6–5 heading into a game at RFK against the heavily favored Redskins. Aikman hurt his knee; Steve Beuerlein took over and finished what became Johnson's breakthrough game as a budding "genius": a 24–21 victory. Johnson was lauded by CBS's John Madden for his pull-out-the-stops approach—for his onside kicks and Hail Marys.

In the preseason, I had nudged Johnson in print to sign a quality backup for Aikman, who had proven to be injury prone. My choice had been Beuerlein, a former starter for the L.A. Raiders who would provide a proven stand-in, just in case. Like Walsh, Beuerlein was mostly about intangibles. "A winner," said Johnson. Aikman probably rolled his eyes and thought I was starting another "I Want Steve" campaign. But Beuerlein was the wise move, and Johnson made it.

With Beuerlein at quarterback, the Cowboys won six straight, including their first playoff game under Johnson, at Chicago. Aikman, who said he felt healthy enough to play against Chicago, was stunned when media members called on Tuesday to tell him Johnson was sticking with Beuerlein. "I was told all along I was going to start when I was ready," Aikman later told me. "That really bothered me. I felt I was misled intentionally. I didn't feel I was being handled as up front and honestly as I should have been. At that point, Jimmy and I had no relationship at all to speak of. The only time I was in his office was when we were arguing about something."

That same day Jerry Jones angered Johnson by telling reporters that "Troy is the franchise quarterback." Now, Jones says, "It had become unclear who the number one quarterback was. It was fuzzy, the way it was being described [by Johnson] in the media. I wanted to clear that up."

Now, Jones makes it clear that "Jimmy didn't move to Troy's camp until after Troy won the Super Bowl."

My first face-to-face clash with Aikman came the night of the play-off win in Chicago. We both were aboard the flying party that was the team plane as it returned to Dallas. Neither of us had played. Though Aikman had a couple of beers, he was one Cowboy who wasn't in a celebratory mood. I was typing my column in a row near the front of the coach cabin when Mark Tuinei commandeered the P.A. system and said, "Skip Bayless, report to the back of the plane." I thought it was a joke and kept typing. Pretty soon, the 300-pound Tuinei loomed beside me and said, "Come with me." Tuinei, I was later told, had drunk more than a couple of beers. He lifted me out of my seat by my arm and began pushing me down the aisle. Near the restroom in the back stood Aikman.

Tuinei pushed me up against the restroom door and said, "Troy wants to ask you some questions." Neither Aikman nor Tuinei displayed even a hint of a grin. This was serious business.

Aikman said, "Why have you always been so critical of me?"

"Yeah, why?" Tuinei said, shoving me in the shoulder and banging me against the restroom door. I stand 5'11" and weigh 170 pounds. I had heard several scary stories about things Tuinei had done under the influence. I told him, "Just calm down and let me talk."

And I tried to tell Aikman why I had been so critical of him. Without burning the bridge between me and Johnson, I couldn't share the things the coach had said to me about the quarterback. But I did try to explain what a difficult position I'd found myself in because of my relationship with his agent. I said, "Leigh has told me so much about what a great guy you are that I've worried about getting too close to you and losing all my objectivity. You sound like you'd make a great friend."

At the moment, though, I was beginning to question that.

Expressionless, Aikman mostly listened.

Six months later, Aikman's friend Dale Hansen told me of a conversation he and Aikman had about me. "He just went on and on about things you had said or written, and I finally said, 'Wait a second. Do you know who you are? You're Troy Fucking Aikman. Why should you give a shit what Skip Bayless says about you?'"

Precisely. I sometimes lost some respect for Aikman's mental toughness *because* he let my criticism affect him so deeply.

But that night on the team plane, our discussion was soon interrupted by Johnson, who made a surprise appearance in the back of the plane. He had been warned of potential trouble. Perhaps he envisioned the headline, "Cowboys Win; Sportswriter Flushed Down Team Plane Toilet." Johnson defused the situation by making awkward small talk—very awkward—and I returned in one piece to my seat.

The following Sunday, with Beuerlein at quarterback in the first half, the Cowboys fell quickly behind the Detroit Lions in their Silverdome. A Beuerlein interception—the result of a bad route run by rookie Alvin Harper—was returned for a touchdown. With Detroit leading 17–6 late in the first half, Johnson sent in Aikman. The switch didn't seem fair to either quarterback. Aikman was rusty and ineffective. The Cowboys lost the second half 21–0, and the game 38–6.

I was left wondering how much longer Aikman and Johnson—and Johnson and Jones—would last.

6

SUPER EGO

Sometimes friction is good. You get one guy
all mad over here, and another guy all mad
over there, and all of a sudden all that energy
produces something good.

—*Jerry Jones, August 1992*

By 1991, as the Cowboys burst back on the national scene, the
Best Buddies from Arkansas myth had become a media monster gnawing at Jimmy Johnson's pride. The easy handle for wire-
service reporters and cable-network sportscasters had become,
"Jimmy Johnson and Jerry Jones, roommates and co-captains at
Arkansas . . ." With each reference, it seemed that another ratings
point of fans accepted as gospel that Jimmy and Jerry were having
dinner by night and eating the NFL's lunch by day.

One afternoon at training camp—St. Edward's University,
Austin—Johnson and I leaned against a wall of the media center
and talked about a recent trade he and/or Jones had made for Tony
Casillas. In the papers, Jones was taking credit for doing some of
the wheeling and dealing with Atlanta personnel director Ken
Herock.

"It's embarrassing," Johnson told me. Johnson said his girlfriend, Rhonda Rookmaaker, had been in his dorm room while he,
alone, had negotiated by phone with Herock. After Rookmaaker
read Jones's quotes in the newspapers, she told Johnson, "You can't

let him get away with that." Johnson said he shrugged and said, "What am I going to do?"

Now I second-guess my decision not to write what Johnson told me or to use it on the air. I wasn't taking notes; we were just "vis't-ing," as Johnson would say. So I considered it "off the record." But maybe Johnson, as early as 1991, wanted the truth known, as he bitterly saw it. I recount the dialogue now only because it provides insight into one of the most baffling breakups in sports history. Even now, Barry Switzer says, "I will never quite understand why those two screwed up such a good thing."

This is how.

That day in camp, Johnson rolled his eyes and told me, "My girlfriend knows more football than Jerry Jones."

That line—and others that hit nearly as far below Jones's belt—began getting back to the owner whose life revolves around being general manager. Understand, Jones has just as large and sensitive a male ego as Johnson or Switzer or the biggest, baddest football player who ever lived. For Jones, Johnson's put-down about Rhonda was slightly worse than questioning the GM's heterosexuality. But though they had several heated arguments during the next couple of years, Jones's lust for winning overrode his macho pride. A fistfight would have forced a split. Jones preferred to drain every last Super Bowl drop out of Johnson, then discard him.

Johnson's mistake was thinking that because he was such a great coach, he had the leverage in the relationship. What struck me that day at camp was that Johnson was picking a fight he believed he could win by knockout. "So what are you going to do about Jerry?" I asked.

"Oh, I'm not going to let him get to me," Johnson said with a sniff. "I can handle Jerry."

Famous last words. From the start, a winking Johnson thought he was smarter than Jones. He thought that, as he began to win, he slowly would manipulate Jones out of the picture. But Jones became one long *Twilight Zone* episode for Johnson. Every time he turned on the TV or radio or opened a newspaper or magazine, he saw Jones's smiling face.

Jones had tried to be up front with him, but Johnson hadn't paid much attention. Jones explained to Johnson before he hired him that he was pulling back from his oil-and-gas operation so he could be involved seven days a week, 365 days a year, as general manager of the Dallas Cowboys. Though Jones once said, "I could coach the shit out of this team," he insisted to me he did not want to coach. He said he did not want to help formulate game plans or to call plays or to instruct players during practice. But: He definitely wanted to be involved in—or at least be informed about—all personnel decisions. He wanted to participate in—and have the final word on—trades, drafts, and free-agent decisions. Just as important, he wanted his coach to simply keep him in the loop. That was the key, really: Just tell him about the new fake field goal that had been cooked up for Sunday's game. Tell him which young defensive lineman was unblockable in practice and which veteran defensive back was on his last legs. Tell him who was hurt and who was faking it. Just *tell* him.

Jerry Jones just wanted a coach who treated him like a partner and pal instead of the plague. Jones has admitted to me he gets "defensive" when I write that he just wants to be "one of the boys." He says, "That's not true. I didn't get into this so I could hang around out there [at practice]." But from talking to those close to Jones, he loves to be liked, especially by his inner circle of friends, and he considers himself an ex-player who's still part of the old gang.

But even at Arkansas, Johnson saw Jones as a little geeky and nerdy—as a guy who wasn't very cool but thought he was, who just didn't get it but thought he did. Johnson, not Jones, was the one who looked like a million bucks in suits. Johnson had "the Hair": the perfectly styled and sprayed creation with sleek curves like the Corvettes he loves to drive. Jones eventually had the hairpiece. No one speaks the salty language of coaches with better command than Johnson, an F-wordsmith. Johnson thought Jones, in effect, sounded like a white guy trying to talk black when Jones tried to speak "coach."

Johnson's fundamental (to use one of Jerry's favorite words) problem with Jones was that he had paid his coaching dues and Jones hadn't. He resented the hell out of Jones's wanting to buy his way back into the coaching fraternity. It wasn't enough that Jones had played as high a level of college football as Johnson or any Cowboy assistant. Johnson simply couldn't stand sharing any credit with *Jerry Jones* for the dynasty he was building. In truth, did Jones deserve a little credit for the Casillas trade? Some, said insiders. Did he deserve some for the two trades that made the 1992 Super Bowl defense—for Charles Haley and Thomas Everett? Quite a bit, said insiders. But by '92 Johnson had gone from being amused by Jones and making fun of him behind his back to sarcastically trying to humiliate Jones in front of other staffers.

Yet Jones always had the last word—or laugh. Jones, who has a slow but deadly trigger, occasionally would unload on Johnson behind closed doors and turn him into something the public never saw: an intimidated employee. Said a Johnson loyalist who once overheard Jones chewing out Johnson: "I was amazed by how meek Jimmy was." Said Larry Lacewell, "There was a side of Jimmy that was afraid of Jerry. He knew there was a limit to how far he could push. He knew who the boss was." Jerry was boss, and Johnson couldn't stand it. When the ESPN cameras peeked into the Cowboy war room on draft day, Johnson knew his coaching buddies around the country saw Jones sitting next to him, giving final approval. In football circles, this was a form of castration.

In the end, it was Jones who indicated to me he was successfully manipulating Johnson—"coaching the coach," as Jones's guru, Raider owner Al Davis, taught him to do. Jones said, "Oh, coach Broyles warned me about what he called the 'Jimmy Package.' The disloyalty, the puffing up [with condescending ego], the ability to be charming one day and surly the next. But I always thought and still think Jimmy is a great coach. *A great coach.* And I believed I could live with the rest of it because I believed we would win."

Jones believed he could harness Johnson's nuclear coaching power for a short time. For sure, Johnson attacked rebuilding the Cowboys with obsessive energy Switzer probably didn't have by 1989. Few if any coaches could have done what Johnson did in such a short time. Johnson created a crisis-a-day force field that only a few good men would survive. What Troy Aikman called Johnson's "incredible sense of urgency" was almost frightening. Players didn't love Johnson; they feared the crazy SOB. Yet they knew he was crazy smart—that he usually jerked the right strings during games.

But from the start Jones knew Johnson heaped so much pressure on his players (and himself) that losses drove him over the edge, made him irrational, even self-destructive with his late nights of chain-drinking his trademark Heinekens over ice. Jones told me, "I just hope Jimmy doesn't wind up in a mental institution." Jones said those words with an air of, *If he does, we'll observe a moment of silence, then go on about our business of winning Super Bowls.*

After resigning at Oklahoma in 1978, Larry Lacewell returned to his alma mater, Arkansas State, where he was head coach and athletic director until 1989. His '86 team lost to Georgia Southern in the Division 1-AA national finals. In 1990 Johnny Majors hired him to be defensive coordinator at Tennessee. That's where Lacewell was when he got the call from Jimmy Johnson in early 1992.

His old friend and sparring partner wanted Lacewell to come to Dallas. Johnson said he needed help with the draft. But Lacewell realized right away that Johnson also needed help with Jerry Jones. "He needed me to be a buffer," Lacewell said. "I think he was pretty desperate at that point."

Initially, Lacewell was better than Bufferin for Johnson. Not only was he Johnson's Xs-and-Os mentor, but Lacewell had a knack for commiserating with and calming Johnson. Lacewell is a round-faced, white-haired banty rooster of a man with a Fordyce accent you could pour on hotcakes. He can tell a story as artfully as Johnson manages a game. Lacewell is a jukebox of classic stories about times that seemed so bad at the time. Jimmy Johnson stories. Barry Switzer stories. Bear Bryant stories. Funny-wise and funny-sad stories that make you laugh and ponder. Stories about the meaning of life and coaching, which for Lacewell are one and the same.

Sometimes hearing Lacewell laugh at the punch line is as good as the punch line itself.

In 1992 Johnson wanted "Lace" around to help keep him sane. Besides, Lacewell knows talent, and with the decades of relationships he had made around college football, he would be the perfect complement to Johnson in the scouting department. Lacewell was named director of college scouting.

But the relationship didn't evolve quite the way Johnson envisioned.

As former Oklahoma coach Gary Gibbs says of Lacewell, "He always knows which way the wind's about to blow." Lacewell soon sensed that Johnson's was an ill wind. The expectations and media mania had turned Johnson into a guy Lacewell didn't know. Lacewell says, "I get here and start reading about this guy who lives by himself and hates Christmas, and I didn't know that Jimmy Johnson." He had become what Lacewell calls "an actor." Lacewell says, "Most coaches are actors to some degree—you almost have to be. But Jimmy was the master. It was almost silly how he was always trying to show everybody how tough he was, running off asthmatic kickers [as he did with a made-for-minicam tirade in '89] and cutting Curvin Richards [the backup running back who fumbled twice in the fourth quarter of 1992's final regular season game, which the Cowboys led comfortably]. I'm reading about how Jimmy works such long, hard hours, and I had to laugh. He and I had our biggest falling-out because that was exactly what he wouldn't do. I mean, all that stuff was for the media, and Jimmy was very convincing. I sometimes wish Switzer had a little more actor in him. He's actually too honest for his own good. But sometimes it was like Jimmy was even trying to convince *me*, and I didn't need any convincing. I already knew he was a great coach."

As he prepared for his first draft, Lacewell mentioned a college player he personally had evaluated, and Johnson began rattling off facts, figures, and opinions about the kid. To Lacewell, Johnson's tone was almost condescending, as if to say he knew what Lacewell knew and a lot more. Lacewell was impressed—until he discovered Johnson had a scouting service directory from which he was repeating opinions. Lacewell's incredulous attitude was "Jimmy, this is your ol' buddy Lace you're talking to."

Meanwhile, Lacewell began spending more and more time with the man he was supposed to help Johnson "handle." Says Lacewell, "Right away I knew Jerry Jones was the most amazing man I'd ever been around. I don't always immediately understand what the man is saying—I mean, he can talk in circles until you're lost. But he knows exactly where he's going. The man is absolutely brilliant, and I enjoy the hell out of his company. People don't often see this side of him, but Jerry Jones can be very funny. Honestly, I never could understand why Jimmy didn't like him."

Of course, Johnson soon assumed that Lacewell had defected. Perhaps Lacewell had figured out that Johnson was a prohibitive underdog against Jones. Perhaps the survivor in Lacewell signaled him to ingratiate himself with the boss so he wouldn't get fired when Johnson did. But Lacewell genuinely was stung by the way this "new" Jimmy treated him. In a way, Johnson drove him to Jones.

Jones says, "Believe me, Larry was loyal to Jimmy. But ultimately my decision to fire Jimmy was very influenced by Larry, and not by anything he ever said. It was because of what I observed— the way Jimmy made Larry feel so uncomfortable . . . that 'puffing-up syndrome' around a man [Lacewell] who really does understand the game. There should have been no bullshitting Larry. That's like trying to kid your brother. There didn't need to be any 'Goddamn, I'm the greatest.' I mean, Jimmy was the best man in Larry's wedding.

"I know enough to know *nobody* knows for sure whether a [drafted] player can play or not. I reacted [negatively] to the perception Jimmy was creating that he was the guru and that every decision was strictly his decision. It's a 'we' thing. We have coaches and scouts involved who have been doing this for twenty, thirty years. It's a 'we' thing.

"All that really concerned me."

Something else concerned Lacewell: the only-in-Dallas pressure eating at Johnson. "I'd be around him sometimes at night," says Lacewell, "and he'd have five beers and just be rip-roarin' drunk. I understood that was happening almost every night, and that really bothered me for Jimmy. I just don't think he realized what a toll it was taking on him. He was headed for burnout real fast."

After a while, Larry Lacewell did his best to avoid Jimmy Johnson, by day or night.

If Johnson is an accomplished actor, he must have been Paul Newman in *The Hustler* the night of December 14, 1992. To this day, I still don't believe what happened.

First, something nearly as shocking happened on the thirteenth when the Cowboys played at Washington. Something nuts always happens when the blood-rival Cowboys and Redskins play. One team almost always humiliates the other. This time, the young Cowboys had the better team. They had won three straight to improve to 11–2. The Cowboys led the defending Super Bowl champs 17–7 at half. Up in the pressbox, Lacewell told Jones, "You are looking at a Super Bowl contender." The Cowboys led 17–10 early in the fourth quarter with a third and goal at the Washington 2 yard line. A touchdown probably would have iced the game at 24–10, and Johnson's team would have clinched the NFC East.

But Aikman threw an interception. Then Michael Irvin fumbled. Then Aikman fumbled in his end zone and the Redskins recovered. And Jimmy Johnson's talk-of-the-NFL team, which had been built on mistake-free execution, had gone up in turnover smoke. Washington won 20–17. No doubt Johnson's big-game doubts about Aikman resurfaced like sharks off the Miami coastline.

I rode the team plane home that night, but I didn't need Johnson to rescue me from Tuinei. Several players and flight attendants needed Tuinei to rescue them from Johnson. Johnson threw some vicious fits, humiliating several backup players who were standing in the aisles. Johnson's tantrums were fortified by (according to one flight attendant) ten Heinekens he drank on the flight.

"A lot of players were extremely upset," Aikman told me. "Here we'd done everything we could for the guy. We played our guts out and it was only our third loss. It was like he sold out on us."

Aikman's friend Dale Hansen told me, "Troy thought what Jimmy did was chickenshit." Referring to two of the defenseless targets Johnson attacked, Hansen said, "Frank Cornish? Tommie Agee? Come on. Guys like Troy and Daryl Johnston and Mark Stepnoski were sitting there just shaking their heads at Jimmy. Did he seriously think losing hurt him any more than it did those guys?"

Many players were so disgusted by Johnson's behavior that they opted not to attend the next night's team Christmas party. Only about half the team showed up. I bumped into Jones that afternoon, and he shook his head, grinned, and said, "Great timing for a Christmas party, huh?"

Perfect timing, as Jones's luck would have it.

Aikman, as the quarterback, decided he should bear the burden of small-talking with the maniac coach everyone at the party was trying to avoid. Aikman and Johnson chatted briefly about the loss and team morale. Then Johnson mentioned his tropical fish, which are his passion, his sanity-saving escape after fourth-quarter squalls. For Johnson, who lives for the ocean, his saltwater fish tanks were his private cove in landlocked Dallas. Some nights, Johnson watched his fish until sunup.

So what were the odds that Troy Aikman, tough-guy quarterback from rural Oklahoma, would have an unquenched desire for tropical fish?

I am not making any of this up.

Aikman first wanted an aquarium when he lived near the ocean in Cerritos. "Don't ask me why. I just wanted one, and it never quite worked out." So Aikman and Johnson talked for maybe forty-five minutes about Johnson's tanks. The following day, Tuesday, was an off day, and as fate would have it, Aikman bumped into Johnson at the team's Valley Ranch complex. "Jimmy said, 'Got a minute? Let me run you over to the house and show you my fish.' I said, 'Shoot, let's go.' That was the first time I'd ever been to his house. He talked me into buying a tank [and later took Aikman to a store to help outfit him]." For Aikman, the most important feature in his new house is its custom-built saltwater tank.

Incredibly, after Johnson's team-plane tantrum had offended an Aikman who considered him slimier than a salamander, Aikman and Johnson struck up a fish-watching, beer-drinking friendship. Talk about a fish story. Only in Dallas.

Aikman says, "It's funny: The fish tank represents great times in my professional life. I remember the time spent getting that thing going and the things we were trying to accomplish on the field. Jimmy and I would go to the aquarium store together for things, and he'd come over and help me set things up. It was through the fish that a very special relationship developed—one I was very proud of. I then had the relationship with Jimmy I had with Norv. I could be very open and honest with him, and he listened."

If Aikman hadn't said these things to me with such an earnest joy, I might have laughed out loud. Was he talking about the same Jimmy Johnson who had caused him such pain? When you least expect it, the deadeye quarterback can be so jarringly naive and easily influenced, so vulnerable, perhaps even gullible.

A Cowboy dynasty began with a conversation about tropical fish at a wake of a Christmas party.

Heading to Atlanta the next Sunday for a Monday night game, Aikman felt "more pressure on my shoulders than I'd felt for any game in my life." He responded by hitting 15 of 17 for 196 yards and two touchdowns—in the first half. Dallas beat Deion Sanders and Atlanta 41–17. Aikman suddenly was swept along in an invisible undertow the likes of which few quarterbacks have experienced. After the interception he threw in the fourth quarter of the Washington game, Aikman went five games (including the Super Bowl) and 135 attempts without throwing an interception. I've never seen a quarterback so hot for so long at such a critical time. The Cowboys won five straight, including the Super Bowl 52–17 over Buffalo.

Jerry Jones was quietly amused and pleased by the sudden, improbable Aikman-Johnson friendship, Now, Jones says, "Once Jimmy saw that Troy was turning the corner, he jumped on that bandwagon sure as the sun's in the sky."

On Sunday morning of Super Bowl XXVII, in my "parting shot" on ESPN's *The Sports Reporters*, I took a shot at myself, saying how wrong I had been about Aikman. He saw it or perhaps Leigh Steinberg told him about it. The next morning, when I bumped into Aikman at the hotel, he said, "What you said on *The Sports Reporters* meant more to me than anything that happened yesterday."

That sentiment from Aikman meant more than anything that happened to *me* all season. But Aikman had been named Super Bowl MVP. That was a wonderfully weird conclusion to a weirdly wonderful month.

Even after that first Super Bowl victory, many Cowboy assistants and front-office members half-expected Jones to fire Johnson or for Johnson to quit. Yet to use Jones's word, he was "greedy" for Super Bowl trophies, and he was willing to live with Troy's new friend Jimmy for another year.

But without Emmitt Smith, the 1993 Cowboys lost their first two games. Smith and Jones were locked in a hotly covered contract battle, with Jones getting as much ESPN airtime as Chris Berman or Joe Theismann. A steamed Johnson basically blamed Emmitt's absence on Jones, for getting intoxicated on the breathless attention and trying to impress the world with his shrewd machismo. After the two losses, it looked as if Emmitt had won the leverage. Johnson was ready to lead a lynch mob of players and fans after Jones. Yet somehow Jones took advantage of Emmitt's impatience to rejoin teammates who obviously needed him. Jones did make Emmitt the NFL's highest-paid running back, but just barely. Before season's end, his four-year, $13.6 million deal would seem like chump change compared to the late-December deal Jones gave Aikman: eight years, $50 million. Considering his value to the team, Emmitt was a bargain for Jones—who even won a last-minute right-of-first-refusal clause for Emmitt's next negotiation. Yes, Emmitt conceded unrestricted free agency in 1997, giving Jones the right to match any offer and keep Emmitt.

Jerry wins again.

So did the Cowboys, thanks to Emmitt Smith. He was named the regular season MVP and won the rushing title. Smith also was the Super Bowl MVP as Dallas beat Buffalo again, 30–13. Naturally, no team had ever won the Super Bowl after an 0–2 start.

Jerry wins.

Yet that off-season, proven superstars Emmitt and Aikman continued to lose members of their supporting cast to free agency. Over the '93, '94, and '95 off-seasons, the Cowboys lost four offensive starters (John Gesek, Kevin Gogan, Mark Stepnoski, and Alvin Harper), four defensive starters (Tony Casillas, Jimmie Jones, Ken Norton Jr., and James Washington) and several special-teams stars such as Kenny Gant and Matt Vanderbeek. After winning Super Bowl XXX, they lost defensive starters Russell Maryland, Larry Brown, Dixon Edwards, and Robert Jones. Jerry Jones often was criticized for letting other teams outbid him, but he told me, "This isn't like baseball, where you have to pay five million dollars for a second baseman who hits .230 because you can't find another second baseman who can hit .230. In football, if you have a nucleus of stars—I mean great players at the key positions—you can plug in players around them at more minimal salaries and still win."

So who deserves the most credit for what is turning into a Cowboy dynasty? Aikman? Emmitt? Johnson? Jones? Or should the four share equal amounts? Given the Jones-Switzer theory that "stars win," consider . . .

- *Aikman:* Clearly, Jones believed in the quarterback before Johnson did. Johnson deserves some credit for having the courage to demote David Shula, but the hiring of Norv Turner, who unlocked Aikman's talent, was mostly luck. Without Turner, Aikman might have turned into yet another talented quarterback (Warren Moon, Jim Everett, Jeff George) who was never quite mentally strong enough to harness his physical tools into a championship package.

Though a few Cowboy coaches quietly consider Emmitt the team's MVP, Jones believes Aikman is slightly more valuable by virtue of the position he plays. Jones is right: The NFL is a quarterback's game.

• *Emmitt:* Early in the 1990 draft, Johnson tried unsuccessfully to trade up for defensive impact players such as defensive end Ray Agnew (who went tenth to New England) and linebacker James Francis (twelfth to Cincinnati). Yet though Johnson had traded just three days earlier for a running back—former first-round pick Terence Flagler from San Francisco—give Johnson credit for being shocked that Emmitt Smith was sliding. Having coached in college against Florida's Emmitt, Johnson knew that despite average 40-yard dash speed for a running back, Smith had "the Gift." He was simply very hard to tackle. So Johnson, encouraged by Jones, spent a third-round pick to trade from the twenty-first spot in the first round to Pittsburgh's seventeenth. There, Johnson grabbed Smith. But what if one of Johnson's deals had clicked for Agnew or Francis? Though Johnson detests the word "luck," he and Jones seemed to create a lot of it.

• *Michael Irvin:* While coaching the University of Miami, Johnson told former Cowboy personnel director Gil Brandt that Irvin wasn't fast enough to be anything above a second-round pick. Brandt took him in the first round in '88. After Irvin did major damage to his knee in Johnson's first season, Johnson instructed personnel director John Wooten to shop Irvin for a trade. But Wooten and receiver coach Hubbard Alexander say they lobbied Johnson to hold onto Irvin because of his work ethic and the respect he generated in the locker room. Johnson deserves no credit for Irvin's emergence as a star under Norv Turner. Johnson does deserve an honorable mention for keeping Irvin from getting into major off-field trouble.

• *Charles Haley:* It's doubtful, though not impossible, that the Cowboys would have won Super Bowls XXVII and XXVIII without Haley's pass rush. Johnson says he encouraged the deal, but Jones pulled it off (for basically only a second- and third-round pick) with the man who would become his primary rival, San Francisco general manager Carmen Policy. Though Haley was a three-time Pro Bowl pass rusher just entering his prime at twenty-eight, he finally had become more trouble than he was worth to the 49ers. He constantly makes life miserable for his coaches and teammates. Johnson tired of Haley, too, and wanted to trade him after the '92 and '93 seasons, but Jones resisted.

• *Leon Lett:* Though he's an emerging force at defensive tackle, he was a shot-in-the-dark seventh-round pick. Pure luck.

• *The offensive line:* Collectively a superstar, one of the greatest units ever. Without this group, neither Aikman nor Emmitt would be able to maximize his potential. Much of the credit should go to the coaches, first Tony Wise, now Hudson Houck, one of the game's best teachers. Wise (with Johnson's encouragement) stuck with Mark Tuinei and Nate Newton, who probably wouldn't have lasted with the Landry regime. Tuinei and Newton turned into Pro Bowlers. Pro Bowler Mark Stepnoski was a terrific second-round pick by Johnson, and Stepnoski's replacement, Pro Bowler Ray Donaldson, was a terrific free-agent pickup by Houck. On the right side of the line, guard Larry Allen and tackle Erik Williams could be two of the best ever to play side-by-side. Allen, because he played at little Sonoma State, took an Emmitt-like plunge through the first round. Only because Cowboy scout Tom Ciskowski was all but turn-ing blue did Lacewell (with Houck's blessing after a quick review of Allen film) decide to take Allen in the second round. "If he isn't already," says Houck, "he'll be the best offensive lineman in the league." Williams had that distinction before a near-fatal car wreck set him back. But he's still very good. He was Johnson's third pick in the third round—after Johnson had taken an offensive lineman from Cal named James Richards, who was a bust. Again, Williams was mostly luck.

• *Deion Sanders:* Strictly an against-all-odds Jones obsession. "If Jimmy had still been here," says Jones, "believe me, there would be no Deion. It's a little thing called dwelling on the negatives." Jones believes Johnson would have scoffed that Jones and his ego had gotten carried away with a half-season player who isn't a quarter-back or a pass rusher. Sometimes, Johnson did provide a valuable devil's-advocate balance for the plunger's enthusiasm bubbling over in Jones. But in this case, Sanders was worth the $13 million bonus and $35 million package.

Jerry wins again.

As the clock ticked down on a second straight Cowboy Super Bowl victory, this one in Atlanta's Georgia Dome, Larry Lacewell congrat-ulated Jimmy Johnson on the sideline. They hugged. Then Johnson noticed the clock had stopped. "He jumped back up there [near the sideline] and put his hands back on his knees and started yelling at the players on the field. He knew the camera was still on him, and he was 'coaching.' My God, it was 30–13."

Jerry Jones already had seen and heard enough. In another Cowboy first, Johnson had told ESPN during Super Bowl Week that he'd be interested in coaching Jacksonville's expansion team. *What?* The coach of a team that could win four or five straight Super Bowls saying he wouldn't mind leaving for an expansion team? Then, two nights after the Super Bowl on *The Late Show with David Letterman*, Johnson wondered out loud if Jones had pocketed $20,000 of the $60,000 the league had given the Cowboys for a team party. Jimmy vs. Jerry was getting uglier by the interview.

Says Lacewell, "I just felt like Jimmy had lost heart for everything, and it wasn't just because of Jerry. He had just put so much pressure on himself for so long that he wasn't himself anymore. He basically had told me, 'Lace, you do the draft [by yourself].'"

Which led several insiders to theorize Johnson had a Cowboy death wish, whether he would admit it to himself or not. It's possible he wanted to force Jones to free him from the out-of-control expectations to be his coaching creation, Jimmy the Genius. It's possible Johnson just didn't think he had enough energy left to live up to that image.

For sure, Jones didn't like what the open warfare was doing to him. "I was turning into something I didn't like. It was making me something I'm really not." Making him defensive, suspicious, unhappy even with two Super Bowl trophies in his office.

Jones says that in the next seven weeks he began talking to family members and confidants about doing what the world would consider unthinkable: firing Jimmy Johnson. Privately voicing high-risk ideas is Jones's way of bringing them to life, just so he can turn them over in his hands and see how they feel. Do the ideas grow or turn to dust? This one grew quickly, he says. "The instant I sensed any kind of plan [by Johnson] to distance himself from me, when in fact the central relationship in the organization has to be ours, that was it. When I lost the enthusiasm to do excessive things like spending almost $45 million in bonuses [as Jones did on his '95 team] or to do Nike deals or even just go to [scouting] combines, just because of how guarded he might be, I just finally lost my tolerance. I knew we had to stop it. There was no changing colors in Jimmy or me. You have gangrene in the finger, you cut it off."

Jones says the incident that pulled the pin on the explosive relationship was the last of many similar attempts by Johnson to embarrass and undermine him in front of others. This one occurred at an ABC party during the league meetings in March of

1994. The site was Orlando's Pleasure Island, a Disney World tribu-
tary. Jones and Lacewell were working the crowd when Lacewell
spotted a big table surrounded by Johnson and girlfriend Rhonda,
Chicago coach Dave Wannstedt and his wife, new Washington
coach Norv Turner and his wife, Bob Ackles and his wife, and
Brenda Bushell. Jones had fired personnel man Ackles (who now
works for Johnson in Miami) and Bushell, who had been brought
in by Johnson to be the Cowboys' TV coordinator. Lacewell left a
glad-handing Jones to say hello to the group with so many Cowboy
ties. Alcohol was flowing. Johnson was presiding, telling "Jerry stories." A moment later, Jones approached as if he were entering a
family reunion. His first hint should have been that no one immediately made room for him at the table. So, still standing, he leaped
before he looked. He proposed a toast before noticing Ackles and
Bushell were present.

If looks could kill, Johnson soon would have been charged with
murder.

Nobody toasted.

Jones proposed a second modified toast.

Johnson glared. A couple of those present attempted a half-
hearted half-toast, so as to defuse the situation without inviting
Johnson's wrath.

Jones finally got the message. Doing a quick burn, he said, "You
goddamn people just go on with your goddamn party."

And Jones wheeled and stormed away.

Johnson chided Lacewell. "Lace," he said, "you better go after
your boss so he doesn't do something stupid."

Back at the headquarters hotel for the NFL meetings, the Hyatt
Grand Cypress, Jones's emotions teetered between relief and rage as
he sat in the bar. He finally knew exactly what he was going to do.
As a group of writers that included two from the *Dallas Morning
News* left the bar, Jones warned them not to go to bed and miss "the
story of the year." Make that story of the decade.

Contrary to published reports, Jones now insists he was not
drunk. He wouldn't want to give Johnson the pleasure of thinking
he was in anything but his right mind. "It wasn't done because I
was drinking or because I'd just had a problem with Jimmy."

In the presence of Ed Werder and Rick Gosselin of the *Dallas
Morning News*, Jones dropped the nuclear warhead that he was
thinking about firing Johnson and hiring Barry Switzer. Jones, in
fact, had already been making research calls on Switzer.

Referring to Johnson's desire to coach elsewhere, Jones

reminded the writers that "there are 500 coaches who would love to coach the Dallas Cowboys."

One of the writers asked, "Five hundred who would love to or five hundred who *could*?"

And Jones impulsively said something that would haunt Barry Switzer the rest of his born days. Jones said, "I think there are 500 who could have coached this team to the Super Bowl. I really believe that." Injured pride inflating, Jones added that *he* could have done just that.

Later that night, several people heard Jones refer to Johnson as "the little cunt." Yes, it was time for this relationship to end.

Considering Jones's belief that "we all ride Troy's coattails," it seems odd that he would risk the fragile psyche of a quarterback who finally had bonded with his coach. If the quarterback is the key, wouldn't Jones try coexisting with Johnson just to keep Aikman in his often unbeatable comfort zone? Yet Jones wasn't too concerned because, after all, Aikman had chosen to play for Switzer at Oklahoma. When the owner first bounced Switzer's name off Aikman, he got a positive response. "Oh, at the time, I had no problem with the choice," Aikman says.

The problem Aikman had was with the choice to fire Johnson. But he did not protest to Jones. No ultimatum was delivered. Aikman views himself as nothing more than a highly paid employee, not as a "partner," as Jones calls him. When I asked Aikman if he blamed Jones for not trying to finesse the situation for one more year while the team attempted to win an unprecedented third straight Super Bowl, Aikman said, "I've never felt that way, and I told Jerry that. As the owner of this team he has the right to make decisions he wants to make. I've always kind of laughed at the thought of Jerry 'meddling.' If I owned a football team and wanted to call every play and stand on the 50-yard line, I would. Whether it's best or not for the team is insignificant. He has that right."

After all, near the end of the '93 season, Jones had given Aikman an eight-year contract that basically guaranteed he would finish his career in Dallas. By the way, Jones insists that even before that deal was completed, Johnson expressed reservations about sinking $50 million into Aikman.

Aikman's emotions were caught in the Jerry-Jimmy cross fire. Leigh Steinberg, a Jerry fan, stuck up for Jones. Steinberg says, "Yes, during a negotiation Jerry can be vindictive and petty and borderline dishonest and clownish and overreaching. But he is brilliant. He's great for the Dallas Cowboys and he's the best thing that's happened to the NFL in the last ten years." Aikman agrees, saying, "I can't imagine an owner wanting to win more than Jerry Jones does. I feel good about the fact I can go to bed at night knowing he wants to win football games. As a quarterback, what more can you ask for?"

A sighing Jones now sympathetically answers Aikman's question with, "The right coach." Johnson was perfect for Aikman. Switzer is perfect for Jones. But in its own ugly way, the Aikman-Switzer relationship has grown nearly as unworkable as Jimmy vs. Jerry.

Aikman was stunned the day it finally actually happened. On March 29, 1994, Jones and Johnson met at Valley Ranch and gave reconciliation one last absurd attempt. Then Jones gave him $2 million and they agreed to do one last press conference without any mudslinging. Publicly, they said they "mutually agreed" to split. Privately, Jones said he fired Johnson.

So ended friction that was better than fiction.

Johnson went home and called Aikman. "It was very emotional on my behalf," Aikman says. "But he seemed very content. I think there was some relief, and for that I was happy . . . But it amazes me it got to the point it did. One of Jimmy's big speeches to the team—especially around Pro Bowl time, when some guys would get left off—was that if the team has success, everybody will have success. There will be plenty of credit to go around. Yet it didn't apply with those two. That was the shame of it all."

Aikman had grown to cherish the way Johnson ran every practice with Super Bowl Week urgency and intensity. Aikman couldn't stand mental breakdowns or cutting up at practice, and Johnson wouldn't stand for either. "Usually," says Aikman, "when I was upset about the way a practice was going, Jimmy already was upset. As complex as Jimmy is, he's very simple in one way: He's about winning. I always remember what he said to the team after that Washington game. It was his way of trying to apologize. He said some people go through life being asked how they're doing, and they'll say, 'Oh, I'm okay.' He said, 'I've never had those days. My days are either great or horrible. When I win, I'm at the top of the world, and when I lose, I'm at the bottom.' That's how I remember Jimmy: either bouncing around the halls happy as could be or mad at the world."

7

ENEMY TERRITORY

Be careful what you wish for . . .

Becky Buwick was driving. Barry Switzer sat in the passenger seat, head resting against the window, eyes closed, still out of it from the anesthetic. Buwick, a girlfriend of Switzer's, turned onto Castlewood Drive, just south of the University of Oklahoma, and saw the media pack in front of Switzer's town house. "Oh, my God," she said. Camera crews, reporters, the works—and Switzer was in no shape to be interviewed.

It was close to noon on Monday, March 28, 1994.

She parked in the driveway, jumped out, and hurried to help him out of the car. The media approached. "Please, not now," said Buwick. As the University of Oklahoma gymnastics coach, she had some experience dealing with reporters. She tried to hustle him through the minicam gauntlet and into the house. As if Switzer's image weren't stained enough, this had the potential for "Switzer Too Drunk to Meet Press in Afternoon."

Switzer wasn't drunk, though he half-wondered if cocktails had inspired Jerry Jones's shocking statement about him at the NFL meetings in Orlando. Jones supposedly had told some reporters in a bar that he just might fire Jimmy Johnson and hire Barry Switzer—that he should have done it two years ago! It had made the papers, and now it was all over ESPN and CNN. Fire the guy who just coached back-to-back Super Bowl winners? Damnedest thing

Switzer had ever heard. Almost as crazy as, well, hiring Barry Switzer to coach the best team in the NFL.

Hell, Switzer didn't know the NFL from the NHL. He had never followed pro football, not even as a casual fan. In the five years he had been out of coaching, Switzer hadn't watched a single pro game start to finish. At that moment, Barry Switzer couldn't even have told you in which division or conference the Dallas Cowboys played. On his weekly TV show, which aired in Oklahoma City and Tulsa, he picked NFL games for silly laughs. Example: "I'll take the Redskins over the Cowboys. You know what happened to Custer."

And now, still drugged up, Switzer wondered if ol' Jerry Jones had just been acting silly down at those meetings. Jones had an oil-and-gas office in Oklahoma City, so they had crossed paths at some social gatherings. One thing Switzer knew for sure about Jones: He knew how to have a good time.

But this is why Switzer hadn't laughed off what Jones supposedly said: Jerry himself had called from Orlando to apologize for any inconvenience he had caused, such as a front yard full of cameras and microphones. But Jones had not said anything like "Oh, I just had a little too much to drink and got carried away." His tone was serious and urgent. He didn't say much more except that "something could happen in a couple of days."

Of course, Switzer's kids had gone nuts, especially Kathy, who was twenty-four. *Dallas! The Cowboys!* Bright lights, big city. Dad, back in the saddle, doing what he does best. But her dad kept trying to calm her down. He kept telling Kathy and his two sons, Greg and Doug, that he wasn't sure he would accept the job even if it were offered. "Oh, Daddy," said Kathy, "you would, too." And her dad told her, "This would be kind of like winning the lottery. It would be neat, but it's a long shot." He didn't want to see her get too excited and get her heart broken.

So on Monday morning, life went on. Switzer kept his appointment with the doctor he calls his "rear admiral" for his colon procedure. "Those things are no fun," says Switzer. Little did he know he was about to embark on something of a two-year colonoscopy in Dallas.

Still groggy, Switzer sprawled across his bed. It was in that position and condition that he answered the phone. It was Jerry Jones again, and he was in no mood for chitchat.

Jones got right to the point. "Do you want to coach again?"

Hell, yes, said Switzer.

Great, said Jones.

"He said I would hear from him quickly," says Switzer.

The next morning, Jones and Johnson met one last time. Then, together, they met the press one last time. The Buddies from Arkansas were officially ex-buddies. Jones had already called Switzer at his house in Norman.

Naturally, Switzer was in the shower. Kathy yelled to him, "Daddy, it's Jerry Jones!" He wrapped a towel around himself and took the phone. "He was very terse, quick," says Switzer. He wanted Switzer and his family to get down to Dallas as soon as possible and meet Jones and his family at the home of his vice president of marketing, George Hays. They would have some pizza and beer, negotiate a long-term deal, then introduce Switzer as the new Cowboy coach at a press conference the next day.

Switzer hung up, did a little dance with Kathy, then called his oldest son Greg at the University of Arkansas. Switzer told Greg's answering machine, "We won the lottery."

Larry Lacewell was double-stunned. No, this couldn't be happening. Stuff like this only happened in some TV show like *Dallas*. As sick and tired as Jimmy and Jerry were of each other, Lacewell still couldn't believe that two guys so talented, so unbeatable as a team, had actually split.

Now Lacewell was faced with an even bigger second shock: Jones wanted to replace Johnson with the former best friend of Lacewell's who had betrayed him sixteen years earlier.

With Barry Switzer.

What goes around had come all the way back around. Jones, moving quickly, gave Lacewell the opportunity to veto the move, if he absolutely could not work with Switzer. Says Lacewell, "I honestly believe if I'd said it wouldn't work, he wouldn't be here."

Says Jones, "I gave Larry every opportunity to tell me if he had any second thoughts."

And there it was: Sixteen years later, the opportunity for revenge appeared in Lacewell's hands like Macbeth's murder weapon. "Is this a dagger which I see before me / The handle toward my hand?" Suddenly, Larry Lacewell had the perfect chance to commit the perfect career-ending crime. All Lacewell had to tell Jones was "Jerry, you just can't do this to me," and Barry Switzer would probably still be living in Norman today, in relative obscurity, once and forever a has-been.

Who knows? Maybe Lacewell would even be head coach of the Cowboys. Moments after Johnson and Jones announced their divorce, Lacewell told me he would be interested in the job. Assistants Joe Avezzano and Butch Davis were campaigning for it, and

Jones had considered former Arkansas coach Lou Holtz, who was at Notre Dame. But who knows? Jones has as much respect for Lacewell's overall command of football as he does for Johnson's or Switzer's. Lacewell and Jones had grown close. If Jones would hire Switzer, why not Lacewell?

We'll never know because Lacewell blessed Switzer.

"Well, I didn't say anything to keep him from getting the job," Lacewell says. "I told Jerry the positives and the negatives, and I said to remember that I hadn't been around him for sixteen years, which is a long time. But basically, Jerry asked me if he would screw it up, and I said no, he will not screw it up. Barry Switzer will take a lot of things with him to the grave, but one of 'em will not be that he's a bad football coach."

Jones says, "What Larry did was very impressive. It took a far better man than a lot of us would have been to basically give Barry a stamp of approval. You cannot imagine how much I valued that, coming from Larry."

Lacewell and Switzer had run into each other a couple of times over the previous few years. They had chatted. Things were okay. Time had closed Lacewell's wound, but time hadn't healed it.

That's in part because Larry Lacewell remains married to the same wife, Criss. And now they were faced with attending staff parties and outings with a single Barry Switzer? Yes, but things would be different this time. Lacewell's home life no longer was built on quicksand. He was drawing on a new spiritual strength. After he left Oklahoma he had slowly put his life back in order. He reconciled with Criss. They had a second child, another son. Lacewell rededicated himself to being a better father, husband, and human.

"Look," he told me the afternoon Johnson was fired, "the Good Lord put us on this earth to forgive and forget, and I'm trying." His eyes glistened. "I will make this work [with Switzer]. It won't be the way it used to be, but I can work with him. But I can promise you I will not be going out with him every other night."

Lacewell has held to that vow.

Lacewell has made it work with Switzer.

In fact, Switzer might not have made it in Dallas without his old buddy from Arkansas—the little big man from Fordyce.

At 65 or 70 mph, it's a straight, flat, mindless drive of about two and a half hours from Norman south to Dallas. Pauls Valley . . . Ardmore . . . cross the Red River . . . Gainesville . . . Denton . . . Dallas. Barry Switzer had made the drive many times on recruiting raids, but he had always returned. He had always been the enemy in Big D. The Dallas media was out to get him, or so he thought. "Ten years after the 'spy incident,'" he says, "the damn Dallas media was still bringing it up. It was always something negative to sell papers."

Switzer had sold lots of papers in Dallas the second week every October. For years he had been the J. R. Ewing of Texas-OU Week— the one figure off which neither side could take its eyes. Switzer electrified one of college football's greatest rivalries. For sixteen years, his personality loomed above the game like the giant cowboy figure, maybe five stories tall, called "Big Tex," who greets the droves of Texas and Oklahoma fans who jam the State Fair Midway hours before kickoff at the fairgrounds' Cotton Bowl. Many of them have been up all night, raising hell downtown on Commerce Street, perhaps even getting hauled in to jail for a couple of hours. Then, in the morning light of the midway, they meet again and form a sweaty cattle drive of Oklahoma crimson and Texas burnt orange, milling, taunting, eating the fair's famed corny dogs for breakfast, chasing hangovers with beer, trying with double vision to win stuffed animals for the little lady. The Texas Longhorn fans give Oklahoma Sooner fans the "hook 'em, Horns" sign (index and little fingers up) as if shooting them the finger. OU fans return fire by pointing the "hook 'em" sign straight toward hell.

Inside the Cotton Bowl, a *Last Picture Show* kind of stadium that never seems to change, seating is split right at the 50. Half the stadium is crimson, half orange. The Oklahoma half includes the south end zone ramp, down which both teams must walk from their locker rooms. Often the teams meld almost like fans on the midway into a reddish orange before bursting separately into the arena. Says Switzer, "I always got a kick out of the fact that both teams entered on the Oklahoma side. I always thought that was a big advantage for us."

Then every fan in the stands makes a steep bet on the outcome: his or her pride. This isn't anything like a home game. The losing fans must file back onto the fairgrounds and take another three hours of ridicule from the winners as they all hit the midway and exhibits again.

There's nothing quite like it. It hasn't been quite the same without Switzer.

So there he was, heading south in his BMW toward enemy territory, and something strange was happening. He wasn't lead-footing it as he usually did. He was going fifty, fifty-five, and he didn't feel like going any faster. His lottery-winning elation had given way to a sobering reality. What the hell had he gotten himself into? "All of a sudden," he says, "I realized it was time to say, 'I do.'"

If you know Switzer, you know the marriage analogy is the most frightening he could use.

"It was one of the slowest drives I've ever had to Dallas. I mean, I was having really mixed emotions. I thought of all the personal commitments I'd made to all my financial partners. I thought of all the time I'd been able to spend with my children—the trips to Italy, the skiing trips, the quality time I'd finally been able to spend with them after all my years in coaching. I mean, I was so content. And here I was about to go back into this structured, regimented lifestyle that's a helluva lot tougher—something I never dreamed would happen. The farther I drove, the worse I felt about it. I was really depressed."

Barry Switzer, never one for hard work, was coming out of semi-retirement for a job that had been held by a Jimmy Johnson known for fanatically hard work. Switzer was about to subject himself to the can't-win pressure of taking over a team with an opportunity to make Super Bowl history by winning a third straight. And Switzer was wondering, "Why?"

A year or so later, Troy Aikman would wonder the same thing. Aikman told me, "I asked Barry if he could go back to college football now and recruit with the same energy he used to. He said, 'Hell, no, that's why I got out of it.' And I understood that. But I saw a quote where he said winning was no longer as important to him as it used to be, that his family and friends are more important to him. And I appreciate that. Right now winning Super Bowls is a priority for me because I'm trying to build a career. But when I'm through with this at age thirty-five or thirty-six, I won't take winning nearly as seriously in other games I might play. But if you're going to coach this team, winning better be a priority for you. So I thought, 'Why would he want to do *this*?'"

Why, Barry? Why do it to yourself? To your team? Especially to your quarterback, who can drive himself so crazy trying to win?

"Oh, I did it for the challenge," Switzer told me. "Coaching was something I'd missed. The competitive challenge. And being involved in the ego part of it, the glamor. I never *had* to have that, but I missed it."

Especially when you've been a has-been. Sure, he missed being Barry Switzer, big-deal coach. His love-hate of the public attention, the autographs, the Polaroid poses, and the small talk is much more love than hate. He loves walking into a restaurant and having every head turn. He loves walking into a gentlemen's club and having the working girls fall all over him. He missed all that dearly.

But he knew he would have to pay a killer price to have it again. Daughter Kathy says, "Sometimes I really think he did it for the kids. He gave us a chance to say no, because we'd have to be back in the media fishbowl again. But he knew we'd love it. And he knew it would mean more money, so he could make even more sure his kids would never have to worry." Kathy keeps her father's financial ledgers. "I say, 'But, Dad, you already have enough.' And he's like, 'You can never have enough money.'"

But for Switzer, there were slightly easier ways to make a million bucks a year. So why? "Well, the other thing was that I did it for Jerry. I mean, I knew he really wanted me. I was the only one he wanted. He wanted someone he could grow with. Hell, I'm a very, very emotional guy, and that meant a lot to me. Jerry's quick like me. Quick to show all his emotions. He's very compassionate, very caring. He's gracious. A good person with a beautiful outlook on life. He really cares about his family the way I do. He has a lot of friends you'd say are 'nobodies,' like I do. Jerry was a guy I wanted to be with . . . Hell, I knew what he was going through with Jimmy. Jimmy knows I know what a fraud he was. He spent a lot of those 'long hours' he worked building his mystique.

"Jerry knew. Jerry was an owner I wanted to work for because *he played the damn game*. He can look at the tapes and understand why you're winning and losing. This thing has been successful because Jerry understands football. Jeff Lurie [a fantasy-football player who made his money in the entertainment industry and bought the Philadelphia Eagles] will never, ever understand. He'll always be susceptible to outside influence from the fans and the media. Jerry, he's one of us. He's got the pachyderm skin of a coach."

That sentiment was all Jerry Jones ever wanted to hear from Jimmy Johnson.

Jones also told Switzer, "I just hope that someday coach Broyles says the same things about me that he said to me about you."

So what the hell, thought Switzer. It would be he and Jerry against the damn world. He and Jerry would have some laughs. He'd make a lot of money. He'd get famous again. Maybe he'd get to take his kids to a damn Super Bowl. Somewhere around Denton, maybe thirty miles north of George Hays's house, he got a little more comfortable with the whole deal.

And maybe, deep down, Barry Switzer realized why he was really taking this job.

Because he just couldn't turn it down. Hell, who could?

*   *   *

Not to spoil the Jerry-Barry party, but allow a brief interruption for two small points. Troy Aikman probably would appreciate the perspective. Jerry Jones was about to hire a coach with attention deficit disorder on the recommendation of a retired coach who hadn't spent much time around Switzer since 1965.

Just as Jones was deciding it was time to hire Switzer, Switzer was figuring out something that had haunted him since grade school. Why did his mind wander so much? Why couldn't he sit without tapping his feet 100 mph? His family and friends wondered why, in the middle of any conversation, in person or on the phone, he suddenly would tune out? Was he that distracted by the latest football crisis? That self-absorbed? That bored with what you were saying? Says the ex–Mrs. Switzer, "I used to have people ask me all the time if he was hard of hearing."

Switzer's brother, Donnie, had another theory. Wasn't Barry impulsive and restless with a short attention span? Isn't that the classic description of attention deficit disorder? Though some doctors question whether the condition actually causes chemical imbalance in the brain, others estimate that between five and ten million adults in the United States suffer from ADD—and more than half never know it. No longer is ADD considered only a children's affliction. It's now thought to be incurable, but treatable. Switzer had begun reading a book on ADD about the time Jones called to offer him the job.

Soon after taking the job, Switzer met with Cowboy team psychiatrist Dr. Mark Unterberg, who agreed Switzer displayed many ADD symptoms. Unterberg prescribed Ritalin, a drug from the amphetamine family that (many doctors believe) actually works to counteract hyperactivity in an ADD sufferer.

Time-out: Jones had just hired a coach who needed to take an amphetaminelike drug to keep from occasionally checking out mentally? And if his mind wandered, would he forget to take his Ritalin? Imagine how Jimmy Johnson cackled when Aikman told him Switzer had ADD. Aikman wasn't immediately informed about Switzer's disorder. Stifling a grin, Aikman told me, "At first [during spring minicamps] I'd walk over and try to strike up a conversation with him, and after a while he wouldn't even be listening. I'd think, 'Hell, he doesn't even want to talk to me.'"

Switzer says he tried the Ritalin for a while and just didn't like the way it made him feel. "It just slowed me down too much," he said. "I just didn't feel like I could operate the way I wanted to."

But Switzer realized there was a better drug for ADD, one he had been taking in large doses for years. Switzer says alcohol "evens me out and calms me down, focuses me." A bottle of wine, he says, allows him to stay right with the conversation at the table. Says Kathy, "That really helped explain why he needed to drink." So the new coach of the Dallas Cowboys—the one sitting in the same chair at the same desk in the same office Tom Landry occupied—needs a couple of shots from a special flask just before he leaves the locker room for kickoff?

"No, no, no," Switzer told me. "It doesn't affect you when you're doing anything that requires intense concentration, like coaching a game or playing chess. You're okay as long as you're doing something that requires you to lock in."

As honored a coach as Broyles was, several who still observe him closely say he no longer is as locked in as he once was. At seventy-one, he remains Arkansas's athletic director, but observers say he isn't as in touch with today's sports world. The last time he was around Switzer on a daily basis was when Switzer was an Arkansas assistant coach.

Yet, as Larry Lacewell says, "Frank Broyles hired Barry Switzer."

One flew into the cuckoo's nest? Maybe. But it has never been wise to bet against the gut feelings of Frank Broyles and Jerry Jones.

To the party/negotiation at George Hays's house Switzer took his attorney, the former attorney general of Oklahoma, Larry Derryberry. Yes, to join Jerry and Larry, Barry took Larry Derryberry—his real name. If his name had been Larry Jerrybarry, you'd have to wonder. But considering the routinely bizarre things that happen to Switzer and Jones, an attorney named Larry Derryberry is to be expected.

Switzer also was accompanied by Kathy and her husband, Heath, and Switzer's youngest son, Doug. Jones brought along his wife and children. Why the families? Jones and Switzer were raised in a culture in which families worked and played together. Neither man, no matter how busy, is ever far from his kids. When Kathy was in grade school, her dad used to take her with him into Oklahoma's weight room.

So the contract negotiation would take place after Jones could observe the families interacting. This was a relationship the Jones family never had with the Johnson family. Jimmy, who divorced his wife soon after taking the Cowboy job, wasn't interested in being a part of one big happy front-office family.

From a distance, Kathy had watched Johnson's sons, Brent and Chad, share a little of Jimmy's spotlight in Dallas. She had known

Brent and Chad since they were all kids—her mom remains close friends with their mom—and Kathy had envied the Johnson boys. Now that spotlight was about to swivel like a cannon toward the Switzer family. "And really," says Kathy, "none of us had any idea of what we were getting into." The first thing she remembers the Jones kids telling her was that "you better be ready. Your life is going to change. This is the big time."

Jones remembers "feeling a lot of warmth" between the families. Then, later that evening, negotiations began. Much later, Switzer and Derryberry were left thinking they and Jones were awfully far apart on several contractual issues. Switzer and his attorney resolved to hold their ground and went to bed "for a couple of hours," says Switzer. When they reconvened with Jones early the next morning, Jones said, "I've had a good night's sleep." And he stunned them by giving them everything they originally had asked for, says Switzer. "Larry and I looked at each other and said, 'Well, that about covers it.' Then I said, 'Jerry, would you like one more night to sleep on it?' That cracked everybody up."

Switzer adds, "You ain't going to beat Jerry Jones out of anything. But he's liable to give you *everything*."

It had come up during negotiations that Switzer owed $70,000 because he had signed a note for a friend who had defaulted. Jones said he would take care of it. "I later heard that Barry has a lot of money," says Jones. "I don't know that for a fact, but that's what I heard. But it didn't matter how much money he had, I wanted to show him how much this meant to me." Jones wanted to start fresh with a coach who could be his close friend and business partner. Jones wanted to show Switzer from the start that he would pave his side of their two-way street with generosity and loyalty. The truth was, Jerry Jones just liked the hell out of Barry Switzer. "You just can't help having fun around him," Jones says.

In some ways, Switzer had always been the kind of man Jones envied: a man's man, a ladies' man, a powerfully built leading man who at fifty-six sometimes acted twenty-six. A two-fisted football man respected by players and coaches alike. A charismatic man equally comfortable running the streets with the guys or sharing a huge table and a three-hour dinner with the women and children. A man who isn't afraid to show his emotions and to tell you he loves you.

Switzer sometimes says and does outrageous things that Jones would love to say and do, if he weren't the owner of the Dallas Cowboys. In some ways, Jones lives through Switzer. Yet for Jones, choosing Switzer ran so much deeper than that. There was a defi-

nite method to the madness of hiring a man no one else would have
hired. Jones knew Switzer was a blank slate, a coach with no NFL
experience and none of Johnson's "I am the greatest" ego. Jones
knew Switzer would be perfectly content to become head coach of
the NFL champions and make no changes. Jones knew Switzer
wouldn't object to keeping Johnson's coaching staff intact—which
Jones considered essential to preserving the championship continu-
ity and chemistry. Jones knew Switzer wouldn't at all mind working
closely and talking football and sharing the stage with him. As Oklahoma athletic director Donnie Duncan told me, "Barry is the easiest
coach to get along with in America." Jones knew that Switzer was
so grateful for the opportunity and contractual generosity that he
would go along with pretty much anything Jones wanted to do.

Well, pretty much. "We did set parameters," says Switzer. "What
happens between the stripes [on the field], that's my business.
Drafts, trades, football management—that's us [he and Jones]. Marketing and promotions—that's Jerry. But we do both shoot from the
hip. Sometimes I'm not sure which area I'm in, his or mine."

Switzer chuckles. He doesn't get caught up in neutral-zone violations. "I don't get worked up about the little stuff," he says. Yes, he
was the perfect choice for Jones.

Jones knew that if Switzer just wouldn't do anything stupid, the
Cowboys could win again, if they stayed healthy. Then the football
world would step back and say, "Well, Jones did it with Johnson,
and he did it with Switzer." In a way, Jones quietly enjoyed the criticism Switzer began to take. The more Switzer was ripped, the better Jones might look when the two of them stood up on the Super
Bowl victory stand.

For the second straight day, the media massed in the theaterlike
team meeting room at the Cowboys' Valley Ranch headquarters. As
Switzer followed Jerry Jones up onto the stage, confirming almost
surreal rumors, I had one last flash of, "No, this can't be happening."

(The night before, Ted Koppel had interviewed me on *Nightline*
about the Jimmy-Jerry breakup. In the final seconds, I had volunteered that it looked like Jones was going to hire Barry Switzer.
That's what everyone I trusted at Valley Ranch thought would happen. As my segment ended and I unhooked the microphone from
my tie, I thought, "I just made a fool of myself on national TV.")

As Switzer began answering media questions, he seemed a little
different than I remembered him. A little more on edge, more
defensive, sort of manic-giddy. He later told me, "I hadn't had much

sleep. I was running on empty. And remember, it had been a while since I'd done a press conference like that." He seemed to be trying desperately hard to convince the "enemy" media that taking over the repeat Super Bowl champs was no big deal because he had won three national championships at Oklahoma. Finally, someone in the audience asked the kind of sophomoric question that made legitimate reporters glance at each other and roll their eyes: "Coach, do you have a message for Cowboy fans?"

Switzer's response made an indelibly bad first impression on fans around the country. That response was used repeatedly on ESPN's *SportsCenter* for the next twenty-four hours, with host after wise-guy host joking about how Switzer needed to calm down a little. Thank God for Switzer they didn't know about his ADD. To this day, Switzer's response is often played as a goofy intro before I'm interviewed by Cowboy-hating radio talk-show hosts around the country.

Switzer's "message to fans"? He suddenly raised his voice and sounded like a bleary-eyed Sooner fan on the state fair midway. Switzer said, "We got a job to do and we gonna do it, baby!"

Switzer was trying to be loose and cool and funny. Watch this: He would give a silly answer to a silly question. But no one out in viewerland heard the silly question. Around Dallas the next few months, fans were mocking Switzer's silly answer. So, perhaps, were some of Switzer's new players, who were trying to figure out who this guy was and why he was coaching them.

In Switzer's heyday at OU, national images were formed as much by newspaper and magazine stories and still photos as television clips. Switzer had now blundered back into a sports world bombarded and dominated by ESPN. The next indelible *SportsCenter* image: the trash can.

The one thrown across the locker room by Michael Irvin.

Switzer's next mistake came during his first remarks to his new team. The Cowboys had been built in Johnson's us-against-the-world image—and that included the team and coaches against that greedy egomaniac owner. Johnson had thrived on his good cop–bad cop relationship with Jones. Johnson ingratiated himself with his players and assistants by privately siding with them during negotiations and bad-mouthing Jones. So what did Switzer do? He immediately told his players how much he admired Jerry Jones.

That, coupled with the shock of losing a coach Irvin had won championships with in college and the NFL, sent Irvin over his emotional edge. When a pack of minicams approached, his form of no comment was to grab a trash can and hurl it across the locker room. For TV viewers, the obvious translation was "Irvin's ready to tear up the place because his crazy owner fired Irvin's guy Jimmy and hired that crazy Switzer."

For a while, the one place Switzer could avoid flying trash cans and insults was at Boo's house.

As a toddler, John Blake's teddy-bear face earned him the nickname Boo Boo, after Yogi Bear's sidekick. Half the nickname stuck: "Boo" Blake turned into a round mound of nose tackle out of San Springs, Oklahoma, who played for Switzer at OU from 1980 to 1983. He made All-Big Eight second team his senior year, but more important, he made friends with Switzer. Blake wound up living in an apartment a football field away from Switzer's house. When Switzer's kids squabbled, Blake often mediated.

This is how much Switzer trusted young Blake: When Switzer divorced in 1981, daughter Kathy moved with her mom to Little Rock. But a couple of years later, at fourteen, she decided to move back to Norman and be with her dad. Her mom says, "She just felt like her dad needed her." Switzer sent Blake with a U-Haul to pick her up and bring her back. (And a week or so later, when she decided she had made a mistake, Blake moved her back to Little Rock.) Kathy says they passed through a highway tollbooth while she had fallen asleep with her head on the edge of Blake's lap. The attendant wondered what was going on between a white teenage girl and a large black man. Soon, here came a highway patrolman to check things out. Kathy quickly set the officer straight.

Blake first coached under Switzer at OU in '86, when his nickname expanded to "Back-'em-up Boo." On the sideline, Switzer constantly yelled to his youngest assistant to keep the players back from the white boundary line. "Back 'em up, Boo!" was Switzer's constant refrain.

Blake remained on the staff of Switzer's successor, Gary Gibbs. But in the summers of '91 and '92, he worked with Cowboy coaches at training camp as part of the Jerry Jones Minority Coaching Fellowship. Jimmy Johnson enjoyed Blake's sunny personality and the way the players responded to him. So, with the franchise under NAACP pressure to add black staffers, Johnson hired Blake to coach the Cowboy defensive line in '93. (Butch Davis, who had handled the defensive line, had replaced Dave Wannstedt as defensive coordinator when Wannstedt became head coach in Chicago.)

Gibbs tried to keep Blake. Gibbs called me to see if I could find out what average salaries were for NFL defensive assistants, so he could compete financially for Blake without going overboard. Gibbs respected Blake's football knowledge. But he particularly didn't want to lose Blake's recruiting charisma. Blake can talk a young football player's language, especially if he's black. Whites light up to him, too, but when Blake turns it on, he can speak poetic rap. On the dance floor, he can still spin into the "sweet" moves that won him some college contests. No doubt all this appealed to eighteen-year-old recruits who thought, "Here's one coach who's still cool." In some ways, Boo Blake was just an overgrown kid with a heart as big as Switzer's.

But after a Super Bowl season on Johnson's staff, Blake was, in effect, put on probation. Johnson reprimanded Blake in a staff meeting, saying, "I didn't hire you to become a friend to the players. I hired you to coach 'em." Several assistants on that staff say Johnson was leaning toward firing Blake when Johnson got fired. Blake insists that wasn't the case. For sure, if Johnson had fired Blake, his dream of returning to be head coach at his alma mater would have been damaged severely.

Instead, when Jones decided to fire Johnson and hire Switzer, Blake went from probation to jubilation. Blake, too, had hit the lottery. In effect, "Back 'em up, Boo" became assistant head coach of the Cowboys. One moment he dreaded being called into Johnson's office. The next he could breeze unannounced through the private entrance off the restroom behind the head coach's desk, flop down on the couch, and use the phone on the coffee table.

Life is strange.

In a league in which loyal assistants can be nearly as important as good players, Switzer now admits he felt as if he were "flying solo" with his predecessor's staff. He had only one assistant he could trust. Until Switzer could find an apartment, he moved in with Boo Blake and his wife, Freda.

Naturally, the one player Switzer automatically counted as an ally was the only player on the Cowboy roster with an Oklahoma tie. Switzer had been told how close Troy Aikman and Jimmy Johnson had grown, and Switzer told me, "It'll take a little time with Troy." But he didn't expect Aikman to be throwing any trash cans.

Right away, though, Switzer and his family and friends were shaken by a quote they read from Aikman in Randy Galloway's column in the *Dallas Morning News*. "I don't need any more friends," Aikman said. The quarterback's point was that as long as the Cowboys continued to win, his relationship with the new coach would be just fine. But when Aikman read the quote in the newspaper, "it came across as harsh," he says. He went to Switzer and tried to put the quote in better perspective, he says. To Aikman, the new coach shrugged it off. Fine. No big deal.

But the quote had hit Switzer's loyalty-alert button, and the alarm wouldn't stop. His family and friends wouldn't let it. To those around Switzer, it sounded suspiciously like Aikman had declared his allegiance to Johnson and Norv Turner. A seed had been planted from which a briar patch would grow.

Right away, Troy Aikman was irritated. Publicly, he had been supportive of the Switzer hire. Even privately, he had told sportscaster Dale Hansen, one of Dallas-Fort Worth's most influential media voices, "You're going to love this guy." For that matter, says Hansen, "I was telling everyone [in the media], 'You're going to love this guy.' Sure, as a Nebraska fan, I hated what he had done to Tom Osborne. But Barry Switzer was the greatest coach [for TV reporters] I'd ever been around." One year before an Oklahoma-Texas game, Switzer interrupted practice to let Hansen's photographer shoot footage from the vantage point of the middle linebacker against the wishbone. On camera, Switzer said something like, "Tell [Texas coach] Fred Akers we're going to run right and run left and let's see if he has anybody who can catch us." Says Hansen, "It was wonderful stuff. I was actually very excited about working with Switzer again. That's why it's so hard to believe what happened."

Right away Aikman was not pleased with the sideline crowd at Switzer's first minicamp practice, about a month after he was hired. Neat freaks Aikman and Johnson always agreed that no one should be at practice who didn't have a function. Now on the sidelines were Switzer's kids, friends, and several of his former Oklahoma assistants and players.

Switzer later admitted he made a mistake letting his ex-assistants hang around, because Cowboy vets began kidding Cowboy assistants that they were about to be replaced. But Aikman was more concerned about an ex-Sooner who was acting like a Cowboy assistant—about the former OU quarterback who had "big-timed" him when he was a freshman. Aikman first saw Danny Bradley working out in the Cowboy weight room—a players-only sanctuary to Aikman. Then Bradley showed up the first day of minicamp dressed like a Cowboy coach. He began making little suggestions, especially to the younger receivers. He encouraged them, congratulated them. Aikman was thinking, "What the hell is this?" When Bradley, uninvited, sat in at a quarterback meeting led by offensive coordinator Ernie Zampese, that was it for Aikman. He complained to Switzer, who said he'd "take care of it," says Aikman.

The "coaching" stopped, but Danny Bradley didn't go away. Where there was Switzer, there often was his "son" Bradley, who operated as something of a personal assistant to the head coach.

Later, Bradley called Aikman's mother to see if she could help set up a meeting between him and Troy. Bradley is a handsome, clean-cut, well-spoken young man whose charm is especially effective on moms. The first time she relayed the request to her son, he sighed and tried to tell her he was just too busy. When she relayed a second request from Bradley, Troy gave in and met with him.

Bradley basically wanted to talk Aikman into approving him for some sort of position on the front-office or even coaching staff. Aikman said, "Danny, I've been trying to get Rick Nueheisel [now head coach at Colorado] hired here [as an assistant coach] for a couple of years. He's a good friend of mine, and I can't even get him hired." Aikman says tears came to Bradley's eyes as he told Aikman he needed this job.

Aikman didn't help Bradley get a Cowboy job. But he didn't try to keep him from getting one, either. Eventually, Danny Bradley wound up with a newly created position called "director of player programs," for which he was paid about $25,000 a year. To supplement his income, Bradley began working for a cellular phone company. But for the Cowboys, he began counseling especially younger players, trying to uncomplicate their lives by answering the many overwhelming questions they face: where to live, where to (and not to) have a good time, what to wear on road trips, how to find the right investment advice, etc.

Ironically, Bradley would lose his job for the role he played in complicating Aikman's life.

That spring, as the "Cowboy coach Switzer" reality sank in, I talked often with several of his close friends about their concerns for him. I heard: "They'll chew him up and spit him out down there in Dallas" . . . "If they win the Super Bowl, the media will say he won with the great team Jimmy built. If they don't win the Super Bowl, the media will say Jimmy would have won it. Barry can't win" . . . "He could ruin what was a great career" . . . "He just doesn't want to work that hard anymore" . . . "He's going to have to watch himself out in public. He can't get away with the same stuff he does in Norman. Now he has Tom Landry's old job, and they'll run him out of town if he's caught doing anything a little crazy."

Right away, Switzer left some indignant Dallasites in his nighttime wake, especially after a bottle of wine with a group of old friends. In that condition, the Frank Switzer in Barry sometimes seizes control, and he's liable to ignore some basic rules of society.

Sometimes, when he has had a little too much to drink, the Barry Switzer who grew up with outdoor plumbing might decide to relieve himself, well, outdoors. He has been known to do so in a restaurant parking lot, for instance. But one Saturday night during that first minicamp, Switzer was among friends at a hotel with an atrium lobby. Up on one of the floors, they stopped Switzer just before he urinated over the railing down into the lobby. Figuratively, Switzer would soon feel like doing just that on many Cowboy fans and Dallas-Fort Worth media members.

But as his first training camp approached, it was clear Barry Switzer had a lot to learn about his new job.

8

BATTLE LINES

Machiavellianism: The view that politics is amoral and that any means however unscrupulous can justifiably be used in achieving political power.
—Webster's Collegiate Dictionary

As training camp opened, Barry Switzer had been briefed repeatedly by his few Oklahoma allies on the political minefield into which he had been thrown. The more Switzer learned, the more his insecurity and paranoia flared. Switzer, who built his Oklahoma staffs on loyalty, perhaps felt the way nineteen-year-old Aikman had when he found himself running OU's wishbone: alone and unsure. Switzer's emotions became an unpredictable minefield.

Mostly, he stayed in the background.

Occasionally, when threatened, he attacked.

In Aikman's eyes, Switzer was about to go after the wrong two people—the Cowboy radio network broadcasters who are friends of the quarterback. In Switzer's view, he was merely defending himself against Aikman's first attempt to undermine the coach by turning the media against him.

One of the broadcasters, Dale Hansen, calls what happened at the end of camp "a defining moment" between Switzer and Aikman. For sure, the battle lines were about to be drawn between their allies. Cowboy camp was about to become camps.

*   *   *

Ironically, when Switzer took the Cowboy job, the least of his loyalty worries were the quarterback who had played for him at OU
and the two team-approved radio broadcasters. His primary concern was a coaching staff with ties to Jimmy Johnson reaching back
to Oklahoma State.

Switzer learned that these assistants had been brought by Johnson from Miami to Dallas in 1989: defensive coordinator Butch
Davis, secondary coach Dave Campo, receivers coach Hubbard
Alexander, running back coach Joe Brodsky, and kicking coach
Steve Hoffman. Aikman had grown close to Alexander, Brodsky, and
especially special-teams coach Joe Avezzano, who joined Johnson's
staff in 1990.

Tight ends coach Robert Ford was hired in '91, and offensive
line coach Hudson Houck and linebacker coach Jim Eddy in '93.
New members like Switzer were highly respected offensive coordinator Ernie Zampese and first-year NFL assistant Mike Zimmer,
who would handle nickel backs. Switzer doubted he could trust the
two guys who had wanted his job, Davis and Avezzano. He thought
he'd be okay with Houck and Zampese, West Coast guys who were
recommended by Norv Turner before he left for the Redskins.
Switzer couldn't yet be sure about the rest.

So more than ever, Switzer leaned on his confidants. John Blake
and Danny Bradley constantly fed back to Switzer what they heard
from players. Switzer and Larry Lacewell were reestablishing their OU
rapport, and Switzer listened to Lacewell's advice on how to handle
the almost hourly crises generated by the prima donna–laden, media-
hounded Dallas Cowboys. "It was just so different for him," says
Lacewell. "Back when we were winning thirty-something in a row [at
Oklahoma], he didn't have to deal with these kinds of problems."

At Oklahoma, says Lacewell, assistants learned to "steer"
Switzer—to point him in the right direction, then let his people
skills and instincts kick in. Though it took a while, Jerry Jones
learned what a powerful asset Switzer's naiveté and vulnerability
can be. After the 1995 season, Jones said, "People around him just
want to reach out and help him so badly. That ADD—hey, that's no
act. But Barry is just so receptive, so eager for you to tell him every
possible thing you can to help him. That quality really makes players want to play hard for him."

Strange but true. Switzer's contradictory "vulnerable strength"
eventually made nearly all his Cowboy players defiantly protective
of him—all but the quarterback, who wanted a coach he could look
up to, not look after.

But Switzer's problems mainly arose when Jones and Lacewell weren't around to help steer him, and others were all too willing.

When he was in town, Dean Blevins was a constant companion of Switzer's. Blevins, another former Sooner quarterback, was probably the most powerful TV-radio voice in Oklahoma. Blevins, ten years older than Aikman, was more like a younger brother than a son to Switzer—more of a dinner-and-drinks friend than Blake or Bradley. But Blevins was out of the Blake/Bradley mold: a sharp, personable young man from an upstanding background (Blevins father is a Baptist minister) whose value system occasionally blurs in Switzer's force field. Like Blake and Bradley and several other ex-Sooners still close to Switzer, Blevins is eager to please his ex-coach and sometimes gets entangled in what Switzer's children call his "dysfunctional behavior." As much good as there is in Switzer, his real children and his Sooner sons must sometimes remind themselves: Do as he says, not as he does.

Why does Switzer choose to hang around with so many guys so much younger than he is? Switzer will be fifty-nine on October 5, 1996. Psychologist Don Beck says, "Really, Barry's mind-set hasn't changed since 1973 [when he became head coach at OU]. There has been very little growth or evolution." More and more, Switzer puts himself down about "getting old"—something he battles as stubbornly as he does the "damn media." He refuses to let his chronological age dictate his behavior. He and friends like Blevins are going to go out and have fun, by God.

Do he and Blevins ever have a winking, laughing blast. That first summer in Austin, they became late-night legends. Even when they're not together, they often update each other by cellular phone during their nights out. Blevins is a handsome charmer, which makes him a hit with the ladies and television viewers. With no formal training, Blevins turned himself into Oklahoma City's dominant sportscaster—a glib, opinionated, hardworking ex-quarterback with great TV hair and a pipeline to Barry Switzer. The coach tells Blevins just about everything that's going on inside the team and doesn't appear to mind that Blevins often uses inside info on the air. The tradeoff: Blevins has little or no on-air objectivity about Barry Switzer.

Blevins would have done well in the media business without any help from Switzer. Blevins is talented enough to be a sideline reporter during ABC college football telecasts. He's charismatic enough that he recently met in Washington with President Clinton, who talked with Blevins about running for senator. But Switzer has been a powerful professional connection for Blevins, just as Blevins has been a powerful supporter of Switzer's.

Like Blake, Blevins hit the lottery when Switzer got the Cowboy job. Switzer basically assured Blevins he would help get him a Dallas media job. At Oklahoma, power plays were a snap for Switzer, who once had an OU radio play-by-play man removed from the job for airing part of Switzer's postgame remarks to the team, in which the coach used an obscenity.

In Dallas Switzer needed a friend in a high media place. He wanted Blevins to have a Dallas TV job and he wanted Blevins to be part of the Cowboy broadcast team.

If you were a Cowboy fan living within five-state radio range of Texas Stadium, you knew Brad and Dale. Many Sundays, Brad Sham and Dale Hansen were an even better team than the one they covered for the Dallas Cowboy radio network. Sham did the play-by-play; Hansen provided very colorful commentary.

Called "professor" by some assistant coaches, the pipe-smoking, sometimes bearded Sham had been part of the Cowboy broadcast team since 1976. As "the Voice of the Cowboys" and a beloved talk-show host, Sham had grown close to Tom Landry and Tex Schramm. Though he never quite seemed to get over the way Jerry Jones treated the two icons, Jones had treated Sham with respect. Early on, it behooved the new owner to build his credibility by aligning himself with Sham, who hosted Jones's weekly TV show. But early on, Jones often had to grin and bear Sham's pomposity, according to several sources close to Jones. Sham sometimes took himself as seriously as he always took his work. Says one source, "It was like Brad had come to believe he sat on this all-seeing, all-knowing throne above the Dallas Cowboys. He actually seemed to believe his opinions were even more important than the owner's or the coach's."

Hansen doesn't take his Cowboy opinions quite as seriously, but his ego is another matter. Chuckling, he readily admits his ego barely fits in his offensive lineman's physique. Hansen is very good on TV and radio, and he knows it. So does Jones. Hansen has a big voice, quick wit, and commanding delivery. He makes fun of the various hair colors he has tried over the years and of his roller-coaster weight, but he knows he's the market's proverbial 600-pound gorilla. He does the top-rated sportscasts on Dallas-Fort Worth's top-rated TV station, WFAA Channel 8.

Yet here's what Switzer initially failed to grasp (or respect or believe) about Sham and Hansen: Both were close friends of Troy

Aikman's. At least, they and the quarterback say they're close friends, though the broadcasters and the quarterback clearly have some ulterior motives for their relationships.

Hansen says, "Aikman and I are better friends. He has more *respect* for Brad. Don't underestimate how close Brad and Troy are."

In Dallas-Fort Worth one other media member was in the Hansen-Sham league in power and influence. Randy Galloway is the lead sports columnist for the *Dallas Morning News*—the market's dominant paper—and host of the highest-rated evening talk show on WBAP-AM. You guessed it: Aikman says Galloway is "a friend of mine," and Galloway rivals Hansen and Sham as an Aikman worshiper.

The Cowboy quarterback, close friends with the market's three most influential media members?

It's unusual for a city's biggest star athlete to become more than superficial "friends" with media types. Most athletes learn to "play the game" by being friendly with or at least civil to key media members. Sure, pat them on the head and maybe they'll help create a favorable image for the athlete and treat the athlete better in print or on the air when the athlete has a bad game or gets arrested. But to most athletes, the media is a necessary evil populated with inferior humans who wanted to play sports and couldn't. Most would consider it beneath their dignity to be actual pal-around friends with even one media member.

But Aikman is a little different. Aikman has "buddies" who aren't pro football players. He says, "My sense of worth and self-esteem is not based on how many games I win as a quarterback . . . When I'm done playing . . . I'll support the Cowboys, but my life won't depend on them. I won't be worrying about what coverage the Redskins are playing this week. I'll be sitting up in the stands telling jokes with my buddies."

Maybe Aikman will be sitting up there telling jokes with Hansen, Sham, and Galloway. But you have to wonder if Aikman's insecure streak made the superstar quarterback a little more willing to develop friendships with these three. Of the consistent public praise heaped on him by Hansen and Galloway, Aikman says, "Dale and Randy have been very good to me." For his part, Hansen admits, "I love the guy. But I'll be the first to admit I've played this deal [being close to Aikman] for all it's worth [to enhance his credibility among viewers and listeners]." Did Aikman enjoy a similar professional bonus from these relationships? Did he have the peace of mind of knowing he would always be given a positive spin no matter how he played or acted?

After winning back-to-back Super Bowls, Aikman's flanks were protected by the equivalent of the U.S. Marines, Navy, and Air Force.

For a while, training camp was as rough on Dale Hansen as on the rookie head coach. The *Dallas Observer*, an alternative newspaper, had done an investigative story on Hansen's after-hours behavior. Other media outlets approached Hansen for reaction to the story. Feeling battered, Hansen looked up one day after practice and there was Aikman, who hadn't forgotten the advice Hansen had given him two years earlier.

"Just remember," Aikman told him, "you're Dale Fucking Hansen."

Translation: You're bigger than anything any *Dallas Observer* can throw at you. Aikman soon would remind Hansen he was bigger than anything any overmatched, out-of-control rookie head coach could throw at him.

From the start of training camp, Aikman had surprised Hansen by reversing field and telling him it wasn't going to work with Switzer. Hansen says, "All of a sudden Aikman went from 'You're going to love this guy' to 'I can't stand this.' The discipline wasn't there during practice. Aikman had seen the shootin', dopin', and rapin' at Oklahoma. He had experienced the boom boxes on the sidelines during practice. He had lived it. You could say it was a quasi-scar. And now it was happening again."

It would have been one thing for Aikman to share such strong sentiments with a teammate, but he was confiding in the TV guy with Dallas-Fort Worth's biggest audience. Hansen was understandably stunned and swayed by Aikman's perceptions, which began to color his public appraisal of Switzer. Sham and Galloway no doubt were hearing some of the same complaints from the quarterback and began to be more openly skeptical and critical of the new coach.

For sure, Switzer wasn't Jimmy Johnson. The previous Cowboy coach wouldn't tolerate a star or a sub being a millisecond late for practice; Switzer shrugged off occasional stragglers. Johnson boiled over if players started jacking around during practice; Switzer seemed to enjoy occasional boys-will-be-boys clowning, as if it broke the monotony. "Hell," Switzer told me. "Michael Irvin is the worst one out there about that [goofing around]. What am I supposed to do, cut him?"

Switzer didn't take curfews too seriously, perhaps because he didn't want to feel like a hypocrite. Switzer, of course, isn't one to be in bed by ten each evening. Curfews, an irritated Switzer told me, "are rat-turd things made to be broken. I don't like 'em."

Hansen says, "That's the kind of attitude that sets off Aikman. I mean, Switzer is *paid* to be hypocritical. He's got to think, 'I'm not your buddy. I'm your coach.' What Aikman has been taught all his life is that if you party until three in July, you can't win in January. My question is, Does Switzer treat his players this way out of respect or neglect?"

Aikman told Hansen of an exchange he and several players had witnessed between Switzer and trainer Kevin O'Neill, who had been a confidant of Johnson's since their days together at the University of Miami (and who rejoined Johnson after he was hired by the Dolphins). When Switzer questioned O'Neill about something, the trainer lashed back, basically telling Switzer not to tell him how to do his bleepity-bleepin' job. Switzer did not get mad, according to the players. He basically shrugged off O'Neill's reaction and walked away. As he left, Aikman and the others looked at each other and said something like, "I don't think Kevin would have done that to Jimmy." Hansen: "It was like, the fucking *trainer* can even get away with that?"

But what really had Aikman on edge was that practices—at least to Aikman—were so chaotic. He told Hansen that one day Avezzano seemed to be running practice. The next day, Butch Davis seemed to be in charge. The next, Zampese. The next, Hudson Houck, who was said to "hate" Butch Davis, and vice versa. To Aikman, Switzer was such a nonfactor during practice that a power vacuum had been created and four assistants were competing at practice and in meetings to become unofficial head coach. Sham says he was being told similar stories by several players other than Aikman. Says Hansen, "For Aikman, it was like, 'Goddamn it, Barry, take control!'"

Aikman later told me he was much more volatile during those camp practices than he had been in his life. I had told him before camp that Switzer thought he was mature enough to take an even stronger leadership role. Yet what Switzer thought was a compliment—even a tribute—Aikman viewed more as Switzer's shirking responsibility. Aikman said, "Regardless of how strong a leader I might be, there has to be leadership at the top. If I'm given the power to cut and sign players and make decisions as to who's playing, I'll lead this team as well as anyone can. Otherwise, there's a limit to what I can do."

Switzer had agreed to be a live guest on Hansen's Channel 8 sportscast on the final Thursday night of camp. For all the wrong reasons, it would become perhaps the most memorable interview of

Switzer's (and Hansen's) career. For sure, it further molded a public perception of Switzer as the un-Landry—a wild man who didn't have much control of himself or his team.

Yet it was Hansen, like a kid playing with a loaded gun, who accidentally fired the first shot that morning, when he was interviewed live by KLIF talk-show host Norm Hitzges. Hansen remembers most of the exchange being pretty tame. "Understand, here I had been beaten up for being Jerry Jones's whore. I had a stack of letters from people saying, 'How could you let Jerry Jones do that to Jimmy Johnson?' And I was saying, 'Well, gee, I can understand what happened between Jerry and Jimmy.' And up until that point, I was a Switzer fan. I mean, I was picking the Cowboys to win the Super Bowl. Then Hitzges asked me if I had any concerns about the team and *boom*."

Hansen, who can be as impulsive as Switzer, basically repeated Aikman's concerns—without, of course, attributing any of them to Aikman. Hansen told KLIF listeners about the power struggle among assistant coaches. Hansen even went public with the "shouting match" between Switzer and trainer O'Neill (and later apologized to O'Neill for doing so).

Hansen had dazzled Hitzges's audience with his inside info— while breaking his own story on KLIF. "Typical mouthy me," he says. This reinforced Switzer's belief that Hansen "basically is an idiot."

Sham scolded his partner for going public with a story they hadn't had time to research completely. But this raises a question: Should Cowboy management allow the broadcasters on its radio network to investigate and report stories that are damaging to the team? Was it fair to Jones for Sham and Hansen to be treated as Cowboy "family"—to be the only two media members allowed to circulate among the players and coaches on the field before games—then use the information against, say, the new head coach? Most Cowboy players viewed Sham and Hansen more as "one of us" than "one of them" (print journalists who aren't to be trusted). Should Jones allow Sham and Hansen, after informal chats with players or assistant coaches, to put on their journalist hats and do investigative stories on team problems for their radio or TV stations? Should Jones tolerate team broadcasters breaking a story about how the new coach—upon whom Jones had staked his NFL reputation—was losing control of the team?

Doing homework for game background is one thing; breaking controversial stories another. Understand, Jones is as open-minded about objective game commentary as any owner in sports. Jones says, "If we stink it up, I want them to say we're stinking it up." But until Switzer arrived and began to complain, Jones had spoiled Sham and Hansen by never critiquing them. That in part was because Jones is so busy before and during games that he rarely if ever listens to the broadcasts.

But, says Sham, "I never felt conflicted . . . It would be hypocritical to ignore a huge problem on the team. What's your motivation? If it's to break a story for the story's sake, that's a point [against broadcaster reporters]. But if your motivation is to always be a step ahead in knowing what impact something might have on the football team so you can address it leading up to and during games, that's fine."

I've challenged Hansen to quit the Cowboy broadcasts and concentrate on breaking Cowboy stories for Channel 8 or the radio station for which he now works, KLIF. Sometimes, it's as if Hansen has a "death wish"—that he all but dares Jones to fire him in subconscious hope he'll be freed from his split reporter/entertainer personality. Yet Hansen admits he likes the check he makes for doing the Cowboy games. And more important, he knows his popularity on Channel 8 is enhanced by—if not dependent on—his affiliation with the Cowboys. Hansen says, "In this town, you better be identified with the Cowboys, or you don't make it [as a TV sportscaster]."

At the psychological core of the looming conflict between Sham/Hansen and Switzer was homage. Switzer wouldn't pay it. Sham and Hansen wanted the rookie coach to treat them with a little more respect than he treated other media members. If Switzer immediately had taken Sham and Hansen into his confidence, told them a few harmless secrets, along with how great they were, they wouldn't have been nearly so quick to investigate the "power struggle" on his staff. Like most broadcasters—or humans—Sham's and Hansen's opinion of a coach or player correlate directly with how the coach or player treats Sham or Hansen. As great a player as Aikman is, if he had been a jerk to Hansen, would Hansen have been "president of the Troy Aikman Fan Club"? No. If Switzer had taken the politically correct approach for a coach in such a politically unstable climate and buddied up to Sham and Hansen, would that have helped his credibility with Aikman? Almost certainly.

But at first Switzer couldn't seem to believe Aikman's allegiance to two pompous broadcasters would be stronger than his Oklahoma ties to Switzer. As psychologist Beck says, "To Barry, it was like Troy had broken the code." The once-a-Sooner, always-a-Sooner code. Then again, Aikman wound up a Bruin. His school ties are to

UCLA. He still keeps in touch with his UCLA coach, Terry Donahue, "who's a good friend of mine," says Aikman.

Switzer soon offended Sham, who says, "It took me two and a half months [after Switzer was hired] to get five minutes with him. I said, 'I'm really looking forward to working with you. The former coach [Johnson] and I got off on a bad foot, and I think I can be helpful to you. The best way for me is to have general knowledge of the way things are going. If I know about [something that's going to happen], and I'm not steered in the wrong path, I can present your side of the story.'" But, says Sham, "his response was terse, almost aloof. He said, 'I think you'll find I'm honest to a fault.' Had he just listened and said, 'Hey, that'd be great. I could use another friend . . .'"

Hansen suspects Switzer was looking for a reason to go to war with him. Hansen wondered: Was it because he is a vocal Nebraska fan (from the days he worked in Lincoln)? Or was it because Switzer wanted Dean Blevins to have his job? Hansen: "My argument is still that Switzer came to town with a chip on his shoulder or the agenda of 'getting' me."

Yet after Switzer heard what Hansen said that morning on the Hitzges show, the coach didn't exactly have to invent a reason to attack Hansen.

Several times in interviews for this book, people close to Switzer and Aikman mentioned the game most of us played when we were kids. Some call it "Operator." You remember: You whisper something to the first person in the circle, who whispers it to the second, and so on, until the final person in the circle says your line out loud. Hansen says, "Sure, you'd tell the first kid, 'The woman wore a red dress and blue shoes.' And it would come out, 'The woman was a communist.'"

Becky Buwick calls the game "Die Laughing." She kept telling Switzer to read distorted newspaper stories and "die laughing."

Over the next two seasons, the Switzer and Aikman camps sometimes would accuse women in red dresses and blue shoes of being communists. But nobody would die laughing.

Larry Lacewell rode in a golf cart with Switzer through the Austin night across the St. Edward's University campus toward Channel 8's outdoor setup. Lacewell knew Switzer's fuse was lit. Lacewell wanted to be there just in case he had to pull Switzer off Dale Hansen.

The interview, before a small audience of fans, began around 10:30 P.M., Dallas time. Hansen and Switzer sat in canvas-seated director chairs, turned slightly toward each other. Both were dressed casually, Hansen in jeans, Switzer in shorts. Hansen opened with a "generic" question about how well camp had gone. Switzer responded with either a subtle dig or a Freudian slip, saying Oliver Stone couldn't have written a better script.

Then Hansen brought up the recent trip to Mexico City for an exhibition—a financial windfall for Jones in an overflowing Azteca Stadium (attendance: 112,376). But the travel arrangements for America's Team had been amateurish if not nightmarish. The team plane was too small and cramped. The delays were maddening. On the return trip, the Cowboys were forced to sit for four hours on the runway before taking off. Several players, including Aikman, had shared their fury with the equally steamed team broadcasters. Players and broadcasters concluded that Jones had booked the "economy" flight for his team and pocketed the savings and that the previous head coach would not have let Jones get away with it.

Now, on camera, Switzer's tone and demeanor immediately changed. His voice rose with sarcasm. "I didn't know you were a Mexican official," Switzer said. Switzer began to lean toward his interrogator, chin jutting, finger jabbing to within an inch or two of Hansen's face. Even on the TV screen, you could see Switzer's jaw and neck muscles flaring. When he's mad, Switzer's jaw muscles can look as scary as a pit bull's.

Switzer continued his Mexico City defense with "Jerry Jones is a great guy. But I've gotta convince you of that."

"Do you need to convince the players?" Hansen shot back.

A defensive Switzer took the offense. Instead of answering that question, he said, "I want to ask you something. You made a call to Hitzges. A controversy on our staff?"

"A power struggle," said Hansen, adding that there are "like five head coaches."

Now Switzer was over-the-top hot. Vocal cords straining, he began driving home his points by punching Hansen in the upper arm with a brass knuckle—a "big-ass ring," says Hansen.

Switzer said, "Dale, I've got the second-fastest gun on this team [to Jones] and I can fire anyone I want—other than the ones [players] with the great contracts."

Hansen tried to add some perspective to his "power struggle" contention by noting that Jimmy Johnson often has said the biggest mistake he ever made was keeping Howard Schnellenberger's staff when he was hired as head coach at the University of Miami in 1984. ("Maybe it made Switzer mad that I brought up Jimmy's name," says Hansen.)

Switzer said, "These guys [assistants] and I get along great."

Then Switzer went for the verbal knockout punch, even if it landed slightly below the belt. "You guys fabricate things. Read the *Dallas Observer*."

Switzer referred to the story about Hansen's alleged carousing. Without anger, a still smiling Hansen said, "You don't have to take a cheap shot at me."

Switzer said, "Dale, we're supposed to be at the same school." Switzer, still using college terminology, was saying that he and Hansen were supposed to be on the same team—that he didn't want to get down and dirty but that Hansen had broken the "family" bond by firing the first shot.

Hansen ignored the "same school" line and, reinforced by Aikman's off-the-record concerns, hammered away: "You've got assistants versus assistants, and players want you to step up and do something about it."

Switzer: "I don't think you know what you're talking about and they [players] don't either."

Bam: another shot in the arm.

A moment later, a manic Switzer said, "I think I'll go fire a player!"

Bam.

Followed by: "You know, I can go back to Norman and sit on my couch. I came to Dallas with more money than Jimmy Johnson!"

Interview officially out of control.

Switzer: "You fabricate! You said Tony Casillas had a brain tumor!"

Hansen started to defend himself. ("Now I was pissed," says Hansen.)

Switzer interrupted. "You told Jerry he [Casillas] had a brain tumor!"

Hansen: "I did not tell anybody that. I asked a tough question . . ."

Switzer: "You were wrong about that."

Followed by: "I think I'll go have a screaming match with Kevin O'Neill!"

The moment the show ended, Switzer said, "What's wrong with you, Dale? We work for the same guy, the same organization."

Hansen said, "No, you don't get it. I don't work for Jerry Jones. *You* do."

Hansen was hurt that Switzer had stooped to bring up the *Observer* article. "He knew I was having problems with the article. That was vindictive." But Hansen was outraged that Switzer had accused him of reporting that Casillas, a former Cowboy, had a brain tumor.

As Dean Blevins later said, "Occasionally, Barry would hear something secondhand and he would react without getting the facts completely straight. But he has worked to get better at that."

The rumor had circulated throughout camp that the Cowboys were interested in resigning defensive tackle Casillas, but that something was wrong with him. I had heard everything from "brain tumor" to "burnout." Like Hansen and other reporters, I had asked Jones, Lacewell, and Switzer what they knew. But no one reported that Casillas had a brain tumor. Hansen merely had asked Cowboy officials about it.

Hansen says, "With the people I cover, I've always wanted a relationship of 'I fire at you, you fire back at me.' Take your best shot. Just don't take an inaccurate shot."

All of Switzer's ring shots were very accurate. One caught Hansen right on the bone, on the backside of the biceps, "and that son of a bitch *stung.*" To this day, Hansen fans say to him in public, "How's the shoulder?" Hansen says, "Twenty years from today when I die, they'll say in my eulogy, 'We all remember when Barry Switzer . . .'"

Switzer supporters thought the coach had made a fool of Hansen. The Aikman camp—including the quarterback—thought Switzer had made a fool of himself.

Hansen: "As egotistical as this sounds, part of me was saying, '*He* was fucking with *me*?' I mean, what's the risk-reward?"

Later, Jones told Hansen that Hansen had "pricked Barry's Achilles heel," which Jones defined as Switzer's "concern over managing an inherited pro staff that had had success." So the following afternoon, hoping to clear the air, Hansen approached Switzer as he sat in his golf cart after practice. Hansen says Switzer told him, "Well, of course there are problems on this staff. Hudson Houck hates Butch Davis, who wants to be head coach, and Joe Avezzano thinks he's the head coach. But I'm dealing with it. Hell, every coach in America has to deal with this kind of thing."

Hansen says Switzer didn't seem that upset and even boasted, "We made good TV, didn't we?"

Hansen: "He even said the *Observer* remark was over the line." According to Hansen, a couple of weeks later, Switzer even told him they needed to go out and have a couple of beers and really get to know each other.

Then, just "two or three" nights later, Hansen and his wife and some friends were on their way to a restaurant. The car radio was tuned to Randy Galloway's show. Switzer was the guest. "And he trashes me," says Hansen. "He even says, 'Pick up the *Dallas Observer* article and you'll see everything you need to know about Dale Hansen.'" Challenged by Galloway on some of the same issues Hansen had raised, Switzer swung back just the way he had on Channel 8.

Hansen says he was so upset he turned the car around and drove back home. "I said, 'I'm telling you, Barry Switzer is out to get me.'"

Aikman was not pleased about the way Switzer was treating his buddy Hansen. Yet the irony was, though Switzer couldn't yet see it, someone was out to "get" him, too. That someone was Aikman, who by confiding in his media pals had turned the watchdogs loose on his new coach.

The following Sunday morning, as Brad Sham prepared for that night's exhibition game at Texas Stadium, he got around to reading a radio-TV column by Barry Horn in Saturday's *Dallas Morning News*. The headline suggested "Hansen's job not in jeopardy," Sham recalls.

"And I just flipped."

Time out, thought Sham: Switzer had accused Hansen of making up a story (on Casillas)—"the worst thing you can accuse a reporter of," says Sham—and now there was doubt about *Hansen's* job security? Sham was beginning to wonder about Switzer's.

Soon he would be wondering about his own.

That night, just before kickoff, over Jerry Jones's airwaves, Sham did a commentary that said, in effect, listeners could not believe anything Switzer and Jones said. "Really," says Hansen, "he was just stating the obvious. No president or GM or CEO can always speak the absolute truth in public. His point was, you're better off listening to a Hansen, a Sham, a Galloway."

But Sham concluded by saying Switzer owed Hansen an apology. Hansen says, "Brad's commentary was eloquent, as always, and the second he finished I knew he was dead in the water."

By the next day, Sham had been removed as host of Jones's TV show. Soon he was told he no longer would be doing a weekly interview with Switzer for the pregame show. Sham: "As I've said, it was absolutely the wrong place for me to say what I said, and he [Jones] was completely within bounds to do what he did."

Sham says he tried to apologize to Jones, but wasn't allowed to see him for a week or so. After eighteen years of quality service, Sham felt he at least deserved a chance to explain himself before any action was taken. When he finally did meet with Jones, the owner said, "I don't know what *I* was doing in [the commentary]." Hadn't Sham's complaint been with Switzer? Jones couldn't get past the fact that Sham basically had called the owner a liar.

Did Sham attempt to talk to Switzer? "I frankly didn't care what Switzer thought, nor do I care now."

But Switzer, he says, immediately tried to get him and Hansen fired off the Cowboy broadcasts. "He thought this was Oklahoma," says Sham, "where he could fire broadcasters. But Dale wasn't going to be fired because of what Channel 8 brought to the postgame show, and Jerry couldn't fire me [because of Sham's existing contract with KVIL]. But he could make it unpleasant."

Sham continued as play-by-play announcer through Switzer's first season. "But Brad suffered," says Hansen. "It was painful."

The Cowboys' annual kickoff luncheon is held the Tuesday before the season opener in a ballroom at the Grand Kempenski Hotel in far North Dallas. Hansen's stand-up routine is usually worth the $1,500 corporations pay for a table. But this time, Hansen refused to emcee. "I told Jones that under the circumstances, it cannot be done. They will not laugh."

Sham took the microphone and opened with, "Welcome to the Cowboys' version of *Family Feud*." Hansen says, "It was a pretty good line, and nobody laughed. I was sitting eight rows back, and I said, 'You're dead.' Roger Staubach [sitting at a nearby table] sent me a note that said, 'I paid fifteen hundred dollars to hear you. Get up there.' And I said, no, the players are uncomfortable. The assistants are uncomfortable. The audience is uncomfortable. They showed the reedited highlight video [of the previous Super Bowl season], and there was no Jimmy. Jerry was all over it. But there was no coach."

Jones soon signaled to Hansen and the two stepped quickly into the Grand Kempenski kitchen for a private conference. Jones told Hansen, "I've come off looking like an asshole." Jones begged Hansen to accompany him to the mike and make jokes at Jones's expense. "He wanted me to say something like, 'I hate to interrupt the MVP of the highlight film . . .' But I just wouldn't do it.

"Jones got up there and tried some jokes and nobody laughed. Of course, at that point a lot of 'em were thinking, 'You're the asshole who fired Jimmy Johnson and shit on Brad Sham.'"

Several times during Switzer's first season he privately vowed he would not return in 1995 if Hansen returned in the Cowboy radio booth. But Hansen won that power struggle. Hansen returned. He's the market's 600-pound gorilla. The franchise quarterback is his friend.

Even now, Dale Fucking Hansen refuses to play along with what he describes as a Jerry Jones PR charade that took place during 1995's training camp.

Jones interrupted a practice to lead Hansen from the media contingent on the sideline out to Switzer on the field. With mini-cams rolling and photographers clicking away, the two shook hands. Later Switzer told reporters that "everything is behind us."

Now, Hansen says, "That was phony as a three-dollar bill."

Switzer also was unsuccessful in helping Dean Blevins acquire a Dallas media platform, on the team radio network or at a TV station. Blevins, says Hansen, "started calling Channel 8 looking for a job [as number two man and eventual successor to Hansen]. Blevins is saying, 'I'm Barry's boy. Hire me and you'll have a pipeline to the Cowboys.'"

Blevins wasn't hired at Channel 8. But Blevins did replace Sham as the host of Jones's TV show. Blevins is in the TV booth for Cowboy-produced telecasts of exhibition games. Blevins does host Switzer's weekly one-hour radio show on KTCK-AM.

But Blevins still lives in Oklahoma City. He says he did not pursue a full-time TV job in the Dallas market because "so many of the people in the media down there just make me sick."

After the '94 season, Sham was "forced out" as Cowboy play-by-play broadcaster, says Hansen. He immediately was hired to do baseball play-by-play for the Texas Rangers. Hansen says, "I do believe Brad loves baseball, and it is a radio broadcaster's game, but . . ."

No, says Sham, he was not forced out. He says he took advantage of a "fortuitous" opportunity. "I have it on the highest possible multiple authority I could have [remained in the Cowboy booth] at least through '95."

Sham was replaced as Cowboy play-by-play man by Switzer crony Dave Garrett, who hit it off with Switzer while he was still coaching at Oklahoma and who hosted Switzer's weekly radio show during the 1994 season. In 1995 Sham's only link to the Cowboys was hosting Aikman's weekly show on KRLD-AM, which carries Texas Ranger games.

Machiavelli would have been a Cowboy fan.

With Sham out, Aikman asked Hansen if he were going to quit the Cowboy broadcasts. Hansen: "I said, 'Do you want me to quit?' He said, 'No, no, no.' I told Aikman that Brad had told me absolutely not to quit. But I do think it was a defining moment between

Switzer and Aikman. He kept hearing Switzer say he was sick and tired of the media and that he didn't listen to what any of them had to say, when in fact that's *all* he cared about. Aikman's attitude was, 'Bullshit. You fired Brad Sham and you're still trying to get Hansen. Why are you so obsessed with what they have to say or Galloway has to write when you have so many other problems? Maybe if you were more on top of some [undisciplined] players . . . '"

9

DEHYDRATION

To know the Cowboys is to hate them.
—*From* The Semi-Official
Dallas Cowboys Haters' Handbook
by Mark Nelson and Miller Bonner

My cab arrived at Pittsburgh's Hyatt Regency shortly after the Cowboy team buses. It was Saturday, September 4, 1994, the eve of Barry Switzer's first regular season professional football game. Occasionally I travel to road games on the team plane, but I was going on from Pittsburgh to Bristol, Connecticut, site of ESPN, where I play a small part on *Prime Monday*, a weekly ninety-minute prelude to *Monday Night Football*.

This time, I at least made it to the front desk before it happened.

Bruce Mays, the Cowboys' director of operations, usually arrives two or three days ahead of the team to prepare a hotel staff for the onslaught. "They never believe me when I tell them what's going to happen," Mays says. The switchboard, the elevators, the gift shop—good luck. It's all part of what PR director Rich Dalrymple calls "the Cowboy Phenomenon."

And Switzer was walking headlong into it. Like the Pittsburgh hotel staff, he still had no idea what it was like. Unlike millions of Cowboy fans, Switzer hadn't followed the team. A few months earlier, he wouldn't have known the Hail Mary from a Bloody Mary.

And now he had gone down in Cowboy history as the third coach. But how far down?

A few minutes earlier, a beefed-up security staff had supervised the unloading of the buses. At road hotels, a cordoned-off gauntlet allows most of the players and coaches to hurry safely past the happy mob of crazies waving felt-tip pens. The superstars—Troy Aikman, Emmitt Smith, Michael Irvin, and now Deion Sanders— are whisked through a side entrance and up a service elevator. "It's like traveling with the Beatles," says Dalrymple. A mere glimpse of Aikman or Emmitt sets off a cacophony of male shouts, female squeals, and children's shrieks from a couple of hundred people wearing lots of No. 8 and No. 22 jerseys. The lobby is overrun with Cowboy fans wielding cameras and all sorts of memorabilia (trading cards, helmets, footballs) to be autographed.

But wait, isn't this Pittsburgh, the steel-beamed stronghold of the Steelers? It doesn't matter. Cowboy fans still had taken over the lobby, just as they do in San Francisco or Washington or Mexico City. These aren't just fans from Dallas who follow the team. These mostly are Cowboy fans living in enemy territory. These are people who, as kids, defied their Steeler-crazed siblings or parents and fell crazy in love with America's Team. Right now, the only NFL team that comes close to attracting this kind of lobby crowd is the San Francisco 49ers. But is their PR director famous?

If the mob can't get a Cowboy to stop, some fans even yell for Dalrymple. He says, "My God, I'm the PR guy, and these people know who I am [from occasional TV shots of Dalrymple accompanying Switzer or Jones]." And if they can't lobby for a Cowboy's autograph, or even Dalrymple's, they're sometimes left with . . .

Cowboy fans often know me from *Prime Monday* or from another ESPN show I occasionally do, Sunday morning's *The Sports Reporters*. In Pittsburgh, I took my key from the woman at the front desk, turned to pick up my bags, and . . . "Look," yelled the woman about Dale Hansen's size wearing a No. 8 jersey, "there's Skip!" Here she came, waving her felt tip and helmet.

I always say, "You don't really want me to sign that." I gladly autograph my books because I wrote them, but I don't play or even work for the Cowboys and . . .

"Pleeease," she begged. As I signed her helmet, the line quickly formed behind her. I doubted half the fans in it—especially the kids—had any idea who I was. But I probably signed my name on thirty or forty helmets and footballs and scraps of paper before apologizing and saying I had to be somewhere. If I hadn't, I might have missed the next day's kickoff.

This happens to me in nearly every lobby of every Cowboy hotel. This happens to me outside stadiums from the Georgia Dome to Sun Devil, where about half the sellout crowds are Cowboy fans. I get trapped inside the Cowboy Phenomenon. It seems so surreal, when I remember the Cowboy games I used to attend as a kid. The Cotton Bowl was never more than a third full.

Switzer had little or no interest in Cowboy history. But if he had asked . . .

It began with an indelible bloodstain left near the Texas School Book Depository in downtown Dallas on November 22, 1963. Predictably but unjustly, a Dallas without much national image became known around the country as the "City That Killed Kennedy." Dallas was left with two "tourist" attractions: the JFK Memorial and a bad pro football team.

"Big D" is one city without an obvious reason for being. It isn't on an ocean or major waterway. It doesn't have a tropical climate or a nearby mountain range, nor is it blessed with a Bourbon Street or a Disney World. In short, it's a very nice place to live, but you wouldn't want to visit there.

So the city's well-known superiority complex was born of insecurity. It was strangely reminiscent of what happened to the state just seventy or so miles north of Dallas—to Dust Bowl Oklahoma. There, too, it took a football team to win some national respect for a shamed area. But in Oklahoma, OU football became merely religion. In Dallas, Cowboy football became life. "It's intensified in Dallas," Switzer says.

In 1963 Tom Landry's Cowboys were 4–10. But in '64 they improved to 5–8–1, and in '65 to 7–7—and not coincidentally the city's self-image began to improve. Jerry Tubbs, the team's middle linebacker then and later a Cowboy assistant, says, "The Cowboys became a vehicle that projected Dallas as a winner instead of the killer of Kennedy."

Projecting powerful images on TV screens was the specialty of the man most responsible for creating what became known as "Cowboy Mystique." Talk about destiny: a guy born in Los Angeles named Texas? With a background in L.A. PR (with the Rams) and in sports television (with CBS), Texas E. Schramm was hired as president and general manager of the expansion Cowboys. Says Leigh Steinberg, "It's hard to explain just how far ahead of their time Tex Schramm, then Jerry Jones, were."

Schramm was the first to envision the awesome potential of teaming television and football. He put stars on the sides of the hel-

mets—still the most powerful hook for young fans in other cities—
and he experimented until he found just the right shade of metallic-
blue uniform color to please the eye via TV. He took cheerleaders
out of turtlenecks and put them in showgirl costumes. Though original owner Clint Murchison wanted to call the team the Jets,
because the city was becoming an air-travel hub, Schramm insisted
on Cowboys, because of the country's fascination with the Old West.
Schramm even put a new spin on the six-gun motif: space cowboys.
In 1971 he moved the team from the Cotton Bowl to a stadium he
helped design. Texas Stadium, which looked something like a giant
spaceship when it "landed" at the confluence of Highways 183 and
114 in Irving, still has a modern look twenty-five years later.

P. T. Schramm, as I called him, was equally ingenious in helping
create a larger-than-life coach and players. He carefully promoted
Landry as a combination Billy Graham/Gary Cooper. At quarterback, Schramm headlined a wisecracking gunslinger named Don
Meredith, who would go on to real fame and fortune playing the
good-ol'-boy foil to Howard Cosell on *Monday Night Football*. At
receiver, Schramm hyped Olympian-turned-receiver Bob Hayes, the
"World's Fastest Human."

Almost as if scripted, the Cowboys lost consecutive NFL championship games to Vince Lombardi's Green Bay Packers in 1966 and
1967. Schramm's creation not only captured America's imagination,
but its sympathy. A generation of Cowboy fans was Schramm's.
Soon, fans nationwide were seduced by an entertainment package
that combined sex, violence, religion, space-age technology, and
Texas. Schramm fought to keep Dallas in the NFC East so his Cowboys could play once every season before the media in Philadelphia,
Washington, and especially New York. While other teams wanted to
avoid the short week of preparation, Schramm volunteered for the
national TV slot on Thanksgiving Day. Now, other owners complain
about how the Cowboys always get such vast annual exposure just
after the country has finished its turkey dinner.

You can thank Tex for that, Barry.

"While other owners were just concerned about selling tickets in
their cities," says Leigh Steinberg, "Schramm was trying to make the
Cowboys America's Team. He had his own newspaper [the *Dallas
Cowboys Weekly*], and he sent it to every writer and coach in the
country. The son of the sports editor in Des Moines had a Dallas Cowboy poster on his wall; same for the coach's son in Pennsylvania.
Schramm pushed [Cowboy personnel director] Gil Brandt as the
expert on talent, so Brandt was quoted in publications all over the
country. Schramm was quoted on all important league matters. Do

you have any idea what a powerful effect that has on fans everywhere?"

What's more, compared to other NFL teams, the Cowboys were just always so damned interesting. It was as if Schramm had commissioned Larry McMurtry and Dan Jenkins to dream up the Cowboy stars who leaped into the headlines for the right and sometimes wrong reasons. Duane Thomas. Lance Rentzel. Walt Garrison. Bob Lilly. Lee Roy Jordan. Calvin Hill. Cliff Harris. Ed "Too Tall" Jones. Harvey "Too Mean" Martin. Thomas "Hollywood" Henderson. Tony Dorsett.

And of course, Roger Staubach, who surely couldn't have been real. A Heisman-winning Vietnam-vet father-of-the-year who threw probably the most famous pass in NFL history—a badly underthrown pass that Drew Pearson pinned with one arm on his hip and turned into the Hail Mary? Dallas Cowboys routinely did things like that.

Current Cowboy Bill Bates says, "Roger Staubach and Tom Landry were role models for a generation. So many fathers told so many sons, 'You should be like this man [Landry] and this player [Staubach].'"

Yet the Cowboys were always such a magnetic mix of good and evil, skill and luck. As former Cowboy pretty boy and All-Pro safety Charlie Waters once told me, "There's this inexplicable dynamic in this locker room that just keeps making people do wild things."

The "dynamic" still operates at full force. Jerry Jones? Barry Switzer? Is this NFL football or *All My Cowboys*? A large part of the Cowboys' appeal has been turning into a daily soap opera for men and women. They don't just win or lose football games, they take you on a roller-coaster ride without the safety bar from love to hate, elation to deflation, cold hard fact to fantasy finish.

But mostly, Schramm's teams won. As Rich Dalrymple says, "We're a little like Notre Dame. People everywhere adopted us as their team just because they wanted to identify with a winner. All the PR in the world doesn't matter unless you win."

Most longtime fans probably have forgotten about the incongruous number of Landry players who had drug problems (Hayes, Henderson, Martin, Golden Richards) or personal problems (Rentzel, Rafael Septien). On and on it went; Dallas can be a temptation-ridden trap for the Cowboys it worships. But Landry's Cowboys won. In hindsight, they were all Staubachs.

If possible, the current Cowboys are more followed—more loved/hated in and out of Dallas—than Schramm's teams were. As much as Switzer was interviewed as a college coach, he was nearly overwhelmed by his media duties in Dallas. "I spend half my time talking to the damn media," he says. Each week Switzer also does his own TV show and two radio shows. If you're a member of the organization and you don't have your own show, you're considered a leper.

Before the 1995 season, the league office asked each franchise to list its weekly TV or radio shows concerning the team. The questionnaire had twelve lines. The Cowboys had thirty-seven shows—surely a league record by far. Says Dalrymple, "From the first day, Jerry said, 'Tex was the master [of promotion]. Let's do what he did, only better.'"

Jones, Aikman, and Irvin had TV and radio shows. Stephen Jones had a radio show. Ernie Zampese and Dave Campo had a radio show. Special-teams coach Joe Avezzano had a radio show—the *Coach Joe Show* on KTCK-AM, done before a packed Thursday night house at Cowboys, a honky-tonk which probably should be called Cowgirls. Yes, the special-teams coach—a frustrated country-western singer—had become a celebrity. So had deep snapper Dale Hellestrae. He and Mark Tuinei—who's from Hawaii—cohosted *The Snapper Pineapple Hour* on KLIF.

Only in Dallas.

Says Dale Hansen, "The Cowboys *are* Dallas, Texas. The Mondays of the stockbrokers, the oilmen, the bankers, and the 7-Eleven clerks are determined by the Cowboys' Sundays. I don't think it was any coincidence that when the Cowboys began to slip in the '80s, so did the Dallas economy."

All of which can be troubling for Aikman, who told me, "In my own quirky way I try to justify what I do. Playing in Dallas has been extremely rewarding, and I can't imagine playing anywhere else. But it's also been a lot of heartaches and very frustrating. There is a lot of pressure. I've had discussions with Roger Staubach about it . . . Roger told me he once got booed at Texas Stadium, and it upset him just as it would me. When I think of Roger, I think of him just the way everyone else does: This guy is the greatest of all time. I would have thought he never had experienced anything like I was going through. But he has."

That's also Dallas.

Aikman continued, "But one great thing about Dallas is that it's nice to play where people really care about winning. In some places they've become accustomed to losing."

I said, "Do you ever step back and think that some of these folks should get a life, that they're asking you to carry their self-image too far for them?"

He said, "I consider it a little sad that some people's happiness and sense of worth depends on whether we win on Sunday. At the same time, I once made a comment to a fan that I've always been amazed at salaries that pro athletes get when there are doctors and teachers who do so much to help mankind, and they don't live the lifestyle we do. I said, 'There's something wrong with that.' And this person said, 'That may be true, but there are a lot of people who get tremendous gratification and happiness from watching you all. There are people with illnesses, people in nursing homes who live for what the Cowboys do. So you really are making a difference.' Put in that light, I feel better about it."

Three Rivers was roaring the next afternoon. The stadium was packed with black and gold and late-summer hope. Some national experts were picking the Pittsburgh Steelers to make the Super Bowl, and what better opening day barometer than the defending champs, before Madden and Summerall and a national-TV audience?

For the Cowboys, led by "Barely" Switzer, the un-coach, this appeared to be a little too much barometric pressure. Yet when you (and perhaps Hansen) least expected it, the only "power vacuum" was the Pittsburgh offense, which totaled 126 yards. Steeler quarterback Neil O'Donnell was sacked nine times (four by Charles Haley). An unsacked Aikman hit 21 of 32 passes for 245 yards. Emmitt Smith ran for 171. The Cowboy offense rang up 442 yards. The game wasn't nearly as close as the final score: Dallas 26, Pittsburgh 9.

I still think it's the best overall game the Cowboys have played in two seasons under Barry Switzer. So much for the training-camp concerns of the Aikman camp.

Had many of Switzer's players made a reverberating statement? Had they said, "We're so talented we can beat anybody, whether Jimmy Johnson or Barry Switzer or Albert Schweitzer coaches us"? Or had they made Jerry Jones look brilliant by saying, "Barry Switzer is a welcome change for us"? When I asked Switzer, he said, "The only statement they made was that when we're completely healthy and rested and anxious to play a football game after a long pre-season, we're very difficult to beat. Hell, players win. It doesn't make any difference if Jimmy Johnson or Barry Switzer or Skip Bayless coaches this team."

There's an idea: If Jones *really* wanted to show the world he could win with any coach . . .

But moments after the Pittsburgh game, Haley said, "We'd been under the whip too long from Jimmy. Barry is perfect for us because he's so laid back. He treats us like men."

Though Aikman and the troublemaking Haley got along surprisingly well—they respected each other's talent and win-or-else obsession—they had radically different views of Switzer. Soon, a picture of Haley with Switzer's daughter Kathy would sit on the coach's desk. Haley would call Switzer "a friend of mine." When Haley would come down with the flu, Switzer would run antibiotics by his house. Switzer got to know Haley's mother, his wife, his kids.

Especially the black players had warmed to Switzer's honesty and zest. He didn't take things too seriously—the media did enough of that for the Cowboys—and he didn't play games. He told them exactly where they stood with the organization. But he constantly emphasized what he liked most about them. He constantly encouraged. He was always in a pretty good mood. He was always kidding around about some crazy something. He wanted each player to feel good about himself so whatever unteachable talent he had could be maximized. "Hey," Switzer says, "when I played, I was always better when a coach was patting me on the back."

While Landry and Johnson motivated by fear, Switzer actually motivated by love. As early as the 1994 season opener, a majority of Cowboys had been won over by their new coach's style. It showed that afternoon at Pittsburgh.

Aikman later told me, "Barry's approach is different, but that doesn't make it wrong. Maybe most of the players liked that approach. I didn't view it as a team problem as much as something I had to come to grips with, because it was different from the way I see things. I didn't feel a need to go in and bring attention to it."

Coming off their muscle-flexing win in Pittsburgh, the Cowboys didn't take a bad Houston team too seriously. That was partly because the head coach didn't take the Oilers too seriously. This was where Johnson might have picked a fight with a media critic or even a player, just to refill the air with tension and refocus the team. But Switzer wasn't going to lie to them.

The Cowboys stumbled around and barely beat the Oilers, 20–17. Aikman—14 of 25 for 228 yards—didn't look himself.

The following Wednesday night, I saw him before the taping of a weekly TV show he cohosted with Pat Summerall. For the show I did a short "insider" segment each week and always enjoyed a preshow chat with Summerall, a rare media star whose humility and dignity match his stature. Aikman's moods on these nights fluctuated from withdrawn to cautiously approachable. But on this night, Aikman didn't have his usual impenetrable air. He seemed a little shaken, even vulnerable. Before the show, I was talking football with Summerall out in the hallway when Aikman walked up. To Summerall's routine greeting of, "How you feeling?" Aikman responded, "I'm not sure."

And he explained he was feeling so inexplicably out of sorts that he was going to check himself into a hospital for tests. Like most unusually gifted athletes, Aikman has an irrational fear of disease. But especially to a control freak like Aikman, it's horrifying to imagine some killer disease infiltrating the temple that is his body. He has told friends that he has an unnatural fear of contracting the AIDS virus. A friend says, "He's extremely cautious and says he always uses protection." But what if something went wrong? What if something unimaginable happened?

Of course, his friends roll their eyes and tell him to relax.

But this time, Aikman was sure something was wrong. He wanted tests done. He was going to the hospital.

The following Monday, before Dallas played Detroit, I asked team officials if Aikman planned to play. I was told he was fine, as far as anyone knew. Aikman played, but once again neither he nor his team played up to their opening day standards. At Texas Stadium before ABC's *Monday Night Football* cameras, Detroit took Dallas into overtime and won, 20–17.

The next Wednesday night, when I asked Aikman how the tests had gone, he said, "Oh, everything was okay. They just said I was suffering from dehydration. I just need to drink more liquid."

A star quarterback in his sixth season checks himself into the hospital and finds out he isn't drinking enough liquid? Maybe. But Aikman's dehydration probably was exacerbated by stress. His highly ordered world had been turned upside down, and Aikman was struggling to get his balance.

During the Detroit loss, as I recall, Aikman looked to Switzer on the sideline for a signal on whether to accept or decline a penalty. Later, Aikman said, "I really don't think he was even paying attention." Was it Switzer's ADD? Or did Switzer figure Aikman could make the call on his own? The referee awaiting the decision said something like, "I need to know what your coach wants to do." And a fuming Aikman said, "So do I."

More and more, the quarterback saw dangerous signs. All-Pro tackle Erik Williams, after the whistle had blown, drew a 15-yard personal foul for hitting a Detroit player out-of-bounds. The undisciplined penalty wiped out a long run by Emmitt Smith. No reaction from Switzer. Aikman sensed a chance to make Super Bowl history slipping through Switzer's cracks. The mistake-free machine built by Johnson was leaking Oklahoma crude.

*   *   *

Barry Switzer was stunned by the reaction to his first loss. Until then his attitude had been, "Hey, this pro football is a breeze." That Monday before the Detroit game the father of Lion great Barry Sanders had called Switzer. (At Oklahoma State, Sanders had played against Switzer.) Willie Sanders wondered if Switzer could get him a sideline pass at Texas Stadium. Switzer got him one. "I thought that was funny," Switzer said.

He did not think Tuesday's media and fan reaction was funny.

Switzer's friends and family said he took it—the reaction, not the loss—so hard that he was ready to quit. Several in his camp told me he was saying things like, "If they're going to get so upset about one loss, then fuck 'em. I'm going back to Norman." Though Switzer is too proud to show his pain in public, his forest-fire emotions range from rage to tears when he's hurt or scared.

As worked up as the media and fans around Oklahoma City got after a Sooner loss, this was different. This, to Switzer, got personal. Rarely had media people in Oklahoma attacked him for his coaching. He was too powerful, too intimidating. He could humiliate them in front of their peers, shut off their access to the program, maybe even jeopardize their jobs. But not in Dallas, where there were too many media outlets that reached too many fans. Jones was not going to let him fight back by shutting off media access to players or by refusing to do his regularly scheduled media sessions each day. In Dallas, he couldn't control the media. Worse, attacking the Dale Hansens only had the tar-baby effect: The more he swung back, the more he splattered the media's increasing skepticism all over himself. After the Detroit loss, the majority of the Dallas-Fort Worth media probably viewed Switzer as a former college coach who had lost touch and was in over his head. The tone of that week's criticism on the talk shows and in the papers was: "Johnson wouldn't have let the Cowboys lose to an inferior team on a Monday night. Blame it on Switzer."

When the Cowboys lose, fans will not accept that the other team was just better. Somebody in the Cowboy organization must take the fall. Switzer had become the easiest target this side of Baghdad. Yet, just as Switzer believes players ultimately win, he believes they lose, too. Did *he* fumble twice in overtime against Detroit?

"I really took it hard," he says.

By then, he had moved into a small furnished two-bedroom apartment in a complex about six miles from Cowboy headquarters. He lived alone. He ate out every night. He rarely did more than talk on the phone or sleep at his apartment. But he spent some long nights there.

"I've basically been a loner all my life," says Switzer, who also describes himself as "gregarious." Sometimes, Switzer can feel alone in a crowd.

The man who helped talk Switzer out of his post-Detroit depression was right-hand assistant John Blake. Switzer listened to Blake, who had a knack for cheering him up, helping him remember the positives. Blake says, "I was really worried about him. That was as bad as it got." Blake smiles. "But that German, man, he's a tough old rug."

As a team, the Cowboys were turning into a tough old rug. They responded to the Detroit loss by crushing division opponents Washington, Arizona, and Philadelphia. Then came the good news–sad news day and night of October 23. In a game at Arizona, having lost Aikman to a concussion, backup quarterback Rodney Peete rallied the Cowboys from 21–14 down in the fourth quarter to a character-driven 28–21 win.

On the flight home, the team was as raucously relieved as I'd seen it. The Cowboys had won a sweaty, bloody street fight against a Cardinal team known more for its toughness than talent. And for the rest of the night, the Cowboys were ready to celebrate. We landed around ten, and Highway 114 back toward Dallas turned into a high-speed caravan of Mercedes and luxury trucks. Many of the Cowboys headed for a hot spot off Greenville Avenue called Iguana Mirage.

About five hours later, a little after three A.M., a concrete embankment was no mirage for Erik Williams. Alone, he was headed home along LBJ freeway. He was legally intoxicated. His Mercedes 600SL left the exit ramp to the Dallas North Tollway traveling "in excess of seventy-five mph," said police, and careened uphill 250 feet into the embankment. He was not wearing his seatbelt, but the car's airbag deployed.

It remains a miracle to many players and coaches that he survived the crash. "Big E," as they call him, was one big 330-pound mess. Of his many injuries, the worst were to his face, which required major plastic surgery, and to his right knee, in which, one doctor told me, "everything is torn that could be torn."

Switzer also was amazed by the way John Blake took over the hospital room. "He was unbelievable," said Switzer. "He touched some hearts." For a number of black players, Blake was as much a counselor and leader as a coach. Blake turned the room into something of a faith healer's revival, leading players in prayer in a tearful circle around Williams. They held hands. They hugged. Many of them knew they could have been the one in that wreckage. "There was just so much love in that room," Blake told me. "It was a very powerful thing." Williams's recovery would be nearly as miraculous as his escape.

One afternoon around midseason I was talking with Switzer in his office about nothing in particular, probably the new house he was having built. Switzer is unlike any football coach I've been around: He isn't much interested in talking about what's going on in his business. Some coaches use writers to keep them informed about behind-the-scenes developments in rival cities. Not Switzer. All he wants to know about what's going on with the Redskins or Giants is right there on their game tape. When it's time to play them, he'll study their tapes until he has a coordinator's grasp of their offense and defense.

But most fans and even players couldn't appreciate Switzer's grasp of the game because he rarely demonstrated it in public or team meetings. "Jimmy," says Lacewell, "made sure he said things that led people to believe he was more responsible for things than he was. Switzer won't do that." In fact, Switzer often referred to other people as "coach." Equipment men, media members, anybody. He'd say to me, "Coach, the reason that happened was that . . ." But calling me "coach" diminished the power of his title. *He* was the coach. It was as if he was saying, "Coaching isn't that hard. Hell, you could do it." Coaching was no big deal to him until he was criticized for never doing anything.

But—see if you can follow this—Switzer was tormented by not receiving any credit for not screwing it up. Not screwing up a team built in Johnson's image was a major—but subtle—accomplishment.

Then again, if fans had heard this midseason exchange I had with Switzer, they would have called for his job. I brought up the hottest team in the AFC, San Diego. He said, "Will we play them in the playoffs?"

"Well," I said, trying not to grin, "only if you and the Chargers make it to the Super Bowl. They're in the other conference."

"Huh," he acknowledged without much interest.

In his Tuesday press conference before a game in Cincinnati, Switzer compared the Bengals to "Iowa State." He was trying to say that no matter how bad Iowa State used to look to his Oklahoma teams, Iowa State almost always gave the Sooners trouble. Of course, Cincinnati coach David Shula, son of the NFL's most respected coach, took the analogy as an insult. To the Shulas, no doubt, Switzer was some cocky yahoo from Oklahoma who had been handed pro football's most talented team.

Just as Switzer had "predicted," the Cowboys fell behind "Iowa State" 14–0 before beating probably the NFL's worst team 23–20. When it ended, Shula trotted straight to Switzer and shook his hand. That done, Shula threw an arm around Switzer's neck, pulled Switzer's ear close, so the photographers around them couldn't hear, and said, "You can stick Iowa State up your ass."

Switzer sometimes got irritated when he read what a "great motivator" he was supposed to be. No, he said, a coach cannot motivate an athlete because motivation must come from within. A coach can only *inspire*. Before the Cowboys played another regular season "game of the year" against San Francisco, this one at Candlestick Park, Switzer read me something a psychologist friend had sent him. It said, "The higher an athlete's self-image, the greater his or her motivation . . . For example, athletes who keep personal issues bottled up inside themselves negatively affect their own self-images. . . . An athlete who is 'stuffing' his feelings inside rather than acknowledging and resolving them is more susceptible to making errors."

That, ironically, described the most important Dallas Cowboy.

It's difficult to assess Troy Aikman's performance at Candlestick. The Friday before the game, he banged his throwing thumb on a blitzing defender's helmet and doubted on Saturday night he would be able to play. He even tried the controversial anti-inflammatory drug DMSO on the thumb. He played. He said, "The thumb affected me on a few throws, but I don't think it affected the outcome of the game."

But did feelings about Switzer that Aikman was "stuffing" make him more susceptible to making errors? His three highly unusual interceptions—two thrown with the Cowboys at San Francisco's 16 and 7 yard lines—were the difference in the game. In Aikman's three previous wins over Steve Young's 49ers (two in NFC championship games), Young's offense had made the crucial mistakes. This time, the 49ers made no turnovers and won, 21–14.

Switzer was heavily criticized by the Dallas-Fort Worth media for his nonchalant approach to a game that perhaps could have destroyed what was left of San Francisco's confidence against Dallas. Yet as a team, the Cowboys played well enough to win. They won the total yardage battle, 408 yards to 308. The one player who didn't respond well to Switzer's approach to the game was the

quarterback. Apparently, DMSO doesn't work on the subconscious.

Injuries often dictate Super Bowl champions. Injuries are dictated
mostly by luck—bad luck. Cowboy team doctor Robert Vandermeer
says, "It's mostly luck. It just goes in cycles. Some years are meant
to be."

On December 19 at New Orleans, on the Monday night stage,
Emmitt Smith pulled a hamstring. He returned three weeks later in
a playoff game against Green Bay, but reinjured the hamstring on
his seventh carry. So the Cowboys returned to San Francisco for the
NFC championship game with a one-legged Smith and no Erik
Williams. At right tackle was sensationally talented rookie Larry
Allen—who had turned his ankle so badly against Green Bay that he
shouldn't have played against the 49ers.

Some years just aren't meant to be.

Still, Switzer seemed relieved that his team at least had gotten
back to the conference title game. Some of the pressure was off, or
so he thought. Without a healthy Emmitt, the Cowboys were underdogs. Switzer was enjoying the role. He was looser than I'd seen
him all season. He told me, "Wouldn't it be something if we won the
motherfucker?"

Again, he wasn't quite prepared for what was about to happen.

On the game's third play, Aikman threw an interception that Eric
Davis returned for a touchdown. Former quarterbacks Joe Theismann and Phil Simms said on ESPN that the obvious read on the play
was a "backside" throw to Alvin Harper, who was left in single coverage with Deion Sanders. Perhaps Aikman didn't trust Harper against
the NFL's most dangerous ballhawk and defensive player of the year.
So Aikman tried to thread the ball to Kevin Williams and misread the
intentions of Davis, who looked like he was going with Michael Irvin.
"The second I let it go," says Aikman, "I knew it was trouble."

That interception wound up being the mistake of the year. No
matter the circumstances, in a game of that magnitude in a hostile
stadium, a quarterback cannot throw an early interception that gets
returned for a touchdown. The stadium ignited. The high-fiving on
the 49er sideline said, "Hey, we *can* beat these guys in a playoff
game." From that moment on, Aikman played probably the most
courageous game of his career. But the Cowboys were constantly
playing uphill.

Soon, they were playing up Everest. Irvin fumbled. The 49ers
scored. Kevin Williams fumbled. The 49ers scored. Just 7:27 into
the game, Dallas was down 21–0.

"It was eerie," says Switzer. "All I could do was grin and ask my assistants if it was really happening."

By then, perhaps, the pressure was off Aikman and he relaxed and let his heart and talent take over. "Troy was gallant," says Switzer. "He got the shit beat out of him and still threw the hell out of the ball." With about six minutes left in the game, down 38–28, Aikman went deep for Irvin on Sanders. Replays clearly showed Sanders interfered, putting a hand across Irvin's arm as he went up for the ball. But no flag was thrown.

And Barry Switzer, accused all season of being little more than a cigar-store Oklahoma Indian on the sideline, finally did something dramatic. Incredulous, he ran onto the field and began demonstrating to a referee what Sanders had done to Irvin. Switzer bumped the ref. Now a flag was thrown—on Dallas. Instead of a first-and-goal inside the 49er 10, the Cowboys wound up with third and 25 at their 42. That was it. The 49ers soon were Super Bowl–bound, 38–28.

Switzer had gone from scapegoat to just goat.

Later, he said, "I was upset and embarrassed. I thanked God they didn't get me on TV, the things I said to ref." Fortunately for Switzer, Fox cameras didn't even get a shot of him bumping the ref. "I mean, if we score there and make it a three-point game with that much time left? I'm telling you, coach, the 49ers choke."

Instead, the 49ers had won the right to blow out that team Switzer had asked about, San Diego.

Perhaps Aikman felt as if he were trapped in Dante's *Inferno*. His punishment for losing to the 49ers was that Switzer coached him once more, in the Pro Bowl. The losing coaching staffs in the conference championship games always handle the conference all-star teams in Hawaii the week after the Super Bowl.

During the game, telecast by ABC, Switzer got hungry and sent daughter Kathy for hot dogs. (From his many conversations with Cowboy players, Dale Hansen uses this analogy on Switzer: "He's like your goofy dad. Do you love him? Sure. Does he love you? You better believe he does. But does he embarrass the shit out of you in front of your friends? Does he ever.")

Partly because his back was bothering him, Switzer took a break during the action and sat on the bench eating his hot dog. ABC's cameras did not miss this unusual scene. ABC's *Monday Night Football* announcers—Al Michaels, Frank Gifford, and Dan Dierdorf—were critical on the air of Switzer's apparent disinterest in the game. League officials were furious. They have enough trouble convincing fans that players take this game seriously, and now the NFC's head coach was eating a hot dog on the bench.

Later, when I asked Switzer about it, he seemed surprised anyone was upset. "Hell, the players are over there all week playing golf and laying out by the pool. Nobody takes that game seriously."

Aikman, in fact, was criticized after the 1993 Pro Bowl for leaving before the game was over to catch a flight. But Aikman had thought he was through for the day. This time, as Switzer sat eating his hot dog, several Super Bowl champ 49ers kidded Aikman and other Cowboys by saying, "Hey, you better tell your coach there's a game going on out there."

And Aikman said something like, "We've been trying to tell him that all year."

10

CANCER

Nice guys finish last.

—*Leo Durocher*

One afternoon that spring of 1995, Switzer showed up for an interview looking like, well, a million bucks, his approximate annual salary. Gone was the face pinched by playoff pressure. Switzer was golden brown after another of the all-day, all-night bass fishing escapes he takes with John Blake, various players, and buddies from all walks of life. Though he hadn't been to bed, Switzer looked remarkably rested and healthy. A year in the Cowboy crosshairs hadn't aged him a bit. Though he still smokes occasionally, he tries to eat fish, pastas, fruits, vegetables, bread, and cheese, balanced off by red wine, he says. "Smoking doesn't cause cancer of the colon or of the liver," he says. "It's what you eat." In Italy, he has seen "eighty-, ninety-year-old men who smoke their cigarettes, but they eat right. I try to stay away from the red meat, the butter, the oils."

Switzer's physique and tan had brought to life a navy suit the way few fifty-seven-year-olds could. He was about to meet some doctor for lunch. He had invested with them in diagnostic clinics all over the country and recently had cut the ribbon on one in Syracuse, New York. He was moving and shaking. He was back in control after a long year of on-the-job training. Now he knew what was going on, he said.

He had spoken a couple of times with Troy Aikman. "I know what's going on with that kid," he said as if he couldn't believe anyone ever thought he didn't. "I know about the problems with Danny Bradley [trying to "coach"]—Troy would have been better off if he hadn't had that. I know Troy's raw from having to talk so much about me, from having to define [their relationship].

"Troy is a player who's a great player who doesn't want to lead the football team. He wants to be told what to do. I knew that at Oklahoma. He leads by demonstration, by his performance. He wants to be told what the fuck to do."

Switzer was going to start telling him and his teammates what to do, he said. No more Mr. Nice Guy?

Before the start of a minicamp practice, Switzer delivered an explosive speech to the team—a brave-new-world warning. Pointing and yelling, he told his players, "I told you it was your fuckin' team last year. You had won two Super Bowls, so we did it your way. Now it's my team. Now we're going to do it my way. I'm pullin' in the fuckin' reins."

Then Switzer ordered his team to do something that would help cause season-long problems for the quarterback who would cause season-long problems for the coach.

Switzer told his players and coaches, "The cancer that destroys great teams comes from within. You guys must help police yourselves. Goddamn it, come and tell me these problems and I'll be the surgeon and cut the cancer out. Don't blame me if I don't know about it. If something's wrong you come tell me, and if for some reason you can't find me, you tell John Blake about it. He always knows where I am."

In effect, in front of the team and eleven other assistant coaches, Switzer had anointed Blake assistant head coach, a title that was unfilled. The thirty-four-year-old Blake was, by three years, the youngest coach on the staff. During the 1994 season, after Gary Gibbs had been fired at Oklahoma, Switzer had campaigned for Blake to get the job. Instead, the OU board of regents had turned to an elder statesman who had never been in the Sooner family— Howard Schnellenberger. That decision proved to be a mistake.

So probably did Switzer's impulse to empower Blake. He hadn't really meant anything by mentioning the one called "Boo." Really, Switzer was stating what had been obvious: that he and Blake were very close and that Blake usually knew where he was.

But several team insiders said the "cancer" speech put Blake in a difficult spot with his fellow assistants. As if they didn't resent Blake enough, now Switzer had acknowledged Blake's authority before the team and staff. Yet to several older assistants, Blake more than ever was acting like a player around the players. He especially infuriated older white assistants by talking what they called "jive talk" with black players. Of course, Switzer considered Blake's rapport with black Cowboys a strength, and he relied on Blake to keep him informed about team undercurrents. But other assistants thought Blake was much better at interacting with players than teaching them. They questioned Blake's football knowledge and the development of his younger defensive linemen.

This surprised me and made me wonder if the older assistants were mostly jealous of Blake's relationship with the head coach. Gary Gibbs and Larry Lacewell—whose opinions I value—had told me Blake was "a good young coach." Johnson did hire him in the first place. Though I'm no coach, after many football discussions with Blake, I found him to be something like Switzer: much less insightful about players' strengths and weaknesses and much more fluent in Xs and Os than he let on in public. Blake wasn't a polished public speaker and shied away from doing interviews. He tended to run his words together and perhaps struggled to combine languages—black lingo and white coachspeak. So as much as Switzer thought of Blake's head-coaching future, Blake was perhaps the least-known Cowboy assistant. Blake, rarely interviewed on radio or TV, did not take advantage of the Cowboy Phenomenon.

For the wrong reason, that would change.

I told him he should do more interviews because most fans would warm to him. Like Switzer, Blake had a little con man in him that could aid in, say, coaxing some players into playing harder. But the politician in Blake would have played well on TV. Blake, forever upbeat, tended to exaggerate and embellish. Everything and every player was almost always "great, baby." Lacewell sometimes challenged Blake in staff meetings to be more objectively critical of his players. But to fans looking for the bright side, Blake would have been refreshing and entertaining.

Blake was a chip off Switzer's block: His heart was big and good. He was intelligent in some areas, naive in others. He could be a little insecure and immature—but endearingly so. He was loyal to a fault.

I personally liked Blake and felt some of the staff and most of the media really didn't know him—mostly because Blake wouldn't let them. He wasn't even close to the other two black assistants, Hubbard Alexander and Robert Ford, who didn't seem to have much use for Blake. A number of Johnson's old assistants were quietly, angrily concerned about how Switzer's "blessing" of Blake might affect impressionable young Cowboys. Veteran players such as Aikman were also leery of Blake and didn't have much respect for him as a coach. Should his words carry that much weight? Word had gotten around that when Butch Davis had left to become head coach at the University of Miami, Switzer had pushed for Blake to replace Davis as defensive coordinator. Jones preferred linebacker coach Jim Eddy, who at fifty-five had been an NFL coordinator for Houston. Switzer and Jones compromised on secondary coach Dave Campo, who was forty-seven.

Blake acknowledged to me that Switzer's remarks, as well-intentioned as they were, hadn't made his life any easier. In the weeks leading up to training camp, Blake had determined that he had to get out. "Gotta get me a job," he said. He had to use his status as a Cowboy coach and his relationship with Switzer to get a college head-coaching job. Perhaps Blake struck up a relationship with me because he knew I was on ESPN during football season and thought I could help spread his name. Perhaps he talked to me because I was one of the few media people who was open-minded about Switzer.

We began to talk a lot about football, life, and one of my favorite subjects, exercise.

Blake knew he had to lose weight. He had been well up over 300 pounds when Switzer pushed him for the Oklahoma vacancy. He knew the board of regents had hesitated to hire a fat guy as head football coach. But now, by running three miles sometimes twice a day and watching what he ate, Blake was in the process of dropping around 100 pounds. That took, well, guts.

As camp opened at St. Edward's University in Austin, I would drive through the dark down Congress Avenue to do my morning radio show at the campus media center. Nearly every morning about 5:30, amid what was left of the streetwalkers and street people, I would see John Blake, slowly but surely, jogging alone down Congress. Trying, perhaps, to run his way out of Dallas.

Until his final throw of the NFC championship in San Francisco, Troy Aikman had believed Dallas would win. Home alone, he tried to watch the Super Bowl, but a moment after Steve Young hit Jerry Rice for the 7–0 touchdown, he turned off the TV.

In April, when I reported that Jerry Jones had genuine interest in signing Deion Sanders away from the 49ers, I asked Aikman if he approved of the longshot attempt. Many in the media considered Jones's pursuit of Deion either a PR stunt or budget-killing madness. Wouldn't Deion—a cornerback who wouldn't be available until after the baseball season—want a fortune? Didn't Jones have about three dollars left under his salary cap? And wouldn't it hurt Aikman's competitive pride for the world to think, "If you can't beat him, sign him"? Aikman surprised me. He said go, Jerry, go. "Hey, I'm all for whatever it takes so I don't have to sit there and watch another Super Bowl on TV. If it takes people criticizing us for signing Deion, and it means us winning the Super Bowl, I can live with that criticism."

Aikman even was trying to see Switzer in a new light. "We've had some good talks about what needs to happen this year," he said. Aikman liked what he had heard in Switzer's "my team" speech. "I really think people will see a new Barry Switzer this year."

Privately, Aikman was telling friends how important it was for him, as the quarterback, to stay positive throughout camp. During Switzer's first camp, Aikman had let all the little things get to him quickly. Not this time. He was going to be more patient and tolerant because Switzer had promised to be more demanding.

Yet when I asked Aikman to describe the Switzer he was getting to know again, he had an ominous answer: "I think he's the same person I knew at Oklahoma. He's extremely loyal to people, to the point he's taken advantage of."

Even as Switzer's second camp started, a grinning Jimmy Johnson seemed to be everywhere. He was all over television and still wrote a weekly column for the *Dallas Morning News*. By phone he kept in touch with Aikman, with several Cowboy assistant coaches, and with trainer Kevin O'Neill. The "Jimmy prison," some in the organization called it. His former assistants remained in the Jimmy prison even after he was fired. What if Switzer started weeding them out and bringing in old friends to coach under him? Or what if Jones fired Switzer and the next head coach insisted on bringing in his own staff? What if Jimmy decided to come back down from his ivory TV tower and coach again? Maybe he would hire back that old gang of his, who couldn't afford not to keep in touch with him, even if taking Johnson's calls was disloyal to Switzer and had to be done on the sly.

To my knowledge, all of Johnson's old assistants liked Switzer and enjoyed working for him. How could they not? He gave them almost total autonomy in their coaching areas, he rarely criticized or second-guessed them, and he always gave them credit in interviews. No doubt they all had more respect for Johnson as an NFL coach, and their dedicated sides longed for Jimmy, glaring over their shoulder, driving them when they got lazy. But the coaching staff pretty much shared the attitude of most of their players: After winning two Super Bowls under Jimmy's whip, Switzer was a welcome relief.

Yet during heat-crazed afternoon workouts, you could almost feel Jimmy's ghost peering down on the practice field from somewhere up in the Main Building, a Texas landmark erected in 1888 with creepy Gothic-revival turrets and spires of buffed white stone. You could feel Jimmy in the chow hall, Jimmy in the media center, Jimmy in the golf carts that players and coaches use to escape the autograph hordes. Perhaps Jimmy's cackling ghost even haunted the dorm-room dreams of Switzer and Jerry Jones.

In many ways "Switzer's team" was still Jimmy's, and Johnson knew it. On Fox's postgame show, Johnson had appeared almost gleeful after the NFC championship game when he had been able to criticize Switzer in I-told-you-so tones. Now, Johnson was predicting Miami would beat San Francisco in the Super Bowl—and that the Cowboys were going to slip. Johnson knew that many Cowboys still had so much respect for him that his prediction would eat at their confidences: *Damn, if Jimmy says we're going to slip, maybe we're going to slip*.

Jerry Jones had become obsessed with beating Jimmy Johnson, and the only way to do so was by winning a Super Bowl with Switzer. Jones was trying to will victory. Jones was openly saying that the Cowboys had the best team and that the Cowboys should and would win the Super Bowl, barring injuries. I'd never heard anything like it. An owner of a pro football team was saying, "Anything short of winning the Super Bowl is unacceptable." The Cowboys weren't going to play it a game at a time, but a season at a time. How was Switzer supposed to inspire his team for regular season games against inferior foes when all that mattered was what happened in January? How would you like to enter a season thinking, "If we don't win the championship, we've failed"? That's the unheard of position in which Jones put his team. That's the position in which he liked to put himself. But now Switzer was having to operate under the weight of (1) a salary cap and free-agency system that Johnson never had to contend with and (2) a win-or-else mandate from the owner.

Switzer didn't complain and he didn't make excuses. He kept saying, "We have the most talented team. We'll win if we stay healthy. I don't want to go into another [NFC] championship game without a healthy Emmitt."

Remember: When following the Dallas Cowboys from a distance, nothing is ever quite as it appears. Perceptions constantly formed by the media become reality to fans. "Really, all our star players become actors, just like big movie stars," says Larry Lacewell. Case in point: Emmitt Smith, "the NFL's most courageous player."

Is Emmitt the best all-around running back? Yes. One of the all-time great money-time competitors? Bet on it. Decent kid with solid character? Check.

But does Emmitt really have a high pain threshold? Who knows? Is he a hard worker? Not compared to most players. Is he easy to coach and handle? Not always.

Reality: Emmitt is a great player who can be a great actor.

Let's start with the great player. Why were sixteen players taken ahead of Emmitt in the 1990 draft? Too many scouts confused speed (Emmitt's is average for a running back, somewhere in the 4.55 range) with quickness. As Norv Turner used to say, "He has great quickness in a confined space." Emmitt is so quick and so strong—and so compact at 5'9" and 209 pounds—that tacklers simply can't quite get a hold of him. The strength isn't so much in his upper body as in his legs and hips. No Cowboy can leg press more weight for his size than Emmitt. His lower-body strength, says running back coach Joe Brodsky, "is just dominating."

But those tangibles are girded by dominating intangibles. Like all great backs, Emmitt has vision and instinct that cannot be taught. He senses a hole about to open. He feels a blindside tackler about to strike. He runs to daylight that Brodsky can't draw up on the blackboard.

So the coaching staff long ago gave up on precise blocking schemes. Sometimes during the 1991 and 1992 seasons, you could hear in the pressbox as offensive coordinator Turner, one floor below, yelled, "Hit the hole, Emmitt!" Meaning, run to the hole the linemen were trying to open. Now, says Brodsky, "We just say [to offensive linemen], 'Get on your guy.'" Nothing fancy. Just pick the nearest defender and drive-block him. Rarely do the Cowboys pull their guards and ask them to run interference for Emmitt on what coaches call a "toss sweep"—Aikman tossing underhand to Emmitt, who runs 10 or so yards laterally before cutting upfield. That isn't playing to Emmitt's strength, which is what coaches call running "north and south." So Aikman just hands it to him, and the little big man with the rare radar runs wherever his instincts take him. Runs hard, every snap, with very little wasted motion. Runs mostly between the tackles, ducking behind five linemen who weigh between 300 and 370 pounds. Runs behind the best blocking back in the business, Daryl Johnston, a 250-pound four-wheel-drive pickup. Runs a defense into the ground.

John Blake offered a unique interpretation of Emmitt's great-ness: "Emmitt's essence is his will. He doesn't wear you down physi-cally but mentally. So many backs go down on the first hit, but Emmitt's legs keep churning. He frustrates a defense because, by the fourth quarter, they know he's tired, and he knows they're tired, and he's still going just as hard as he was in the first quarter. How many times have you seen him break one in the fourth quarter? They've been trying to stop him all day and finally one guy doesn't wrap him up and he's gone. Once he gets in the open, he doesn't get caught from behind. It's will. His mind is focused on the goal line. You don't see him mess around and lose 10 or 12 yards, like Barry Sanders. He is always moving forward."

The bigger the game, the more relentless and dependable is Emmitt. He has never been a fumbler. After watching him average fifty catches a season for six seasons, I can remember only a couple of drops. His hands are at least as good as Michael Irvin's.

Like Irvin, Emmitt simply loves to play pro football for the Dal-las Cowboys. Do you realize what an advantage that is for Jerry Jones, to have a great player who still has a kid's love of a brutal game? Do you realize how many good players play pro football sheerly for the money? (Unlike Irvin, Emmitt wasn't a particularly cool guy in college. Irvin, his NFL role model, taught Emmitt how to dress and act when he arrived in Dallas.) Emmitt still has a Peter Pan side fascinated by cartoons and video games. If the Cowboys awarded varsity letters, Emmitt proudly would wear his letter jacket to the mall. Part of the reason he continued taking off-season classes at the University of Florida until he finally received his undergraduate degree on May 4, 1996, is that Emmitt likes being around college kids and loves being big man on campus. Emmitt Smith, a twenty-seven-year-old bachelor, is much more interested in being a kid than becoming a father.

He has one of the best smiles in sports—a genuine kid-in-a-Disney-store smile he flashes often. He loves to score touchdowns. He loves the attention.

And, according to many Cowboy coaches and players, Emmitt sometimes plays the spotlight for all it's worth. Rewind to the final regular season game of 1993, Dallas against the Giants at Giants Stadium for the NFC East crown. Emmitt fell on his shoulder late in the first half and suffered a "grade two" separation. No doubt it hurt, but how much? For a journalist, the most difficult aspect of covering pro sports—especially football—is knowing how hurt a player really is. For that matter, coaches, general managers, and team doctors are often frustrated by the same question. If only we had a machine that could be connected simultaneously to an injured athlete and, say, to a skeptical journalist. If only for a minute the journalist (or coach or GM) could feel the athlete's pain and say, "Oh, come on, that's not so bad." Or: *"Turn it off*—my God, no way you can play with that." That, of course, might bring into question the journalist's pain threshold—mine is inordinately high, from years of dealing with psycho athletes and coaches—but such a machine might have lent some perspective to Emmitt's accomplishment that bone-chilling day at Giants Stadium.

Many pro football players play every Sunday with "grade two" separations, but you don't hear about them because they're not Emmitt playing the Giants for all the division marbles. Teammates said Emmitt cried like a baby at halftime. Several told him to forget trying to play in the second half. But, with his arm hanging limp at his side, Emmitt played. As he often has, Emmitt took over a game the Cowboys won in overtime. John Madden made a special trip to the locker room to tell Emmitt it was the most courageous performance he had ever seen. ESPN commentators were comparing Emmitt's courage to the kind Ali and Frazier demonstrated while nearly beating each other to death in Manila.

Yet as gutsy as Emmitt was, several of his coaches and teammates thought he enhanced his performance with some melodramatic theatrics. Several of Aikman's confidants say that—as deeply as the quarterback respects the running back—Aikman is sometimes amused by the way Emmitt acts (or perhaps overacts) when he's injured. Late in the 1994 season, when he pulled his hamstring on Monday night in New Orleans, Emmitt writhed for several minutes as if a rattler were clamped on the back of his leg. Says an Aikman friend, facetiously, "Troy thought Emmitt was going to die." Not that a pulled or torn hamstring isn't a serious injury, but for a moment, I thought he had blown out a knee or fractured his leg. Before the ABC cameras, he was driven by cart to the locker room. Perhaps Emmitt, knowing he might be hampered the rest of the season, was as hurt emotionally as he was physically. Perhaps, as Aikman dreads disease, Emmitt fears the injury that might end the pro football life he loves. Perhaps he doesn't have nearly as high a pain threshold as his idolaters want to believe.

Or perhaps this is all part of the overall psych job he does on defenses. One moment, defenders are wondering, Is he or isn't he hurt? The next, Did he or did he not just run through six of us for a touchdown? That's another reason why, occasionally, I've referred to him as "Emmy" Smith.

For sure, Emmitt loves the media attention he receives when

he's hurt, and his pride flares when he's publicly criticized for not taking better care of his body. Emmitt's talent is purely natural. He has never been a particularly attentive or enthusiastic practice player or a weight-room warrior because he hasn't had to be. (I laughed out loud when I first saw Emmitt's Reebok commercial, about how some guys work harder in the preseason.) Another of Switzer's naive rookie-year mistakes came when, trying to impress the media with his working knowledge of the Cowboys, he simply repeated what his assistants often told him: that if Emmitt were going to prolong his career the way Walter Payton did, Emmitt was going to have to work harder in the off-season. The next day, urged by many in the organization, a sighing Switzer sought out Emmitt and explained his way out of a potential clash without further offending Emmitt. Switzer treads softly around Emmitt. Switzer says, "He's his own man. He's not a follower. He can't be led. He'll stand his ground on his values and principles." Wrongheaded as they sometimes are.

Before and during the '95 season, Emmitt did appear to work harder than he ever had. Perhaps his pride was pricked by the inadvertent criticism from Switzer—and blatant public warnings from me. I've always been an Emmitt fan. On ESPN, I constantly sided with Emmitt during his '93 contract battle with Jones, and Emmitt later thanked me for it. But something I said on radio—something he heard about "from a friend"—angered him during the '94 off-season. Something about how he had never been much for off-season workouts, which wasn't exactly a scoop. Though I didn't apologize, I did try to explain myself to him. He wouldn't listen. He stayed mad and refused to talk to me. One coach told me, "You deserve a game ball for helping motivate him."

Ah, life with the Cowboys. As Switzer sometimes tells his friends, "A big part of this job is dealing with prima donnas, and we've got a bunch of 'em."

During camp Switzer often was hamstrung by the condition of Emmitt's hamstrings. Both were tight, Emmitt said, obviously enjoying the daily suspense he caused. Was he "hamming" it up? Or should Switzer hold Emmitt out of practice? Play him even sparingly in exhibition games? The constant media questions and guessing game wore out Switzer, who sometimes said, "I'm getting too old for this." The height of hamstring lunacy: Emmitt pulled up lame and limped out of the light Friday practice before the Saturday-night exhibition opener. It looked bad; Switzer was dejected. That cinched it: Emmitt Smith was going to be slowed by hamstring pulls all season, if not the rest of his career.

Yet a little while later, when Emmitt was late for the buses, several coaches were stunned to see him sprint at what looked like full speed. Sound the trumpets: The season was saved. Switzer could relax, for a few more minutes.

She was there almost every practice, often with her dog, an Akita named Oskie who probably could have started at linebacker for her dad's team. "An O.J. dog," she calls it, flashing a feisty, irreverent wit her dad envies. If Kathy Switzer weren't his daughter, Barry Switzer probably would marry her. Remember *Semi-Tough's* Barbara Jane Bookman, the ideal guy's girl who could outdrink and outcuss most males while remaining the perfect lady? At twenty-six, Kathy Louise Switzer is a Barbara Jane for the '90s—an attractive tomboy who doesn't smoke or drink or eat anything unhealthy. She looks a little like her dad, with her mom's spitfire personality. With brown hair highlighted by the sun, she looks equally comfortable in an evening dress, boots and jeans, or workout wear. During practice, she'll chat with the media guys on the St. Edward's sideline; after practice, she sometimes plays catch with a football, displaying an arm and hands most media guys never had.

Kathy Switzer, weight lifter and runner, was hoping to get her master's at the University of Oklahoma in health and sports science and exercise physiology. She also was hoping to accompany her dad to the Super Bowl. It's not that she loves football or even the Cowboys. "I'm not a Sooner fan or a Cowboy fan," she says. "I'm a daddy fan."

During camp, Kathy goes everywhere with her dad, from practice to whichever watering hole he and Jerry Jones and the gang might choose to close. Sipping bottled water, Kathy often serves as designated driver. She doesn't always approve of her dad's behavior, but she loves him unconditionally and knows the love is returned.

"One thing that's very impressive about Barry Switzer," says Larry Lacewell, "is that no matter what he did, those three kids never quit on him. I've never seen anything like the love they have for him—or, for that matter, the love Jerry's three kids have for him. I've told them both how fortunate they are to have that."

The three Jones children are each about three years older than the corresponding Switzer children, who also go boy-girl-boy. Stephen Jones and Greg Switzer are the oldest. Charlotte and Kathy are middle children. Jerry Jr. and Doug were born exactly three years apart on September 27. To Jerry Sr.'s delight, the families match up well socially.

But as much as Barry Switzer loves his boys, his daughter is the love of his life. She says, "I don't defend Dad on a lot of things. I've always said he was a great dad and a lousy husband. But my dad was not in the minority [of dads who cheated on moms]. I appreciate my mom because she was a great role model. If I had seen her stay [instead of filing for divorce], maybe I'd have dated guys who cheated on me and lied to me, and thought it was normal. But she had the self-esteem to stand up and be strong."

Though her dad has been through several girlfriends, he has made his daughter a constant. She says, "I've had friends from high school and college whose dads have had girlfriends or remarried and had nothing to do with [their daughters]. They are so jealous of my relationship with my dad. I'm so lucky. It's rare for a man in his glamor profession to be so consumed with his kids. Football is meaningless to him compared to his kids."

Her dad, she says with loving sarcasm, was the perfect role model: "He made me see what not to do." She stays on him about his diet. Sometimes, he'll just have to have a cheeseburger, so they'll stop at Wendy's and she'll have a plain baked potato. When he stays at her house in Norman, he smokes out on the porch.

"My dad is the luckiest son of a bitch on Earth. He still eats junk food. He doesn't work out. And he's still gorgeous."

Why? Switzer's family and friends share this theory: Despite his faults, he's blessed because of the love he spreads. Kathy says her dad never got too big for the littlest people. "It's unbelievable the lives he supports [financially]." He helps support ex-players and childhood friends. "He always says, 'I got lucky,' and he wants to help those who didn't." Just being around him, she says, is an inspiration to many. "He can make you believe in yourself—he just makes you happy being around him. Wherever he goes, he touches people—and not just famous people. I see a lot of famous assholes. But out in public, people just love him. They flock to him. He just has the biggest, most wonderful heart."

During camp, Kathy Switzer was trying not to break her dad's heart. She had decided to get out of her marriage. Her husband, she said, is "the greatest guy in the world." They were best friends. But she wasn't sure she was in love with him or that she was cut out for being a housewife/mother or even for marriage.

Through camp, Kathy and I became friends. I appreciated the pain she was experiencing. I went through a divorce at her age. But I couldn't quite understand why she was so afraid to tell her dad that she had failed at marriage. Of all people, wouldn't he understand?

She said, "He just doesn't want me to wind up lonely, like he is."

For a while, says Kathy, her father had a strong relationship with (perhaps significantly) a licensed professional counselor in Norman named Ann Jones. Kathy believes her dad would have married Ann Jones. He still drops by to see her from time to time. "But," says Kathy, "she wouldn't marry him because she knew he wouldn't be faithful."

Barry Switzer has his father's fatal flaw: He'll always have an eye for the ladies and perhaps he'll always be lonely. But Kathy is always there for him—Kathy, who doesn't believe in sex without love. (During her senior year in college, Kathy was enraged to hear that a guy she briefly dated as a freshman was telling members of his fraternity's pledge class how he "plugged" Kathy Switzer. After seeking instruction on how to throw a punch, she had the bouncer of a Norman nightclub hold the guy while she "right-hooked his ass," bloodying his nose. The next afternoon, members of the football team were calling her Tysonette.)

Other media people were amazed during camp when they heard that Kathy went with her dad and Dean Blevins to a topless bar down the street from St. Edward's. I wasn't at all surprised. She rolls her eyes at their lust, but she accepts it as part of life. "It's a man's world," she says. She lets them gawk for a while, she tells them when it's time to get back to the dorm—and she makes sure they get there in one piece.

Though current girlfriend Becky Buwick accompanied Switzer to Cowboy away games, he insisted Kathy go, too. During camp, Kathy and Oskie (an old college-football nickname for an interception) sleep in an adjoining dorm room. "Once a night I'll hear dad say, 'Goddamn it, Oskie, get off my bed!'"

Finally, Kathy asked John Blake to break the news of her divorce to her dad. She didn't want to be there when he went into one of his tirades. She says he took it better than she thought he would. After all, he loves her far more than he does football.

For two reasons it was remarkable that Erik Williams was ready to ease back into camp drills. His knee had been so badly damaged in his wreck that, at first, doctors weren't sure he'd be able to walk without a limp let alone play pro football. But his availability had been further clouded by an off-season incident involving a seventeen-year-old topless dancer who accused him of sexual assault. She and Williams had "partied" together several times. Incredibly, Williams had risked a probation violation—risked jail and his Cowboy career—to involve himself with this girl.

The case wound up before a Collin County grand jury, which voted not to indict Williams.

One day, in response to a caller's criticism he heard on my radio show, Switzer told me, "I cannot be held responsible twenty-four hours a day for the actions of all fifty-three people on this team. These are grown men. I can't baby-sit them when they leave here. These things happen to players everywhere—in Cincinnati, in Buffalo, everywhere."

Tom Landry made the same argument about the many of his players who stumbled onto the police blotter. Many of Landry's players considered him hypocritical: a Christian who coached a violent game played on Sundays, a cold-hearted man who often treated his players without compassion. Switzer is quite the opposite. Switzer's players know he cares about and understands them—perhaps to a fault. They know he's out there at the "gentlemen's clubs," too. They hear stories about how he sits with his feet up, coolly smoking cigarettes between his thumb and finger, flirting with the harem. (During a 1995 press conference, Switzer mentioned that after practice, players go home to their wives or girlfriends or to "the men's clubs"—an outrageously honest statement from the head coach.)

Landry and Switzer separately have argued that no matter how the coach conducts himself, a percentage of players will stray. Nothing a coach can do, they say.

The key, says Troy Aikman, is how the coach reacts when players' off-the-field behavior affects a practice or even a game.

Usually, players are given Wednesday nights off during camp. On this particular Wednesday, Switzer even pushed the curfew back an hour. Something like thirty-seven players broke curfew, thought to be a Cowboy record.

The next day as the players stretched before practice, Aikman was infuriated to hear the head coach laughing about the "unprecedented number" of violators with several guilty players—even comparing "girl" stories with them from the night before.

Then Switzer "punished" the team by cutting practice short. (Switzer says he had to because of a team activity scheduled that afternoon.) Aikman wanted to see Switzer run his hungover players until their swollen tongues dragged in the grass. He wanted Switzer to cut a player, just to make an example of him. As practice ended, Aikman asked Switzer why no one was being disciplined. Switzer responded, "What do you want me to do, cut Michael Irvin?" Irvin had missed curfew.

Switzer knew Irvin's reputation for partying as hard as he played—just as Irvin knew Switzer wasn't exaggerating when he told the media, "None of my players have done anything I haven't done." Irvin obviously was more afraid of Johnson than of Switzer. Irvin had indicated as much when, within earshot of Aikman as another practice had ended, he remarked that he could get away with more now that Switzer was coaching. Would a whip-cracking Johnson have kept Irvin from getting himself in the image-ruining mess he did following the season? No, says Switzer: "You can warn players a hundred times, and they always think you're talking to the one next to 'em."

Aikman obviously didn't want Switzer to cut Irvin. But Aikman thought something dramatic needed to be done to show the undisciplined half of the team it couldn't keep getting away with near-murder. Aikman later told me, "We have twenty-five guys you could yell at every day, and it wouldn't matter. They'd still bust their butts and do the things it takes to win. But there's another twenty-five who do just enough to get by. Those twenty-five need discipline."

That day, Aikman's newfound patience went up in the smoke coming out his ears. Forget it: same old Switzer. The "my team" speech? Bullshit, said Aikman. Just a lot of big talk to get the media and the quarterback off his back. Just one big con job. How could Aikman trust Switzer and Blake to "cut out the cancer" when they—in his eyes—*were* the cancer?

Switzer's greatest strength as a coach is his incredible charisma, which pulls people to him, a contradictory "vulnerable strength" that made nearly all his Cowboy players defiantly protective of him—all but the quarterback, who wanted a coach he could look up to, not look after.

"If Jimmy had still been here," says Jones, "believe me, there would be no Deion. It's a little thing called dwelling on the negatives." Being superstitious, Jones reneged on the final dollar of the record-breaking $13 million bonus. It went in the books as $12,999,999.

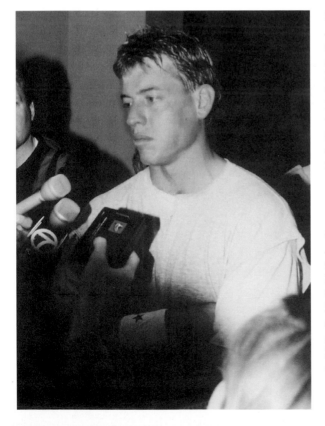

By the end of the season, Aikman was sick of answering questions about his relationship with Switzer, who blamed his problems with Aikman on the media. "It's created because y'all ask him all the time. Everybody keeps bringing it up. Rubs you raw. It's kind of like jock itch—you can't get rid of the thing."

OPPOSITE: Switzer suffers from Attention Deficit Disorder, although no one knew it when he was hired to coach the Cowboys. Aikman said, "At first I'd walk over and try to strike up a conversation with him, and after a while he wouldn't even be listening. I'd think, 'Hell, he doesn't even want to talk to me.'"

Larry Lacewell, the man at Jerry Jones's right hand. Switzer says of him, "I trust Larry Lacewell's football judgment more than anyone I've ever been around."

At the press conference announcing his hiring, Switzer seemed on edge, defensive, trying desperately to convince the "enemy" media that taking over the Super Bowl champs was no big deal because he had won three national championships at Oklahoma. He later admitted that the drive to Dallas "was one of the slowest drives I've ever had. . . . The farther I drove, the worse I felt about it. I was really depressed."

A moment some of Switzer's friends—and all of his enemies—thought they'd never witness: Barry Switzer holding the Super Bowl trophy.

While angry voices across the NFL accused Jones of destroying the league, Jones put it all on the line for his team. In just seven years he would fire Tom Landry, hire and fire Jimmy Johnson, hire a new coach with no NFL experience, and pay a part-time player a record $13 million bonus. Oh, and he also won three Super Bowls.

When John Blake, a devoted Switzer follower and former Cowboy assistant, got his wish to become head coach at Oklahoma, Aikman got his wish too—no more John Blake. *Photo courtesy of the University of Oklahoma.*

On the morning of the Super Bowl, commissioner Paul Tagliabue blasted Jones on national television: "Jerry Jones dishonors the agreement he made when he came into the NFL partnership. He takes what does not belong to him." Later that day Jones took exactly what belonged to him, his third championship trophy, which was Tagliabue's chore to present.

Irvin's bizarre touchdown celebrations are legendary, resembling eerie sacrificial dances. In the Thanksgiving Day victory over Kansas City, "The Playmaker" made perhaps his greatest catch ever, leading to this performance.

Irvin has always played big brother to Emmitt Smith, whom he calls "my boy." But while Irvin craved the Dallas night life, Smith took comfort in the simpler pleasures of video games and cartoons. And while Irvin spent the off-season embroiled in controversy, Smith graduated from college to fulfill a promise he made to his mother.

Irvin pulls away from Steelers' safety Myron Bell in the Super Bowl, although the Steelers mostly shut down the Cowboys. Irvin would have only five catches for 76 yards, with no touchdowns.

During the season several team officials feared Irvin was using drugs, but they had no proof. A Cowboy official privately admitted, "It's amazing he hasn't gotten into trouble. He's often in places he shouldn't be." Three months later Irvin would be indicted on drug charges.

OPPOSITE: Jerry Jones is drawn to humans who do rare things, and Deion Sanders, says Switzer, is "almost like from another planet," a description Jones loves.

While Aikman's perfect form has made him probably the most accurate passer in NFL history, his complex personality has made him one of its most perplexing characters. His brain power runs amok, turns on him, eats at his psyche, makes him crazy.

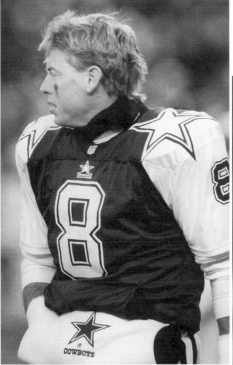

"The shine is off the star," Aikman said privately after the season. "We're headed in the wrong direction."

Aikman spent much of the season battling the team's "self-inflicted problems."

Emmitt Smith celebrates his second touchdown of Super Bowl XXX . . .

. . . but Pittsburgh was extremely successful in taking Smith out of the Super Bowl, especially in the second half; he had only nine yards on seven carries.

The infamous fourth-and-1 play that earned Switzer the headline, "Bozo the Coach." On consecutive plays against the Eagles, Switzer, the ultimate players' coach, put the game in the hands of his players. Both times the Eagles stopped them cold. TV analysts called the plays "Dumb and Dumber."

The Big Three. Which was the one player the Cowboys felt they could not win without? Not Troy Aikman or Emmitt Smith, but Michael Irvin. "Don't even talk about it," Switzer said, as if merely asking about it might conjure evil spirits.

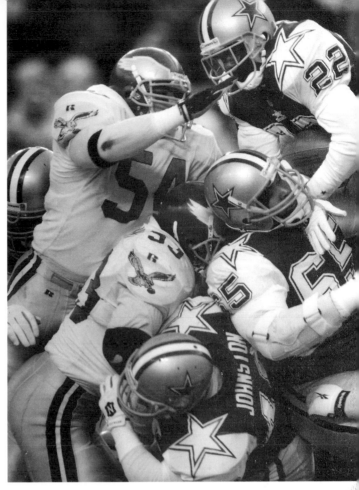

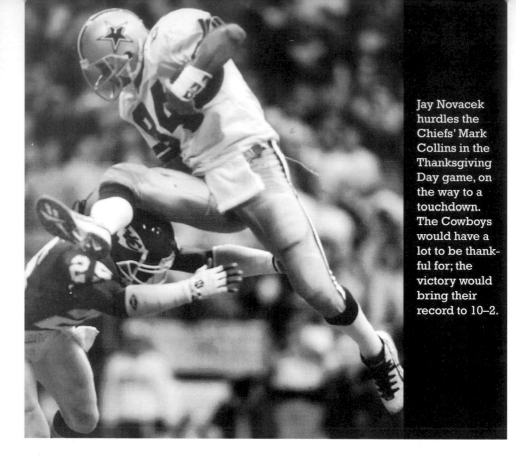

Jay Novacek hurdles the Chiefs' Mark Collins in the Thanksgiving Day game, on the way to a touchdown. The Cowboys would have a lot to be thankful for; the victory would bring their record to 10–2.

Charles Haley, returning to action in the Super Bowl after a two-month recovery from back surgery, finishes off a sack of Steelers' quarterback Neil O'Donnell. Before Haley became a Cowboy, said Jerry Jones, "we couldn't even spell Super Bowl."

11

PLANET JERRY

T'hell with patience. Let's kill something.
                    —*One buzzard to another,*
                              from a plaque on
                         Jerry Jones's office wall

To the outside NFL world, Jerry Jones was out of control. It appeared he had declared war on the league, that he was going to defy its sacred one-for-all rules, to sue it to smithereens, to Jerry-rig it so that he, Jerral Wayne Jones, would win every Super Bowl. Would the movie of his life be called *A League of His Own*? Would this outsider, this interloper, this chicken-fried Steinbrenner, this smiley Al Davis, turn into the "Grinch Who Bought Football"? Would we some day read, "Jerry Jones won his tenth straight Super Bowl as his Dallas Cowboys Inc. beat his Dallas Cowboys Ltd."?

The Devil and Mr. Jones? Not only had he figured some diabolical way to sign Deion Sanders, but this egomaniac made a pizza commercial with his "man" "Prime Time"! Soon, no doubt, Jones would buy Pizza Hut and do his own commercial, playing off the company's "both" slogan. "Jerry, which Sanders do you want, Deion or Barry?" Both!

Yes, completely out of control.

At least, that was the bitter sentiment echoing through the league in September of 1995. In *Inside Sports* magazine, NBC's Mike Ditka said with bite-his-head-off venom: "What Jerry Jones is doing is going to destroy what this league was and what it should be. For that reason, I can't bring myself to pick [the Cowboys] to go to the Super Bowl."

Jones's rival, San Francisco president Carmen Policy, said, "The man's gone too far . . . What he's doing is contrary to the image of the NFL. If it were up to him, he'd turn our uniforms into race-car uniforms . . . There is money, and there is class. The two aren't synonymous."

Even Green Bay quarterback Brett Favre, on his way to an MVP season, got into the act, calling Jones "a silly man with a lot of money."

Nearly all the old-guard NFL owners acted as if Jones had bought the biggest mansion on their stately block and turned it into a disgustingly successful amusement park, JerryWorld. Cleveland owner Art Modell told *Sports Illustrated*, "What would football be in Green Bay without sharing [league] revenue? They'd have igloo suites instead of luxury suites. Their pregame meal would be blubber!"

Yet what Modell really feared was that if Jones did own the Packers, he'd figure a way to sell ice to the Eskimos.

The stuffy old yacht club of NFL owners had a new member, a wildcatting supersalesman who wouldn't take "whoa" for an answer. The nouveau riche new guard was supposed to behave just as reclusively as owners who inherited their fortunes or whose families acquired a ground-floor franchise without debt. Jones indirectly was told to shut up, stay in the background, take his lumps, and share the wealth. Each of the thirty owners gets an equal share of league revenue. Such capitalistic socialism had long made the NFL the financially soundest and most successful of all pro sports leagues.

Yet after a year or so of observing NFL owners, Jimmy Johnson told his assistants, "There are only four or five owners in the league who really care about winning. The rest will fire their coach every three years to make it look like they want to win, but all they care about is making money."

So which, Johnson was asked, is Jones?

"He's both," said Johnson.

Both.

Jones soon decided that this one-for-all dog wouldn't hunt—not when club membership cost him $140 million. Jones began to rock the yacht. Jones says he began trying to take the old guard's thinking from the 1950s into the next century. Says Leigh Steinberg, "Jones thinks in terms of having one of the world's premier corporate entities while other teams are still trying to learn how to count the number of shoulder pads in the locker room."

The truth is, Jones probably inspired more fear than anger in his NFL frat brothers.

Jones says he wanted to increase revenue for every team, but the boys at NFL Properties wouldn't listen. So Jones finally got mad. Jones decided to get his fellow owners' attention. No one can top Jones when it comes to getting attention.

Jones fired the first shot late in camp. It wasn't just that he announced a rule-breaking alliance with Pepsi, but the way he did it that offended other owners. Like some of his stars, Jones can't help flaunting and taunting. Perhaps if he had just wrapped his suggestions for Properties with a ribbon of humility, he might have been hailed by the media as a visionary instead of a mercenary. But that's not Jerry.

"Today," he says of the resulting lawsuit and countersuit, "I regret the NFL got involved in getting us in court. Today, I would have preferred working through all this with dialogue. But I had tried that on numerous occasions. In the real world, it's very difficult to make decisions and have change without having urgency. This was the only way I could have created any urgency."

Red, white, and blue cowboy boots, that's how.

At the press conference, Jones hiked up his pants and let the photographers get a lensful of his garish new Pepsi boots, which basically said to the NFL, "Pepsi this." Pepsi reportedly had paid Jones as much as $40 million for ten years of pouring and advertising rights at Texas Stadium. Yet Coke had paid to be the official soft drink of the National Football League.

Fine, said Jones, but the Cokes of the world weren't paying enough. Each team's one-thirtieth share of properties sales was only $3.5 million—chicken feed! Jones's argument was that the league as a whole could make more money if each team were given the right to market its logo in its region—and if each team were put on an incentive plan. Jones didn't want more than his share of the league's major source of revenue, television. No, he was just trying to upgrade a minor source. Says George Hays: "Jerry never said he wouldn't share [properties revenue]. He just said, 'Let every team handle its own logo because each team can do better than somebody on Wall Street does [selling the entire league].' Green Bay *can* compete with Dallas, when you consider how Packer-crazy that entire state and region are. But they've never tried to market. Teams like Cleveland don't even have marketing departments. And one of the worst marketers is San Francisco. [Owner Eddie] DeBartolo doesn't want to market. They're doing about seven percent [of overall properties sales], so it's not just about winning."

In 1994 the Cowboys did about 29 percent of properties sales. So why, Jones wanted to know, should he spend so much time and money marketing the Cowboys—flying all over creation making speeches and appearances—if his take would always be one-thirtieth of a ridiculously small pie? He wanted cuts based on a sliding scale of performance, yet he all but guaranteed that the worst sellers would make more than the current $3.5 million. Says Hays, "Under Jerry's plan, I promise you the ones who just sit on their butts would make five million."

But were other owners going to be quick to change, to listen to Arkansas Jerry, to say, "Maybe you're right"? No. Too much fear and jealousy. After all, Jones owned the NFL's most marketable team, and he controlled most of the revenue produced by Texas Stadium (the City of Irving gets 8 percent of stadium profit). Key point: Teams do not have to share their stadium revenue, and Texas Stadium generated $37 million in '94, more than double any other franchise. Jones's comeback? Any other owner could have risked buying the 3–13 Dallas Cowboys for $140 million when the franchise, as Jones said, was "a piece of shit."

Still, the other owners merely watched and fumed while Jones two-stepped with Pepsi. For the moment, he was merely Jerry, Jerry, quite contrary. But then came opening night at Giants Stadium. *Monday Night Football* with Al, Frank, Dan, and America looking on. Cowboys vs. Giants? For a while. During the second quarter, Jones turned it into Jerry vs. the NFL. Down to the sidelines he went with seldom seen Nike chief Phil Knight. If that weren't enough camera magnetism, Nike darling Monica Seles tagged along. For the next seven minutes, ABC's cameras had little choice but to keep an eye on Jones-Knight-Seles. What might Jones do next? Handed a press release, ABC's announcers had little choice but to talk about Jones's new and controversial alliance with Nike. For Knight, it was like a free infomercial, considering many viewers hit the restroom or kitchen during regular commercial breaks, when each minute costs about $700,000. Now Knight had a captive audience. Whatever he paid Jones to get Texas Stadium wallpapered with swooshes—reportedly more than $2.5 million a year for seven years—was probably worth it to Nike just for those seven minutes. A friend vacationing in Scotland sent me the front page of the newspaper featuring a picture of Jones and Knight.

Taking Knight and Seles down to the sideline turned out to be a brilliant marketing maneuver—which was no spontaneous suggestion by Jones. He and his advisors carefully plotted it. Even the team cooperated: Jones would have been tarred and swooshed by media critics if the Cowboys had lost, but the players didn't even seem to notice Jones's scene-stealing as they rolled, 35–0. "It was like an Andrew Lloyd Webber opening," says Switzer.

But Jones's fellow owners noticed—especially old guard New York Giant owner Wellington Mara, who was not amused. "It pissed him off royally," says George Hays, choosing an appropriate adverb. It appeared, perhaps, that Jones was trying to upstage the halftime ceremony honoring retired Giant quarterback Phil Simms. (I talked to Simms two days later, and he said, "I didn't even notice what Jerry was doing. It didn't bother the ceremony at all.")

Asked recently if he has any regrets about the Knight episode, Jones said, "None at all. Nike has wanted to be involved with the NFL for five years. The greatest sports marketing people there have ever been not involved with the NFL? That was ludicrous." Of the many "petty" excuses Jones heard, one was "being afraid of Nike overinfluencing the NFL. If we don't have enough confidence and stability to deal with that . . . "

But the key, Jones notes, was that his grandstanding "did create urgency."

The five owners who govern Properties (saying they were acting without NFL commissioner Paul Tagliabue's involvement) sued Jones for $300 million. Jones countersued for $750 million. (You half-expected the NFL to counter-countersue for a billion and for Jones to counter-counter-countersue for a trillion.)

Jones envisioned doing exactly what he watched Raider owner Al Davis do when Jones was a wide-eyed rookie owner in 1989. Later, Davis became Jones's friend and advisor. (Imagine: Tex Schramm's bitter enemy—to whom Schramm shot the finger during a game at Texas Stadium—became Jones's one friend among owners.) At one of Jones's first owners meetings, he watched Davis move from owner to owner, smiling and collecting checks—something like $750,000 installments they owed Davis after losing to him in court. So, countersuing, Jones dreamed of, *How we doin'*, *Wellington, and do you have my check?*

"An Al Davis wannabe," Carmen Policy calls Jones.

But though Davis and Jones are kindred rebels—and frequent dinner partners—they come in very different packages. Davis, "Darth Raider," is reclusive and doesn't appear to care how he's perceived by fans. Jones wants to be rebellious—but wants desperately to be portrayed as a good guy and a great league-loving owner. Jones wants both. "I know I'm getting the lesser of it PR-wise," he says of the lawsuits. "I know sports fans view me as negative. But what I feel very confident will happen is that we will win and ultimately some of the things I have advocated will be done . . . People will say, 'Ol' Jerry's kind of a maverick, but Jerry wasn't just for Jerry.'" And when the lawsuits end? "I want to be able to jump back on the other side of the table with [all the other owners] and yell at somebody else."

A few weeks after he made his deal with Nike, the NFL finally made a deal with Nike. "That obviously reinforced me," Jones says.

Says Michael Ozanian, who analyzes sports franchises for *Financial World* magazine, "Jerry Jones will become the Harvard case study on how to buy a franchise, make it profitable, and get the most price appreciation."

But will he be remembered as the man who took the league up or down with him? Will Jones, in maximizing profit, destroy much of what is sacred to faithful NFL customers? He has offended many Landry-Schramm customers. But of course, they can't quit watching their Cowboys, because Jones has put a consistently terrific product on the field. So does he want to win every Super Bowl? He says, "I'd be a fool not to realize that great competition made the NFL what it is." He knows it would hurt leaguewide interest for the Cowboys to win ten straight championships.

But, say, eight out of ten . . .

Jones finally won some respect from Art Modell. Not long after calling Jones "the devil," Modell replaced Jones as the world's most hated owner. Modell broke league rules by taking a lucrative offer to move his Browns to Baltimore. A tearful Modell said he needed the money to compete for free agents. What, he didn't make enough from the NFL's oldest revenue source, ticket sales in 80,000-seat Cleveland Stadium? No, he said, he needed a new stadium with luxury boxes, and the city wouldn't build him one.

Basically, Modell's problem was that he couldn't keep up with the Jerry Joneses. Was Modell emerging from the dark ages? Or had he sold his soul because of "the devil"?

At a midseason league meeting, says Jones, Modell told him, "You have the biggest balls I have ever seen." By then they were squarely on the line. Lawsuits were one thing, $13 million bonuses for injured, baseball-playing cornerbacks quite another.

In a way, Jerry Jones's pride might have cost him a third straight Super Bowl. The more obvious reasons were injuries to Emmitt Smith and Erik Williams and the three early turnovers at San Francisco. Yet after the Cowboys' second straight Super Bowl victory, Jones did grow dangerously proud of a new salary cap he had helped ramrod. After just five NFL seasons, Jones was becoming quite an NFL force—a Hall of Fame candidate. In 1992 he was named to the prestigious five-man competition committee. In 1993 he was influential in convincing old-guard owners to break their ties with CBS and negotiate a landmark $1.6 billion deal with upstart Fox. Then Jones pushed for what he thought would be a landmark "hard" cap, meaning each team could spend X-amount, period. Why would an oil-field plunger suddenly want a strict budget? Jones is a frugal plunger. He'll stop to turn out the lights in an unused Valley Ranch room. Given the option of outsmarting his rivals with or without a salary cap, he predictably chose the less expensive way.

But he and son Stephen didn't look as hard for ways to beat the new system as they might have if the Cowboys hadn't just won back-to-back championships. The 49ers, who had lost back-to-back NFC championship games to Dallas, got out their magnifying glasses.

The most talented and risky player on the 1994 market was Deion Sanders, who had been with Atlanta for five years. Says Jones, "The Atlanta people have told me they would have tried to re-sign him, but they thought it was a hard cap, too, and they just didn't think they could compete with the kind of dollars they were hearing." As Sanders conducted his "Deion Over America" tour, several teams, including New Orleans and Miami, were said to be offering up to $4 million a year. Jones was intrigued by Sanders and scheduled a Dallas stop for him. But Mr. Salary Cap also decided Deion's desires were well beyond his budget, and Deion's visit was canceled.

Besides, Jones had to wonder how Deion's "Prime Time" ego would squeeze into the Cowboy locker room. Deion was committed to playing pro baseball. Imagine paying $4 million for a guy who shows up in November and might disrupt championship chemistry. But one afternoon I had an enlightening chat with Emmitt Smith. He said, "I'm tellin' you, I would restructure my deal if it would help get Deion in here." I said, "But you have maybe the best cornerback tandem in the league [in Kevin Smith and Larry Brown]." He grinned and shot me a little "dumb sportswriter" look. And he said, "We are talking *Deion.*"

Emmitt, along with other Cowboys, sometimes kidded about how sorry Larry Brown's hands were. "Larry Brown," Emmitt said with affection, "couldn't catch a cold butt-nekked in Alaska." Emmitt's point: As solid as Brown had been, he wasn't in Deion's league. Nobody was. I'd never heard Emmitt speak of another player with awe. Deion inspired awe in Emmitt and Michael Irvin.

Ego clashes? No way, said Emmitt. He and Michael and Deion were good buddies—"homeboys" from Florida. (Emmitt, from Pensacola, played for Florida. Irvin, from Fort Lauderdale, played for Miami. Deion, from Fort Myers, played for Florida State.) I began beating the Deion drum, on radio and through my columns. But to Jones, Deion remained a risky luxury. Jones did not ask Emmitt to refinance.

Until the end, the 49ers weren't in the Deion derby. Then, bulletin: "Deion Signs with Niners." Hmmm, thought Jones, concerned but not alarmed. Deion took considerably less base salary (only $1.2 million) with incentives that could get him to $2 million. Hmmm, thought Jones. What was this about deals with Nike and Sega that would supplement Deion's income? If the 49ers had helped arrange those deals, that would be cap circumvention. Yet what were Eddie DeBartolo and Carmen Policy doing with several of their high-dollar player contracts? *Hmmm.* Tearing them up, giving stars big bonuses, then lengthening the deals?

The 49ers were leaping through a cap loophole—one, incredibly, the owners' lawyers left right there on the bargaining table for NFL Players Association negotiators. The collective bargaining agreement carried no restriction on up-front bonuses vs. contract length. An up-front bonus, which a player immediately received in full, could be prorated annually against the cap over the length of the contract. So, for example, a $10 million up-front bonus on a five-year deal would count only $2 million a year against the annual cap. If a player would take the minimum $178,000 base salary, he could have what amounted to a guaranteed deal: a huge up-front bonus check to spend immediately. Very few NFL contracts had been guaranteed (against injury or poor performance) the way most are in baseball and basketball. But getting a large portion of the contract upon signing served as a guarantee.

Soon, that loophole would cost owners millions in bonuses—especially Jones. But for a while, Mr. Salary Cap fought the loophole, saying the 49ers and other teams were violating the "spirit" of the collective bargaining agreement. After the '94 season, Jones officially complained to the league and actually thought San Francisco might be penalized by a fine or draft choices. But Jones was told that nothing could be done until the collective bargaining agreement runs out after the 1998 season—that teams (and free-agent players) couldn't be penalized for taking advantage of a deal structure the agreement allows. Obviously, the NFLPA would cry foul. "Spirit" wouldn't stand up in court. No, what Jones and other owners had proclaimed a "hard" cap was in reality expensively soft.

Suddenly, Deion was a 49er. They didn't even have to wait on him to finish baseball season. There wasn't one. "I really believe," says Larry Lacewell, "that the baseball strike cost us the Super Bowl. It would have been so much harder on them if he hadn't been available until midseason."

From the start Deion fit in beautifully with all the 49ers except Jerry Rice. Several 49er sources told me Deion would frustrate Rice during practice by covering him so tightly. Then he would humiliate Rice by pulling his hands away at the last second from a pass he could have knocked away or even intercepted. The message to Rice and everyone watching, "Oh, I think I'll let you have that one, Jerry." But Rice's resentment of Deion certainly didn't affect the team, which developed a new swagger walking beside Deion. Says Barry Switzer, "His free spirit just permeates a locker room. It's something to behold."

For years, the 49ers won in Joe Montana's image: low-key, classy, confident. They walked on the field knowing they had "Montana Mystique" and their opponents didn't. They had the greatest clutch quarterback ever—as the Cowboys first found out in "the Catch Game" (Montana to Dwight Clark) that ended their Super Bowl hopes in early 1982. When Steve Young replaced Montana, the magic died. Young began to make the big mistake in the big games—especially against Dallas. Until Deion arrived, the 49ers just didn't appear to believe they could beat the Cowboys. But San Francisco had acquired the one human who strikes competitive fear in the hearts of Emmitt and Irvin and many Cowboys. Deion was the difference. Deion intercepted a pass in each of San Francisco's victories over Dallas. Deion changed both games by allowing the rest of the 49er secondary to play double-coverage on every receiver except the one Deion took man-to-man.

Soon after Deion helped end Jones's hopes of a history-making third straight Lombardi trophy, Mr. Salary Cap said "spirit" be damned. Deion had signed for only one year in San Francisco, and Jones vowed to do whatever it took to outbid the 49ers for him. Lacewell says, "Everything that happens in this building [Cowboy headquarters] is all about beating the San Francisco 49ers . . . Jerry finally said, 'Okay, if those are the [salary-cap] rules, watch this: I can play that game better than anybody.'"

The luxury-suite revenue and the new Pepsi and Nike deals helped give Jones a luxury some owners didn't have: cash flow. He began using the "San Francisco method" to re-sign many of his stars or to create cap room by restructuring their deals. Jones began writing check after up-front bonus check. The total soon would exceed $40 million in cold cash.

To a chorus of media scoffing, Jones publicly acknowledged he was pursuing Deion. The critics said Jones would have to wreck his budget for a half-a-season cornerback who had hurt his ankle playing baseball and said he needed surgery. Indeed, exploiting the cap loophole carried one penalty: If injury or poor performance forced a team to cut a player, the remainder of his prorated bonus counted against the next year's cap. So, for example, if a big-bonus player failed after two years of a five-year deal, the team would be severely strapped the following year. Big cap hit; no player.

But Jones was using his thinking cap. "My mentality was, I wanted to build a team talent-wise that would be remembered and distinguished, not just in the '90s, but in contemporary times. I mean, twenty years from now, would people be talking about the Dallas Cowboys the way they would Babe Ruth?" The salary-cap, free-agency system precluded the Cowboys from being as deeply talented as they were, say, in 1992, the first Super Bowl season. But what about adding one more superstar?

Jones: "I'm thinking of a collection of athletes, and I'm seeing the MVP in the NFL on defense is out there, free as a breeze. You don't have to give up a thing [in compensation to the 49ers] to get him. And I'm asking myself, 'Why?' I *do* look a gift horse in the mouth. I said, 'Give me the logic of why a player of this ability is available.' All I'd ever heard was that he was 'the best.' If he had been there for us in '89 or '90, he wouldn't have been proven. And if he only had been in Atlanta, you wouldn't have a read on him. His flamboyance would have made you wonder what he would do to your chemistry. But he had proven his ability to meld and be a positive influence for a good team."

Still, outbidding San Francisco—and Al Davis's Raiders—for Deion was scary, says Jones, "because with the team we already had, you might be able to get there [the Super Bowl] without him. So this was a much bigger decision than Herschel Walker. This was much more controversial. The criticism I had gotten [for firing Johnson and hiring Switzer] had bothered me much more [than the criticism for firing Landry]. You'd think you could use two Super Bowls as a way to establish credibility. But I'm one of the few people who can figure a way to be involved in two Super Bowls and *still* have everything to prove."

Of course, Jones didn't just routinely take advantage of the cap loophole. No, he planned to send up a mushroom cloud: a record $13 million up-front bonus for Deion Sanders. Jones's message to rival owners: Don't mess with me.

Jones met with team leaders, then the team. He says he received nothing but positive feedback. Finally, he asked Larry Lacewell to sit with the coaches and study the Deion tapes, "just to make sure he wasn't spending all this money on a bill of goods," says Lacewell. To his astonishment, Lacewell noticed that on the championship game's pivotal play—the uncalled pass interference—that Deion slipped completely down as Michael Irvin came off the line and still caught him. "I told Jerry, 'I've never seen anything like him.' I said, 'It's not my thirteen million. But the only regret I've ever had in life is when I knew I had an opportunity and I didn't do everything I could to take advantage of it. I don't know if we'll win the Super Bowl, but I know we'll have a better chance with this guy. If we win the Super Bowl, that thirteen million will seem like chicken feed.'"

Though some reporters speculated that Jones was bidding against himself, he says no, "I was convinced Deion had other options." The final negotiating session between Jones and Deion's agent, Eugene Parker, took place at the one of Dallas's most exclusive hotels, The Mansion on Turtle Creek. Very late on a Wednesday night/Thursday morning, Jones left the room for a final conference with his son. To the father, the son is the perfect counterbalance: the rational, unemotional chemical engineering major who played college football mostly on wits and who thinks like a conservative coach. Sometimes, Stephen says with a chuckle, "Jerry gets on a mission [to beat the odds and get something done] and I have to stop him early before he gets too focused."

Now, Stephen thought it was time to at least slow down his dad.

Did Deion's bum ankle bother Stephen? Deion's mother had been quoted as saying the injury (sustained three months earlier when Deion slid into third base) could be career-threatening. But Cowboy doctors had examined it and were convinced it wouldn't be a problem. "The ankle was never an issue," says Stephen. Was baseball an issue? No, the elder Jones had a feeling Deion was about ready to give up baseball and concentrate on football—especially if the Cowboys would allow him to be a full-time receiver as well as a cornerback. Not only did Jones want Deion to play offense, but he said, "San Francisco missed the boat not using him more as a kick returner." To cinch matters for Jones, starting cornerback Kevin Smith had ruptured his Achilles tendon on opening night and was lost for the season. Deion had gone from a luxury to almost a necessity.

But perhaps best of all, this was Jones's chance to get even with DeBartolo and Policy, to buy their defensive MVP toy and psychological security blanket right out from under them. Signing Deion was as much about taking him away from the 49ers as making him a Cowboy. *What are we waiting for, Stephen?* Jones was ready to Deion-dance back down the hall and do the deal.

Stephen Jones decided his dad was, well, out of control. *He's going to pay $35 million for five years for a guy who doesn't even play quarterback?* "No question," says Stephen, "I thought it was too much money and too big a gamble." Stephen stood at the door, fists balled, blocking his dad's exit. Jerry shook his head in amazement and said, "What are you going to do, Stephen, punch me in the nose?"

Jerry says it took him a few more minutes to get Stephen "on the same page." Jones says, "Stephen's the keeper of the vault—that's his charge. I've had very few budgets in my life. I've had a lot of nice things said about what a prudent businessperson I am. I'm very frugal and practical. But when it comes to investing and buying, I've always been a risk-taker. I've never let not having money on hand keep me from doing something. I've always been able to borrow anything I wanted—maybe that's a frailty. That can be painful. But Stephen hadn't been involved in every step of the negotiations, and that night, hearing for the first time where we were at, he was taken aback by the numbers. But once I got him comfortable with what it was going to take, he was okay. Of course, he had hoped the deal would be more akin to the one Deion had in San Francisco, where he took less salary and bonus and depended more on his opportunities off the field . . .

"But Deion wanted both."

Being superstitious, Jones reneged on the final dollar of the $13 million bonus. It went in the books as $12,999,999. Yet because Deion had agreed to take a "mere" $178,000 in minimum base salary for each of the first three years, the cap impact was a palatable $2,035,143 ($178,000 plus $1,857,143, the prorated portion of the bonus divided by seven years). The Jones boys tried to beat the system by extending the deal to seven years by giving Deion easily made first-year incentives that could void the final two years of the contract. Naturally, the NFL charged Jones with cap circumvention, and naturally, Jones called a press conference and charged the league with trying to intimidate and undermine the Cowboys. Jones said, "This is not about Deion Sanders's contract. This is about sticking it to the Dallas Cowboys."

Eventually, Jones agreed to increase Deion's cap impact by $411,000. But today, Jones talks about Deion as if he were a steal. Jones has come to enjoy Deion's company at least as much as any Cowboy's. I've never heard Jones—who keeps a healthy employer-employee distance from his other stars—speak so fondly of a player.

Perhaps Jones sees some of himself in Deion: What you see on TV isn't necessarily what you get in private. Each wants to dominate, to shock the world, but each cares foremost about his children. Each has used the media to carefully craft a public image, which doesn't necessarily coincide with his self-image. Says Jones, "When I think how different Deion is from his image, I've never seen anything like it. It's like with the stars of stage and screen: I don't know if [off camera] James Cagney was really that little bull-dog."

Jones is drawn to humans who do rare things, and Deion, says Barry Switzer, is "almost like from another planet," a description Jones loves. It's almost as if, athletically, Deion isn't controlled by the same gravitational pull other earthlings are—as if he can run faster, jump higher, and play stronger than his 190 pounds. At the scouting combine before he was drafted, Deion agreed to run one 40-yard dash. Just one. He slipped out of his warm-up suit, barely warmed up, and said he was ready. *Bang:* He ran in the 4.2s, an unofficial combine record. He immediately slipped back into his warm-ups and left. Around players and coaches, he isn't obnoxiously arrogant, just matter-of-factly confident. He just knows he's better than everyone else.

No mortal can play cornerback the way Deion does. It doesn't matter how quick or slippery or crafty or physical the receiver is, Deion confronts him in nose-to-nose "press" coverage. He hunkers low in his presnap crouch, one foot behind the other, hands circling in a hypnotic, martial-arts motion, the cobra ready to strike. His powerful chest and shoulders are disguised by his sleek arms and legs, and with his incongruous upper body he can strike an immediate blow that knocks the biggest wide receiver off his route and sometimes immobilizes small receivers. Then he's so quick and smart that he almost *becomes* the receiver, moving in maddening harmony with the man's every juke and cut and all-out burst. It's as if the impulses sent by the receiver's brain are going also to Deion's muscles, and he mirrors the poor man's every movement with blithe boredom. Most rival coordinators have learned to ignore the receiver Deion is covering. But occasionally, baited by the apparently disinterested Deion, cocky quarterbacks dare to throw for the receiver he's covering. No cornerback can break on the ball with such incalculable speed. Says Cowboy backup quarterback Wade Wilson, who used to practice against Deion when they were Atlanta teammates: "You just can't convince yourself that if a receiver looks that open and you put the ball in the right spot, he can catch up to it. But he can."

No cornerback has softer hands, quicker leaping ability, or a better sense of hands-to-ball timing than Deion. (Two who have coached him, Denver head coach Mike Shanahan and Atlanta head coach June Jones, say he could be in Jerry Rice's league as a receiver if he dedicated himself year-round to learning the position and developing a rapport with Troy Aikman.) If cornerback Deion gets his hands on a pass, he almost always intercepts it, and he almost always runs a long way with it. In uniform with a ball under his arm, Deion is the NFL's fastest man. He isn't a pretty runner, like Rice. Nothing smooth or graceful or effortless about his style. It's a blur of hands and feet. Here, there, everywhere, *touchdown!*

Then he prances and dances. He plays the "Prime Time" role he created, the act that has generated extra millions in commercial-making, rap singing, and club-owning. "I don't play the game of football," he says. "I *entertain* the game of football." But here's the kicker: Opponents do not complain about Deion's high-stepping or soft-shoeing. Opponents seem to realize there's Deion, then there's "Prime Time." For sure, they know he earns the right to dance. They know he's once-a-century.

The white media especially resents Deion because, in part, he's everything they were always taught not to be as an athlete. He's not even courageous: It's like Deion is the only man on the football field who isn't playing a contact sport. His only injuries are pulls, not breaks. While he can match bumping, grinding, hand-fighting macho with any receiver, he tackles only when necessary. While his endurance is unparalleled—for the Cowboys he has played more snaps in a game, including kick returns, than probably any pro player in modern times—he won't risk his body against kamikaze ball carriers, unless it's to prevent a touchdown. He avoids punishing contact; he doesn't get dirty. He is to football what a young Ali was to boxing or Gretzky has been to hockey: above it.

Yet Jerry Rice is perhaps the only Deion teammate who didn't care for Deion. The rest swear by him, as do all his coaches. "A caring, good person," says Switzer. "Beneath the glitter, very down to earth. He was a catalyst for me with Michael [in helping develop their relationship]." Coaches and teammates describe Deion as quiet, hardworking, and dedicated to knowing everything he can about his opponent. Off camera, Deion actually tries to blend. In Atlanta, Deion became fishing buddies with safety Scott Case, a white guy from Oklahoma with whom Deion would reunite in Dallas. Yes, Deion escapes from "Prime Time" by fishing or playing with his kids.

In Atlanta, Case marveled at young Deion's confidence. Case, who called defensive signals, would duck into the defensive huddle and call some complicated coverage. Deion would grin at him and say, "Case, you guys do whatever you want. I got my nigger." Ho hum: Deion knew his every-down responsibility was to take one receiver completely out of the picture—and he did. (Now, in the Cowboy locker room, Deion often can be heard referring to black teammates as "my nigger," as in, "What's up, my nigger," which he pronounces "naggah." Lots of blacks call other blacks that term, but Deion uses it often, with endearment. Perhaps it's a constant reminder that his race has come a long way. There was a day when it would have been difficult to imagine a rich white man from Arkansas writing a young black man a $13 million check.)

In Dallas, Deion would go fishing with various Scott Cases and John Blakes—not exactly big names. They told me stories of a Deion I didn't see or know. The meet-the-press Deion isn't so lovable or admirable. In fact, Deion brazenly bites the media hand that helps feed him. Who can forget the mean-spirited way Deion responded to announcer Tim McCarver's criticism by repeatedly dousing him with water in the locker room? Several times in 1995, Deion chastised the gathered media or verbally attacked a single critic. Sick of reading his salary in the newspapers, he said, "Every time you mention Troy Aikman's name, why don't you put his salary beside it?"

"Prime Time" will use the media, but Deion makes sure his teammates see he won't suck up. He plays no politics. He wants no friends at the *Dallas Morning News* or Channel 8. His attitude is that the media needs him more than he needs the media. In group interviews, Deion can get be disgustingly arrogant, even surly. Image? Reality? Listening to Jones rhapsodize about Deion, you'd think he was talking about Wally Cleaver. Or does Deion have some Eddie Haskell in him? He definitely doesn't bite the hand that pays him.

Jones says, "He is a very trusting individual. He wants to take you for your positives and look for the best in you. Many times people have said I'm naive about some things, and I see that in him. He likes to have a relationship, until you mess it up. But I don't know that I've ever met anyone as easy to talk to as he is. He is disarming on a one-on-one basis. I was immediately comfortable the first time I sat down with him. He is highly intelligent—maybe one of the smartest people I've been around—in the areas he's smart in, of course. But he is so genuine. So unhurried. He doesn't chatter. He's good with conversation. He just has a charisma, a glow about him. And he's evolving into an exemplary young person with his focus on his two young children [Deiondra and Deion Jr.] and his wife [Carolyn]."

So Jones now sees Deion as an even sounder investment than he originally thought. For sure, Deion's hourly wages will drop dramatically because he'll be available for spring minicamps, training camp, and the entire season. "Spending more time with his children," says Jones, "was a key to his decision to quit playing baseball."

So, he says, signing Deion "was a big bang for '95. But in my mind that was just one-fifth of the deal." He has the man from another planet for four more years. Kryptonite, anyone? Jerry wins again.

In mid-September, though, nothing seemed nearly so certain. While Deion, insisting on ankle surgery, wouldn't be available until October 29, the rest of the NFL was saying, "That's it. Jones bought himself another Super Bowl." A Cowboy source told me, "In a way, the assistant coaches feel sorry for Barry. It's like Jerry has done his part: He has given Barry the best team. Now the pressure's on Barry to win it all. If we lose, it'll be Barry's fault. Who knows? Maybe that's the way Jerry wants it."

Just in case Troy Aikman's contract needed to be restructured, Leigh Steinberg was on the scene at Valley Ranch toward the end of the Deion negotiations. During some downtime, Steinberg mentioned to Jones his concerns about the Aikman-Switzer relationship. Jones suggested he call in the coach so Steinberg, Jones, and Switzer could share some ideas. Great, said Steinberg, who didn't know Switzer. Jones sent for Switzer.

"I must have been in there four hours," said Steinberg. "No Barry Switzer." Typical, thought Steinberg. As Aikman's agent and friend, he had expected Switzer to get to know him. As the agent for Steve Young, Steinberg hears regularly from San Francisco coach George Seifert, who just checks in to make sure everything's okay with his quarterback. As Drew Bledsoe's agent, Steinberg keeps in touch with New England coach Bill Parcells. But when Jones first introduced Steinberg to Switzer, in a social setting, "Switzer acted like he didn't know who I was or care to know," said Steinberg.

I kept telling Steinberg about Switzer's positive qualities, but what more could I say? Once again, Switzer was making the politically incorrect move. Steinberg is Aikman's most trusted advisor. Obviously, Steinberg had no reason to talk Aikman out of his serious doubts about Switzer.

A few days later I suggested to Switzer that it "might be" a good idea to get to know Steinberg. I told him how Steinberg talked occasionally to Seifert and Parcells. Switzer seemed receptive, saying,

"Hey, I haven't been around as long as those guys. I'm still learning about stuff like this."

Still, Switzer made no effort to get in touch with Steinberg. Getting closer to Aikman just didn't seem to be a priority for Switzer. In early September, he appeared to have no idea how deeply the camp curfew-busting episode had affected Aikman. Switzer was about to get his first hint.

That Sunday, the Cowboys beat John Elway's Broncos 31–21. Switzer was ecstatic—until family and friends told him that night about an interview Aikman had done for NBC's pregame show. In it, he called the Cowboys "an assistant coach's team." Aikman later told me he didn't intend that remark as an insult to Switzer. Wasn't Switzer the first to say he delegates to his assistants? Still, Aikman had damned Switzer with no praise.

That night, Switzer's mood fell from jubilant to brooding. He let those around him convince him that Aikman had made him look bad on national TV. "Where's the loyalty?" he asked, as he had even more red wine than usual.

So why, you ask, didn't Switzer pull Aikman aside on Monday and say, "Hey, where did we go wrong?" Why didn't he communicate with his quarterback? Why didn't Barry Switzer, whose strength is his one-on-one rapport with athletes, use every kilowatt of his charisma to win over the most important player in his life? He didn't for any or all of three reasons. He was (1) too proud to "crawl for that kid," especially when Aikman remained friends with so many of Switzer's enemies; (2) a little intimidated and baffled by Aikman; (3) using his old "Oklahoma Method" of ignoring problems until they took care of themselves.

As the leaves turned, Switzer and Aikman spoke less and less.

It would be another month or so before I would ask Jerry Jones about the Aikman-Switzer tension. During September, he was tough to catch because he was so busy being Jerry Jones. Said George Hays, "Jerry has created his own entity, like the Cowboys." What next, Jerry dot com? Steinberg says, "Jerry's rise coalesced with the explosion of cable TV. He realized what a huge celebrity-making machine it is, with its dozens and dozens of shows in search of content." Jones never met an interviewer he didn't like. He almost relishes being grilled by antagonists, such as Mike Ditka, because he believes he can convert them.

Said PR director Rich Dalrymple, "If we win this thing [the Super Bowl], Jerry will become a cult hero."

Soon, Jones and Deion made one of the most loved/hated TV

commercials of the season, the "both" ad for Pizza Hut. It was shot in and around Texas Stadium—nearly eight hours and 138 takes worth—and it ends with Jones asking, "What'll it be, Deion—$15, $20 million?"

"Both," says Deion.

"Both," Jones repeats, as if he should have known.

If possible, the owner upstages the superstar in the ad, which first aired during the first installment of *The Beatles Anthology* miniseries on ABC. Had Jones arrived, or what? Jerry, Deion, and the Beatles on national TV.

"Are we having fun yet, Jerry?" Switzer constantly asked him. Jones rarely had fun with Johnson. So he and Switzer used their inside-joke question to keep reminding each other that the object was to have fun.

Funny, but the only person in the organization who always seemed to be having fun was the owner.

12

BREAK LOVE

It's always something around here.
—*Mickey Spagnola of* The Insider, *leaving the Cowboy complex without seeing Troy Aikman behind him*

And it never has anything to do with football.
—*Troy Aikman*

Y ou'd have thought Barry Switzer had just won the Super Bowl. He was over the top, if not the rainbow. In the Metrodome locker room, his brief postgame talk to the team had turned into what looked more like an "I just won the lottery" commercial. Switzer was *happy* and he wasn't afraid to show it. Switzer calls this "getting nekked with my emotions."

The media normally wouldn't see or hear what Switzer said to the team, but NFL Films had been allowed to capture it for *Six Days to Sunday,* which aired on TNT before hitting the video market. Cameras went behind the scenes for a week with the Cowboys and the Minnesota Vikings, culminating in their Sunday night game. So for fans who had grown up or grown old with Tom Landry's glacial emotions, this inside view set in stone Switzer's image as the Oklahoma wild man who had lost control of himself and his team.

Switzer was "nekked" happy because his team had just won a game it easily could have lost. The Cowboys hadn't played particularly well, but had survived 23–17 in overtime—thanks to two small blessings. With thirty seconds left in regulation, after Viking quarterback Warren Moon had once again taken advantage of 5'10" Cowboy cornerback Clayton Holmes, flipping an 8-yard touchdown pass to 6'3" leaper Cris Carter, Minnesota had opted to kick the extra point and settle for overtime. The next day, the Cowboy coaches took an informal vote and almost unanimously agreed they would have gone for the two-point conversion and the win—probably gone right back to Carter on Holmes. But perhaps the Cowboy coaches had lost sight of how intimidating it is to risk a do-or-die shot at slaying the Dallas dragon. From their viewpoint, they felt fortunate just to get to overtime. They felt even luckier after they won the overtime toss and soon faced a third-and-six.

Troy Aikman hit—no!—Cory Fleming on a "drag" route for 16 yards. Deion Sanders eventually would make Fleming and Clayton Holmes expendable, but for the moment, Fleming was all the Cowboys had as a third receiver on passing downs. As an NFC East scout told me, "What are they thinking, using Cory Fleming? He's too slow to play in this league."

Apparently, Fleming's first professional catch so stunned the Vikings that they couldn't regroup quickly enough to contain Emmitt Smith, who on the next play broke off-tackle and went untouched 31 yards for the winning touchdown. And in the locker room, Switzer was yelling, "Cory Fleming caught a pass! Cory Fleming caught a pass! Cory Fleming caught a pass!"

As Switzer emoted, the *Six Days* camera caught Jerry Jones, in coat and tie, struggling to help Charles Haley pull off his jersey over his shoulder pads.

After Lacewell saw the scene on TNT, he said, "That's the essence of Jerry Jones. That defined him better than anything I've seen. There he was, genuinely trying to help Haley get his jersey off, pulling as hard as he could. He just wants to be a part of everything so badly, to be involved, to help."

Switzer was the one who was about to need help.

Though the team was 3–0, two very important Cowboys were not happy. As usual with this team, public perception (a crazy-happy Switzer) did not match unreported reality: Sitting in front his locker, Charles Haley listened to Switzer's gushing and muttered, "Fuck that. We played like shit."

Aikman thoroughly agreed with Haley. If you could have heard Aikman on the plane ride home, you might have thought the Cowboys had lost. Aikman shared his complaints with a small group of players (and with Dale Hansen and Brad Sham). But word of the quarterback's dissatisfaction spread through the players' section and irritated a few of the veterans—"What does he *want*?"—who complained to assistant coaches such as John Blake, who told Switzer. Aikman later heard "from some media people" that Switzer criticized his negative attitude. Aikman says, "I definitely wasn't happy with the way we'd played. Yet I heard Switzer was saying, 'Why is Aikman motherfucking everybody? He didn't play so hot, either.' Terry Donahue [who coached Aikman at UCLA] always told me, 'Appreciate a win, because sometimes you play well and don't win.' But this [the 1995 season] wasn't about one game at a time. I knew what our goal was, and I didn't like the way we were preparing for it."

Aikman resented being seen as the boy who cried wolf. He saw several very real wolves down the schedule, waiting to take bites out of the Cowboys' goal. Wasn't it Super Bowl or bust? Was he the only one left in the franchise who how much total team concentration and dedication are required to win a championship in the thirty-team NFL? Was he going to have to be the head coach as well as the quarterback? He knew full well that Jimmy Johnson would have found the Cowboys' overall performance in Minnesota extremely unacceptable. In fact, in the same Metrodome locker room in December of 1993, Johnson had blown up at the defense for drifting mentally and allowing a late Viking touchdown that cut the Cowboys' final margin of victory to 37–20.

So, the day after the overtime win, Switzer thought, "Okay, big boy. Here goes." Switzer responded to Aikman's criticism by doing something he hadn't yet dared: He criticized Aikman in front of the team. Well, sort of. At the end of a longer, calmer, more analytical and objective assessment of the Minnesota performance, Switzer said of Aikman's on-and-off 24 of 38 for 246 yards: "And we can't throw the ball in the dirt." Which was a nice, safe way to say, "And by the way, Troy, what the hell was wrong with you, bouncing so many passes to receivers? It's hard for us to put a team away on the road when you make that many bad throws."

So was Aikman shocked and stung by the criticism? Or quietly delighted that the head coach had shown the team that even the quarterback wasn't above his wrath?

Aikman was neither.

Apparently, Switzer's criticism was so sanitized that it went right over Aikman's head. After the season, when I asked Aikman how it felt for Switzer to finally get on him in front of the team, he had no recollection of it.

Incredible. Switzer and Blake thought the head coach had taken a bold step with the franchise quarterback—while Aikman still thought Switzer was in his eat-drink-and-chase-Mary mode. Blake told me, "Really, Troy wants coach Switzer to get on him, and coach isn't completely comfortable doing that. But he finally did this time."

If, as Switzer says, Deion is from another planet, then Switzer and Aikman were living on different planets or at least in parallel worlds. It was as if they were talking about different Minnesota games, attending different team meetings, speaking different languages—clinging to opposite ends of the elephant. So many of their reactions to each other were based on "I heard he told so-and-so." If this conflict weren't about to turn so vicious, it could be viewed as comical or at least juvenile. But this was no "Who's on First" routine. "Who's Gone First" would be more like it.

John Blake was feeling good about his new svelte self and the performance of his defensive linemen, who had been dominantly disruptive in the first three games. Blake was feeling light enough on his feet to regain some of the form that won him college dance contests. During one lunch hour in his office, I was openly skeptical about his dancing ability in hopes of goading him into a brief performance. As luck would have it, his favorite Janet Jackson video, "Runaway," came up next on VH1 (the cable station several coaches use as office background music), and Blake went into a slick, convincing spin. It appeared his ability to start and occasionally star at nose guard for Oklahoma was based more on his light-footed agility than any macho mean streak. Blake was not your stereotypical ex–defensive lineman still capable of suffering a psycho flashback and breaking all the furniture in his office. No, Blake was a gentle soul who motivated his players with one-on-one soul talk instead of group humiliation. "Boo" Blake was active in his church and close to his pastor. Like Switzer, he was quick to tell his players or close friends how much he loved them.

Ironically, while Bud Light's relentless "I love you, man" commercial was based on "Johnny's" transparent insincerity, John Blake and his head coach preached genuine love. Switzer really did love you, man.

Blake had even come up with a pro football battle cry based on love. Occasionally when I walked down the hall with him, one of his players would pass and Blake would say, "Gotta break some love, baby." Break what? Blake explained, "You know how your mama used to whip you because she loved you? She would *bring love* to you. So we need to *bring love* to our opponents, but we want to break it off in 'em."

Sure, this being the NFL, and not the Ice Capades, defensive linemen couldn't just *bring love* to opponents who need to be shown the error of their ways. No, a defensive lineman's love for an enemy quarterback must be broken off in him like an arrow, to teach him a lasting lesson.

Hence: "Gotta break some love."

In the next few weeks, though, Cowboy players and coaches would be breaking love off in each other, and John Blake would want to break one neck, Charles Haley's. Haley tormented Blake, who was just three years older. Of course, Haley would have gotten on Gandhi's nerves, but Blake and Haley's teammates called him "Dog," short for "Bad Dog," as in "beware of."

Blake was losing sleep and feeling "stressed" over Haley because Blake couldn't quite understand why Haley had to make life so difficult for his teammates and coaches. Haley wasn't self-destructive, he was team-destructive. Vintage Haley: Before a defensive line meeting, Blake told Haley that a teammate was having problems with his girlfriend and asked that Haley "please lay off him just for one day." Blake might as well have thrown a raw steak in front of a bad dog. Haley proceeded to tell the teammate in sickening detail how he had slept with the girlfriend the night before—a very bad joke. Haley couldn't differentiate between what was affectionately funny ribbing and over-the-line insulting.

Why, Blake wondered, was Haley still such a nightmare when he was playing for his dream coach? Unlike Jimmy Johnson, Switzer didn't care that Haley rarely practiced. Switzer let Haley do and say whatever he wanted, as long as he was ready to play by Sunday's kickoff. Switzer actually liked Haley. Switzer appreciated his talent, his football savvy, even his financial acumen. "He's smart as hell with his money," said Switzer. Switzer saw the good in a Haley who could be a nice guy around fans in public and who was always great with kids.

But Charles Haley has a revoltingly rude and crude side that has prompted black teammates to call him the "missing link" or "Cong" and leave monkey dolls or pictures of monkeys in his locker. When his 49er teammates angered him, Haley sometimes responded by defecating in their lockers or urinating on their cars. But the Cowboys and their coaches had worked to be more tolerant of (if not oblivious to) Haley's nonstop low-blow needling. They learned to be careful when kidding Haley back, because he could be a very defensive end, a sensitive bully. Haley sometimes took the most innocuous comments by teammates and coaches as insults to his manhood or as racial slurs. Haley's feelings were constantly on injured reserve.

"Charles," says Blake, "is not a fighter." Returning a Haley insult didn't mean having to whip Haley. It meant having to repair his pride. Remember, upon re-signing Haley in the off-season, Jerry Jones pretty much had said the Cowboys couldn't win a Super Bowl without their pass-rush specialist. Who wanted to be responsible for damaging Haley's psyche and costing the team a game? So everyone tried to live with Charles Haley.

Blake said, "Jimmy couldn't control him. [Former defensive coordinator] Butch [Davis] couldn't control him. But coach Switzer and I have done a pretty good job of handling Charles. You just have to let Charles be Charles and hope he doesn't disrupt every-thing you do."

Blake's biggest concern was that Haley was stunting the growth of the player Blake considered his prize pupil, 6'6", 288-pound Leon Lett. "Big Cat," as he's called, had Blake's shy, softer personality. No "Bad Dog" in "Cat." Lett had Deion-like athletic gifts, without Deion's savvy, work ethic, or confidence. Lett is so quick and strong for his size that it's sometimes unfair. "Leon," says Blake, "could be the best [defensive lineman] who ever played—better than Reggie White. He's a better athlete than Reggie, and he's not dumb. He won't talk [to the media] because he's afraid he'll sound dumb. But he knows football. To play well, Leon just has to practice hard and study. Leon could be better without Charles around. [Tony] Tolbert and Russell [Maryland] are dedicated enough that it doesn't matter. But Charles isn't a good influence on Leon. Charles knows exactly what he has to do to get ready. In meetings, Charles will be acting a fool and cracking on everybody until I say, 'Charles, this is the guy you're going against.' Then it's . . ." Blake locks his eyes on an imagi-nary screen. "Charles will find a weakness in a guy and really exploit it. He is so quick, and much stronger than most people think. But he mostly beats guys because he's smarter than they are."

Yet Haley wasn't so smart off the field. "I try to tell Charles how big he could be if he handled the media the way he's capable of, but he won't listen." Haley almost never talks to the media during the week and often uses the brief interviews he allows after games to complain about something or somebody. "Then," says Blake, "Charles always gets upset about things that are written."

Everyone in the organization respected Haley's four Super Bowl rings and his rage to win, but they waited like bullied kids with lunch money for the next opportunity Haley would seize to remind them just how important he was. He was holding them hostage: Jones had given him a $3 million up-front bonus on a four-year, $12 million contract. So, for instance, if Haley quit, or had to retire because of injury, he still would count $1.5 million against the 1996 salary cap. The Haley contract, said several insiders, "might have been our one mistake."

This should come as no surprise: While Barry Switzer didn't voice much postgame disappointment in the 34–20 victory over Arizona, except to say it "got ragged," Aikman went public with his concerns. The Cowboys had nearly let a hot-handed Arizona quarterback Dave Kreig cut their cushion to seven in the fourth quarter, thanks to a fumble by rookie running back Sherman Williams. Again, given the same opening, Jimmy Johnson would have done more overacting than Al Pacino in *Scarface*. Aikman eased into the Jimmy role by telling the media: "A football team needs to learn it's a sixty-minute game . . . What took place in the last four minutes was frustrating . . . I'm not complaining about the fact we're 4–0. I'm talking about the little things we need to work on."

Little things? A few days later I spoke with Leigh Steinberg, who said Aikman was so upset with Switzer's attitude during the fourth quarter that he just didn't think he could play another season for the guy. Steinberg cautioned that Aikman, like many of his NFL clients, tends to overreact during the season. But: "Troy said that during the fourth quarter, Switzer acted like he didn't even care. It was like he had lost interest in the game and quit paying attention, and Arizona almost got back in the game. Troy was just beside himself."

Of course, the Switzer camp was frustrated by Aikman's critical postgame quotes. Their general reaction: "Troy, no team in NFL history has played the perfect game—no penalties, interceptions, fumbles, drops, missed tackles, off-line passes . . . "

Switzer felt so good about the 4–0 start that he allowed himself to scan the schedule and told confidants, "We've got a chance to run the table." Barring injuries to stars, the Cowboys would be favored to win every game. Especially the next one, against the 1–3 Redskins in Washington.

A source in the Redskin front office later told me, "We knew we had a chance when Switzer was asked about the [Dallas-Washington] rivalry and he [flippantly] said, 'It takes two teams to have a rivalry.' He was being honest. But you can't say that to your players when you're having to go through a sixteen-game season. You have to keep getting their attention. You have to say, 'God, the Redskins beat the hell out of Arizona, they nearly won at Denver and Tampa Bay, and they were six-all with the Raiders going into the fourth quarter.'"

Washington coach Norv Turner later said to me, "We were in the perfect spot."

The weather even cooperated. It was the best I've experienced in the twenty-two games I've covered at RFK, which I call Rickety Field for Knuckleheads. It was a picture-postcard day in a mug-shot neighborhood. Usually, it's suffocatingly humid in September or game-ruining cold and windy in November or December. But for the Cowboys, this October 1 game, which started and finished in daylight, was played under deceptively tranquil skies.

The Redskins won the toss and quickly wound up in a fourth-and-19 hole at their 16. "This one," I thought, "is going to get messy." They punted Dallas back to its 45, but here came the Cowboys, ripping off big gains. "Blowout," I thought. I didn't think much about a third-and-3 at the Redskin 14. I had seen Aikman convert these things as routinely as he signs autographs at a card show.

Then it happened.

Aikman took a short drop. As he merely touched his right toe to the grass, to plant and throw, his leg retracted like a landing gear and he began to fall backward. He still got rid of the ball, though his unexpected plunge perhaps pulled the short pass off-line, and Daryl Johnston couldn't quite snag it. Aikman went down as if hit in the back of the right calf by a sniper's bullet. I'd seen this several times before.

"That's it," I said to no one in particular in the pressbox. "Season over." Surely Aikman had torn his Achilles tendon. It always happens when an athlete least expects it, as if the mighty warrior Achilles is still up there, getting even for his vulnerable heel by randomly victimizing the tendon named after him.

But a few minutes later, this routine announcement was made in the pressbox: "The Cowboys say Troy Aikman has a strained calf and that he probably won't return." Come again? I was surprised enough that Aikman's Achilles wasn't involved, but he probably wouldn't return with a strained calf? Surely one of Aikman's calf muscles was torn. Otherwise, a Troy Aikman with a reputation for being tougher than Tombstone would take a pain-killing injection and drag a bawling calf muscle back onto the field, especially if the game stayed close in the third or fourth quarter.

Midway through the third quarter, the Cowboys fell behind 27–10. No Aikman. Strange.

Now we got our first look at what would become Switzer's Achilles heel—the heat-of-battle decision-making ability of Switzer and his staff. On the following Cowboy series, they suddenly faced a fourth-and-2 at the Washington 17. Still plenty of time, 3:26 left in the third quarter. Go for it? Or take a 34-yard field goal? For a moment, confusion appeared to ensue on the Cowboy sideline. (Afterward, a stormy Switzer, usually so complimentary of his assistants, blamed "one of my assistants" for wrongly telling him it was fourth-and-"less than a yard.") With many of the offensive players on the field lobbying to go for the first down, Switzer finally decided to take the field goal. As Emmitt Smith came off the field, he made the mistake of expressing his disappointment to Switzer, who unleashed some "nekked" anger on him. This was not acting. This was Switzer, jumping in Emmitt's face and yelling that he had been given "the wrong fuckin' information" and that no coach in his right mind was going to go for it on fourth-and-2 with so much time left!

Taken aback, Emmitt backed off.

Emmitt's legitimate reason to scream came with about five minutes left in the game. Trailing 27–20, the Cowboys moved to first-and-goal at the Washington 9—thanks mostly to Emmitt. On first down, he carried for 4 yards, but unfortunately for the Cowboys, that would be his last carry of the day. By calling two straight pass plays, offensive coordinator Ernie Zampese chose to put the game in the hands of backup quarterback Wade Wilson. Twice Wilson looked to Michael Irvin, who was wearing Redskins like new jewelry. Twice Wilson had to go to secondary receivers, one for no gain and one incomplete. On fourth-and-goal at the 5, with 4:20 left, Switzer quickly called for the field goal.

I agreed with the decision, and said so the next night on ESPN. What were the odds, with Irvin having to hand-fight two Redskins in a tight space, of Wade Wilson (or even Troy Aikman) throwing a touchdown pass from five yards? Not great. Why not cut the lead to 27–23, trust your defense to hold the Redskins, as the Cowboys had the last quarter and a half, get the ball back with maybe two minutes left, and go for the win?

Several in the organization did not agree with that logic. At least one assistant coach in the pressbox threw his headset in frustration. But the next day, when Larry Lacewell gently tried to cross-examine Switzer about his thought process, the coach was in no mood for constructive criticism and began to boil. Ironically, Switzer had made the conservative choice—the one he would be ridiculed for not making two months later on a fourth down in Philadelphia. Switzer later told me he followed the same protocol he always does as the Cowboys approach a critical point: "I'm on the headset with Ernie, Robert [Ford] and Jason [backup quarter-

back and potential coach Garrett], and we're constantly talking
what-ifs as we move down the field. So I said to Ernie, 'You want to
take the field goal?' And he said, 'Damn right.' Robert and Jason
were all for it, too."

Yet at Oklahoma, Switzer was connected by headset to
Lacewell, then Gary Gibbs—two defensive coordinators he knew
and whose flash-point instincts he trusted. If, from the pressbox,
Lacewell or Gibbs said, "Go for it!" Switzer went. But even in his
second season in Dallas, he didn't feel completely comfortable with
Zampese. Switzer didn't second-guess himself on taking the field
goal, but he said he made a mistake by not ordering Zampese to run
Emmitt three straight times from the 9 yard line. That's the head
coach's job (though that never had been Switzer's strength). It is not
Switzer's job to tell the coordinator which running play to run, just
to provide overview direction such as, "Emmitt's rolling. Let's keep
giving it to him." Even Zampese later admitted he should have ridden Emmitt two more times. But Switzer still had too much respect
for Zampese's NFL-made reputation. If it was possible for a man to
feel alone in a packed stadium, Switzer, with most of Johnson's old
staff, felt alone.

Of course, Switzer would have looked brilliant if the Cowboy
defense had held and the offense had roared in for the winning
touchdown. But Redskin running back Terry Allen continued to rip
off key gains on the way to 121 total yards on thirty carries. The
Redskins killed the clock and the Cowboys, 27–23, and Cowboy fans
everywhere suddenly had to know What Went Wrong and Who Gets
the Blame.

On Monday, Aikman and Wilson pretty much answered both
questions by saying they would have gone for the touchdown with
4:20 left in the game. That's all that talk-show callers needed to
hear: Switzer got the blame.

To understand what happened next—and more important, what
would happen after the Washington-at-Dallas game on December 3—listen to a story Lacewell tells about Switzer from the
national championship season of 1975. The Sooners were Orange
Bowl–bound, thanks in part to halfback Horace Ivory. But a graduate assistant hired by Lacewell told Lacewell that, while on dorm
duty, he twice had told Ivory his girlfriend would have to leave.
Ivory got mad and told the graduate assistant, "I'll be here a lot
longer than you will." Lacewell got madder and "made the mistake"
of saying to Switzer, "How far are we going to let these guys go? Are
we in control here or are they?" Mostly, Lacewell just needed to vent

to his best friend Switzer. Sufficiently unburdened, Lacewell went Christmas shopping. When he returned, Switzer had dismissed Ivory from the squad. "I was shocked," says Lacewell, who hadn't wanted the head coach to go *that* far. The Sooners still beat Michigan 14–6, but that was Lacewell's first indication of just how careful a trusted assistant must be when telling Switzer about a player problem. It's like smoking in the forest.

John Blake was still learning this. He once marveled to me, "The littlest thing can set him off." But he still perhaps didn't quite appreciate the firepower at his fingertips. On Monday morning after the Washington loss, Lacewell sat in with Blake and the other defensive coaches reviewing the wreckage on tape. They quickly confirmed that one player besides Aikman had been missing in action. Charles Haley had complained that his back pain had flared again, and Switzer had held him out of the starting lineup. But Haley had played much of the game. And again and again, Norv Turner had run Terry Allen at Haley, who had registered two whole tackles (and no sacks). So the coaches sat and cussed Charles Haley. They cussed how many times he ignored the defense called and refused to play his "technique" and cover his assigned gap. They cussed how he insisted on lining up in a left-handed stance at right end. They cussed how he often freelanced and went for spectacular stat-building sacks that never materialized.

So actually, the Cowboys had played without their best offensive and best defensive players. It appeared to the coaches that Haley pretty much had taken the day off (and Switzer already had granted the guy Monday and the usual Tuesday off so he could stay in his native Virginia).

Blake made the mistake of venting about Haley to Switzer. That afternoon, Switzer blamed much of the loss on the defensive line for not playing its technique. Switzer might have gotten away with only saying that, but he named the perpetrators: Tony Tolbert, Leon Lett . . . and Charles Haley. Lacewell said, "Switzer was trying to do what everyone wants and be a tough guy. He was trying to criticize Haley as part of the defensive line and it backfired. He had to eat crow. He didn't have any choice. I mean, Haley was going to quit."

In a story splashed across the top of Friday's *Dallas Morning News* with the headline "Switzer apologizes to defensive linemen," Switzer was quoted as saying, "I made a mistake, and I'm man enough to admit it . . . I think that it's wrong for me to cite individual players. There is no need to criticize, and I'm not going to do it anymore. It doesn't help them emotionally to prepare and focus the next week."

Switzer's version to me: "I chewed their fucking asses out in the [Monday] meeting, when they deserved it and they knew it." Haley, however, wasn't present. "Then I made the mistake and mentioned the same thing to the media. John Blake came to me and said, 'Coach, Leon and Tony don't mind getting their asses chewed, but if you bring the media into it, you put them in a position of having to respond to all those damn microphones and cameras in their faces, and neither one of 'em is very comfortable doing that.' So I went out [on Thursday] and pulled the defensive line aside and said, 'Look, I'm not apologizing to you fuckers for chewing your asses out, just for saying it to the media.' That's what everyone missed."

Aikman, though, thought he understood perfectly. Charles was in charge. Or Lett or Tolbert or Blake or anyone but the head coach, who publicly had been backed down by his defensive line. Aikman had never heard anything quite like it. The inmates were officially running the asylum. Several in the Aikman camp told me something like, "That was the end of whatever respect Troy had left for Switzer."

But Lacewell, trying to see both sides, said, "I can understand why Troy is upset. But he has to understand that Switzer didn't apologize for Switzer. Hell, ninety percent of the coaches in this league wouldn't have swallowed their pride and apologized. But Switzer did it for the team. What if Haley had quit? Then all the players would have been saying, 'That idiot Switzer.'"

As usual, Barry Switzer, coach of the 4–1 Cowboys, couldn't win for winning.

Switzer says that over the months, he had mentioned a couple of times to Aikman to be careful about his ongoing relationships with Norv Turner and Jimmy Johnson. "I told him, I'm not going to interfere with those relationships—I'd be stupid to even try." In Switzer's world, friendships prevail. "But I told him some things will have to be filtered out. I think he's smart enough to realize what the agendas are. I told him he has to understand the agendas of people like Hansen and Galloway. It's obvious they want to see me fail."

But several in the Switzer camp were beginning to wonder if Aikman wanted to see Switzer fail. Remember, these were well-intentioned people who cared deeply and sometimes blindly about him: John Blake, Danny Bradley, Dean Blevins, Becky Buwick, Switzer's children, and other ex-Sooners who remain in constant touch with Switzer.

The suspicions took shape that week when Aikman—though limping—was able to practice on Wednesday, Thursday, and Friday.

Several Switzer loyalists asked me something like, "Where was the $50 million man when we needed him Sunday? He can practice now, but he couldn't even come back in the game and at least hand off to Emmitt?" What happened, they wanted to know, to the "toughest man in the NFL"?

They began to wonder if Aikman had, in effect, taken a dive—and as far-fetched as that seems, I could understand their suspicion under the far-fetched circumstances. By this point, the Switzer camp had no doubt about how much Aikman disliked playing for Switzer and how much he missed playing for Turner. I have no doubt that if Aikman could have snapped his fingers and made Turner the Cowboy coach and Switzer the Redskin coach, he would have. In phone conversations with Turner, Aikman had brought up the idea as wishful thinking—as in, "Man, I wish you could . . ." But Turner says he never kicked around the idea with Aikman even as a "wouldn't it be nice . . ." He says he told Aikman it just wasn't going to happen. He was in the second year of a five-year deal. He was committed to rebuilding the Redskins.

"I don't *want* that job," Turner said emphatically after the 1995 season. Turner knew, from the inside out, what an ordeal it would be serving as Jerry Jones's ringmaster.

Still, no one in the Switzer camp knew Turner felt that way the week after the first Washington loss. They understandably wondered if Aikman had used a minor injury as an excuse not to return to the game—perhaps to undermine Switzer or perhaps just to help his soul mate Turner establish his credibility in Washington. The Redskins had gone 3–13 in Turner's honeymoon season, and after a 1–3 start, they appeared headed for a similarly hopeless finish. Redskin fans would start losing their patience. But to either coach, a Dallas-Washington game can have the same impact as the Texas-Oklahoma rivalry: Win one, and your fans will forget about several other losses. Win two in a season, as Turner eventually would in '95, and a 6–10 finish will be remembered fondly by fans as "the year we beat the world champion Cowboys twice." Whether he did so knowingly or subconsciously or unwittingly, Aikman eventually did Turner two huge favors in '95.

Was the first favor exaggerating the severity of his calf strain? Aikman and Turner both scoff at that conspiracy theory. Turner says, "That's the most absurd thing I ever heard." Aikman first strained the muscle in practice the week before. Several weeks later, team doctor Robert Vandermeer told me, "If he wasn't hurt, it sure was a great imitation. He's still tender." Aikman says that the Saturday night before the game after the Redskins, against Green Bay at

Texas Stadium, he told teammate and friend Dale Hellestrae, "I made a mistake [by practicing and saying he would play in the game]. I shouldn't play. I can't move. I've been watching the tape [of the previous year's playoff win over Green Bay] and I'm going to be a sitting duck against those guys."

Hellestrae said, "So why are you playing?"

Aikman said, "I just feel like I have to."

So why, wondered those in the Switzer camp, hadn't he felt the same way in Washington? Why wouldn't doctors have to put a straitjacket on him to keep him from limping back onto the field with anything short of a torn Achilles?

Because it hurt too much, says Aikman. The strained calf was simply so painful he couldn't run or even drop back to throw, he says. "In fact," Aikman told me two weeks after the season, "it *still* isn't right."

That Sunday, as he warmed up for the Green Bay game, he told Wade Wilson to "stay loose" because "I didn't think I'd last too long." But though Aikman limped occasionally, he did more than last. He played perhaps his best overall game of the season, hitting 24 of 31 for 316 yards and two touchdowns and outplaying Brett Favre (21 of 41 for 295, one TD, one interception). Without a turnover, the Cowboys won 34–24.

Sometimes, an injury heightens an athlete's concentration. A quarterback is so concerned about how the injury will hinder him that he plays completely within himself, only attempting the throws and maneuvers he is most confident in executing. Maybe Aikman was so unstoppably effective because he didn't heap pressure on himself to carry the team on the field and the sidelines. Maybe, this time, he said to himself, "Just take it a play at a time and do the best you can." Jerry Jones says, "I like it when Troy's all concerned about his calf and he gets cautious and throws the ball away like he should and doesn't even think about running out of the pocket. Now we're talking about Marino—a guy who could last six or eight more years."

Then again, you can imagine what Switzer's family and friends thought after watching such a great Aikman performance seven days after he sat out nearly all of the Washington loss.

After Green Bay, Switzer tried to joke to the media that "I'll take a pulled calf every time to get that kind of performance." But privately he was concerned about the depth of the Aikman-Turner relationship and how it was affecting the quarterback. His suspicions were stoked by those of the family and friends he trusted. They were saying what Blake said: "Obviously, you have to wonder if Troy's trying to get Norv back here." Didn't they talk by phone every week?

They did. But, says Turner, "if he [Switzer] only knew the number of times I've given Troy a pep talk." Several times when the Cowboys struggled during the '95 season, says Turner, he reminded Aikman of similar struggles in '92 and '93—years in which the Cowboys eventually won the Super Bowl. Turner says he heard through the grapevine that the Switzer camp wondered what his intentions were in keeping in frequent touch with Aikman. To plant subtle but negative thoughts in Aikman's head about Switzer? After all, it's a cutthroat business. Said Blake, "Seriously, does Troy really think Norv and Jimmy really and truly love him, or do they love what he did for them? He helped get Norv a head-coaching job, and he helped make Jimmy a legend."

Turner says, "I was really upset that they thought I was undermining. That is so far from the truth."

Truth? Through all the pressure and paranoia, the overreaction and miscommunication, I was finding it more and more difficult to identify the truth, which was one thing to the Switzer camp, another to the Aikman camp, yet another to Charles Haley, a camp unto himself.

As Lacewell says, the Cowboys' Valley Ranch complex, is the "greatest show on Earth." Originally designed by Tex Schramm, it sprawls at the base of a long, steep hill in the middle of a booming community out near the airport. Hundreds of media people from around the country know the way to Valley Ranch, which on many days is the sports equivalent of one big grocery-store checkout rack of tabloid stories. Dissension! Lawsuits! Denials! Threats! Vows! Hurry, hurry: At least one headline story happens on the slowest news day at Valley Ranch. Says Switzer, "A quiet week around here would be a distraction."

Maybe the one-story building, with its miles and miles of hallways (some as yet unexplored by man), is overelectrified. On any given day during the season, FOX, ESPN, ABC, NBC, CBS, CNN, HBO, and six or seven local radio stations have run enough cable into and around Valley Ranch to blow up Russia. Maybe so many billions of rival ESPN electrons and FOX protons are colliding that brain waves are altered, and suddenly Charles Haley is speaking in tongues to the multiplying cameras, making stop-the-world statements he soon won't remember making.

That's about the only way to explain what happened next.

Following Switzer's apology, the Cowboy brass was so concerned about Haley's emotional instability that they prepared themselves for the worst. Might he come out for the Green Bay game in uniform, then walk up into the stands and watch the game with his family? Might he suddenly strip naked during player introductions and walk out of the stadium, never to return? These reactions wouldn't have surprised the front-office executives, who often called Haley a "time bomb."

Yet what Haley *did* do surprised everyone in the organization, especially the head coach.

Switzer had planned to take Jones's private jet to see his son Doug play quarterback in a Saturday night game for Arkansas Pine Bluff. But he decided to stay in Dallas—a sacrifice for Switzer, considering his love for his kids—mostly because Haley was ticking. Sunday morning before the game, Switzer talked with Haley, just to see how he felt physically and emotionally. Remember, Haley had been Switzer's biggest supporter among players—Switzer's buddy—and the coach usually had a pretty good read on the hieroglyphics flashing through Haley's head. Switzer says, "I had been told by the trainers that Charles's back was so bad that he might not even dress. So Sunday morning, I said to him, 'How's the back?' and he said, 'It's okay.' So I said, 'You tell me when you feel like playing, and we'll try to get you in some nickel [passing-down] situations.'" Switzer felt good about the exchange with Haley and told John Blake to monitor Haley.

Midway through the second quarter, Blake asked Haley if he felt like playing. Blake said, "We need you, big man." Haley said, sure, he'd play. And, just as an injured Aikman was doing a Lazarus on the Packers, so did Haley. Three times he made great escapes and would have sacked Favre, if not for the quarterback's unusual athletic ability.

Several assistants speculated that Haley's postgame explosion was the result of simply being ticked about missing the three sacks. If that's so, you dread to think what have happened if he narrowly had missed four or five sacks. Would lives have been endangered at the nearest post office?

Haley told the media, "They can do the stuff to fuck with my mind this year, but they'll never get me back in this uniform again . . . I don't know what's going on. They have reduced me to a second-string player, and that's not me. They can give the public any excuse they want about my back, but I live to play on Sundays regardless of what's going on . . . I'm being blamed for everybody's play."

Forgive me if I don't even attempt to explain any of that. Haley even blamed Switzer for apologizing to him. Haley said, "He made the point sincere [to the media], so live with it. Don't come back and apologize. That's bullshit. I don't play that."

Randy Galloway wrote in the *Morning News:* "Here's a guarantee—once Haley's comments reach San Francisco ears, they will be treated as the most joyous news from Dallas since Jimmy Johnson left town." Galloway quoted Aikman as saying, "I told Jerry before the game, if we don't win this one, all hell could break loose."

But they *had* won, and all Haley had broken loose.

Switzer was at a loss. "I was shocked," he told me the following week. "But I think he went home and reconsidered. I know his wife and his mother said to him, 'What are you *doing?*' I went to him Monday and said, 'Where the hell did we go wrong?' After we talked about it, he was fine."

From "I'll never wear this uniform again" to "fine"? Blake tried to explain: "Charles told me, 'I don't know if I can get back.' He was trying to tell me he was feeling really down. He said, 'I don't know if I can come out of it.' The way you handle Charles is you tell him you love him. Charles knows coach Switzer loves him. But Charles has so much pride that he couldn't take coach Switzer criticizing him." Blake sighed. "We should have just gone on and started Charles [against Green Bay]. From now on we'll start him, and if he can't go, we'll pull him."

It should also come as no surprise that for most of October, Switzer suffered flulike symptoms and exhaustion that forced him to take occasional afternoon naps in his office.

It was a Wednesday, about 12:30 P.M. I happened past Switzer's office and out he came, looking college-preppy in a Polo pullover shirt, shorts, and loafers without socks. Like Aikman, Switzer has a chewing-tobacco side and an "L.A." side. "Want to see my house?" he asked me.

A moment later, we were in his BMW, covering the 2.2 miles to the only security development in Coppell, called River Chase. There, across a canal from the golf course, is Switzer's haven from the Valley Ranch madness—about 4,000 square feet of two-story, three-bedroom French contemporary. (Actually, it's four bedrooms if you count the walk-in closet off the downstairs master bedroom.) At the time, the house was maybe two-thirds completed. Switzer stopped at the front door to confer with a worker in a torn, dirty T-shirt and cowboy hat. Though Switzer didn't seem to know the man, he asked him, "You like the random stones around the door or the mortar?"

Though the man didn't appear to know much English, he listened carefully and said, "Oh, stones."

Switzer nodded and studied the door some more. Yes, stones.

This is Switzer's dream house, so far removed from his childhood home without indoor plumbing. Vintage Switzer: Originally, the wrong toilets were installed in his new house. When his kids discovered the first one, they told their dad it was like "a 7-Eleven toilet." Switzer was angry. All but winking at each other, they hurried to the next bathroom. "Another 7-Eleven toilet!" Now Switzer was cussing. Egging him on, the kids moved to another bathroom: "7-Eleven!" Now Switzer was in a rage while his kids were breaking up with laughter and telling him it would be okay. They would just have the toilets replaced.

Inside, Switzer proudly showed me where a $26,000 Steinway piano would go for son Greg . . . and where a small backyard had been added beside the pool for Kathy's dog, Oskie . . . and where a $10,000, 250,000-BTU pizza oven would be installed for his friend Patsy Benso, owner of Othello's in Norman. Patsy and his family would come cook Switzer and his kids Italian feasts, just like in Norman. Just like old times. Just 2.2 miles away would be reality and sanity.

On the way back, Switzer said, "Look, I know how bad Troy wants to win this sumbitch [the Super Bowl]. But I guarantee you, he doesn't want to win it any worse than I do. Maybe I don't show it the way he wants me to, but I guarantee you I feel it."

"You really take it hard?" I said.

"It's eatin' me alive," he said, barely audible above the purr of the BMW.

Though I was afraid he'd be late for practice, he suddenly said, "I'm hungry. Want something?" And into McDonald's went the head coach of the Dallas Cowboys. "Ya'll got any hamburgers left?" he asked the kids behind the counter, who treated him as if he were a regular.

13

FAMILY SECRETS

*Let him who is without sin among you cast the
first stone . . .*

—*John 8:7*

On the flight to San Diego, the coaches were informed by
Stephen Jones that linebacker Darrin Smith was no longer a
contract holdout. Smith, who had Pro Bowl speed and playmaking
ability, finally had come to terms (if not his senses). He would be
available for the October 29 game in Atlanta, following the San
Diego game and a bye week. Deion Sanders would also debut in
Atlanta, where he began his NFL career. One good and one great
player were about to add several thousand volts to the Dallas
defense.

Remembered quote from Jerry Jones, early in training camp,
when signing Deion was thought by many to be a hype dream: "Boy,
I sure would like to have Deion and Darrin join us about midseason. That might be just what we need."

How many rival fans would secretly love to have Jones running
their team?

John Blake made his way to the back of the plane and circulated among the players—"my boys"—then returned to first class
and reported to Switzer that "they're excited. They say the house is
built."

Yes, a fortress was built—on quicksand. The Cowboys were

about to have a day at the beach against the Chargers, who were
without starting quarterback Stan Humphries. They were about to
cruise 23–9, to go 6–1 with a week off—and they were one big
happy mirage. Troy Aikman was given permission to stay on the
West Coast for a couple of days. He spent some time with Steinberg. They discussed the possibility of asking for a trade after the
season. Aikman, said Steinberg, had concluded he could not play
another season for Switzer.

Ho hum, another day in paradise.

Another indication of the coach-quarterback communication
chasm came when Aikman said he didn't hear about the Darrin
Smith signing until the morning of the San Diego game. It seemed
ludicrous that the franchise quarterback would be one of the last
Cowboys to hear about such a key development. Wouldn't the head
coach—or the owner—make Aikman feel important by making sure
he was the first player to know?

Jones didn't feel much more rapport with or closeness to Aikman than Switzer did. But by this time, it no longer occurred to
Switzer to tell Aikman anything. If Aikman had so little respect for
him, why should he even bother the quarterback? His moods about
Aikman changed as quickly as North Texas weather. One moment:
sad and hurt. The next: proud and angry.

During 1994 press conferences, Switzer had often used the nickname Cowboy players called Aikman—Roy. (Legend had it some
rookie got flustered and called Troy "Roy.") Switzer would say, "If
we protect Roy, we'll win." But by October of 1995, Switzer no
longer used the affectionate handle.

It pained Switzer loyalists to see how miserable Aikman had
made him. They weren't going down without a fight. If Aikman was
going to the media with "you won't believe it" stories about
Switzer—going for the jugular, trying to get Switzer fired—the
Switzer camp could play that game, too.

On the flight to San Diego, Blake and I talked about Aikman. He
said, "I just don't understand Troy. Why can't he just accept coach
Switzer and make the best of the situation? Coach Switzer ain't
going anywhere."

Meaning, in Blake's view, Switzer wasn't going to quit and Jones
wasn't going to fire him just because one player didn't like him.
Blake believed Jones liked Switzer too much and liked the way just
about every player except Aikman had come to like—even love—
Switzer. Jones was fond of Blake, who had an accurate read on the
owner. Blake knew he was speaking from a position of political
strength.

"Troy," said Blake, "is just so sensitive, so fragile. At times he's so insecure. You wonder if . . . "

Blake tossed out a Switzer-camp theory that had crossed my mind during the Aikman-Johnson cold war. Let's assume Aikman is playing the most difficult position in sports—quarterback in Dallas. To ensure survival, perhaps Aikman learned early on to make sure the right media people knew he didn't care for the coach. Then, if the season was a failure, Aikman could blame the coach. If it was a success, Aikman could tell the Hansens and Galloways that he basically overcame the coach.

So sure, I could see how Aikman might position himself with media friends so that Switzer would take the fall if the Cowboys lost. Maybe he hadn't actually plotted to do so; maybe it had happened gradually, as a subconscious defense mechanism. But several members of the Switzer camp suspected this was happening, which meant Switzer had wondered, also.

Blake also sensed growing resentment of Aikman among the team's black players. Blake said, "The team is mostly black, and he can be aloof, cool, sort of distant to the black players. I mean, sometimes he won't even say hello to some of the guys."

(After the season, Aikman responded: "I know some people may think I'm aloof, but there are times during the season when [while walking through the locker room or down a Valley Ranch hall] I just want to be a guy on the street and go about my business without talking to anybody. I just don't have time to stop and talk." And: "I pride myself on having a good relationship with all my teammates.")

Yet several in the Switzer camp began to wonder if some of the "redneck" in Aikman was showing. Because he comes from rural Oklahoma, dips snuff, drives a pickup, and has palled around with the country-western group Shenendoah, Switzer supporters wondered if Aikman had a built-in cultural bias against blacks. No one ever accused him of being flat-out racist. They just thought he was being harder on black teammates than he should have been. They told me stories about how he "even yells at Michael Irvin."

In Aikman's defense, he yelled more and more at teammates— including Irvin—because the head coach wouldn't discipline them. Aikman mostly yelled at black players because only fourteen of the team's fifty-seven players (counting injured reserve) were white.

But Blake and Danny Bradley said they were hearing grumbling about Aikman's attitude from "many players"—and certainly Switzer was made aware of the potential problem. Other assistants suspected that Blake and Bradley had inspired the player grumbling with grumbling of their own. But though Blake wouldn't name names, I believe several players had complained to him. Probably, he was sympathetic to their complaints, which perhaps was out of line for an assistant coach. But in this case, Blake kept Switzer apprised only because he thought there was real potential for team-wrecking conflict.

"Believe me," Blake said, "I'm trying to help protect Troy." He hoped Aikman understood that "the black guys love coach Switzer." Which was true. "So why doesn't Troy?"

I tried to explain to Blake that Aikman loved Johnson's coaching style and couldn't get used to Switzer's. Blake shook his head. "It's just not fair to the man. If he's such a bad coach, how did he win all those games at Oklahoma? How did we come so close to the Super Bowl last year? Why is Troy so *hard* on coach Switzer?"

I had heard the rumor since 1991. An off-duty Dallas police officer who traveled with the Cowboys and worked security at their hotels first told me that "the word on the street" was that Troy Aikman is gay. Over the next four years, I heard the rumor from two more police officers who worked around the team (and I know they mentioned it to team officials). One officer told me Aikman "was supposed to be" having a relationship with a male member of a country-western band.

But policemen, suspicious by nature, can be some of the worst rumormongers.

When I first asked Leigh Steinberg about the rumor, he said he had heard it, but was mystified by its origin. "Where does this come from?" he said. "Troy definitely is not gay." He laughed. "Well, at least I know he's bisexual." Many times, says Steinberg, he has seen Aikman in action with the opposite sex. On balance, I've heard just as many stories about Aikman's female conquests at country-western bars.

I had heard—okay, read some tabloid story—about Aikman's tumultuous relationship with country singer Lorrie Morgan. Then Aikman was "linked"—isn't that the Hollywood term?—to actress Janine Turner, then to actress Sandra Bullock. Why so many starlets? For one reason, Steinberg and Aikman have had off-season discussions about potential "links." For instance, Aikman told Steinberg he was intrigued by Bullock, so Steinberg contacted her "people," and Aikman and Bullock began a fax-pal relationship that finally led to a date at some Hollywood bash. Despite enough paparazzi photos for a Beverly Hills wedding, Aikman and Bullock did not click.

Imagine: The Cowboy quarterback is such a "catch" that he can scan Nashville or Hollywood and say, "How about *her*?" So why haven't any of the relationships clicked? Are they planned merely as a finite off-season diversion—the equivalent of a trip to Opryland or Disneyland? Or are they arranged merely to provide "most eligible bachelor" publicity?

Friends of Aikman say it's as simple as this: He can't have a steady girlfriend because he's married—to football. Aikman told me during the 1992 season, "I'm not getting married until I'm through playing. It just wouldn't be fair to the woman." In 1994 he told me, "Someday I want to be married and have three or four kids."

Over the years, I've heard through the media grapevine that four or five superstar, team-sport male athletes were gay, or at least "bi," yet not once have the rumors been proven true by a concrete or even a tabloid story, to my knowledge. Not one ex-lover has come forth to tell or sell his story. Not a Greg Louganis among these ex-superstars. Are gay rumors just part of the bargain for single, wealthy star athletes? If, say, they experimented a time or two during their roaring twenties, then settled down into heterosexuality, does that make them gay? In Aikman's case, if a stud quarterback speaks openly of how much he loves spending time with his "buddies" (drinking beer, cooking burgers, playing golf, etc.) and he isn't constantly seen with some Sharon Stone on his arm, is he automatically branded "gay" by many in our macho, homophobic society? Sometimes I've thought Aikman simply wasn't interested in having a relationship with a woman—having to spend X-amount of time with her, call her regularly, give up his independence—but does that mean he wants to have sex with men?

So I didn't spend much time pondering the Aikman rumor until October of 1995, when several members of the Switzer camp told me about new "incidents." They said the team had been informed "by the police" that Aikman "had been in some places he shouldn't have been." Yet Switzer sometimes stayed at the Melrose Hotel, which is in Dallas's gay district. Did that make Switzer bisexual? Of course not.

Furthermore, what should the sexual preference of a pro athlete matter to a journalist? My guideline: Only if an off-the-field involvement affects the athlete's performance during games is it fair game for a reporter. Only if, say, voracious promiscuity or a torrid affair or a messy divorce or a sexual-identity crisis is draining the athlete mentally and/or physically and causing decline in his production would I consider reporting it.

Yet on this point I was asked a difficult image-reality question

by Switzer loyalists: What if the superstar athlete is constantly portrayed by the media as something he isn't? What if Aikman's
image—"most eligible bachelor in sports"—is just a facade? What if
that image helps make him endorsement millions? What if media
members close to Aikman help protect that image by looking the
other way?

Switzer loyalists were "nauseous" over the opening paragraph
of a January 15 *Sports Illustrated* story by John Ed Bradley: "SWM,
tall, handsome, twenty-nine, professional football player, seeks
beautiful, intelligent young woman to help design dream house and
create family equivalent of America's Team. Must like quiet
evenings at home, either cruising America Online or admiring tropical fish tank . . . "

Maybe I imagined this, but I began to feel subtle pressure from
the Switzer camp to "tell the truth" about what a "fraud" Troy is. In
December, Switzer supporters would wonder if "the truth" about
Troy had made him a "very troubled young man" and helped cause
his slump. My response: "What exactly am I supposed to tell the
truth about?" I had no proof of "the truth." Several times I asked
Switzer supporters if they had any indisputable facts or rock-solid
details, and I was told with knowing looks or tones to "just check out
the incidents." So I contacted two Dallas police officers I know, who
said they had heard nothing. Aikman certainly hadn't been arrested,
and the officers had heard no scuttlebutt from coworkers about anything involving Aikman. Nothing, I asked, about officers finding Aikman "some places he shouldn't have been" and perhaps even taking
him home? Nothing. Both officers definitely have heard the rumor—
heard it "for years"—but both agreed that if Troy Aikman had been
found in any situation involving homosexual behavior, word almost
certainly would have spread through the police ranks.

I told several Switzer supporters that my friend Steinberg
insisted Aikman is not gay. One person close to the coach said, "Oh,
it will come out. It may not be until he's fifty or sixty, but it will
come out."

Yet a team source who should know about such matters told
me, "I just don't think there's anything to the rumor." In Aikman's
early Cowboy years, team officials were worried he was a little
naive about the backgrounds or motives of a couple of people who
were trying to get close to him. Team officials warned him. But this,
they say, had nothing to do with homosexual suspicions.

So had these old warnings—like the kids' game "Operator"—
come full circle to Switzer campers as a distorted, "Troy was in
some places he shouldn't have been?"

For sure, Switzer had heard the rampant rumor about his quarterback. I was told that one night after a bottle of wine, when he
was particularly down about something "demeaning" Aikman had
said publicly about him, Switzer lashed out in the company of
friends by saying, "I have to take so much shit off that kid, and he's
gay."

Many team sources told me that most, if not all, Cowboy players had heard the rumor. During Super Bowl Week, when a controversy between Aikman and Blake erupted, Charles Haley told
ESPN, "If Troy let's any of this bother him, then he really is a punk."
Though I wouldn't dare try to interpret a Haley quote, "punk" can
be a derogatory term for homosexual.

By late in the season, several NFL executives or coaches had
asked me about the rumor. Callers, I was told, were asking about it
on Philadelphia all-sports station WIP. Several Dallas-Fort Worth
radio talk-show hosts were asked by callers about the rumor. A man
at the Cowboy Super Bowl victory parade wore a sign that said,
"Troy, I want to have your baby."

Then, incredibly, the rumor hatched an offspring: that I was
writing a "Troy is gay" book. I'm not sure how that rumor started or
if the Switzer camp or even the Aikman camp gave it wings. But
word spread through media circles that I had on-the-record material from several of Aikman's ex-boyfriends. Operator? That is hilar-
iously and completely untrue.

Only in Cowboyland.

Only when you're caught in the Switzer-Aikman cross fire.

Time-out, you shout. The Switzer camp would want to "expose"
and presumably humiliate and ultimately tear down the player who
could do the most to win Switzer a Super Bowl? Well, some in the
Switzer camp believed Emmitt Smith was more valuable than Aikman. But the realities were that (1) the Cowboys weren't going to
win a Super Bowl without Emmitt *and* Aikman and (2) by this time,
the Switzer and Aikman camps had lost sight of reality.

Many people around Switzer knew that if Aikman got him fired,
they might lose their jobs or their celebrity-by-association. Even if
you can't understand it, do not underestimate how betrayed they
felt by Aikman's breaking the always-a-Sooner code. Because the
Switzer camp believed Aikman and his "henchmen" were trying to
"get" Switzer, they at the very least wanted to hear Dale Hansen and
Randy Galloway having to field calls on their radio shows and publicly admit "their boy" was gay. In Switzer's world, the term is
"queer." In Switzer's men-will-be-men world, a man could suffer no
greater humiliation than to be exposed as a "queer."

Fire was being fought with fire, as bizarre and twisted as it all might seem.

A month or so after the season, Hansen asked me if it was true I was doing the "Troy is gay" book. No, I said, chuckling, "unless you tell me you're his lover." Hansen said he had heard the rumors "for a couple of years," but had never seen or heard any proof of them. Hansen said he told Randy Galloway, "If it's true, then I'm converting." But, said Hansen, "Galloway did not think that was at all funny."

Hansen told me this story: One night after a Cowboy game, Hansen, Aikman, and several Cowboys went to a country-western bar called Borrowed Money. Of course, the women were coming at Aikman like blitzing 49ers. Several, said a laughing and perhaps exaggerating Hansen, "probably would have stripped right there and done it with him in the middle of the dance floor." But while Aikman's poor teammates were striking out more than Texas Rangers, Aikman just wasn't in the mood. He soon tired of the near riot he was causing and left. A few nights later, Hansen stopped by Borrowed Money and a bartender said, "Well, that clinches it. Aikman's gay." The bartender said several of his regulars had watched Aikman turn down one potential Miss Texas after another, and the regulars had concluded that no red-blooded American heterosexual male would do that.

"Maybe that's how a rumor like that gets started," said Hansen. I told Hansen that you keep hearing the rumor from so many sources that after a while you think, "Well, where there's smoke . . ." Hansen said, "Okay, but here's what I don't understand: If there's anything there at all, why hasn't *Hard Copy* or the *National Enquirer* done something on it? With someone as big as Troy Aikman, wouldn't there be some kind of leak somewhere?"

Hansen made another good point: "I've never seen Emmitt Smith with a woman, or heard about him having a relationship with a woman, but I've never heard any rumors about Emmitt being gay."

But Aikman definitely has heard the rumor about himself.

He also heard the rumor that I was writing the "Troy is gay" book. He called me about three weeks after the Super Bowl and said he wanted to meet with me and tell me a couple of things. A few days before, he had declined my request to interview him for this book. As Hansen said, "He thinks you're Barry's boy."

Later, when I told members of Switzer's camp that Aikman had decided to talk to me, and that I needed their reactions to some of the points he had made, several said, "He only talked to you because he wanted to try to convince you he isn't homosexual."

I did not tell Switzer supporters how my conversation began with Aikman. He interrupted my first ice-breaking question to tell me, unprompted and quite emphatically, "I am not gay."

I was a little surprised and very relieved he just came right out with it, the way he might say, "I am not left-handed." I wasn't looking forward to saying, "Uh, let me ask you something . . . "

He went on to say his administrative assistant, Verna Riddles, had received mail from people claiming to know male lovers of his. He said he has no idea where all this started. He said, "How can I fight this? Am I supposed to keep a girl around even if I don't care anything about her, just so I can keep everybody off my back?"

One morning in mid-October, during a commercial break of a weekly radio show I did with Jerry Jones, I jumped on the phone so I could speak to him off the air. I plunged. I said, "Jerry, this Aikman-Switzer stuff is getting pretty serious." Jones was somewhere in California. He sounded uncharacteristically irritated as he said, "Is it so bad that I should jump back in my plane and fly home?"

I said, "I don't know. It seems pretty bad to me."

I didn't know whether Jones knew considerably more or considerably less than I did.

He said we could discuss it in his office, when he returned, and we did. Jones said, "Let's get this straight: Troy is the most important person in the franchise. No doubt about it. He's more important than Barry. That's just the way the game is designed in this day and age [with rules favoring the passing game]. Troy and I talk more than you might think, and I'm aware of Troy's concerns as well as Barry's. I think they both are at fault to some degree, and I believe I can help in subtle ways—that's ultimately what my job is. But I cannot look like I'm undermining by talking to Troy behind Barry's back. I still say for the long haul, Barry was absolutely the best move I could have made. He is committed for the long haul. I was just in there [Switzer's office] and I could see the fire, the intensity. Every day he gets a little more 'off the couch,' if you know what I mean."

Aikman probably was thinking more along the lines of "off his rocker."

But Jones wasn't ready to step in and do anything dramatic because the Cowboys were 6–1—and soon to be 8–1, after impressive wins against Atlanta and Philadelphia. So Jones pretty much had decided to let Aikman vs. Switzer rock along and monitor the battle the way any good general would, through binoculars. "This situation will be fine," said Jones, "as long as we win. Otherwise, we could have problems. And we could have problems until we win a Super Bowl with Barry—win it *his* way, so Troy can step back and say, 'Hmmm, you *can* do this another way.'"

For the moment, though, Jones actually seemed pleased about the negativity. Remember Jones's philosophy: Some inner conflict is good for a team. Conflict produces internal combustion, which can unify and focus and turbo-power a team. (Larry Lacewell: "We're getting to be like the old Oakland A's. We feud and bicker and win.") Jones thought his conflict with Johnson helped drive the team through consecutive Super Bowl championships. But finally, Johnson vs. Jones became counterproductive, and I thought Aikman vs. Switzer had just about reached that point.

Jones disagreed.

If possible, at the moment, Jones had a more pressing matter. He was doing battle with rumors about his own personal life, which had just materialized in a book called *King of the Cowboys . . . the Life and Times of Jerry Jones,* by Jim Dent, who covered the Landry-Schramm Cowboys for the *Fort Worth Star-Telegram* and the *Dallas Times Herald*. Whispers and winks about Jones's after-hours behavior were at least as prevalent as the rumor about Aikman. Dent wrote that Jones was "the talk of his peers" when an attractive young lady openly accompanied him at an owners' meeting; that Jones had been seen in Dallas in the company of Gennifer Flowers, who claimed she once had an affair with Bill Clinton; and that Jones had carried on a not-so-discreet affair with Susan Skaggs, the Cowboys' director of civic affairs.

About Dent's contentions, Jones was just as adamant as Aikman was about his rumor. Jones said he hadn't had any affairs or been unfaithful, that "I've only seen Gennifer Flowers on TV" and that "Susan Skaggs has never been anything but an employee" and that "I've never done anything that would hurt my family."

Dent also wrote that "rumors of a Jerry-Gene divorce were rampant." Heatedly, Jones told me, "You can bet your house we're not getting a divorce. She doesn't want one and I don't want one. She knows [Dent's book] has zero credibility, and she's not even going to read it. All Gene said was that my mistake was being in the wrong places where that kind of thing goes on."

Bars, he meant. Jones readily admits to "being in places he shouldn't have been." His dad often has reminded him how important it is to release tension by "letting your hair down" periodically. Jones sometimes lets his down in clubs or bars.

Jones continued: "I do have my frailties. I've drunk a lot, and I'm not proud of it." Yet isn't part of Jones proud of his "party animal" reputation? Doesn't he exaggerate his alcohol consumption? Friends describe him more as a sipper than a drinker. Doesn't the male ego in him want to be known as a man who puts away more than his share of booze—and never lets it affect him? Isn't part of his "rumor" problem that he wants both: to be admired by male friends as a "ladies' man" while remaining a faithful husband to the woman he loves? Jones's friends claim that to Jerry the *appearance*—occasional flirting with a cute young thing while out with the boys—is much more important than the *reality*.

Jones on admiring females: "Understand, I've been exposed to this kind of thing all my life [because of his money]. It wasn't like I bought the Dallas Cowboys and all of a sudden women are pushing Gene out of the way to get to me, and I'm thinking, 'Man, I'm really getting good-looking.' You see all the time how a doctor or lawyer gets to an age that the kids are grown, and the first pretty nurse or secretary who comes along, he's out of the marriage. I did not do that. I love Gene very much. We're building a wonderful home."

In fact, when Jones says "bet your house" on his marriage, he almost literally was betting his. Three Christmases ago, he surprised Gene by giving her one of the most conspicuous lots in exclusive, old-money Highland Park—five acres on the northeast corner of the busy intersection of Preston Road and Armstrong Parkway that slope down to Turtle Creek. For many of its residents, Highland Park is a grown-up extension of the snootiest rich-kid sorority and frater-nity on campus, and soon after the Joneses made their "Clampett-like" arrival in Dallas, "humiliating" Tom Landry and all but threat-ening to paint Texas Stadium Razorback red, Mrs. Jones was made aware that she and her husband would have to pay some dues before they would be allowed to join Highland Park society. Now, of course, Highland Parkers probably would pay astonishing sums to be seen at restaurants such as Star Canyon or The Mansion with Mr. and Mrs. Super Bowl. So for the last three years, Gene Jones has busied herself building a mansion at Preston and Armstrong that could serve as the capitol building of Highland Park. To me, the guest house would qualify as a mansion. I've heard several Highland Park-ers sniff about how "garish" the Joneses' creation is, rising above the surrounding white wall like, well, Jerry's middle finger.

Yet, as upset as Gene initially was when she heard about the Dent book, a source close to the family says, "Do you really think she'd ever file for divorce? In a way, she'd have to give up her chil-dren, because you know they're going to stay around the Cowboys.

The games are such a family affair for them. It would be so hard for her to give all that up."

Gene had just one warning for Jerry about Dent's book: "I better not ever see an autographed copy of the thing."

That perhaps goes double for yet another "Jerry Does Dallas" book that hit the bookstores later in the season—the self-published *Jerry Jones and the "New Regime"* by Todd Cawthorn, once a co-pilot on Jones's jet. When I saw the first ad for it—*What?*—I figured Todd Cawthorn had to be a pen name for Rod Serling. A twenty-six-year-old pilot fired by Jones had done a fly-and-tell exposé on him? At this rate, Jones would have an entire bookstore shelf: *Inside Jerry Jones* by his former gardener, cook, mechanic, Pizza Hut delivery boy . . .

When confidants asked Jones about the "co-pilot book," he told them it was "even worse" than Dent's. More and juicier details. All fabrication, Jones told me.

When I bumped into Cawthorn at the Super Bowl, he challenged me about why I'd never done any investigative reporting on Jones's after-hours life. I asked him, "Has whatever he does away from the office ever affected his performance at the office?" Jones, I thought, deserved to be 1995's NFL executive of the year. How many sports executives drink excessively and/or carouse? Many. Is it a Dallas city ordinance that the Cowboy owner must conduct himself in public as if he's Tom Landry? Obviously not, though some fans might think so. Has Jones broken any laws? None, to my knowledge. Was Jones making millions of endorsement or donation dollars because he had duped millions of fans into thinking he's the NFL's answer to Billy Graham?

No. He's just a guy from Arkansas who's doing a great job of running the most famous team in sports.

Sex and drugs have always been part of Cowboy Mystique. If drugs hadn't been so destructive to Landry's teams following his final Super Bowl appearance in early 1979, you could argue that an occasional cocaine casualty helped build the team's soap-opera appeal. After a federal drug investigation involved several prominent Cowboys in the early eighties, rival fans began calling the Cowboys "South America's Team." For my book *God's Coach*, former Cowboy scout John Wooten (now with Philadelphia) told me: "Tom was approached and told we were going to lose this team to drugs. But he just didn't seem that interested in doing anything about it. He just didn't believe the effect it could have. Everything was going to be all right. The team was still close enough to a Super Bowl that just a little more and it would be okay."

For once, was Jerry Jones about to emulate Tom Landry?

From the days of Pete Gent's *North Dallas Forty*, the Cowboys always had titillated Cowboy lovers and haters with sexual perversion (in separate incidents, Lance Rentzel and Rafael Septien pleaded guilty to indecency with ten-year-old girls) and occasional drug-related flameouts ("Bullet" Bob Hayes and Thomas "Hollywood" Henderson). Jerry Jones's Cowboys were beginning to uphold the legacy.

Late in training camp, I had heard from a source in another team's front office that "one or two Cowboys" had violated the league substance-abuse policy. Jones wouldn't comment; breach of a league confidentiality clause carries as much as a $500,000 fine. But he wasn't pleased that someone at league headquarters in New York had leaked this info. Can the league office fine itself? Jones viewed this as yet another example of the league trying to "stick it to Dallas."

In early November the league stuck it to Leon Lett, who had tested positive for marijuana. Lett: gone for four weeks. "Just plain stupid," said a Cowboy front-office source. "Why can't these guys get it through their heads that they have to stay clean during the season, then when it's over, they can go to Jamaica and smoke as much shit and have as many 'ho's' [whores] as they want?"

Yet as Jones later said, Lett's was a "speeding ticket" compared to Clayton Holmes, who figuratively was involved in "a wreck with a fatality." Holmes had tested positive for cocaine. Holmes: gone for the rest of the season.

Vintage Jones: He was going to fight the suspensions—especially Lett's. "We have the best attorneys in the country trying to figure this thing out because we believe the system is flawed. I'm not saying there's nothing there, just that it's very subjective what constitutes stage one, two, and three [test failures]. We may not win, but we're going to contest it."

For once, Jones did not win.

Of course, Deion Sanders would make Holmes instantly forgettable. Lett would be missed, but he would return for the stretch run with fresh legs and (Jones and the coaches hoped) a rededicated drive fueled by public humiliation. But quietly the coaches and front-office execs worried about losing the one star they considered irreplaceable. Not Aikman: Wade Wilson and Jason Garrett were capable stand-ins. Not Emmitt: rookie running back Sherman Williams wasn't Emmitt, but he wasn't bad.

Michael Irvin was the one player the Cowboys couldn't afford to lose.

Irvin had no backup. Deion didn't yet know the offense and couldn't play every snap on offense and defense. Cory Fleming would be cut soon after the season. Rookies Ed Hervey and Oronde Gadsden were raw at best. Irvin wasn't the Hall of Fame lock that Aikman is, but the 8-to–88 connection was becoming one of the strongest in NFL history, especially at critical moments of critical games. No. 8 struggles without No. 88, as the Cowboys would learn in December when defenses began taking away Aikman's first and last resort. Tight end Jay Novacek was also a security blanket for Aikman, especially down near the goal line. But Irvin was the one wide receiver Aikman always could trust to run precisely 12 yards downfield, make a 90-degree cut to the sideline at precisely the right moment—and to fight like hell for the ball if Aikman tried to force it to him when he was covered. Irvin regularly turned potential interceptions into, at worst, incompletions.

What if Irvin went down? "Don't even talk about it," Switzer said to me, as if merely asking about it might conjure evil spirits.

To insiders, the season hung by the flamboyant threads Michael Jerome Irvin wore when he did the town. They knew they couldn't afford to lose him to injury—or incident. They suspected he had narrowly avoided serious trouble on several occasions. Several Cowboy officials feared Irvin was using drugs. They grew suspicious because of his mood swings, the sunglasses he donned immediately after games, and the stretches during which the loquacious Irvin refused to talk to the media. But they had no proof—and hoped they didn't hear about any. Irvin, they said, had never tested positive for cocaine or marijuana.

Like many of Landry's stars, Irvin had become brazen about his nocturnal behavior, as if he were bulletproof, above the law, king of the streets. During the season one Cowboy official told me, "It's amazing he hasn't gotten into trouble. He's often in places he shouldn't be."

Irvin was the Midnight Cowboy.

Perhaps Jones again was fortunate that Irvin's thirtieth birthday didn't come until about five weeks after the season was over. When the incident hit the papers and airwaves, it came as a shock to many Cowboy followers, who just couldn't get over what a great guy like Michael Irvin was doing in a room with two women of questionable repute and about $6,000 worth of cocaine and marijuana. Many of the same fans had been appalled and outraged when Irvin said "shit" on national TV following the NFC championship game, then wouldn't apologize for it. In fact, three days later when TV reporters asked him on camera if he wanted to apologize, he said no, he meant to describe what Switzer had gone through as "shit." He added, "I'll say it again. Shit, shit, shit."

For viewers at home, that clip of Irvin saying "bleep, bleep, bleep" should have been their first hint that he was about to rub their noses in their blind idolatry of him.

Their shock is a tribute to Irvin's acting ability. Of all the acts at Valley Ranch, his was the most convincing. His lovable image might have been the furthest from his shadowy reality. Irvin had done an instinctively brilliant job of using television to create a persona that melted most fans, black or white. For minicam interviews at his locker, or especially for his radio or TV show, Irvin had almost always turned on his charm and wit and a smile about the size of a football. He just always seemed to be having such a great time playing the game he loves. Typical Irvin sound bite: "Baby, we (deep chuckle) are goin' back (chuckle) to *our* house. Know what I'm sayin'? (chuckle chuckle chuckle). The Super Bowl is *our* house. We just let somebody rent it last year."

It was like he was always letting fans in on the inside joke.

Incredibly, Irvin had become a sort of cartoon superhero to kids. "The Playmaker," as he's called, was approved by parents as a tough but benign role model, a player who whistled while he worked, always worked as hard as any player on the team, and always saved the day with the crucial catch. At games or malls, when I often saw children in No. 88 jerseys, I would think, "If only their parents knew . . ." Why didn't I report on the real Irvin? Because frequenting topless bars and womanizing isn't illegal and certainly hadn't affected his performance.

From a distance, most fans forgave Irvin for wearing sunglasses indoors, for wearing more jewelry than Mrs. Jerry Jones—and for wearing out his welcome in rival stadiums with his chest-beating and bizarre touchdown celebrations (a sacrificial dance to Deion's Broadway soft shoe). Irvin always did his share of charity appearances. On TV, Irvin sincerely told you what car to buy. Irvin was occasionally pictured with his nice, beautiful wife, Sandi, the mother of his two daughters.

That's definitely one side of Irvin, but probably not his dominant side.

The real Irvin, ironically, is the one right before fans' eyes on Sunday afternoons. The Irvin who had been involved in one off-field scrape after another is simply an extension of the football player. Irvin the receiver is a shrewd operator who isn't exceptionally fast or athletic. His game is pushing the rules (along with his defender) to the limit. At 6'2", 205 pounds, he is exceptionally powerful in his upper body and hands, and he often outslaps, outjostles, and ultimately outfights smaller cornerbacks for the ball. Like Charles Haley and Erik Williams, Irvin has a rage to win. He works hard during the week, then works himself into a pregame frenzy. He maniacally exhorts teammates and trash-talks opponents. On game day Irvin unquestionably was the team's leader, the one the others looked to for kill-or-be-killed inspiration. Make no mistake: The Dallas Cowboys who have won three of the last four Super Bowls are mostly made up of what Switzer calls "Mandingo warriors."

(One highly respected New York–based commentator recently told me that many years ago during a one-on-one chat Switzer used what the commentator considered a racist reference. He wonders if Switzer has exploited black athletes to get rich and famous. Yet Switzer's love for black players—or blacks in general—is obviously genuine and obviously returned by blacks who know him. How many white coaches could get away with calling his black players "Mandingo warriors"?)

But Switzer's warriors sometimes have a hard time turning back into upstanding citizens at night. As Cowboy doctor Robert Vandermeer has often told me, "The common fan has no idea how violent a game pro football is." Yet fans want their Cowboy gods to leave opponents bloodied and bowed, take two aspirin, and turn back into role models. It doesn't work that way in the real world. Irvin is a warrior, a gladiator, a street fighter—anything but a role model.

Irvin grew up on the rough side of Fort Lauderdale, one of seventeen children. Around the house, Irvin had to outslap and outjostle siblings for just about everything. Of his childhood he told *Inside Sports* magazine: "You only get in trouble with the law if you aren't good at what you are doing. If you don't get caught, they don't call you a criminal. I wasn't the kind to go around shooting people or anything, but I had my problems early on, which is the best time to have them."

If you don't get caught . . .

Out on the streets, Irvin quickly realized that to the football victor went the spoils. But he wasn't born with the talent of an Emmitt or a Deion. He doesn't have Jerry Rice's elegant speed or housefly-catching hands. As Jimmy Johnson once told me, "People don't want to believe this, but Michael Irvin is an overachiever." Irvin worked and willed himself into a star at the University of Miami and again for the Cowboys. Irvin lives to win and to celebrate, and star-crazed Dallas greeted him with a dangerous embrace.

While Irvin and Deion are close, they don't run the streets together much. Deion escapes the demands of being "Prime Time" by going fishing, sometimes alone, or by just playing with his kids. To Deion, "Prime Time" is just a job. To Irvin, "the Playmaker" is his existence. Irvin is not a fisherman. Irvin relaxes by being famous, by playing "the Playmaker," by making royal entrances into the hottest nightspots. Irvin puts down the top of his Mercedes and puts on those granny-shaped shades so that he can be cool and recognized at the same time. Irvin, like many of his warrior teammates, frequents the "gentlemen's" clubs, where he preens and poses. Irvin flirts with trouble. Says a team source, "In the past, Michael has routinely stopped by topless bars the way most guys would stop into the neighborhood pub for a quick drink on the way home from work."

Pro athletes love the topless clubs because they offer sexual arrangements without attachments. Unlike girls they might pick up at a singles' bar, the ones who work at topless clubs aren't going to fall in love with them or wonder why they didn't call the next morning. Says a recently retired Cowboy: "Many of these girls are bisexual. A lot of them will live with a divorced rich guy for a year or so, but a lot of times they'll give sex in exchange for drugs. Most of 'em love cocaine and marijuana. Not alcohol—that's for the college girls. Drugs. Guys [Cowboys] will buy drugs for them to, in effect, pay them for sex."

The ex-player laughed about media reports—and the resulting amazement expressed by fans—about several Cowboys chipping in $300 or so a month to lease a house that can be seen from the practice field. The "white house," as the players called it, was used for sexual liaisons and parties. The ex-Cowboy said, "Lots of players have had places like that, going back into the Landry years." Fitting irony: The "white house" was on Dorsett Drive. According to many sources and reports, Irvin was one of several players who used the house.

It wouldn't matter if Irvin's coach were Switzer or Landry or George Patton, he occasionally would get the urge, head into the night, and try to impress men and women who are nothing but fawning trouble. For Cowboys, Dallas remains a falling Rome. The more they win, the more the people of the night lead them into temptation—and sometimes destruction. Their idolaters often become their assassins. *For you,* says the coke dealer, *"half price."*

Craig James, the former SMU and New England running back who cohosted Irvin's TV show, told the *Dallas Morning News:* "I'm very glad I didn't play professionally in Dallas. Reality is so farfetched from what Cowboy players believe. They believe players can get and do what they want. Most NFL players are put on a pedestal.

Cowboys are put so high, it seems like they are on another planet."

For me, it was rather amazing the Playmaker had developed such a playboy reputation by night while keeping his Cowboy image spotless enough to keep doing his radio and TV shows and commercials. In 1990 he was sued in a paternity case and ordered to establish a trust fund for the child. More recently, he was involved in several criminal investigations. He was one of several Cowboys who received stolen tickets from an airline agent charged with theft—though authorities said the players weren't aware the tickets were stolen. A Plano woman filed a lawsuit accusing Irvin of assaulting her in a nightclub parking lot—an allegation Irvin called "absolutely ridiculous." He was cited for disorderly conduct following a disagreement with a convenience-store clerk. A man told police that Irvin hit him in the face during a charity basketball game. Irvin, who was not charged, was called to testify in the Erik Williams case.

Nothing major. Irvin loudly proclaimed his innocence in all the criminal matters. For fans, these matters went in one ear and out the other. But cumulatively . . .

Not until after the 1995 season, when Irvin apparently was celebrating his birthday, did he finally get caught in a place he shouldn't have been. What excuse could he give his fans after two Irving police officers, investigating complaints of marijuana smoke and possible prostitution, found Irvin and his closest friend and ex-teammate, Alfredo Roberts, in a $119-a-night Residence Inn hotel room with two women who called themselves "self-employed models"? Also present were three ounces of marijuana, two ounces of cocaine, and paraphernalia including rolling papers, razors, a tube used for snorting cocaine, and two vibrators. Though Dallas TV station KXAS Channel 5 reported that the tube, with cocaine residue, was found in Irvin's overnight bag, one of the women claimed all the drugs belonged to her. She was the only one arrested.

Sports Illustrated reported that Irvin, clad only in his pants, initially asked the policemen, "Can I tell you who I am?"

I'm the Playmaker. I make you happy. I catch touchdown passes and win Super Bowls for you. You remember, don't you?

When Irvin made his grand entrance to testify before the grand jury, he wore a full-length fur coat and gilt-edged sunglasses. *Can I tell you who I am?* Irvin argued that he always dressed that way. He told members of the media, "Do you want me to try to be something I'm not?"

As a televised videotape of Irvin later showed, he basically was leading a double life.

As Irvin strode down a courthouse hall toward the grand-jury room, a female security guard left her post to ask Irvin for an autograph. She soon was fired, according to reports.

Another woman asked Irvin to sign her Bible.

Chilling.

But apparently the grand jury was not impressed: Irvin was indicted for cocaine possession, a second-degree felony that carries a sentence of up to twenty years, and for misdemeanor marijuana possession, which carries a sentence of up to 180 days in jail.

About five weeks later KXAS aired a videotape that a "friend" of Irvin's named Dennis Pedini secretly shot about two weeks (according to Pedini) after Irvin was indicted. 5'4" Pedini, who had a background in security work, was called "Inch-High Private Eye" by several Cowboys who knew him. Pedini hid a camera in the backseat of his car, taped an exchange with Irvin, who was riding in the passenger seat, then sold the tape to KXAS for $6,000, according to the station. Pedini, thirty-one, had ingratiated himself with Irvin and won the player's trust by running errands for him and sometimes serving as his driver. A team source says, "Michael's ego just ran away with him. He let Pedini into his life because Pedini would do anything for him, and that made Michael feel cool."

Pedini said he sold the tape to KXAS because he believed Irvin had a drug problem and needed help. In an on-camera interview with KXAS, Pedini said that as the tape begins, Irvin has just returned to the car from buying cocaine. Holding what Pedini says is a packet of cocaine, Irvin talks to a young fan who (trailed by his parents) runs up to Irvin's side of the car.

Irvin says on the tape, "What you know, little champ?"

You hear a little boy's voice say, "I wanna be like you."

Irvin tells the child's parents that "kids know more than we know" because they're "pure in the mind and pure in the heart." Then to the little boy Irvin says, "So see, you know I'm a good man, huh? Forget what they [people] say, huh?"

For that performance Irvin deserved an award at the "Con" Film Festival. But the irony was, while Irvin was abusing the fan-hero trust of a kid and his parents, Irvin's good friend Pedini was taking advantage of Irvin's naive trust.

On tape Irvin laughs and tells the parents their son "has too much sport in him . . . keep [him] away from my daughters."

As Pedini pulls away, the parents say, "We love you, Michael."

Irvin says, "I got God. I don't need love."

As they drive, Irvin says to Pedini, "You want some . . . A couple lines will help you."

Pedini says, "It stunts your growth."

Chuckling, Irvin says, "If that's the case, I shoulda been stunted a long time ago."

For Cowboy fans in Dallas-Fort Worth, that one damning line pretty much ended the long-running act that had been the lovable Michael Irvin.

On tape, Irvin continues, "Boy, I can't wait to get me a line or three." Then he talks about destroying the bag and any possible fingerprints, about how he has beaten a lie detector test, and about how he isn't afraid of taking an NFL drug test.

Though some fans and rival media members condemned KXAS for paying Pedini, and though several stories were done by newspaper and TV stations questioning Pedini's background and credibility, the man on tape certainly looks and sounds like the real Michael Jerome Irvin. In the end, it didn't matter who was responsible for making the tape or how KXAS had acquired it. All that mattered was what was on the tape.

Another Cowboy first: Never before had fans been provided a bird's-eye (or perhaps stool-pigeon's) view of an unsuspecting star athlete candidly talking to someone he considered a friend about using and having used cocaine.

Irvin began blaming his problems on the Dallas media and fans for hounding him and invading his private life. Irvin began threatening to move to another city. His attitude smacked of, *If you'd just cheer me on game days and let me do what I want the rest of the time, I'll win you some more Super Bowls. If not . . .* Some team sources began to use the word "denial" when discussing Irvin.

Predictably, the public reaction to the almost weekly revelations about Irvin was a stunned mix of disbelief and anger. *Our Michael?* But the truth was, Irvin pretty much was being the same Irvin he had always been. The libido that fueled Super Bowl titles also fueled this warrior when he celebrated.

Yes, Jerry Jones was lucky that Irvin hadn't turned thirty before Super Bowl XXX.

14

EARTHQUAKE

Sports do not build character. They reveal it.
—*Heywood Hale Broun*

The last hopeful moment of the season between Troy Aikman and Barry Switzer took place on the flight home from Atlanta. Aikman felt good enough about the team's performance that he wandered up into first class to share war stories with several coaches. The Falcons had been hit by falling stars—by Aikman, Michael Irvin, Emmitt Smith, and the newest Cowboy, Deion Sanders. Cowboys 28, Atlanta 13. At the season's halfway mark, Dallas was 7–1.

As former SMU coach Ron Meyer once told me, "Winning cures cancer."

In this case, maybe it arrested the cancer.

Switzer joined in the victory talk and began (as he calls it) "dog-cussing" Clayton Holmes for letting the team down with his cocaine suspension. Several coaches said Aikman, mostly listening, seemed impressed and perhaps surprised by Switzer's renewed passion. (Larry Lacewell: "That Washington loss really got Switzer's attention. Since then, there hasn't been any ha-ha, hee-hee.")

A few days later, Leigh Steinberg said, "Barry needs to understand Troy is not Gary Cooper [not some unreachable, stoical, mythical figure]. Barry needs to show him he cares. If he would just do that, who knows, they might become friends."

Let's not get carried away. But the good vibes continued through a Monday-night talent show—Dallas 34, Philadelphia 12—and into the following week. It was finally here. "We've felt the pain," said Switzer, "since the minute the game ended last January." San Francisco 38, Dallas 28 in the NFC championship game. But this time would be different. This time would be almost unfair. San Francisco was a spent shell of itself.

The 49ers had lost Ricky Watters to free agency and coordinators Mike Shanahan and Ray Rhodes to head-coaching jobs. They had lost quarterback Steve Young to a shoulder injury and fullback/enforcer William Floyd to a knee injury. They had lost Deion to Dallas. They had lost back-to-back games at home to New Orleans and Carolina. They had lost momentum, face, and (it appeared) hope. They had lost respect in Las Vegas, where the odds makers made Dallas as much as a 14-point favorite for the "game of the year" at Texas Stadium.

The defending champs had no believers left among the media. Not one national expert—including Jimmy Johnson—gave San Francisco a prayer. (I picked Dallas, 42–17.) The media wrote and spoke billions of words about what a nonevent this game would be.

As Stephen Jones so wisely said after the season, "The league tends to end the season after each weekend." Yes, the media, fans, and many executives, coaches, and players tend to overreact to wins or losses by the best teams. Much of the hysteria is fueled by the I-for-an-I competition among the many network and cable TV shows analyzing the NFL. More and more, commentators feel pressured to play the crystal ball game and take an attention-grabbing stand—to crown a champion and eliminate a contender in September.

But before this mismatch, the media no doubt was influenced by Deion Sanders, who told a Wednesday press conference that the 49ers were "in denial" about how the balance of power had shifted seismically to Dallas. (Translation: "Because I'm here and not in San Francisco.") Though the 49ers still had the NFL's top-rated defense, Deion rolled his eyes and said, "Would you rather have the NFL's number one defense or be 8–1?"

Johnson did an interview on the local Fox affiliate in Dallas and said, "This Cowboy team is better than the '92 or '93 team, but the best team doesn't always win [the championship]." Lacewell's analysis: "Is he trying to set up Switzer, or what?" Randy Galloway wrote, "Under the existing circumstances, if the Cowboys lose, nuclear hell will descend upon the city Monday. This is your 'Nebraska,' Barry. Either win it biiiiiig, or lose the kingdom."

Switzer, however, seemed confident to the point of cocky. He flew to watch son Doug play on Saturday night. Just about everyone in the franchise shared Switzer's "we're better, we'll win" approach—except maybe Nate Newton, the team's philosopher-clown. It's sometimes difficult to know when Newton is delivering a monologue or a message, or both. On Friday afternoon, Newton stood shirtless before twenty-five or thirty reporters from around the country and delivered a hilarious warning: "I know I'm just a dumb-ass football player. But I still think this is going to be one of the best games of the year. You can't bullshit a bullshitter. This ain't going to be no cakewalk. Everybody we play comes at us like *we* just won the Super Bowl, and so will the defending champions. I don't want to hear about no fuckin' Ricky Watters or Steve Young. I'm talkin' about their defense. They've gone above and beyond making the right plays at the right time. So they relaxed one week [against Carolina] and got their ass tore up? But don't listen to me. You're the men with the pen. But remember, the Bible was written by man. It was spread by God through man. That's how we wound up with fuckin' Jehovah's Witnesses and fuckin' Baptists and . . . "

Now he was laughing. But he wasn't kidding.

It was a blowout, all right. Barely into the second quarter, it was 24–0.

San Francisco.

The 49ers blew up Dallas, 38–20. Elvis Grbac, thought to be nothing but a hound dog, went 20 of 30 for 305 yards. Just as in the nightmarish championship game, the Cowboy offense opened with tumultuous turnovers by two of its stars, a fumble by Michael Irvin returned for the 14–0 touchdown and an Aikman interception that set up a short 49er field goal. With 6:30 left in the first quarter, Aikman headed to the locker room with a bruised knee and did not return.

Given the buildup, it was perhaps the biggest regular season letdown in Cowboy history. Total devastation and humiliation. No city can overreact to a dramatic loss the way Dallas can. Suddenly, everything was being questioned. With one loss on November 12, it was as if the Cowboys had gone from 8–1 to 2–8. Indisputably, Barry Switzer was 0–3 against San Francisco.

After the season, Switzer remembered, "It was *Friday the Thirteenth Part Two*. Everybody was overconfident, and I couldn't understand that."

Huh?

Switzer said the 49ers "dicked us"—a football synonym for "tricked us." Beware the male sex organ. With Jerry Rice the Niners exploited the "one weakness in our defense," said veteran Cowboy safety Bill Bates. On the game's second play, they split receivers other than Rice to both flanks and motioned Rice into the slot, which forced the Cowboys to cover pro football's best receiver, at least for 10 or so yards, with middle linebacker Robert Jones, who might have trouble covering Jerry Jones. The Cowboys compounded their strategic weakness when (1) Darrin Smith, still overweight and out of shape from his holdout, completely missed Rice with a "chuck" designed to knock him momentarily off stride and (2) cornerback Larry Brown, moved for the first time to safety because of Deion's presence, didn't immediately grasp that he was supposed to pick up Rice. Hence, the NFL's most stunning play of the year: Jerry Rice, running suddenly, completely, inconceivably free down the middle of the Texas Stadium field, 81 yards for the 7–0 touchdown.

Psychologically, the Cowboys never recovered.

With that one play, Switzer and staff confirmed many suspicions that they were distant relatives of Humpty Dumpty. Talk about great falls. Randy Galloway wrote, "Unprepared. Heartless. Clueless. Disorganized. Disgraceful. Overconfident. Outcoached. Outplayed . . . And now Jones's team has taken on the personality not of its head coach. No, even worse. It's the personality of the owner. Big mouth, big show, big wallets, but also big failures without Jimmy around to ride herd with his bullwhip. Jones is out of control. Switzer continued to demonstrate he's out of his league . . . Deion got it all wrong . . . if he's looking for a team in denial, all Mr. Sanders has to do is gaze out at his own locker room Monday morning."

Oh, were Switzer's family and friends steamed about that appraisal. Yet criticism came from more objective sources. Safety Darren Woodson publicly said the Cowboys were "totally confused," and Steve Young (who helped coach Grbac from the sideline) privately said the Cowboys quit trying in the second half. Even a Cowboy official told me, "It's sad. Barry's such a nice guy, but he just isn't an NFL coach, and even worse, his overall staff isn't very strong and even the hard workers are thinking, 'Hey, if the head coach has gone fishing, why should we sit here looking at more tape?' There's no creativity. No onside kicks. 'Lace' knows some things are going to have to change, but you wonder if the man at the top sees this, and if he does, if he'll do anything about it. Is Barry his one blind spot? We were not prepared to play this game, and it starts with the head coach."

*   *   *

Despite his ego, Jerry Jones never overreacts to a loss in public or in private. What's maddening for some Dallas-Fort Worth media members, for many fans, and even for a few Cowboy staffers is that Jones underreacts. For all his "Super Bowl or bust" vows, Jones will not stand in the middle of the locker room following a loss and tell breathless reporters, "Heads will roll." Quite the opposite: "We'll be fine," he always says, politely scoffing at questions about changes. But Jerry, what are you going to *do*? "Same things we've been doing," says Jones.

This comes from years of making and losing spectacular amounts of money on oil wells. Dry holes are just part of what, most of the time, is a great life. For Jones, part of proving his manhood is smiling calmly at adversity, then kicking its ass. If he loses, he does not hide. He humbly makes himself more visible than ever.

That's because Jerry Jones believes he won't have to humble himself long or often.

But at 24–0, Jones figured it was time to humble himself. Normally, he spends a good portion of the first half of home games sitting next to Stephen and Lacewell on the top row of the two-row pressbox, then he makes an appearance in his 50-yard-line luxury box on the far side of the stadium, then he usually blows and goes down to the sideline sometime in the fourth quarter. Does he eat up the TV close-ups? You bet your Nikes. But more important to Jones, he wants to feel part of the day's conquest—to exchange handshakes and hugs and winks and grins and inside jokes with coaches and players. Outside the time he spends with his children, these are the best moments of Jones's life.

Of course, this has triggered criticism among fans, media, and most fellow owners who believe the sideline is the sacred preserve of players and coaches. But this time, Jones no more wanted to walk the sideline than he wanted to strut barefoot on hot coals. "To tell you the truth," Jones told me the following week, "I wanted to stay in the pressbox like this . . ." He put his hands over his eyes. His newest commercial with Deion had just debuted, this one for Nike. A takeoff on the TV show *Dallas*, Jones plays a J. R. Ewing character who says of Deion, "God dang, if I had eleven men like that I could rule the world." Now, it appeared he needed at least eleven to rule the 49ers. Talk about humiliating.

But Jones headed down to the sideline much earlier than he ever had, in part to show the world he wouldn't hide. But he also wanted "to show my support [to players and coaches], to show I was there when everyone was feeling so bad." He also wanted to tell everyone the world had not ended: "People were attaching so much significance to the loss because it was San Francisco. But it's just like losing a Texas-Oklahoma game. It doesn't ruin your chances of winning the Big Eight and going to the Orange Bowl. It doesn't have anything to do with killing or creating our momentum. I mean, do you really think Nate Newton, when he gets out there [the next Sunday] banging heads with the Raiders, that he'll still be thinking about what happened against San Francisco? No way."

But for a moment down on the sideline, Jones lost his patience and perspective. A male fan sitting a few rows behind the Cowboy bench yelled, "Go back to the pressbox, Jerry!" With his pride on the line in front of some of the players, Jones walked to the end of the bench and glared at the guy, who silently shrank back into a group of pro-Jones fans who yelled their encouragement to the owner. Jones turned back to watch the game. The guy came back to life, yelling, "Yeah, turn your back, Jerry." That did it. Jones strode to the retaining wall above which the fans sit, pointed at his tormentor, and said, "Kiss my fuckin' ass."

Later, he said, "I know I shouldn't have done it, but I just reacted without thinking. I guess I was fortunate he didn't come after me. I don't know what I'd have done."

Jones probably would have met him head on while hoping the guy didn't know kung fu or a good lawyer.

Perhaps to save himself from himself, Jones spent much of the third quarter in the locker room, watching some of the debacle on TV with Troy Aikman and Leigh Steinberg. "In my own way," says Jones, "I wanted to tell Troy I knew what he was feeling, as much as I *could* feel it."

On the Cowboys' first offensive play, the 49ers had made another shrewd move, sending Marquez Pope, a tough-tackling safety playing cornerback, on a "corner" blitz. Pope came free and blindsided Aikman a split second after he had released the pass. Down he went, banging his knee on the concrete-based turf. The metal brace he wears turned into a weapon, bruising the knee. Midway through the first quarter, when 49er defensive tackle Dana Stubblefield took down Aikman, he again landed on the knee.

As trainer Kevin O'Neill knelt over him, Aikman angrily said, "I'm hurt worse than you think."

It has come to this for Aikman: The Last American Hero has been portrayed as "indestructible" for so long that he almost has to grab the trainer by the lapels and say, "I'm *hurt*, damn it!" Yet despite his reputation, he has been hurt a lot. Without complaint he endured an unholy beating in his first three seasons. Concussions, shoulder surgeries, knee surgeries, torn muscles—name it, Aikman suffered it, multiple times, making his body increasingly susceptible to similar breakdowns (especially concussions). So he has become brittle tough: easily injured with a high pain threshold. Confused? So, probably, is Aikman. His friends say all this is further complicated by trying to please a father who kept working the ranch with part of his finger cut off.

In the NFL there are two kinds of tough. There is getting the snot knocked out of you, bouncing up, and completing another pass. That's Aikman tough. Can't-be-intimidated tough. Never-quit tough.

Then there is injured tough. No-regard-for-your-body tough. Play-with-broken-bones tough. Aikman is too smart and civilized to be this kind of tough—especially now that he has won multiple Super Bowls and would like to win several more. When he believes he's hurt, he's *hurt*. He is not going to do something stupid and risk hurting himself worse. He is no longer going to be John Wayne Jr.

After he left the 49er game and was taken to the locker room, Aikman said he was having trouble bending the knee. He was walking gingerly—yet he was able to walk. Now for the tricky questions: If this had been a playoff game, would he have returned and played through the pain? If he hadn't been humiliated to the bone by San Francisco's 24–0 lead, would he have tried to keep playing? Was he really hurt worse than anyone thought, or was the pain as much emotional as physical? Did Aikman just want to disassociate himself from the "disorganized disgrace" Galloway would write about—from the coach who was "out of his league"?

Only Aikman knows the answers.

Switzer, again, was left to take the brunt of the blame. His camp was left to wonder if Aikman's early exit had been calculated to set up Switzer for an even harder fall. More important, some of Aikman's teammates were beginning to question the quarterback, according to many sources. Many Cowboys were playing with injuries that would require surgery. Tony Tolbert would need double knee surgery, Charles Haley back surgery, and Dixon Edwards shoulder surgery, just to name three. Deion Sanders was playing with hamstring and groin pulls. As John Blake said, "A lot of players are saying, 'I'm out there busting my ass, playing hurt. Where's he?' I mean, he's a great player—the most accurate passer ever, bar none. But you have to wonder what's going on."

Though Steinberg didn't seem terribly concerned about Aikman's knee right after the game, he did tell reporters on Monday that a "black spot" showed up on an MRI. Low-grade hysteria ensued. Was Aikman gone for the season? Several players wondered

why he didn't show up for treatment, as all injured players are supposed to do. "Where's Troy Boy?" was the mumbled complaint. On
schedule, he practiced that week. He didn't seem hobbled the next
Sunday in Oakland, where he played superbly.

True grit? Was Aikman playing with pain at Oakland? Or had he
healed that quickly? Again, under the bizarre circumstances, these
questions from the Switzer camp reflected only mild paranoia.

Dale Hansen says Pro Bowl safety Darren Woodson told him in
casual conversation that Aikman "quit" on the team against San
Francisco. But when Hansen told Aikman, and Aikman confronted
Woodson, Woodson denied saying Aikman quit. Perhaps Woodson
didn't want to take the fall for a number of players who were upset
with Aikman. Or perhaps Woodson thought Hansen, and in turn
Aikman, had misinterpreted his use of "quit." That word also
applied to not standing on the sideline in civilian clothes during the
second half and not facing the media firing squad after the game.
Aikman did not return to the field, even in jeans. By the time the
media was allowed into the locker room, Aikman was gone.

Several insiders said Aikman left the stadium during the game;
Switzer was left with that impression. Many in the organization
were concerned by Aikman's disappearance—especially after it
became clear he wasn't badly injured. Naturally, it would have
looked better to his teammates if the franchise quarterback had
returned to stand beside them in collapse and among them when
the media descended. His leaving increased the risk that any player
who resented his $50 million contract would think, "Oh, so now he's
too good to be seen with us."

Lacewell suggested to Switzer that he at least talk with Aikman,
just to check signals and see exactly what had happened. But, perhaps
fearing a "chat" could turn into a confrontation, Switzer was reluctant
to call Aikman into his office. This led to another misconception.

Not until after the season did I find out that, during the third
quarter, Aikman was about to walk back down the tunnel to the
field, where he planned to stand in street clothes and watch the rest
of the game. But he was met by a security official, who suggested he
take routine precaution by staying in the locker room. Death threats
had been phoned in to Texas Stadium—perhaps by irate gamblers
or demented fans who expected the Cowboys to win 42–17. With
the Cowboys, death threats have become fairly routine. But still,
why risk sideline exposure when the game was a blowout and Aikman was through for the day?

Jones and Switzer weren't informed of the death threats
because Aikman did not return to the field and was in no immedi-

ate danger. Aikman could have done himself a favor by at least sharing with key teammates—not to mention coaches—this valid reason for his sideline absence. But it was increasingly amazing how little any of the principal figures in the franchise communicated.

Aikman, Jones, and Switzer rarely interacted. The Emmitts and Irvins and Deions—each an act unto himself—seemed to have little feel for the depth of the Aikman-Switzer clash. Often, it seemed that none of the players had much idea how the front office worked: who did what, when, and why. Each star held on to only a small but important part of the elephant.

Often, the right hands at Valley Ranch didn't really know what the left hands were doing. Staffers were sometimes reduced to asking reporters if *they* knew what was going on. Some days, that gleaming machine hailed for years under Tex Schramm as the "most efficient organization in sports" seemed more like a confederacy of dunces. "If you see it from the inside out," one official told me, "it's amazing anything ever gets done around here." Things got done, but not routinely and efficiently and not without a drop-dead deadline. Jerry, Barry, and Larry didn't communicate as much as outsiders would think, because Jones was often tied up with league business, lawsuits, and interviews. Jones was trying to do three jobs at once (owner, general manager, celebrity), and there were only so many hours in a day. So from hour to hour, as a rumor spread up and down the maze of hallways, the truth was spread thin.

One last half-truth: Aikman insists he did stay at Texas Stadium through Switzer's postgame remarks to the team. But he did leave before the locker room was opened to the media. While Deion and Irvin went through stretches of refusing to talk to reporters after games, this was not like Aikman, who always had been classy in defeat. Aikman was not himself.

When Switzer finished his postgame remarks to the media, he returned as usual to the coaches' dressing room, where some of the assistants were still changing back into their coats and ties. The door always remains closed, but through it, from ten feet away, you could hear Switzer yelling. Much of what he said was garbled by the crashing of flying objects, but he clearly ended the tirade with ". . . I'll fire your ass tomorrow." Switzer had probably been detonated by an offhand remark from a defensive assistant about the lack of a pass rush on Grbac. The criticism, probably, was aimed at defensive line coach John Blake, who was taking more and more heat from fellow assistants.

Switzer didn't want to hear a word of it. When he did overhear the remark, he took it as a symptom of staff cancer. Switzer erupted. One more word about Blake and somebody's head would roll.

Yet even Lacewell was growing impatient with Blake. "He's such a good young football coach," Lacewell said. "But he still has some things to learn." One day when Lacewell dropped by Blake's office to offer a suggestion, Blake half-listened and dismissed it with a half-interested, "Yeah, I know that." Lacewell heated and said, "You know, John, when I was at Alabama, a guy named Paul Bryant sometimes stopped by my office just like this to make a suggestion. Even if I had already thought of it, I acted like I was hearing it for the first time." And Lacewell walked out, with Blake following and saying, "Lace, Lace . . . I didn't mean it that way."

That week, after a three-mile jog, Blake sounded more worn out mentally than physically. He wasn't his usual upbeat, "got it covered" self. He sensed turbulence ahead. He said, "I've just got to hang on until I can get a [head-coaching] job."

It wasn't until after the season that I was able to tell Aikman what a critical role Larry Lacewell played during November and December. Behind Valley Ranch's celluloid scenes, Lacewell was especially helpful to and protective of Aikman—something the quarterback did not know. Aikman wasn't even sure of Lacewell's job description and rarely said more than hello to him in the hall.

Yet, while Aikman was trying to play the "Jimmy" role on the field, Lacewell had, in a way, become the Jimmy Johnson of the front office. Yes, the man who gave Johnson his first break in college coaching and who taught him much of his bedrock philosophy had replaced him. This is to take nothing away from Jones, whose instincts, guts, and drive are essential Super Bowl ingredients, but Lacewell's football wisdom saved several late-season days. This is strictly my view—one Lacewell does not share. But following the season, when he was inducted into Arkansas's sports Hall of Fame, Lacewell was equally honored around Valley Ranch with the line, "He should be inducted into the [Cowboy] Ring of Honor."

Lacewell was the franchise conscience. Of Jerry, Barry, and Larry, the latter was the one who said, "Wait a second." The little man with the big man's swagger commanded respect when he walked into any coach's or scout's office. He knew the Cowboy defense as well as any coach; he helped think it up at Oklahoma. He almost always knew whether a player could play or if coaches were fooling themselves. He knew when Switzer had screwed up and when the assistants had gone stale in their thinking. He knew when trouble was brewing; he could feel it in his joints. Talking to him was like reading Mark Twain on football. Lacewell on two bad teams playing a close game: "It was like two dogs barking at each other and one of 'em fainted."

Lacewell ran the draft. Lacewell was the final arbiter on all player-personnel debates. Larry was the one Jerry and Barry looked to for sage advice when the crisis of the hour struck involving drugs or contracts or skinned egos.

Yet at midseason, Aikman asked another Cowboy employee exactly what Lacewell did and why he sometimes hung around practice. Come again? It was as if Aikman thought Lacewell was just another member of the "Oklahoma Mafia" who had a job mostly because Switzer had his job.

That's how little the franchise quarterback knew about the inner workings of the franchise. Sometimes it appeared Switzer kept his job because Lacewell did his job so subtly and wisely.

The week after the 49er game, Lacewell was concerned about Switzer, as were several Valley Ranch staffers. One said, "Barry's going to mess around and make Jerry fire him. If it gets to that point, Jerry will call him in, they'll cry and hug a lot, and Jerry will put a big check in his pocket and send him back to Norman."

Was Switzer spending too much time on a potential restaurant deal? Several staffers wondered. Had Switzer's staff prepared thoroughly and creatively enough for the 49ers? Lacewell wasn't sure. So Lacewell, with the help of scout Walter Juliff, soon began studying the 49ers the way Michener would: breaking down stacks of tapes, charting tendencies, analyzing what works and doesn't work against their offense and defense. No, the Cowboys weren't scheduled to play them again. But everyone at Valley Ranch had circled January 14. Dallas vs. San Francisco, for the fourth straight year in the NFC championship game. "This time, we will leave no stone unturned," said Lacewell, who dedicated himself to solving the 49ers.

The next Sunday in Oakland, at Switzer's request, Lacewell went down on the field before the game and went over a few coverages with secondary coach Mike Zimmer, who had been with the Cowboys just a season and a half. Then, as the game began, Lacewell and Jones sat next to each other in a small booth just off the pressbox. This game, said Lacewell, "will go a long ways toward determining the rest of our season—this one and Kansas City [four days later on Thanksgiving]." In the second half, I noticed Lacewell had moved to a chair behind Jones. Later, he laughed and said, "I was going to get hurt next to him. I think he recovered six fumbles in the first quarter alone."

Lacewell probably broke up a couple of passes himself. Like

Jones, he got awfully worked up for games, his blood pressure constantly edging into the red zone. Lacewell had endured several
angiograms—and soon would live to tell about another one. His
family had been plagued by heart disease, and several times
Lacewell's heart had become such a clenched fist that he surely
thought he was a goner. Soon after the Oakland and Kansas City
games, he was rushed to the hospital again. But he bounced back
quickly, missing only a couple of work days. "Thank the Lord," he
said. "The doctor said, 'Are you under a lot of stress?' And I said,
'Me? Stress?'"

No one suffered any more heartburn over the daily Cowboy
soap opera than Larry Lacewell. In several ways, he was a better
football man than Switzer, but Switzer had one big advantage: His
arteries seemed to be made of stainless steel.

Did Switzer stay late at the office reviewing tape the Friday
night before the trip to Oakland? Hell, no. He and his brother Donnie went to check out the new Bond flick *GoldenEye*. Switzer has
walked unscathed out of nearly as many death-defying scrapes as
007.

The Saturday night before the game, I sat in Dale Hansen's room at
the Cowboy hotel outside Oakland in San Ramon and listened to
his highly entertaining and provocative soliloquy on what was
wrong with the Cowboys. As usual, the focus was on Switzer, and of
course, Hansen's opinions had been provided or substantiated by
008.

Yet as much as I admired Hansen's commitment to showing the
Cowboy world he was no Cowboy shill, I was sometimes stunned by
his fearless stances on Jones's coach. The previous Sunday's San
Francisco earthquake at Texas Stadium had sent Hansen perilously
close to Jones's fault line again.

But when the franchise quarterback is helping write some of
your material . . .

Hansen began with the fan backlash after the 49er loss: "I
detect an arrogance on the team the fans are getting tired of. Erik
Williams. Shante Carver. Clayton Holmes. Leon Lett. That's why
there was such a strong reaction to a simple game in November. It
was like [fans saying], 'You're embarrassing me. You're offending
me' . . . I mean, Jerry could have owned this town. Why does he
continue to make it so hard for people to like him? He keeps raising ticket prices. My God, $28 for parking? You can park in a high
rise in downtown Dallas for $28 a month . . . I really think he's out
of control. I believe in what he's doing [in his battles with the

league], I just don't believe in *how* he's doing it. Why does he have to do the Pepsi press conference [in the Pepsi boots] and Phil Knight?"

From the start, Hansen has been a Jones fan, always taking the "shrewd" side of the shrewd-or-goofy debate about the owner. "But now you sometimes have to wonder," said Hansen, who kept looking [unsuccessfully] for the shrewd side of Switzer. "I mean, I used to be in awe of Switzer when he was at Oklahoma. I used to think he was Barry Fucking Switzer. And I just haven't seen that guy."

Switzer's aura *was* different in Dallas. At Oklahoma, his cock-of-the-walk body language told everyone within binocular range that he was in charge. But in Dallas, where he has suffered from a disk problem in his neck, reducing him to an old-man shuffle and stiff-necked full-shoulder turns to greet people, his presence has been much smaller. At practice he's more of an observer than a commander. An outsider definitely wouldn't know he's the head coach. Switzer knew full well that two Super Bowls had been won before him and that nobody was graduating. So he didn't try to dominate the way he once did in "Switzerland."

But Hansen was asking the same question Aikman was: "What does he *do*? I honestly believe I could have coached the team to 12–4 last year . . . Seriously, would any other owner hire him? . . . A lot of players on the team are questioning his leadership . . . One of the theories the players have [about the early turnovers two straight games against the 49ers] is that Troy and Michael are trying to do too much because they don't trust the head coach."

Hanson said they couldn't even trust Switzer in his postgame press conferences, when Switzer sometimes suddenly went off the Richter scale. Hansen: "I mean, he embarrasses me during those press conferences, and I think he embarrasses Aikman and all the rest of them. Did he do that stuff at Oklahoma? I don't think so."

(When I asked Rich Dalrymple about Switzer's postgame behavior, he said, "You can't coach emotion." But Lacewell mentioned to Switzer that he probably should calm down during group postgame interviews. Lacewell said, "He doesn't need to impress anybody with how much he knows, just make a few simple statements and let the players do most of the talking." Lacewell laughed. "I've listened to him and wondered if maybe he forgot to take his medicine.")

Hansen had his doubts about whether the Cowboys would win the next day. The Raiders also were 8–2. The Raiders knew the Cowboy personnel and schemes because the teams had practiced twice a day against each other for a week during training camp and had played an exhibition game. For the Raiders, this was a "Super Bowl preview"—a chance to prove they belonged in the two-team league with the 49ers and Cowboys.

"But of course," Hansen said with a laugh, "just when I think they're in trouble, they'll probably win by 30."

It looked like Halloween three weeks late. As the Cowboy buses rolled toward the coliseum, the last mile or so was lined with Raider fans with their faces painted a ghastly black-and-white. They looked as if they had escaped from a *Dracula* audition or the rock group Kiss, and almost every one of them welcomed the Cowboys with a single-finger salute. It was like playing an away game at Transylvania. Blood was three bucks a cup at the concession stand. Vendors were tossing boxes of chocolate-covered eyeballs to customers. The meat in the hotdogs came from the bodies of visiting teams.

Said Dale Hellestrae, Aikman's buddy and an eleven-year veteran: "Definitely a hostile environment. But I think that worked to our advantage because we've always been a good road team. And our recent history has been that whenever we've had a setback, we've responded like gangbusters."

With 3:35 left in the third quarter, Dallas led 31–7. The Cowboys had done a San Francisco on Oakland. Only a flashback performance by forty-year-old backup quarterback Vince Evans cut the final margin to 34–21. The best fights were in the stands, among frustrated ghouls. The final gun might as well have been shot at the Raiders, to put them out of their misery. They wouldn't win another game, falling all the way to 8–8 and missing the playoffs.

The Dallas Cowboys had made a statement that would echo into January: They did not quit on Barry Switzer. They basically could have ended their season—maybe even Switzer's career—by rolling over and playing dead. Instead, the Cowboys shouted from Transylvania's peaks that Dallas was still the NFL's best team when challenged.

Switzer was unusually subdued during his postgame interview—thanks to a little reminder from Lacewell. Switzer quickly ended his remarks with "Get with the players. Hell, they were the ones who did the job."

A few feet from Switzer's interview stand, Dale Hansen was preparing to interview Aikman live for a couple of minutes on Channel 8's postgame TV show. Hansen knew Aikman was incensed over a column I'd written in the previous Wednesday's *Insider*, and Hansen and Brad Sham had made Aikman aware that Darren Woodson, if not a few other players, had questioned his early departure from the

49er loss. So, during a commercial, as Aikman took his place beside Hansen and first-year play-by-play announcer Dave Garrett, Hansen said, "Be ready. I'm going to stick you with something at the end." Aikman winked at him and said, "Be careful."

Hansen was anything but. After the predictable questions about how well Aikman and the team had played against Oakland, Hansen fired one last one: "Did you quit in the San Francisco game?"

Understand, not a whisper about the Switzer camp vs. Aikman camp, the quarterback's peculiar 49er-game behavior, or any teammate displeasure with the quarterback had been reported by the print or electronic media. So to even a rabid fan, Hansen's question was a shocker. *Did he what?*

Aikman's answer was remarkably succinct and effective: "If anyone thinks I quit, they either don't know me or they haven't been watching the Cowboys for the last seven years."

Hansen didn't notice, but as Aikman walked away, he turned and gave Hansen a disgusted look. As Mark Tuinei stepped in to be interviewed, Hansen couldn't help noticing what he called Garrett's "deer-in-the-headlights" look. On camera, Hansen said, "What, you think I wouldn't ask that question?"

Aikman definitely didn't think Hansen would. Later, Hansen was surprised to hear Aikman was upset with him. Hansen says, "I thought it was a beach ball [an easy question to answer]. I thought he'd do just what he did, which was give a drop-dead, kick-ass, shut-the-fuck-up answer. But his position was that I *knew* the answer, and that I was giving the whole thing credence merely by asking the question. He said I had no right to ask it. He said, 'Switzer can plant it. Bayless can write it. You *know* better. I don't *need* to address those son of a bitches."

Aikman sarcastically suggested Hansen was trying to be "like your role model Bayless." Meaning, I suppose, Hansen was trying to show he could be a critical journalist and follow up on a question I had raised.

Yet the only question I had raised—at the bottom of my column, after criticizing Switzer for the San Francisco loss—was if Aikman had decided not to return to the game because the 49ers "had his number." For three straight games against San Francisco, very little had gone right for Aikman. So I basically asked if Aikman was stung psychologically. I did not suggest he quit physically. (Said Steinberg, "To question that is like asking Troy if his mother is a whore.") But I did ask, "Should Aikman go blameless for Switzer's 0–3 vs. San Francisco?"

Aikman had made early dramatic and uncharacteristic mistakes in each of the three games. But apparently, by merely raising that question, I officially declared myself a knife-carrying member of the "Oklahoma Mafia" in Aikman's eyes. Did Switzer tell or encourage me to write what I wrote? Absolutely not. Did others in his camp influence me? Somewhat. But again they asked valid questions, which a number of players were asking.

Aikman was becoming just as sensitive and paranoid as Switzer. That went double for their confidants.

Before the Thanksgiving game at Texas Stadium, Hansen mentioned that Aikman was "pissed" at me. But Hansen added: "I get the feeling that deep down, he knows he didn't handle things [during and after the San Francisco game] quite the way he should have." I still naively thought I had a solid professional working relationship with Aikman. So I decided that, if the Cowboys beat Kansas City, I would try to catch Aikman in the locker room and clear the air about the "quit" issue.

The afternoon before Thanksgiving, I wandered by Switzer's office and thought I'd stick my head in and just say hello. I hadn't spoken to him for a while and figured he'd be feeling considerably better about things, even though his 9–2 team faced another difficult assignment: 10–1 Kansas City. To my surprise, there were Switzer and his secretary, Barbara Goodman, watching what sounded like a movie on Switzer's tape machine. Not a football movie. A Hollywood movie. Barbara, who faithfully served Landry and Johnson, is simply the hardest working woman in the show business that is Cowboy football. She works long hours without complaint. She's tirelessly devoted to her boss and her family. She's exceptionally polite to visitors—even reporters—while continuing to chip away at the three or four tasks she's always doing at once. I wasn't sure Barbara ever had found time to watch a movie in her life.

But Switzer is no Scrooge. It was almost Thanksgiving. I could just hear him saying, "That stuff can wait till Monday, Barbara. Pull up a chair and watch this." If Landry had asked her to watch a movie, she might have fainted.

I mention this only because, that night, I was supposed to drop by the Kansas City Chiefs' hotel in North Dallas and see my friend Paul Hackett, who was now the Chiefs' offensive coordinator. But Hackett called about 9 P.M. to say he just couldn't get free. The coaching staff, he said, had even flown in a secretary, and they still had several more hours of computer printouts to study. Of course, head coaches don't usually spend as many hours game-planning as coordinators, but with only three days to prepare for a Thursday game, the contrast between Hackett and *his* secretary and Switzer and *his* was, if nothing else, amusing.

Though the Cowboy coaches were impressed with the Chiefs, who played tough, smart NFC-style defense and ball-control offense, the Chiefs just couldn't match the Cowboys' star power. Irvin made a full-speed, look-Ma, one-handed catch in the end zone that Hackett called "one of the best I've ever seen." Though Hackett had vowed to "get Deion" one time on a post route, the Chiefs failed to do so in four attempts. And a subtle change in what had been a predictable Cowboy coverage momentarily confused Chief quarterback Steve Bono, who was sacked and fumbled away an opportunity to cut the Cowboy lead to 21–19. Dallas prevailed 24–12. "We'll give 'em a better game," Hackett said, "if we're lucky enough to see 'em in the Super Bowl."

After beating the two best teams in the AFC, Dallas was 10–2 with ten days off. Emmitt had sprained a knee, but he told the coaches he thought it would be fine. Happy Thanksgiving: I couldn't imagine a better time to talk to Aikman. I didn't expect him to be jovial or even polite. But I did not expect him to be hostile. After the locker room had nearly cleared out, I approached him at his locker.

As you've read, he let me have it, concluding with "Your sources are a fucking joke."

Now, perhaps, you can better understand the tangled roots of Aikman's rage.

Much later, after the season, Aikman told me that "I yell at my sisters and they say, 'Hey, what's going on?' Then in a little while, I'm fine." This, however, didn't sound like something that soon would be fine.

This wasn't just about "quitting." It was about allegiance, taking sides and politically calculated shots. No matter how I protested, Aikman would not accept that I remained unaffiliated. Aikman's profane bombardment was my first overt indication that Switzer vs. Aikman had gone over the edge. Even at 10–2, trouble loomed. In this case, winning was about to *cause* cancer.

15

THE N-WORD

O! beware, my lord . . .

—*Iago to Othello*

There wasn't much Jimmy Johnson memorial sense of urgency as the Cowboys returned to practice for the stretch run—or stroll. All that stood between Dallas and home-field advantage throughout the playoffs were home games against 3–9 Washington and 4–9 New York and away games against 4–9 Arizona and an 8–4 Philadelphia that had been no match for Dallas at Texas Stadium. Just four more December games, against four division rivals the Cowboys knew like the palms of their hands. Again, perhaps, Switzer was too honest: He told his players all they had to do to clinch home field was win three of the four, so why not do it the easy way? Why not win three straight and relax?

Why (ha-ha) not (hee-hee)?

The lowlight of Thursday's practice was another skirmish between Troy Aikman and receiver Kevin Williams. Aikman didn't think Williams was concentrating on a route that might work—might be important—against Washington. Aikman snapped at Williams, who scowled back. Williams, who had caught only nineteen passes in twelve games, still hadn't won Aikman's respect or trust.

Williams was the un-Michael, Irvin's flip side. Williams you rarely noticed, on or off the field. Though he was a local boy made

pretty good, a Dallas Roosevelt High product who had become a
Dallas Cowboy starter, you didn't read or hear much in Dallas about
Williams, who wasn't much of a talker or entertainer. Williams followed Irvin at the University of Miami, but he never quite filled
Irvin's blue suede shoes. Williams appeared and played smaller than
his listed height and weight of 5'9" and 195 pounds. Coaches affectionately called him "Small Fry." Williams was quick and fast, but
he sometimes got pushed around by the more physical cornerbacks.
Irvin, of course, appeared and played bigger than his 6'2" and 205
pounds and made up for average speed with bullying strength. Irvin
was football-quick mentally; it took Williams a while to catch on. So
Cowboy formations appeared to be an unbalanced teeter-totter of
"Small Fry" and "the Playmaker."

But make no mistake, Irvin respected the one the players called
"K-Dub," short for "KW." Deion Sanders respected Williams so
much as a kick returner that Deion told coaches he didn't think it
was fair for him to just walk in and replace the little man on kick-
offs and punts. Still, Williams tormented Aikman because his mind
wandered and he sometimes ran imperfect routes or dropped perfect passes. For Aikman, Williams could be "the Playbreaker."

Aikman treated teammates with caste-system respect: The more
a player had proven, the less Aikman reprimanded him. Though
Aikman insists he "didn't yell at Kevin any more than anyone else,"
his blowups at Williams were becoming more exasperated and
harsh. As the days grew shorter, so did Williams's patience. How
could he prove himself, he wondered, when Aikman wouldn't throw
to him in games?

That cold, gray Sunday at Texas Stadium, Aikman was forced to
throw to Williams more than usual. The Cowboys were giving a
cold, gray effort against Norv Turner's lowly Redskins, who were
smart enough to attack Irvin the way the 49ers had: by rolling a
safety "over the top" into Irvin's path and taking him away from
Aikman with constant double coverage. Yet against Dallas you
picked your poison: If the safety shaded Irvin, he couldn't break to
the line of scrimmage and become an extra linebacker to help contain Emmitt Smith. The 49ers, with their magnificent front seven,
could control Emmitt without much help from their safeties. But
right away against Washington, as the Cowboys came out in an out-
of-character four-receiver set, it was obvious to Turner that Emmitt
hadn't fully recovered from his sprained knee. So the Redskins
dared Dallas to beat them with Emmitt—or with Kevin Williams,
who had only one man to beat. Turner knew how uncomfortable
Aikman was having to rely on No. 85.

Aikman was in the midst of playing what even Turner, his biggest fan, thought was "the worst game I've seen him play." For the day his nineteen incompletions were three fewer than his previous four games combined. He finished 29 of 47 for a quiet 285 yards. But one of those incompletions—on a third-and-long late in the third quarter with Dallas trailing by 4—caused a reverberating reaction.

Not from the fans, who merely groaned.

From Aikman and Williams, who engaged in a shouting match. The route had been the same one Williams had messed up in practice, and he had messed it up again. But as the two reached the sideline, Aikman's "I told you so" turned profane and insulting, and Williams returned fire.

Finally, Williams said something like, "You don't talk to Michael Irvin like that."

Aikman: "You're not Michael Irvin."

Williams: "You can't talk to me that way."

Which made Aikman even madder: "Who are *you* to tell *me* how I can and can't talk to you?"

What you had were two proud, frustrated athletes losing their heads in the heat of battle—especially the quarterback. This happens every Sunday on many NFL sidelines. But, of course, not every NFL team has a superstar quarterback who's trying to "get" the head coach and vice versa. What happened next you could see coming all the way from Norman.

Like John Blake, Danny Bradley had voiced his concern to Switzer that Aikman was coming across as aloof and condescending to many of the black players—who, said Bradley, had whispered their concerns to him. According to several sources, Bradley feared the problem was one slip of the tongue away from exploding into a full-blown, season-wrecking crisis. Bradley had been expressing his fear to several in the Switzer camp, and with their help, Bradley had been pressing Switzer to address the problem.

It remains unclear who, if anyone, told Switzer this happened, or if he just assumed it himself, by the look of angry pain on Williams's face. But Switzer was under the impression that Aikman had crossed the line and called Williams a racial slur. Over the next few weeks, several in the Switzer camp thought Aikman had lost his head and used the n-word.

Even Dale Hansen, when he first heard about Aikman's reaction to the incident, said, "Knowing that Aikman had routinely yelled all sorts of things at Kevin Williams before, and hearing how Aikman was so concerned about apologizing, you look at it from a distance and say, 'He had to have crossed the line.' But after hearing Aikman swear up and down that he didn't cross the line, I don't believe he did."

When Aikman called me after the season, he wanted to address two issues. You already know one, concerning sexual preference. But he also told me: "I did not call Kevin Williams the n-word."

Black receiver coach Hubbard Alexander supports Aikman. "That did not happen," says Alexander. "I would know about it if it had."

After the season, Switzer shrugged off the issue with "Only he [Aikman] knows what he said."

At the time Switzer was upset over the appearance of what had happened and how it would affect Williams for the rest of the game and season. Remember, Barry Switzer is as sensitive to racism as any white coach on the planet. Kathy Switzer half-kids her dad that he's "too much for the black athletes and doesn't pay enough attention to the white guys in the background."

But at that moment on the sideline, it didn't matter to Switzer whether Williams had been racially insulted, directly or indirectly. It just mattered that Williams had been humiliated. Switzer says, "I made a beeline for that kid and put my arm around him and said, 'Son, I believe in you. You're going to make a play for us. That's why I kept you instead of signing [veteran free agent] Gary Clark.'"

Though neither could see it, Switzer and Aikman were playing an effective good-cop, bad-cop. In the next few weeks, Williams would respond spectacularly to his verbal thrashing. But during and after the Washington game, few involved could see past their own bent-out-of-shape nose. Hubbard Alexander, a former Jimmy Johnson assistant who's close to Aikman, says with irritation that he told Blake and Bradley to get away from Aikman and Williams and let him handle it. He notes that later in the game Aikman and Williams hooked up on a 19-yard completion, which probably wouldn't have happened if Aikman had racially offended Williams. For that matter, as Charles Haley later told Aikman, "If you had called Kevin Williams [the n-word], as much as I like you, you and I would have had a *problem*." There was no mutinous reaction over the way the quarterback treated Williams.

For his part, Williams says the profanity was "as bad as you can get." He says Aikman tried to come back five minutes later and apologize. "But I wouldn't talk to him. He tried to talk to me after the game, but I wouldn't do it. Then he came to me the next day and apologized, and I realized Troy and I shared the same goal, which is just to win."

After the season Aikman told me, "As the older player, I felt I had handled the situation wrong—not yelling at Kevin on the field, but the way I handled it [as the shouting match escalated] on the sideline. I appreciate Kevin—I really do. I thought, 'Boy, I really blew it this time.'"

Maybe, if the Cowboys had beaten Washington, the Aikman-Williams clash would have faded into the afterglow for Switzer and his supporters. But the Cowboys lost for a second time to Aikman's soul mate Turner. The final was 24–17. When it ended, Aikman and Irvin quietly told Turner it just hadn't been the same since he left. Irvin made an auspicious display of hugging and kissing Turner in the Redskin locker room. Aikman camper Randy Galloway wrote, "Just wondering what happens if Norv Turner had been standing on the *other* sideline Sunday as coach of the best team money can buy."

Which again left the Switzer camp wondering just what the hell was going on here. Can you blame them? That night, the conspiracy theory surfaced again like a communist sub. Would Aikman see to it that Turner would soon coach the Dallas Cowboys? Was it just coincidence that Aikman had sat out the first Washington game with a calf pull, then played by far his worst game of the season in the second game? Had he purposely played poorly in a game the Cowboys didn't really have to win just to help Turner and hurt Switzer?

Larry Lacewell's balanced perspective: "Maybe Troy was trying *too* hard to impress Norv."

But in three dreary hours the Cowboys had gone from 10–2 to "Team Turmoil." One of the country's most respected pro football writers, Peter King of *Sports Illustrated*, told me after he left the Cowboy locker room: "You heard divisive comments for the first time. You heard the offense criticizing the defense. You heard guys who don't like Barry Switzer. I think that team is in trouble."

That was King's view without even knowing about the Kevin Williams incident or the Oliver Stones being cast back and forth between the Switzer and Aikman camps.

That night Switzer didn't just blame Aikman for the loss. He privately fumed about how all his prima donnas had decided to take the day off. It was in that agitated state that Switzer was informed by Danny Bradley that he had overheard even Michael Irvin grumbling about how verbally abusive Aikman had been to Williams. For Switzer, after hearing several months of warnings about Aikman and potential racial tension, that did it. Switzer decided to summon Aikman to his office the next morning.

Knowing Switzer's love for the restaurant Othello's, you also have to wonder if he had one too many Iagos whispering in his ear.

Switzer first mentioned Oronde Gadsden to me back in minicamp. "I like that No. 1," he said when I asked about the boatload of undrafted rookie free agents trying to make the team. I soon discovered that Gadsden, a receiver from Winston-Salem State who wore No. 1, was another "Dallas in Wonderland" story: He had come to Dallas the previous January to work as an intern at a hat company owned by Drew Pearson, perhaps the most famous undrafted free-agent receiver in NFL history. Pro scouts weren't impressed with Gadsden's 4.6 40-yard dash speed. But he began working with a track coach, who helped shave his times down into the 4.45 range. Pearson took a look at Gadsden's highlight tape and—right out of a TV movie—encouraged a Cowboy scout to take a look. The Cowboys asked him to drop by and catch a few passes. Gadsden soon signed with the team that had always been his favorite.

"The flash, the glitter, the glory," he says. "The silver and blue. The star on the helmet. I even had Tony Dorsett cleats. When I first got out there I was just in awe of everybody."

At 6'3", 218 pounds, he quickly caught Switzer's eye. "I just like the way he moves," said the coach. Through training camp, Gadsden moved up the depth chart, outperforming Cory Fleming. But Fleming had a year of experience on him, and Gadsden wound up on the Cowboy practice squad. All season, though, Cowboy management assured Gadsden he had a future in Dallas. In fact, as he stood on the sideline in street clothes before the Washington game, Stephen Jones made a point of telling Gadsden how pleased the coaches were with his progress.

Gadsden, with a quick smile and a slow-blinking confidence, doesn't let much bother him.

So there he was, standing on the back side of the Cowboy bench area with about five minutes left in the Redskin game. His buddy Sherman Williams, the rookie running back who was in uniform but didn't play, walked over to him and they noticed, up in the stands, Cowboy mascot Crazy Ray playing the same card trick on some woman that he had played on Gadsden before the game. "She had the same look on her face that I had had," says Gadsden. He and Williams started laughing . . .

. . . and Gadsden got caught with his hand in the cookie jar.

At that moment, Washington quarterback Heath Shuler rolled right and cut loose with an Elwayesque heave all the way back across the field, 44 yards to Leslie Shepherd, who had a step on

Larry Brown. Switzer spun away in frustration, "looked through about fifty people," says Gadsden, and locked eyes with the laughing rookie from Winston-Salem. Switzer made a beeline to Gadsden, grabbed him, shook him, and asked him what was so damn funny. Switzer thought Gadsden was laughing at Brown, which would have been entirely believable.

Not only did Larry Brown's teammates make fun of his hands, they laughed at the way, when he was beaten by a receiver, he seldom could locate the ball. One coach called it "doing the turtle": Brown, chasing a receiver, thrust both arms up in the air and sort of retracted his head into his body, the way a turtle goes into his shell.

Much of the season, Brown had felt like going into his shell. During camp, it looked as if Brown finally (some said fittingly) would lose his starting job if Jerry Jones pulled off the Deion deal. After all, Brown had been no more than a twelfth-round draft choice, a well-spoken but flaky kid out of L.A. by way of TCU who had gone inexplicably AWOL during his first Cowboy camp and nearly was cut. But in football, Brown has a flaky angel that watches over him. He returned with a shrug from his unexcused absence to win a starting job because, well, the Cowboys didn't have anyone better. Though Brown doesn't have such hot hands or much hand-eye coordination, he can run, he can cover receivers, and, when he feels like it, he can pack a wallop for a 185-pounder.

But responsible? During the 1994 season, Aikman asked about twenty-five players to be a five-minute guest on his TV show. Only one stood him up. Larry Brown said a cook didn't show at the restaurant he owned in Grapevine. Brown said *he* had to cook. Imagine Brown, on a Thursday night during football season, back in the kitchen flipping hamburger patties. Perhaps that's one reason the restaurant went under.

Worse, he and his wife, Cheryl, had a second child, Kristopher, who was born three months premature just as the 1995 season began. For ten weeks, Brown went to practice, then to the hospital. Kristopher died the week of the Oakland game.

Yet when Kevin Smith tore his Achilles in the opener, Brown survived again and remained a starter. When Deion hit town, Brown began to intercept some passes. As Norv Turner said of his Cowboy game plan, "We decided to play ten on ten. Wherever Deion went, we ignored that guy [receiver]. Why risk it?" That meant lots of business for Brown. Sometimes, when a quarterback made a really bad throw, Brown couldn't help catching the ball. Somehow, he had gone from potential backup to emerging "star."

But, lovingly, his teammates still laughed at some of the things he did.

After the Washington game, Switzer concluded his remarks to the team with: "That person who was laughing at Larry Brown is going to have a talk with me first thing in the morning, in my office."

Gadsden was there at 8:30 A.M. Switzer told him, "You know why I have to do this."

Gadsden tried to explain, to apologize.

"I understand," said Switzer. "But I have to do this for the team."

Gadsden realized he was being cut. "Well, then," Gadsden said, "thanks for everything you've done for me. I really appreciate it."

Yet he was further confused when Switzer said, "Well, it may not be permanent."

Later that day I talked to Gadsden's agent, Michael Todd, who couldn't figure out (1) if the Cowboys had officially waived Gadsden and (2) why Switzer would choose to make an example of a rookie practice-squadder. Todd said, "That's like hitting a gnat with a sledgehammer. Do you really think Michael Irvin is shaking in his boots?"

Switzer knew the legend of Curvin Richards. When Switzer protested that he "couldn't be an actor like Jimmy," he often added, "What do you want me to do, cut a backup running back?" On the final day of the 1992 season, Richards fumbled twice in the fourth quarter of a meaningless game, and Jimmy Johnson made a media event out of cutting Richards. It was a brilliant move: Richards, as the only backup to Emmitt Smith, was valuable enough to raise eyebrows and doubts. But Johnson knew that if Emmitt went down, the Cowboys almost certainly wouldn't make it to the Super Bowl. So Johnson, the actor-director, used Richards to cement his image as the win-or-else tyrant who would not tolerate mistakes.

With Gadsden, it appeared Switzer finally was desperate enough to try pulling his own "Curvin Richards." But this was like Kevin Costner trying to play Wyatt Earp: Switzer's heart is too big. There wasn't any new sheriff in town; Switzer was firing blanks. When Gadsden went to Nate Newton for advice, Newton told him that Switzer "don't do stuff like that."

The "cutting" of Oronde Gadsden was no more than a note on page five or six of the papers. Many fans wouldn't have known Oronde from the Gadsden Purchase.

By the following Monday, Gadsden had been "reinstated." When he bumped into Switzer in the players' lounge, the coach "joked about everything," says Gadsden. "He said to tell the media he had made me run some laps."

But the Monday after the Washington game, Switzer's next appointment turned into no laughing matter.

Troy Aikman says he tried and failed to reach Kevin Williams by phone on Sunday night. When Aikman arrived at Valley Ranch on Monday, he went looking for Williams, but was told Switzer wanted to see him.

Leigh Steinberg says Aikman walked back to the coach's office half-expecting a pep talk: "You know, a pat on the back, some reassurance that everything was going to be okay."

This mostly is Aikman's recall of his closed-door conversation with Switzer. The coach wouldn't discuss it.

There was no pep talk. Switzer got right to it, saying some concern had been expressed in that morning's defensive staff meeting over Aikman's involvement in the Kevin Williams incident. "Yeah," Aikman told Switzer, "I tried to call him last night and I'm looking for him right now." No problem, Aikman assured the coach. He would handle it.

Aikman remembers, "Now I was waiting for him to tell me the reason I'd been called in."

It took another minute or so of throat-clearing and vague references to fallout from the Williams incident before Aikman realized *that* was why he was making a rare appearance in Switzer's office. He basically had been called on the carpet.

Switzer suggested that maybe he "say something to the offense"—by way of apology, was Switzer's drift—and "it will trickle down to the defense."

Aikman was thinking, Why do I need to say anything—especially to the offense? Didn't this come from the defensive staff meeting?

Switzer told him, "You know how some players are. They might be pretty sensitive to something like this. You know, players like Darren Woodson and Deion."

Several sources close to Switzer say, in hindsight, he wishes he had been clearer on that point. He didn't mean Woodson and Deion *were* upset, only that players of their stature might be. Remember, he had been told Irvin was upset, but he didn't want to pit Irvin against Aikman. Instead, unintentionally, he had pitted Woodson and Deion vs. Aikman—or so the quarterback thought.

Aikman remembers being shaken and confused as he got up to

leave. Again, if the head coach and quarterback had developed any rapport or mutual respect, Switzer could have pulled Aikman aside and said, "Hey, big guy, what's going on between you and K-Dub?" If the coach and quarterback had shared a wavelength, the coach even might have said, "You didn't call him the n-word, did you? No? Well, be careful, because even though you don't intend to, you're coming across as maybe a little racist."

"Gotcha, coach."

But obviously, this coach and quarterback now eyed each other as enemies. From what he had been told by his supporters, Switzer was under the impression that Aikman was one strange guy—possibly a gay racist who wanted Norv Turner sitting in Switzer's chair. Meanwhile, Aikman saw Switzer as Jones's half-crazy, Ritalin-popping puppet who had run amok and was using me and Dean Blevins to mount a media campaign against him. Those views might be slightly exaggerated, but only slightly. Some days, like the Monday after Washington, those views might have been understatements.

It was that insane.

Yet Switzer still knew it was Super-Bowl-or-bust with Aikman. What was he going to do, trade him? Bench him? Cut him? Switzer argues that by dealing head-on with the Williams incident, "I was trying to *help* Troy, and he just couldn't see that. He didn't understand he was being protected. I was trying to defuse the situation. I said to the team [later that day] that things happen in the heat of the moment, and that Troy would say the same things to DJ [Daryl Johnston, who is white] or Jay [Novacek, who is white]."

To an incensed Aikman, that put the incident in a racial context in which it did not belong.

Switzer says, "I told the team Troy had worked it out with Kevin Williams. All of it was innocent. Then [when the story broke at the Super Bowl] people were trying to make it out to be racist. I was trying to cover Troy's ass by making it not racist, by saying he'd chew a white guy's ass out, too."

Blevins says, "To me, it was a bold move by a head coach who nipped a potential problem in the bud. He did defuse it by getting it out in the open. Who knows how long it might have festered?"

A couple of days later John Blake lauded Switzer's move, saying, "It really helped clear the air, and I think it helped Troy think about some things. If he hadn't been bothered by any of it, why did he go back and talk to several of the guys about it?"

Aikman says that was to clear his name, not his conscience.

After the season Switzer sighed and said, "I guess if I'd just kept my mouth shut, none of this would have happened. I guess I just should have let the son of a bitches figure it out for themselves."

In Aikman's view, that's basically what happened.

Aikman says he walked back to the locker room and found Kevin Williams and Deion next to each other in the trainer's room. "So I thought I'd kill two birds with one stone by bringing it up in front of both of them. Kevin and I visited for about thirty minutes. Everything was fine." Aikman notes that, after the season, "my buddies and I" ran into Williams at a restaurant and that Williams joined them for a round of drinks. It's doubtful Williams will be asking Aikman to help him pick out a tropical fish tank, but their sideline clash definitely improved their relationship.

Deion, says Aikman, also seemed to have no problem with what had happened. But Aikman still wasn't sure exactly where he stood with Woodson and the defensive coaches. Tuesday was an off day. But before the next day's practice, says Steinberg, Switzer again brought up the Williams incident to Aikman, this time within earshot of some players. "Troy just walked away," says Steinberg. "He was humiliated. This whole thing was outrageous, unconscionable . . . The incredible irony was that the only reason Troy was yelling at guys so much was because he was trying to play the 'Jimmy' role. Switzer sure wouldn't take that responsibility."

Aikman says, "I don't enjoy that role . . . But I've seen Charles Haley undress a guy [chew out a teammate]. Michael Irvin gets on everybody."

Aikman says that as Wednesday's practice began with team stretching, defensive backfield coach Mike Zimmer walked over and said not to lump him in with the "defensive coaches" who supposedly complained to Switzer. "Then," says Aikman, "Dave Campo came over and told me the same thing, and I'm thinking, 'What's this all about?' Then I looked up and saw Barry and 'Boo' over there watching me and whispering to each other, and it all started coming clear. It wasn't the defensive staff that complained. This was coming from one defensive coach.

"You know, a lot of [defensive linemen] who played for John [Blake] have had problems with him. He's been known to be insincere about things, and he can be insecure. He tells one thing to one person, something else to another. Some [of the defensive linemen] weren't going to re-sign here because of him."

Untrue, says Blake. Leon Lett, he says, re-upped with the Cowboys in part because he and Blake were so close. When Blake eventually did get a head-coaching job, many Cowboys were publicly complimentary of him.

But now that a seething Aikman finally thought he understood, he went to Switzer and asked to talk about the incident in a full team meeting. "I wanted to go around the room and let everyone talk about what happened and see who really thought what. But he said, no, no, he didn't want to do that."

Switzer says, "Why would I want to do that and make a much bigger deal out of it than it was?"

After practice, says Aikman, he was getting treatment in the trainer's room when Blake sat down beside him "and tried to strike up a conversation. He said, 'How's your mother?' I said, 'Fine.' I tried to be as short as possible with him."

Aikman soon left the trainer's room and went looking for Woodson out in the locker room. Blake followed. Aikman found Woodson and asked if they could talk. Blake walked past and exited the locker area through the blue curtains that cover the entrance. "Darren and I start talking," says Aikman, "and I look around and Blake is peeking through the curtains at us. I thought, 'What is going on here?'"

Aikman says Woodson was "furious" that Switzer had said he was upset with Aikman. Aikman says he tried to calm Woodson, but he stormed back to Switzer's office to get some answers. Aikman says, "Woody was told Switzer didn't have time to see him. Have you ever heard of a coach not having time to talk to a player?"

Woodson did talk to Switzer the next morning and apparently was satisfied with the coach's explanation that he had used Woodson's name only "as an illustration."

But Valley Ranch had turned into a Tower of "Babble." Clearly, nobody was communicating clearly. Says Hubbard Alexander, "That one little thing [Aikman vs. Williams] nearly tore up our team. It should have been handled intelligently and squashed."

As fate would have it, Larry Lacewell was at a scouting-combine meeting in Washington the day after the Redskin game. If he had been around, he probably would have tried to "steer" Switzer away from calling Aikman to his office to question him about a racial issue.

I believe I was the first to inform Lacewell of the episode when he returned to Valley Ranch that Friday afternoon. Watching his eyes grow round, you'd have thought I'd just yelled, "Fire!" He heaved a sigh and began to pace in his office. "Let me tell you something," he said. "The highway is littered with coaches and assistant coaches who couldn't get along with a quarterback ... I really believe Switzer was wrong to challenge Troy on this, and making an issue of this is the kind of thing that could get John Blake fired. It's not an issue until you make it one. Hell, Troy throws to Michael. He threw to Alvin Harper. We won two Super Bowls. It's not like he wouldn't throw it to the black guys."

As Lacewell left for Switzer's office to assess the damage, I told him Switzer might have left already. That night, at the University of Oklahoma, he was scheduled to receive what's called a Distinguished Award. Barry Switzer, the "outlaw" coach who had been fired seven years earlier? I felt like I was trapped in a Quentin Tarantino movie.

Lacewell, perhaps, was surprised to find out from Switzer that the man most responsible for prompting his meeting with Aikman was Danny Bradley. Not John Blake. Bradley, the "director of player programs."

Lacewell took that news to Jerry Jones, who agreed that Bradley had to go. Bradley, they believed, was too sympathetic to anti-Aikman sentiment among players and was passing along too much of it to Switzer. Of course, Bradley didn't *order* Switzer to question Aikman; the decision ultimately was the head coach's. But as Jones says, Switzer is a talented coach who needs sound guidance from those around him. His people skills and instincts need occasional direction. Bradley was long on loyalty but short on front-office experience and maturity. Lacewell believed Bradley was not a sound advisor for Switzer.

Lacewell returned to Switzer's office with the delicate assignment of trying to convince the coach to fire his "son" Bradley. Switzer quickly realized the move had to be made.

Then again you can bet your Troy Aikman autograph that tears were shed when Switzer eventually informed Bradley. For Switzer, who has never fired an assistant coach, firing Bradley had to be one of the most soul-wrenching moments of his career.

In a way, Switzer did it for Aikman. Switzer, I assume, even reprimanded Blake. Somebody did.

A few days later a shaken Blake waved me into his office for a moment and said, "Troy Aikman is not racist." Blake hadn't told me Aikman was a racist, only that several players thought he had racist tendencies. So this surprised me. "This has really eaten at me," Blake said. He even had talked to his pastor about it, he said.

I think Blake was trying to tell me that he, too, had overreacted—that maybe some of what he had said was just exaggerated locker-room talk whose bluff had been called. I hadn't written, spoken, or spread any of it, but maybe Blake was shocked that he had helped inspire Switzer to challenge Aikman—and that Aikman had won the political battle by backing down all his detractors.

It's possible Blake feared Aikman would try to sabotage his chances of replacing Howard Schnellenberger as head coach at Oklahoma. It's possible that, when I talked to Blake on December 13, Switzer had told him that Schnellenberger was about to be fired. Switzer, who's tight with OU president David Boren, might have known by then.

But here's the kicker: Aikman knew none of this. He wasn't remotely aware of what Bradley's role had been or even that Bradley had been fired. Bradley's parting was chronicled in the newspapers with a brief, buried note in which Bradley said he had resigned to pursue a private business opportunity.

Aikman definitely knew nothing of Blake's sudden regret.

So why wouldn't Switzer have used the Bradley firing and apparent reprimand of Blake as peace offerings to Aikman? Why wouldn't Switzer immediately have made Aikman aware of the painful sacrifices he had made? Probably because Switzer has far too much pride to let Aikman know he swallowed any.

Aikman, meanwhile, had vowed to Steinberg that enough was enough: He no longer would talk to Switzer.

16

BOZO

Fool me once, shame on you. Fool me twice,
shame on me . . .

On the Sunday morning of the Cowboy game in Philadelphia, I was a panelist on ESPN's *The Sports Reporters*, which is taped around 7:45 a.m. in New York. Naturally, the show's opening segment was devoted largely to discussion and debate about Barry Switzer's Cowboys. Were they alive and well? Or had they been Barryed alive?

I said the signs were not good. I reminded host Dick Schaap of Jerry Jones's declaration that, before Charles Haley became a Cowboy, "We couldn't even spell Super Bowl." Now, you supposed, the Cowboys were spelling it Sooper Boll. That week, Haley had announced, "I'm through." He had retired because of his bad back, which had plagued him for ten weeks. Of course, Haley averages 3.4 "retirements" per season, but this was a herniated disk; Haley soon had very real surgery.

Souper Bole?

Yet when Mike Lupica, the conscience of *The Sports Reporters*, said, "But you still think the Cowboys will win today, don't you?" I lost my resolve. Really, the Eagles had just one rising superstar: coach Ray Rhodes. Otherwise, how seriously could you take a team with ex–Cowboy backup quarterback Rodney Peete as its starter? Around Valley Ranch, the 8–5 Eagles were taken only slightly more seriously than the flock of reporters that most players ignored.

I said to Lupica, "Oh, they'll beat Philadelphia."

With a minute left in the first half, it looked as if the Cowboys had done just that. Larry Brown, who probably couldn't catch a cold butt-nekked in subfreezing wind chill in Veterans Stadium, managed to catch a wind-blown Peete pass. There went Brown, running 65 yards toward the Dallas goal line. With each stride, the crowd of 66,509 grew quieter. Some of these fans would catch pneumonia to beat Dallas: The Vet is a kennel of rabid fans, some wearing green paint instead of shirts.

But now, you could have heard a grenade pin drop. That interception return blew up what was left of the Eagle resolve, I figured. Call it off: Dallas 17, Philadelphia 3. In my pressbox seat, I began packing up my notebook, binoculars, and portable TV. My hands were too frozen to write. I was moving into the heated media lounge to watch the second half on TV.

In the hallway, I passed Larry Lacewell, who grinned and said, "It finally kicked in."

The Switzer Luck, he meant. Lacewell had always believed Switzer's luck was his most valuable quality. It wasn't just any old luck. It was the Switzer Luck, known in Oklahoma as Sooner Magic. Lacewell had seen it in action too many times. When you least expected it, the Switzer Luck kicked in and produced all sorts of minor miracles and perhaps even a championship. Just when you thought Switzer was going to get himself fired, *bang*, his Luck kicked in like a shot of tequila. Lacewell envied the hell out of Switzer's Luck. It could cancel racial rifts and coach-quarterback battles and coaching blunders. It was even powerful enough to overcome the loss of Charles Haley. The Switzer Luck just might cure cancer.

Jerry Jones, who's superstitious, regards the Switzer Luck the way he might *I Dream of Jeannie's* bottle—as an invaluable possession. "That luck," he says, eyes widening, "is something you want to be part of, something you want on your side."

Lacewell kept raising one eyebrow and warning me it was about time for the Switzer Luck to suddenly possess the Cowboys. Later, he said, "I really thought that Larry Brown interception was it."

False alarm.

Farther down the pressbox hall, I passed two Philly writers who were arguing whether Rhodes should yank Peete in favor of failed hero Randall Cunningham. Yet, by the time I made it to the media lounge and glanced at the TV, Peete had taken only 46 seconds to pass the Eagles into position for a 27-yard field goal with three seconds left in the half. Peete had accomplished this into a wind that could bring tears to your eyes.

Somehow, 17–6 seemed much closer than 17–3. Pumping fists, the Eagles ran to the locker room with new life.

At halftime, Rhodes and his staff decided to quit worrying about double-covering Deion Sanders when he entered the game as a receiver. They committed an extra defender to help stop Emmitt Smith, who already had 98 yards. In the second half, Emmitt wound up with just 10 more yards on nine tries. For the second straight game, Emmitt lost a rare fumble. Worse, both bobbles came in the fourth quarter, when the Cowboys were about to score. Rare indeed: Until his fumble in Week 3 at Minnesota, Emmitt hadn't fumbled in 761 straight carries/receptions.

Stunningly, in the second half, Troy Aikman was 6 of 22 for 45 yards. Ed Werder, who covers the Cowboys for the *Dallas Morning News*, called it "possibly his worst big-game performance ever." His receivers dropped a couple in the tricky wind, and there was insider conjecture that Aikman's throwing elbow was sore (he would have cleanup surgery following the season). But now, knowing what went on the previous week, you have to wonder if Aikman's concentration had been scattered all over Valley Ranch.

For all these reasons, the Cowboys found themselves fit to be tied 17-all with three minutes left in the game. Their ball, first and 10 at their 20, wind in their faces. Aikman threw two straight incompletions, then hit Cory Fleming with a pass that appeared to be thrown a little short of the first-down marker. Fleming had to retreat too far for it, then was tackled. The Cowboys were left with fourth down and about a foot at their 29 yard line. The clock was blinking down toward the two-minute warning.

On the Cowboy sideline, there was no hesitation, no debate. Not one assistant coach, near Switzer or in the pressbox, expressed the slightest doubt. Not a single, "Coach, are you sure . . . "

Go for it, said Switzer. Coordinator Ernie Zampese was right with him, ready to send Emmitt behind Pro Bowl blocking back Daryl Johnston, Pro Bowl left tackle Mark Tuinei, and Pro Bowl left guard Nate Newton. The play is called Load Left, and there isn't a better load to run behind in pro football. Furthermore, on short-yardage situations between the 20s, Emmitt was ten for his last ten.

Still, incredulous, I turned to Gary Myers of the *New York Daily News* and said, "I cannot believe they're doing this." The risk-reward wasn't high enough. So Emmitt gets a yard? Now it's first-and-10 at the 30. Come up short and the Eagles immediately are in position to kick a gift field goal for the win. Deep down, did the

Eagles really think they could beat the Cowboys? Not unless the Cowboys made it easy for them. So why not make the Eagles handle a funhouse punt into the wind? Why not, for Peete's sake, put the game back in Rodney's hands and force him to win it—or lose it? Remember the stakes: San Francisco had already won that day, improving to 10–4. If the Cowboys lost and fell to 10–4, the 49ers, with their win over Dallas, would regain the lead for home-field playoff advantage. Just as bad, Philadelphia would creep to within a game of the Cowboys in the division race, whose winner would probably get a first-round playoff bye. An extra week of rest and playing at home are often unbeatable advantages. So, as the season teetered . . .

. . . Load Left was stopped cold.

But wait! The Switzer Luck? A ref had blown his whistle and waved his arms for the two-minute warning an instant before the ball was snapped. No play. Repeat fourth and a foot.

Again, no hesitation or discussion. Go for it, said Switzer. Here, his pride was on the line. If he had called for a punt the second time, it would have appeared to his critics that he had come to his senses and admitted the first decision was foolish. But no, Zampese wanted to go right back at the Eagles with the same play.

Now, though, the Eagles were smelling royal blood. While the Cowboys did not run Load Left as if their season depended on it, the Eagles attacked as if their very lives were on the line. This time, Emmitt barely got out of his stance before he was swarmed like a victim in Hitchcock's *The Birds*. No gain. Eagles' ball.

On the Fox broadcast, John Madden made the harshest comment I've ever heard him make. Madden set the tone for the national reaction by saying, "They deserve to lose."

The Eagles made four yards on three runs, then took their gift field goal from 42 yards with 1:30 left. Philadelphia, 20–17. What most people soon forgot was that the Cowboys did get the ball back at their 20 with 1:26 remaining—plenty of time for a Hall-of-Fame-bound quarterback to do the Canton Shuffle. But, given two Hail Mary opportunities, Aikman threw a Hail Mary Poppins. Twice in that final series, Michael Irvin broke behind rookie cornerback Bobby Taylor, but Aikman badly underthrew him. Yes, it was a tough wind, and perhaps Aikman's elbow and/or psyche were bothering him. But his line-drive deep balls are the perfect wind-cheaters. Marino makes that throw. So does Elway. If Irvin makes the catch, it's an almost certain field goal and overtime. If Taylor can't catch Irvin, it's Aikman's first last-minute, come-from-behind victory as a pro.

Instead, Taylor was able to break up both passes, and the game ended with Aikman being sacked by William Fuller. Up jumped Aikman, and in an ugly scene captured on VCRs everywhere, he screamed at tackle Erik Williams. "Three!" Aikman said shaking three fingers at Williams. Though the Eagles had rushed only three men against five blockers, Williams had confused his responsibilities and let Fuller go.

Though Williams never went public with his feelings, he told several sources he was furious that Aikman had shown him up on television.

Now came the most bizarre postgame locker room I've ever covered. It was as if no one in those cramped, steamy quarters—coaches, players, media—had seen the same game. It was as if each character's dialogue was being written by a different author—from Poe to Dr. Seuss to Hunter S. Thompson.

On the postgame shows, Switzer was getting lambasted for the "Blunder of the Century" by Jimmy Johnson, Mike Ditka, and Joe Gibbs. Along with Madden, each of these critics has coached at least one Super Bowl champion, so this condemnation carried damning credibility. Naturally, as newspaper, TV, and radio reporters were allowed into the Cowboy locker room, they went scrambling to find the players and assistant coaches itching to criticize Switzer's decision.

They found not one dissident—especially not Jerry Jones, who wasn't just giving reporters the company line. Several sources said Jones had been up in the visiting owner's box yelling, "Go for it!" on both fourth-and-a-foot decisions. Not once, on or off the record, did I hear anyone in that locker room so much as say the decision was debatable. (The next day at ESPN, when I saw my *Prime Monday* colleague Sterling Sharpe, he called it "the greatest call ever.") From this I learned a lesson: Players always want to go for it and always will love a coach who lets them. What National Football League player wants to back away and say, "Gee, we better not try to make a foot"? Even Aikman said, "No, I wasn't surprised [by the decision]. I didn't think it was the wrong call. I certainly felt we'd be able to make that."

The next week, a respected coach outside Dallas told me, "Players want to go for it every time. But no coach in America would have gone for that. If you say, 'We can always make a foot,' why not go for it every time you have fourth-and-a-foot inside your 10?"

Yet Deion Sanders, backing Switzer and exaggerating slightly, said, "If we can't get an inch, we got problems."

The logical conclusion: The Cowboys had problems. Whether or not they realized it, the players were blaming themselves—blaming the players directly involved in the play. But here's where it got even crazier. Switzer said he went for it "because I wanted to make a foot to control the ball, because if we kick into the wind, they're going to come back and kick a field goal to win the ball game anyway." John Jett had punted once into the fourth-quarter wind—a 38-yarder with a 12-yard return. With a similar result from the Cowboy 29, the Eagles would have taken over at their 45 and would have had to move 22 yards to give themselves a 50-yard field-goal attempt. So Switzer was saying his defense (without Haley and Lett) was so bad that 22 yards would be a breeze for Peete?

That's what it sounded like. But were defensive players offended by the remark? Deion, while threatening to quit talking to the "negative" media for the rest of the season, said, "You can talk about Deion, his mama, his wife, and his kids, but don't say a thing about the defense."

The head coach had just paid his disrespects to Deion's defense.

Utter madness.

Ed Werder wrote, "Barry Switzer's fourth-and-one decision will live in infamy unless the team wins the Super Bowl, which it doesn't seem inclined to do."

And, of course, Randy Galloway called for Switzer's head, writing, "The collapse of the Jerry-Barry football empire officially reached crisis stage . . . Together they stand, owner and coach, while the Cowboys, as a team, disintegrate into an uninspired, lifeless loser . . . Not only did the Cowboys lose a game they absolutely had to win, the head coach also made a national fool out of himself . . . A month ago, it was Jones who vowed Switzer would be back next season unless he was 'hit by a truck or shot' . . . let the record show an eighteen-wheeler and a bull's-eye bullet struck Switzer and the Cowboys . . . December, the month of champions, now has opened with consecutive losses to mediocre teams . . . [After making the fourth-and-a-foot call, Switzer would have been] immediately fired by any owner in the league other than Jones."

But he was not going to be fired by Jones. The following day at Valley Ranch, two scenarios circulated among whispering staffers: (1) Aikman soon would walk into Jones's office and say, "Switzer goes or I go" and (2) Lacewell soon would have to go to Jones and say, "Jerry, it's just not working."

But that week, Jones put out an unwritten "memo." Jones quietly spread the word that, under no circumstances, would he tolerate one word of criticism of the head coach.

*   *   *

Because I stayed in the Northeast, I saw the next day's *New York Post*. I must admit I laughed out loud at the back page. In "WORLD ENDS" type, the headline said, "BOZO THE COACH." There was Switzer, on the sideline in Philly, wearing this goofy-looking diver's hood to keep his head warm and pointing out to the field. You could almost hear him saying, "Go for it again!"

Switzer's problem was that he sometimes looked or sounded the "Bozo" part.

I took the newspaper back to Dallas, only to hear that Switzer was looking for a copy. Did he want to sue the *Post*? Use the newspaper itself as a prop he could shred during an angry speech to the team? No, Switzer thought the thing was so funny that he wanted to frame it and give it to his kids as a gag gift for Christmas.

That's Barry Switzer. I didn't know whether to be impressed or distressed. If Jones was the only owner in America who wouldn't have fired Switzer, Switzer was the only coach in the world who could have laughed at being ridiculed by a New York newspaper. In a way, his perspective was shockingly refreshing. Here was the coach of probably the most famous team in sports, who had made perhaps the most infamous decision in NFL history, and he was able to step away, laugh, and say, "Hey, it's just one football game."

Yet, another side of me wanted to write a column with the headline "WORLD ABOUT TO END," frame it, and give it to Switzer. He just didn't seem to grasp the magnitude, the impending doom.

That week, I got a call from author and psychologist Don Beck, the director of the National Values Center in Denton who writes a "sports values" column for the *Dallas Morning News*. Beck counsels coaches in all sports on how best to bring teams to their psychological peak. Beck assisted Tom Landry and studied Jimmy Johnson, and in turn Beck helped me on books I wrote about Landry and Johnson. Beck, a native Oklahoman, had even worked briefly with Switzer when he was coaching the Sooners.

Beck again wanted to offer Switzer a few suggestions. "I'm very worried for him," Beck said. "He keeps saying, 'My style is my style.' But a coach has to be able to hang a plumb bob over a team and say, 'What does this team *need*?' Barry's still good one-on-one, but with team dynamic, he's not very good. Jimmy was such a brilliant strategic thinker, but Barry's merely an impulsive thinker. He's not providing any stereophonic balance. I thought his last couple of years at OU he had gone a little sour. He just wasn't monitoring his players any more. I'm afraid he can't fix a team, and this team has a heavy heart. It's puzzled. It has no idea why this is happening. *Twice* it couldn't make a yard . . . I don't think this team ever got over the switch from Jimmy to Barry. There was never any closure. Then it lost a center who was a leader [Mark Stepnoski]. There's no more Tommie Agee, who was a spiritual leader and an anchor for Emmitt. There are no more 'bad asses' on defense [such as James Washington, a notorious headhunter]. It's just not the same team."

All true.

"And," said Beck, "one good thing about Jimmy was that he protected Jerry from Jerry. Now, there's no check on him. His son can't do it, and Barry certainly won't. It's like Caesar always having an aide walk beside him to remind him, 'Thou art mortal.' If Jerry lets Barry fly this thing into a cliff, the rest of Jerry's life could be very sad."

I caught Switzer one day in the hall and mentioned that Beck had a couple of ideas that might help him. Switzer stopped and put both hands on my shoulders. "Look," he said, "we [he and his staff] have been doing this thirty-something years. We know what we're doing. We know what it takes."

Instead of making Wednesday's practice tougher, he made it easier. He joked to the team, "Now I know what you're doing. You're going to make history. You want to go on the road in the playoffs and win the Super Bowl. Now I get it."

Observing Switzer that week, Lacewell said, "He's the most resilient guy I've ever known. I'd be suicidal over this. *Most* coaches would be worried to death. But hell, he's going on like nothing happened."

Lacewell, chuckling with awe, told Switzer that after missing the fourth-and-a-foot on the first attempt, *he* would have punted. "I wouldn't have had the nerve to go for it again, but that's Switzer," said Lacewell, who was just as amazed at Switzer's Thursday-night plans.

Sharing Switzer's apartment at the time was Dale Boutwell, his old running buddy and teammate from Arkansas, one of the unlucky ones. Jones had given Boutwell a job working maintenance at Texas Stadium. But, while on the job, Boutwell had broken his arm. So for now, he hung around the Valley Ranch offices quite a bit and went to dinner with Switzer. That night, they were headed for Bob's Steak and Chop House, one of Switzer's favorite places.

With laughter in his eyes, Lacewell told him, "Switzer, so far no coach has ever been shot over something like this [the fourth-and-a-foot call]. But I'm glad you have a bodyguard with you, because tonight somebody might try."

*   *   *

Bob's Steak and Chop is a classy, classic Manhattan-style steak house owned by a sharp, ambitious, boyish-looking forty-two-year-old named Bob Sambol. Switzer just showed up one night at Bob's, and his group was seated in the restaurant. Switzer loved the food, but diners all around him were eavesdropping on his table's conversation. Switzer noticed a glassed-in room in the back of the restaurant for private parties. So the next time, Switzer asked if his party could sit in the private room.

At the time, it was called the Troy Aikman Room.

It since has been renamed the Barry Switzer Room.

In one stretch, Switzer brought in several large groups, and after three or four hours of wine and dinner, the checks were as high as $1,500. After four or five of these visits, Bob Sambol told the waitress to tell Switzer this one was on the house.

Switzer, says Sambol, immediately pulled him aside and said, "You're young and trying to build a business here. Some day when you're making a lot of money, you can do this for me. But this one's on *me*."

Each Friday in the *Dallas Morning News*, Jimmy Johnson did an as-told-to column with staff writer Tim Cowlishaw. The one that ran on Friday after the "Fiasco in Philly," as the *Morning News* called it, was the equivalent of Johnson coaching Oklahoma against Switzer's Oklahoma State. Did Johnson ever run up the score.

Johnson said, "As bad as the call was, I don't think there would have been such a media uproar if Switzer had come back and said he had a gut feeling, he went against the percentages, and he lost. To act as though it was the right call to make and that it wasn't a terrible risk . . . is nothing short of mind-boggling . . .

"Barry Switzer has been fighting for his credibility for two years now. I truly believe this one call will put his credibility as an NFL coach beyond repair. As they should, the Cowboys' players will stand behind Switzer publicly. But in the backs of their minds, they have to be asking themselves why a decision was made, why no assistant stood up to question the decision and why they are now looking at a much tougher road in the NFC playoffs."

The Switzer camp countered, "Are the players really wondering that, or is Jimmy trying to plant that seed?" Switzer supporters also wondered who at Valley Ranch planted this little tidbit, which Johnson used the next Sunday on Fox's pregame show and for which he received an "information award" from *USA Today* TV columnist Rudy Martzke. "The Cowboys," reported Johnson, "haven't had a full staff meeting since August."

Though Switzer and Jones said there had been several full staff meetings since August, full meetings hadn't occurred on a daily basis because Switzer doesn't like them. Switzer's offensive and defensive staffs usually meet separately, with Switzer popping back and forth between the two because, he half-joked, "my ADD will kick in if I sit in one meeting too long." Yet Johnson presented his zinger with the implication that Switzer's staff never even met. While Switzer shrugged it off as just another "Jimmy leak," Jones was irritated enough to do a little investigative reporting of his own. Some staffers thought it came from an assistant who had been close to Johnson, such as Joe Avezzano; others thought the "leak" was trainer Kevin O'Neill; and still others suspected it came from Avezzano through Aikman, who says he talked to Johnson "maybe four or five times" during the season.

Somewhere Jimmy Johnson was cackling.

One day that week, Jerry and Stephen Jones were brainstorming about what they could do to shock the world and turn around the season. What was the most glaring offensive deficiency? Kevin Williams hadn't been able to replace the game-breaking capability of deep-threat Alvin Harper, a long-striding 6'3" former high-jump champ at Tennessee. Before he had taken the free-agent superhighway out of Dallas, Harper had helped take some defensive focus off Irvin.

So, thought Jerry and Stephen, what one receiver had most terrorized the Cowboy secondary the last few seasons? No, not Jerry Rice. Sterling Sharpe, who could operate with Irvin's muscle and Rice's finesse. Near the end of the previous season, Sharpe had suffered a potentially career-ending spinal injury. Though he continued to rehab and work out, Sharpe wasn't sure if he wanted to risk a wheelchair existence—even death—by returning to pro football.

But that week at ESPN, Sharpe told me that Jerry Jones had left a message to call him. "What do you think he wants?" Sharpe said.

"To see if you want to play for Dallas," I said.

Jones hadn't bothered to go through Sharpe's agent. Jones knew Sharpe worked at ESPN, so he just called the switchboard. When Sharpe called back, Jones wanted to hear "from the horse's mouth" about Sharpe's recovery status and if perhaps he would take less money to win a Super Bowl ring with the Cowboys. Sharpe said he was interested.

Nothing came of it, but this was another case of Jerry Jones thinking big. It was also an indication of how concerned the team was about Kevin Williams. "To be honest," said Jones, "we feel we have our second receiver in place for next season, but Deion's going to need a training camp to get to know the offense."

To completely appreciate what happened next, you need a quick numbers lesson. Of the previous twenty-five Super Bowl champions, none had lost more than one of their last four regular season games. Thirteen had lost one of their final four; twelve had gone unbeaten. Tom Landry's five Super Bowl teams were 19–1 in their last four regular season games. Jimmy Johnson's two championship teams were 7–1.

Historically, NFL champions come together, not apart, in December. Landry preached the importance of "streaking" into the playoffs.

As the 5–9 New York Giants visited Texas Stadium on December 17, the Cowboys were stumbling headlong down the stairs toward 0–3. Later, many stories were written around the country about how Switzer's fourth-and-one call actually unified the Cowboys into an us-against-the-world juggernaut on a mission to prove "Bozo" right. "If that's true," Switzer said, "then how do you explain the way we played against New York?"

The Giants controlled the ball with 244 yards rushing and controlled the clock, 33:05 to the Cowboys' 26:55. Rodney Hampton gained 187 yards and 34 rushes—a rhino crashing through the undergrowth that was the Dallas defense. The Giants converted a ridiculous 9 of 15 third downs.

The Giants did everything but win.

The Giants led at half, 14–6. During intermission, Lacewell did something he wished he hadn't. "I could have kicked myself," he said. In the pressbox, he passed Randy Galloway and just couldn't help himself. Galloway had been so relentless in his attacks on Switzer and Jones that Lacewell said, "Why don't you rip Aikman? Are you watching this?"

In the first half, Aikman had fallen deeper into his slump by completing just 3 of 9 for 66 yards. About three weeks later, Galloway wrote about how a "high-level team official" had criticized him for not criticizing Aikman. Lacewell figured Galloway or maybe Hansen had made sure Aikman knew who it was, yet the truth was that Lacewell was as pro-Aikman as Galloway and Hansen. Lacewell constantly said, "We won two Super Bowls because of No. 8. As he goes, we go."

In the second half, Aikman didn't play much better. Only three outrageously bad calls kept the Giants from blowing the game open. "If we got that many calls, we'd have eleven wins, too," said New

York coach Dan Reeves, not one to whine. Yet with the Giants leading 20–18 and only three and a half minutes left in the game, Aikman threw an interception that looked like it might end the game—and, effectively, the season. Aikman looked as if he had reverted to the pre-Norv Troy: tentative and mistake-prone.

The Cowboys hadn't stopped Hampton yet. How could they stop him from running out the clock now? Hampton powered for 5 yards on first down. But on second down, backup middle linebacker Godfrey Myles, subbing for the injured Robert Jones, met Hampton in the hole and stopped him for no gain. Godfrey Myles? Thank Godfrey. Though it certainly didn't seem like it at the moment, that was the Dallas Cowboys' defensive play of the year. On third and 5, Reeves put the game back in the shaky hands of Giant quarterback Dave Brown, who misfired incomplete. It's an easy second-guess now: But why not run Hampton again just to keep the clock running? Having burned only 25 seconds, the Giants had to punt.

This time, the Cowboy coaches paid no more respect to the punt-return tenure of Kevin Williams. Deion Sanders, the "man from another planet," was called upon to make an out-of-this-world play. About now, a long punt return would be worth about $13 million to Jerry Jones. (Jones says, "Maybe the one thing that separates me from other owners is that I *don't* believe in meddling in the coaching area. But in this case, I had been lobbying the coaches to let Deion return more kicks. I didn't *tell* them. I just lobbied.")

Deion fielded the punt at his 14, threw about 13 million moves on the first wave of Giants, but was rendered mortal by the second wave. Deion made it 11 yards to the Cowboy 25, where they had it first-and-10 with 2:59 left. The feel of the game—the momentum, the players' body language—still favored the Giants. I seriously doubted Dallas could win.

Understand, it had rained in the third quarter, and the turf and ball remained slippery. Aikman grips the ball so unconventionally—down on the end, without touching the laces—that it tends to squirt out of his hand when damp. So what were the odds Aikman would suddenly get a grip on the ball and himself and snap out of his worst slump since he attained "star" stature?

As had the 49ers, Redskins, and Eagles, the Giants were daring Aikman to throw to Kevin Williams. Irvin was seeing double: two Giants mirroring his every urgent juke. But cornerback Thomas Randolph was giving Williams 8 or 10 yards of cushion. Finally, it appeared, Aikman said what the hell and let it fly. Sometimes, he's best that way, when he lets a little Switzer leak into his perfectionist psyche. On first down, he hit Williams for 10 yards. Two plays later, on third-and-7, he went again to Williams, who was as open as a 7-Eleven.

But five hit-and-miss plays later, the game came down to third-and-10 at the N.Y. 38 with 1:14 left. The Cowboys still weren't in Chris Boniol's field-goal range; 55 yards was too far in air thick with moisture. They needed one more significant gain. Desperate to change their luck—or maybe Switzer's—Jones and Lacewell tried watching the last two minutes on the locker-room TVs. One paced up one row while one paced down the other. Jones's pride and reputation—and Switzer's future—dangled.

The call from Zampese had Kevin Williams running a "5 route"—driving the cornerback 15 yards downfield, cutting to the sideline, and actually angling back toward the quarterback, who throws to a point in the flat just beyond the first-down marker. If the coverage "rolls" to Irvin, as it had been, Williams becomes the primary target. The Giants rolled. Aikman, dropping and planting, looked right and cut loose for Williams. Perhaps, at that instant, Aikman wanted to shout the n-word: "No!"

Maybe the ball slipped a little. Maybe Aikman would have felt a little more confident trying to thread the ball through the octopus of arms to Irvin. Maybe, under the complete-it-or-else circumstances, Aikman tried to get a little too "fine," as baseball's pitching coaches say, and guide the ball to an exact spot, and he tightened up and let it get away from him.

Who knows? Maybe, under the crazed Aikman-vs.-Switzer circumstances, if Aikman even subconsciously wanted to do in Switzer . . .

It was not a good pass. "It was not where it was supposed to be," Williams says. "At first I didn't think there was any way I could get to it."

He launched himself . . . and time slowed. Into another dimension Williams flew, feeling a little like Superman—like he had broken free of gravity. Williams describes the actual one second as if it took several minutes. "I'm watching the ball and I'm thinking, 'Hmmm, I'm gaining on it. Maybe . . .' Then it hit one finger—just one—and I was able to control it just enough to get my other fingers on it, and I pulled it into my body just before I hit the ground."

It was an unbelievable catch—for many more reasons than just the catch itself. Kevin Williams had just saved the season. Kevin from Heaven?

With five seconds left, Boniol made his fifth field goal of the game, a teaching-video 35-yarder executed with much more confidence than Aikman's throw to Williams. Dallas 21, N.Y. 20. That was the twenty-second field goal without a miss for the minimum-wage kicker. "He's our MVP so far," said Aikman, who seemed deflated by the win. He added, "We're not going to get where we want to be playing this way." Irvin and even Switzer had similar reactions. The Cowboy locker room quietly reverberated with humiliation.

The only two remotely happy people were Jones and Lacewell, who were trying to stifle grins in the gloom. Lacewell said, "Finally, the Switzer Luck kicked in. Here we go."

Hmmm: the refs' calls, Godfrey Myles, Kevin Williams. Could it be?

Here they went.

17

THE LUCKIEST SOB EVER

I'd rather be lucky than good . . .

Following the New York Giant game, the Switzer Luck manifested itself in startling news from "Switzerland." I was still in the locker room when I heard it from Dean Blevins, who's plugged into the Oklahoma football program. Bulletin: Howard Schnellenberger, after just one 5–5–1 season, was about to be removed as OU's football coach.

Atop OU's "national search" list was college football's hottest name, Northwestern coach Gary Barnett. But president David Boren and the board of regents were leery of bringing in another outsider. Schnellenberger, with no OU roots or connections, had shown almost no respect for the school's tradition and had alienated many ex-players and heavyweight alums. More likely, the next OU coach would come from "within the family." That meant one of three men employed by Jerry Jones: Barry Switzer, John Blake, or Larry Lacewell.

Still in the locker room, Blevins and I turned to Lacewell and asked if he would be interested in the job. He sighed and thought for a moment, weighing his loyalty to Jones against his pride. "Jerry Jones has been so good to me," Lacewell said. "But yes, I would at least talk to them." Remember, this was the job he had finished a close second for when Switzer was elevated to head coach in 1973. Lacewell remains extremely popular in Oklahoma, especially with the school's wealthier, more conservative supporters. Soon there was some talk of coupling Lacewell and Blake as co-coaches for a couple of years until Blake was ready to fly solo. (Blake hadn't been a head coach or even a coordinator on any level.) What an odd but effective couple they might have made: Lacewell as wise old strategist and country-club fund-raiser; Blake as recruiter and "break love" motivator. Lacewell didn't immediately veto the idea, but Blake told me, "If that's what they want to do, I'll just stay right here and coach the defensive line." Ah, youth.

But of all the candidates, one name was on the frothing lips of talk-show callers in Oklahoma City: Switzer! Bring back Barry! The sentiment: "If Cowboy fans don't want him, *we'll* take him."

For Troy Aikman, the next best thing happened: John Blake was named head football coach at the University of Oklahoma. Then again, Aikman was mystified over how his old school could have chosen *John Blake*. Aikman's reaction appeared to say: "Good for us, bad for them."

Blake fell into place only after these dominoes fell . . .

Number One: Switzer declined Boren's plea to "come back and turn the program around." For Switzer, just knowing Oklahoma's hierarchy, fans, and media truly wanted him back lifted his spirits. "You could see the spark back in his eyes," says daughter Kathy. She adds that a little "face" was involved, as in, "In your face, you regents who stabbed dad in the back seven years ago." But Switzer quickly realized that (a) chasing after eighteen-year-old recruits is a young man's game; (b) he would be taking a $500,000 pay cut; and (c) he had made a commitment to Jones, who had stood by Switzer through media torture that would have made many owners crack.

Number Two: Gary Barnett didn't show much interest, and for various reasons nothing clicked with several other lesser-known candidates.

Number Three: The board of regents didn't show much interest in hiring Lacewell.

Number Four: Boren and the board were affected by newspaper updates that second-year Oklahoma State coach Bob Simmons— young, black, and personable—was running up the score on OU in recruiting. Says an OU insider, "Blake probably wouldn't have been hired if Bob Simmons hadn't been hired by OSU."

Number Five: The year before, Switzer had openly campaigned for Blake before Schnellenberger was hired. Switzer told me, "The black high school coaches in Texas and Oklahoma would not let John fail." But Boren had been in power for only a short time and perhaps didn't have as much influence on the decision as he did this time. Boren was heavily influenced by Switzer's opinion. Once it became clear Switzer wasn't an option, Oklahoma fans and media packed "Boo's" bandwagon until it careened out of control. "John Blake," wrote *Daily Oklahoman* columnist Berry Tramel, "should have been hired last time around."

To my knowledge, none of OU's decision-makers was aware of the anti-Blake bitterness harbored by the most famous ex-Sooner football player. Not a hint of it had yet been reported by the media. Yet, thanks in part to the influential voice of Blevins in Oklahoma City, many talk-show callers had turned on Aikman. It was clear to them even from watching Aikman on TV interviews that he wasn't much of a Switzer fan, and Switzer remains godlike north of the Red River. According to several Oklahoma media members, among Sooner fans Aikman was beginning to be perceived as a "whiner." More and more on Oklahoma City radio, Blevins and others were critical of Aikman's performance and attitude toward Switzer.

Perhaps, if OU's regents had known the details, they would have been impressed by the way Blake had defended Switzer in the Aikman conflict.

But when OU hired Blake, Aikman and several Cowboy assistants rolled their eyes at "Boo" quotes such as this one: "Going through another season with the Cowboys has prepared me for things. I'm a more mature coach. The older you get, the more mature you get in several areas. I'm sharper with the Xs and Os now. I'm as good at the Xs and Os as I am at recruiting."

Yet as Berry Tramel wrote, John Blake had "the best college-football job a black man has ever had"—and several black Cowboy stars gave him what certainly sounded like convincing endorsements. Charles Haley told the *Daily Oklahoman*'s Mike Baldwin: "I think John will do a great job. He's a great coach and a good people person." Deion Sanders said, "I'm so happy for him. He's a good man. He's charismatic. He's going to be good with the fans and the players." And Emmitt Smith said, "I'd like to go up there with him and be his running back coach. You think I'm joking? I'd really like to. He's a good man."

More metallic-blue lunacy: Could these stars have been talking about the same guy Aikman and Cowboy assistants were? It certainly didn't sound as if Blake's role in upsetting Aikman had upset the entire team. Most Cowboys didn't know much more than Aikman had yelled at Kevin Williams, who had accepted Aikman's apology. As Switzer later said, "You think those Mandingo warriors care about what's going on personally with Troy?"

Only if it affects Aikman's performance, which was certainly the top priority of Jones and Lacewell. If Blake hadn't been hired by OU and the Cowboys hadn't won the Super Bowl, might Jones and Lacewell have tried to steer Switzer into firing Blake? Possibly. As much as the owner likes Blake—they still keep in touch—Aikman's unhappiness might have rendered Blake expendable . . . unless maybe the Haleys, Deions, and Emmitts stood up for Blake.

So complicated—unless the Switzer Luck kicked in.

Did it ever. Not a drop of bad blood was shed. A potential PR nightmare became a PR dream: Ah, yes, another "sharp young Cowboy assistant" got a prestigious head-coaching position. Blake got his dream job. Aikman got rid of a bad dream.

And it happened right on schedule, just as the playoffs were starting. Three veteran Cowboy assistant coaches said that if the "cancer"—Blake—hadn't been removed, the Cowboys couldn't have won the Super Bowl. Whether that's a bitter or jealous exaggeration is irrelevant. Blake became a godsend of a scapegoat. He was "demonized," as psychologist Don Beck says. No matter Blake's true guilt, he was loaded down with all the sins of December and sent on his way to Norman.

About 350 members of the Sooner football "family" turned out for John Blake's welcome-back press conference, described as "more of a coronation" by one media observer. Perhaps the only "family" member in attendance who wasn't all hugs and smiles was Barry Switzer.

According to several close to him, he looked drained and glum. Perhaps he wasn't comfortable being thrust into a glad-hand setting with regents who had voted to fire him. For sure, as pleased as he was for Blake, he was not pleased about losing the only assistant he trusted. He told a couple of old friends he was "pretty miserable" in Dallas.

Blake brought tears to some eyes with his introduction of Switzer, "a guy who means so much to me." Blake told the crowd that his connection with Switzer was so strong that he couldn't yet leave him. Blake said, "I have a commitment to make sure the Dallas Cowboys have every possible chance to win another Super Bowl, and I'll stick with that commitment. I'll work diligently with the Cowboys and I'll also use the phone and travel when coach Switzer allows me to get out and recruit."

Yet with only about five weeks left until national signing day for recruits, how was Blake going to play catch-up with Oklahoma State's Simmons while preparing his Cowboy defensive linemen for the playoffs? Doing both jobs did not make sense. Yet Blake and Switzer were going to attempt the arrangement until, on Lacewell's suggestion, Jones intervened. The day after Blake's "coronation," Jones quietly arranged for him to become the full-time Oklahoma coach.

In a laughable example of what's wrong with sports-talk radio, Switzer was blasted by at least one host I heard for "selling out" to OU and letting Blake leave early. The host warned that the Cowboys were in trouble without their defensive line coach. I wondered if Aikman happened to be listening to this host.

Earlier that day, Rich Dalrymple had pulled Aikman aside and said, "Jerry wanted me to let you know that Barry let John go." Translation: That Switzer rushed Blake into his new job—sort of "fired" him from his lame-duck Cowboy job.

Aikman said, "Rich, don't try to tell me that. I know Jerry did it." Dalrymple told Aikman to calm down and quit being so hot-headed. But Aikman said, "No, Rich, I just won't accept that."

Five days after the New York Giant game, a strange story by Mike Fisher appeared in the *Fort Worth Star-Telegram*. The headline: "Aikman questions his future." The sub headline: "Conflict with coach may lead to change." Yet not once in the story was Aikman quoted as saying anything about Switzer. The strongest Aikman quote: "At this time, it's ridiculous for me to say I'd retire. For sixty minutes, I get to do what I enjoy. But this has not been an enjoyable year for me, in regard to things outside the football field. I do still get the spirit of competition, the camaraderie with the guys, the emotions. But beyond that, everything that's happened has taken a lot out of me."

Dale Hansen, who works with Fisher at radio station KLIF, says Fisher told him he "crafted" the story with Aikman, with whom he had been close in the past. Yet, according to Hansen, Aikman said he was misled about Fisher's intentions and that Aikman was angry about the story.

Switzer basically dodged the issue by giving his standard reply: All that matters is that he and Troy share a commitment to winning. Yet in the next couple of days, Switzer said something to reporters about how Aikman ought to be happy making $6 million a year. Aikman read the quote and later told me, "Whatever wealth I've been able to accrue is irrelevant to how I feel about playing football. I was offended by that."

So now, on December 22, we had the first public hint of something not quite right between Switzer and Aikman. We had Aikman mad at Fisher for "manipulating" him into being quoted in a story that didn't quite live up to its billing. We had Switzer mad that Aikman apparently had put Fisher up to the story. Finally, we had Aikman mad at Switzer's reaction to a story for which Switzer basically held Aikman responsible.

Just another day at "Happy" Valley Ranch.

That week, former Cowboy personnel director John Wooten, now with the Eagles, crossed Lacewell's path along the college scouting trail. As Lacewell began to talk about all the Cowboy problems, from injuries to internal conflict, Wooten interrupted. "Larry, don't give me any of that stuff. You think you got problems? I'll take your problems. I'll trade you teams right now. I'll take your eight Pro Bowlers on offense—and you got two or three more who should have made it [including Daryl Johnston and Erik Williams]."

Wise and prophetic perspective from Wooten.

The first hint that Santa was going to be very good to some bad little Cowboys came the night after the Giant game, at the annual team Christmas party. Early arrivals had turned off the Monday-night game after being turned off by yet another San Francisco outburst: 21 quick points. But Michael Irvin arrived bearing gifts and good tidings: Turn the game back on! Minnesota had caught the 49ers, 27-all, in the third quarter. At home, the 49ers eventually prevailed 37–30. But their defense hadn't been able to stop the Vikings, who had taken advantage of a very uncharacteristic four 49er turnovers.

A sign?

Just four days later, the 49ers had to fly cross-country to play an early Sunday game against division rival Atlanta, which was 8–7. Simultaneously, Philadelphia was playing at Chicago, which was 8–7. If the 49ers won, they clinched home-field advantage over Dallas. If the Eagles won—and Dallas lost its final game on Monday night at Arizona—they won the NFC East and a first-round bye. So for the Cowboys, two of the most important games of the season would be played while their team plane was in the air, bound for Phoenix.

Call it the flight of the phoenix. The closer the plane drew to Phoenix, where the Super Bowl would be played in four weeks, the more the Cowboys rose from their own ashes. (Larry Brown had added to the self-inflicted misery by missing the flight.) Rich Dalrymple sat in his seat at the front of the coach section with his battery-operated TV in his lap. In and out it faded, teasing and tormenting the growing crowd around Dalrymple's seat. *Steve Young, going deep for Jerry Ri* . . . Static and snow. *Rodney Peete . . . scrambling right . . . throwing . . . INTERCEPshhhhhhh* . . . Static and snow. Reclining in his front-row, first-class seat, Switzer didn't pay much attention to the commotion, choosing instead to listen to a tape Kathy had made him for his portable tape player: a little Streisand, some Neil Diamond.

Finally, Dalrymple's TV locked into a signal long enough to provide a final score from Chicago: Bears 20, Eagles 14. A small roar went up around the TV. Now for the big one. The 49ers had led early, 14–3. But in the third quarter, Atlanta had rallied for a 22–21 lead. Dalrymple frantically surfed through the snow for a clear channel. This much he could piece together: For the Falcons, an injured Jeff George had been replaced at quarterback by Bobby Hebert. Great, said several of the Cowboy coaches who questioned George's fortitude under fire. Atlanta, they thought, had a little better shot with Hebert. The Switzer Luck? Hebert threw two second-half touchdown passes. With 19 seconds remaining—and Dalrymple's TV providing a view through a Georgia Dome snowstorm—Young's pass for Rice was . . . intercepted by Kevin Ross! The Falcons had done it, 28–27! The news whipped back through the plane as if the cabin pressure had suddenly dropped. It was as if a door had been opened and all the tension has been sucked out. Says assistant coach Robert Ford, "It was like the plane started *breathing.* We landed and went right out [to Sun Devil Stadium for a brief walk-through rehearsal], and suddenly you could see the bounce was back in everybody's step. The Giants had really beaten us up physically, but you could actually see everybody coming out of it. I said, 'The Cowboys are back.' "

Just before the plane landed, Switzer grinned and shook his head. "Hey, I've been saying all along, 'You've got to wait till the whole thing's over.' When you win a championship, you've got to be good and you've got to be lucky. Somebody has got to help you along the way. Somebody has to beat somebody else when you least expect it."

Dean Blevins on Switzer: "Through December he was the calm in the eye of the storm, just sitting back watching the madness fly. No one on the outside could see what he was doing, but the players and coaches saw it."

Well, many did.

Several Switzer supporters said that when the San Francisco

score was announced on the plane, Dale Hansen looked "crest-fallen." Again, Larry Lacewell couldn't contain himself. He walked back near Hansen's seat, and though he used a stage voice for all within earshot, his sarcasm was intended for Hansen's ears. Lacewell said, "Well, I guess [San Francisco coach George] Seifert didn't have 'em focused, did he? It's all his fault."

A common criticism of Switzer was that he didn't have the Cowboys "focused."

For once, Hansen kept his mouth shut. But, he says, he was thinking, "You're defending this guy after what he did to your wife? You can do a lot of things to me: Call me names, hit on my daughter, but you do *that*, and that's it."

But Lacewell wasn't just defending Switzer. He was doing his form of Neon Deion post-touchdown celebration over all the right moves Cowboy management had made. Lacewell says, "Really, I was defending Jerry Jones for hiring Barry Switzer, and for signing Ray Donaldson [instead of Mark Stepnoski], and for keeping Derek Kennard [who had replaced the injured Donaldson]. I was defending the Dallas Cowboys."

For Lacewell and probably many Cowboy players and coaches, Monday, December 25, was, well, slower than Christmas. "Longest day I've ever spent," Lacewell says. Who knew which Arizona team would show up? Would it be Buddy Ryan's loyal pit bulls, who would clamp down on the Cowboys and fight for Ryan's coaching life? Or the 4–11 Cardinals who couldn't wait to get out of Phoenix and take a vacation? For sure, Ryan's job was in jeopardy, which made the Cowboys even more unsure of what Ryan might try to pull on the season's final Monday-night stage. After all, this was the coach who—according to several Cowboys, who heard it from several Eagles—once placed a bounty on the head of Cowboy kicker Luis Zendejas. Ryan sometimes acted like the sergeant, too long in combat, who had gone over the edge.

The Cowboys figured the early part of the game would determine how quickly the Cardinals called it a season. The Cowboys won the toss, and Kevin Williams returned the kickoff to the Cowboy 34. On first down, Aikman had to dump a safety-valve pass to Daryl Johnston that was a little low. Johnston couldn't hold it. Second and 10: Aikman went to his new best friend, Kevin Williams, who had outquicked Seth Joyner and was running free. The pass couldn't have been thrown any better. Williams dropped it. "I was so excited I was hyperventilating," says Williams, who for the first time was a prominent part of the game plan. "I just said, 'Calm down and get a grip on yourself.'"

Before this moment Aikman probably would have locked Williams in his doghouse for the rest of the game. But on third and 10, with the hope and noise rising among Cardinal fans, Aikman went back to little No. 85 on a post route called 585. It's difficult to say which was more difficult to make: the throw or the catch. For sure, both were dangerous, with Cardinals flying around like rabid bats. Williams suddenly shot up and snatched the ball, as if he were suddenly on fast-forward and the rest of the game on rewind. Then Williams inspired teammates with, for him, a first: a spontaneous celebration. Up he jumped and did a little march in place and an exaggerated first-down signal.

Kevin from Heaven.

Three plays later Aikman hit Williams with a 29-yard touchdown pass—Williams's first of the season—and you could almost see the Cardinals practicing their golf swings on the sideline. The Cardinals kept single-covering Williams, and Aikman threw him multiple passes. Williams wound up catching nine for 203 yards. "We've created a monster," said Switzer, who had nearly created one out of Williams after the Washington game.

By Super Bowl standards, the Cowboys weren't particularly sharp. Aikman threw an interception that Aeneas Williams returned for a touchdown, and two fumbles were lost. But this time, who remembered? Emmitt Smith, the NFL rushing champion, scored his NFL-record twenty-fifth touchdown of the season—a team joy— and overall the Cowboys felt pretty good about themselves for the first time since Thanksgiving. The final was 37–13.

Were they on the kind of flawless roll that carried them through San Francisco to Jerry Jones's first Super Bowl championship following the 1992 season? Lord, no. But this beat the frozen hell out of, say, having a short week to prepare for a wild-card playoff game in Green Bay. When you least expected it, the Dallas Cowboys had a week off to prepare for, potentially, two home playoff games.

That off week Cowboy coaches passed the time by watching horror movies: *Sunday the 13th*, parts one through sixteen, starring the Detroit Lions. The NFL's top-rated offense no was longer stored in missile silos in San Francisco or Dallas. For the first time in NFL history, a team had two 100-catch receivers (Herman Moore and Brett Perriman), a 1,500-yard rusher (Barry Sanders) and a 4,000-yard passer (Scott Mitchell). The Lions led the NFL in yards gained and points scored. One Cowboy coach said, "Let's face it: We're average on defense, so Detroit is not a good matchup for us. Detroit will move up and down the field on us, so we'll have to outscore 'em. But unfortunately, their defense is better than you think." Furthermore, the Lions had won in Dallas on a Monday night during Switzer's first season. They wouldn't be awed by a rare visit to the "Stadium with the Hole in the Roof."

Dallas would probably get the winner of Detroit at Philadelphia, so Cowboy coaches spent the week studying Detroit.

As, well, luck would have it, All-Pro Detroit tackle Lomas Brown lost his head one day that week while two reporters were taking notes—one, Ray Didinger, from the *Philadelphia Daily News*. Brown said the Lions would make the Eagles quit, which soon made huge headlines in Philly. Eagle personnel director John Wooten said, "Lomas can't come in here talking that stuff. What has Detroit ever done? And he's saying we're going to quit after the first quarter? That's the one thing [coach] Ray [Rhodes] preaches: Never unball your fists. We don't quit." By Saturday's kickoff, Rhodes had transformed the Eagles into fifty-three Rocky Balboas ready to knock the snot out of Detroit's Apollo Creeds.

After a December to remember, Detroit's Scott Mitchell turned back into just another ugly face at the Vet. Mitchell threw four interceptions before being replaced by Don Majkowski, who threw two more. In the most shockingly lopsided score of the season, Philadelphia led 51–7 on the way to a 58–37 ticket to Dallas.

Switzer spent that Saturday in Norman helping son Greg buy a wedding ring.

The next morning at Valley Ranch you could have cut the relief with a butter knife and spread it on the coaches' bagels. The Lions sleep tonight. The Eagles had a lot of fight in them, but to Cowboy coaches, they were still the Eagles, and this was a playoff game at Texas Stadium. The Eagles weren't explosive enough on offense to exploit that "average" Cowboy defense. When Aikman wasn't in a funk or a slump, the Eagle secondary was no match for him. Thank you, Lord: The Eagles provided a very favorable matchup for Dallas.

The following Saturday, the day before the Philadelphia-Dallas divisional playoff game, it happened again. For the Cowboys, this must have seemed like the eleventh or twelfth day of Christmas. But in the NFL context, this was the greatest gift. You half-expected a Dallas newspaper game story to begin, "It came upon a midnight clear."

Green Bay had done it.

The Packers had eliminated the 49ers. Rather, the 49ers had fallen on their once mighty swords, committing four turnovers to Green

Bay's none. The Packers, with little to lose, had caught the 49ers flat-footed by getting tough with them, attacking and intimidating them. In the beginning, the Packers did to San Francisco what San Francisco had been doing to Dallas: a fumble by 49er Adam Walker was returned 31 yards for a touchdown. In football, it's difficult to overcome the emotional swing of an early turnover returned for a touchdown. Early in the second quarter, Green Bay turned 3Com Park into a memorial service, 21–0. The Cowboys knew the feeling.

So after Steve Young returned from shoulder surgery, the 49ers never quite regained the bossa nova–like offensive rhythm that Dallas had found nearly unstoppable. Young didn't appear quite as fearless about taking off from the pocket and supplying a running game the 49ers lacked without Ricky Watters. As impenetrable as San Francisco's defensive front seven was, the Deion-less secondary had no antidote for Brett Favre Disease. Once Favre was allowed to ease into an early groove, he turned into a bigger, stronger-armed Joe Montana. Favre was unconscious hot, hitting 21 of 28 for 299 yards and three touchdowns. In his last nine games, Favre had thrown twenty-one touchdown passes to just two interceptions. That kind of quarterback magic can cancel several team deficiencies, and Green Bay still had several.

Jerry Jones had made this point to me in training camp: "In this day and age, with the rules favoring the offense, you win championships with offense. Growing up, we were always taught that cliché that you win with defense. But that's no longer the case in the NFL. You can't have a 'give-up' defense [one that can't stop anybody]. But a Dallas and a San Francisco have been winning Super Bowls with their offense."

Very true. San Francisco's offense hadn't been able to overcome Favre. For Dallas, the Wicked Witch of the West had fallen, 27–17.

Lacewell gladly filed all the 49er research he had done. Even at Texas Stadium, could Switzer's Cowboys have broken through their psychological barrier against San Francisco? It would have been difficult. San Francisco was a bad matchup for Dallas—especially if the game had been in San Francisco. Could Aikman have risen to the occasion? Risen above the game? Maybe. But not likely.

Green Bay, which had lost five straight games under Favre at Texas Stadium, was a favorable psychological matchup for Dallas.

So, unbelievably, by Saturday night, January 6, the Dallas Cowboys knew they had to beat only Philadelphia and Green Bay at Texas Stadium to reach the Super Bowl. "No team," Jones told me, "will ever have a better chance to win a Super Bowl than we have right now." Yet if you had told the Cowboys on the night of December 17, following the Giant game, that they would find themselves in this lottery-winning position, they would have wanted you drug-tested.

Really, the Cowboys had earned none of this. In December they had played three poor games and one mediocre game. The Cowboys had merely watched as the 49ers and Lions, the NFC's most dangerous teams, had flamed out. Really, the Cowboys hadn't played an impressive game since Kansas City on Thanksgiving. Remember what a worthy Super Bowl foe Cowboy coaches thought the Chiefs would make? The following day in Kansas City, in weather fit only for beast, former Cowboy kicker Lin Elliott missed three field-goal attempts and the Chiefs were eliminated by Indianapolis 10–7.

This was getting creepy.

As much respect as Lacewell had for the Switzer Luck, he also was aware of Switzer's biggest coaching deficiency. On a staff Switzer hadn't hired, he had no sounding board, no trusted devil's advocate to help with bang-bang in-game decisions. Lacewell had filled that role for years at Oklahoma. Now, with a Super Bowl begging to be won, Lacewell wanted to eliminate any potential fourth-and-a-foot fiascos. For Sunday's game at Texas Stadium, Lacewell went undercover and again became Switzer's conscience.

In the pressbox just before kickoff, I wondered why Lacewell and the Joneses, Jerry and Stephen, weren't in their customary seats. Through binoculars, I scanned the middle luxury-box level of the stadium and caught sight of a small, shadowed, sparsely furnished box just to left of the end-zone Stadium Club. Its lights were turned out, but there was just enough sunlight out in the stadium to illuminate three inhabitants: Larry, Jerry, and Stephen. Only if you looked hard through binoculars could you make them out; TV cameras wouldn't be able to spot them.

Lacewell had a phone line to the bench, to be used only in case of emergency.

But on this day Switzer didn't face a single potential "Bozo" decision. The Switzer Luck was riding shotgun.

Near the end of the first quarter, with Dallas up 3–0, the Eagles were driving for the lead. To Cowboy fans, Rodney Peete probably looked dangerously comfortable, hitting three of his first five throws for 28 yards. Now it was third-and-4 at the Cowboy 12. Peete rolled right . . . looked . . . looked . . . and decided to run for it. Cowboy safety Darren Woodson greeted him right at the first-down marker. Peete didn't hesitate. Peete lowered his head and tried to run over a basically stationary Woodson, who simply lowered *his* head and flexed his trapezoid muscles, which flared like an extra set of shoulder pads.

Not only was Peete stopped short of the first down, but he knocked himself silly. The Eagles took the field goal while Peete took a wobbly walk toward the locker room. He could not return. Says John Wooten, "If Rodney didn't go down [with a concussion], I really believe we could have hung in and made it a game. I'm saying, 'Slide, Rodney! Slide!'"

The Eagles were forced to play Randall Cunningham, Philadelphia's star-turned-sub. Cunningham had left the Eagle practice site in Vero Beach, Florida, the previous week to be with his wife in Las Vegas while she had their first child. Cunningham, perhaps, figured he had played his last game as an Eagle. Wooten says, "He could have been back by Thursday morning. He didn't get back until Friday night. He missed our last two practices. He didn't even know our game plan. We were completely limited with him in there. I told Ray, 'Well, he told us what he thought of us.'"

Cunningham looked as woeful in Dallas as Aikman had looked in Philadelphia. The Eagles who had shocked Dallas and electroshocked Detroit suddenly turned back into harmless overachievers.

The Cowboys moved quickly to first-and-10 at the Eagle 21. That's when Deion took the game, popped it in his mouth like bubble gum, and blew a big bubble that popped all over the Eagles. Deion ran a reverse to his left, found what looked like thirty or forty Eagles waiting for him amid bear traps and camouflaged pits full of spikes, said, "Ta ta, fellows," and took off the other way. Sanders was running an unassisted double-reverse! Once he turned the far corner, he was traveling the speed of (spot)light. I've never seen a human run that fast with a football under his arm. No Eagle came close to touching him. You could see the Eagles collectively deflate. They had to know they did not belong on the same field (or planet) with Deion.

The Cowboys eventually won 30–11.

Dean Blevins, who worked for ABC and three radio stations (two in Oklahoma City, one in Dallas), hosted *The Jerry Jones Show*, and wrote a column for the Oklahoma edition of *The Insider*, didn't have an assigned seat in the Texas Stadium pressbox. He usually found an unused one, but the heavy newspaper turnout for the Philadelphia game relegated him to standing room only.

With about four minutes left in the first quarter, Aikman underthrew Michael Irvin. Philly's Bobby Taylor tipped it and Mark McMillian intercepted it. Later, I was told that several writers saw and heard Blevins bang his fist and curse. Of course, Blevins was rooting for his ex-coach and friend Switzer. But the writers interpreted Blevins's body language as being anti-Aikman, as if Blevins were saying, "There he goes again." One told me, "I wish Blevins would conduct his vendetta somewhere other than the pressbox." Blevins says the vendetta charge is "sick."

Dale Hansen was told at halftime about Blevins's "outburst," which didn't surprise Hansen. From his partner in the team's radio broadcast booth, Hansen was hearing what also sounded like an anti-Aikman bias. Hansen was getting increasingly irritated by the descriptions of first-year play-by-play man Dave Garrett, a native Oklahoman (from, ironically, Henryetta) chosen by Jones and Switzer (mostly Switzer) to replace Brad Sham. Garrett had hit it off with Switzer when Switzer was coaching at Oklahoma. In 1994 Garrett was the host of Switzer's radio show.

Hansen counted seven times during the game that Garrett referred to a "bad pass" by Aikman. "I finally had to say something [on the air] like, 'Dave, that one didn't look so bad to me,'" says Hansen. "I'm wondering, 'Was he *told* [by Switzer] to do this?'"

Garrett says, "That's silly. Just listen to the tapes. No way was I hypercritical of Aikman." Garrett was so disturbed about having created any perception that he was anti-Aikman that he called the quarterback, who told him not to worry. "I have no problem with you," Aikman told Garrett.

For Aikman, the Philadelphia game was an average performance. For the record, Aikman was 17 of 24 for 253 yards, with one touchdown pass and one interception.

Hansen also told me of a story burning the phone lines among Aikman campers—a story, if true, that could finish forever what was left of the Aikman-Switzer relationship. No doubt Aikman heard the story. He has his Iagos, too, and he sometimes reacts (or overreacts) as emotionally as Switzer to what his supporters whisper in his ear.

This time, the Aikman camp heard about a gathering of Switzer and his co-conspirators over drinks at a bar. Present, Hansen heard, were Blevins, John Blake, Danny Bradley, Dave Garrett—and I. I've never been in a bar with Switzer, nor have I ever been in the same room with that group of people, nor do I have any knowledge of this alleged meeting. But in it, allegedly, Switzer called Aikman "a loser, a quitter, a baby, a pussy" and encouraged his assassins to spread the word.

To my knowledge, this wasn't even a distorted Operator story. This was complete fabrication.

Switzer's supporters say there was no such gathering and no such statement made by Switzer. Garrett says a *Dallas Morning News* columnist asked him about it, as if he might actually write about it. Garrett told him, "I honestly have no idea what you're talking about."

Still, the week after the Philadelphia game, Hansen told me he had talked to Aikman about whether the quarterback would march in after the season and tell Jones to fire Switzer. "He said he absolutely would not do what Magic [Johnson] did to [ex–Los Angeles Laker coach] Paul Westhead. He said, 'I don't want that blood on my hands. That's Jerry's area.'" Hansen also had heard that Aikman's parents would not stand for his trying to fire a coach. Even at twenty-nine years old, Aikman still honored his mother and father.

But, concluded Hansen, "I have serious doubts about whether Troy Aikman will be here next year." Meaning, he would demand a trade or retire. As much as I knew about the psychological blood that had been shed, hearing Hansen say that with such conviction the week of the NFC championship game still jarred me.

Psychologist Beck was right: The Cowboys had never experienced any closure over the loss of their "father," Jimmy Johnson. They had never been allowed to mourn his passing or exorcise his ghost or merely to forget and go forward. Jones never missed an opportunity to trade jabs with Johnson through the media. For Jones, this endless game of macho "gotcha" was ego-inflating, because it kept him on the same stage with Jimmy the Genius. But Jerry vs. Jimmy had a negative effect on Jones's current coach and team: It kept Jimmy "alive." Stephen Jones said he suggested several times to his dad that he cool it. "Really, they both needed to move on," Stephen says. "No matter what either one of 'em said, it sounded like sour grapes."

But finally, just when Barry Switzer needed it most, Jimmy Johnson's media career ended on Friday, January 12, when he succeeded Don Shula as head coach of the Miami Dolphins. Now, the Wicked Witch of the East was dead. No more hovering. No more undermining. Now Johnson was back in the arena, on a level playing field. You could almost feel the fog of Jimmy's hair spray lift off Valley Ranch.

That week I told Beck about a little speech Nate Newton gave to the team before the Philly playoff game. Newton said, "Whatever starts your engine—money, cars, women, whatever—start your engine right now. This is what it's all about." Beck, as amazed by the team's turnaround as I was, said, "That speech is fine as long as the team knows *how* to win. They were able to remember the *how* that Jimmy taught and instilled in them. But as it's turning out, Barry was actually the perfect complement to Jimmy's rigid style. Barry's strength in one-on-one relationships has been very important late in the season. Very few coaches could have done, in tandem, what Jimmy and Barry have done. Now, whether Jerry planned that, I don't know."

The first thing Jerry Jones said about Barry Switzer was "I think he'll be the perfect complement to Jimmy."

But Switzer wasn't about to compliment Johnson. At his Thursday press briefing that week, Switzer said he couldn't understand how any owner (Miami's Wayne Huizenga) could pay that much money ($2 million) to a coach (Johnson) who has been out of coaching for two years. This again prompted my up-the-down-staircase debate with Switzer over the value of coaching. Later that day, he again got exasperated with me and said, "All I'm saying [about Johnson's salary] is that it's the fuckin' players. It's just amusing to me that a guy from outside the arena starts believing in the mystique you all [in the media] create. *You* make us into a genius. It's our fault if we start believing it. I mean, look at what happened to Bill Walsh. He goes back to Stanford and he loses because *he doesn't have the fuckin' players*. Is he still the same guru he was [with the 49ers]?"

"So," I said, "Jerry wasn't exaggerating when he said 500 coaches could win a Super Bowl with this team?"

"Well," Switzer said, "not 500. But several could. The question is, how do you define 'coach'? In this job [as Dallas Cowboy coach], the hardest thing to do is to control yourself—control your own emotions."

Switzer, of course, had more emotions to control than most coaches. Yet he had done a quietly magnificent job of keeping his lid on through December. Jones says, "Barry handled it so well. I'm so proud of him. He's the guy you want flying your plane when you're in the storm. He never wavered. Jimmy's great as long as everything is stable around him. But I'm not sure how he would have held up through everything we went through."

PR man Dalrymple says, "That quiet toughness of Barry's really made you want to see him succeed. He was able to absorb all the heat [for the team] and deflect it at the same time."

As Switzer says, he is one thick-skinned son of a bitch.

Yet you didn't exactly see a *Sports Illustrated* cover story entitled, "Barry Switzer, Dallas's Unsung MVP." That week, I was interviewed by six or eight out-of-town radio shows a day, and the hosts routinely referred to Switzer as (at worst) a buffoon or (at best) a figurehead or puppet. Jones says, "I don't think Barry ever will *not* be criticized because he always makes it look so much easier than it is. Even when I was in school and he was a very young coach, he was very excitable, but everything always seemed so easy for him in adverse situations."

Jones says no one outside the coaching staff has a sense of the subtle suggestions Switzer makes in offensive or defensive meetings. "I wish people could watch him operate in those meetings,

making suggestions about technique or scheme or whatever without having to 'show-dog' it [upstage assistants]. His ability with the
Xs and Os is still very underrated."

So what is coaching? As Lacewell says, "It's so many things. It's
what you do in the [coaches] meetings during the week. It's in-game
coaching. It's talking to the team. It's dealing one-on-one with players. But one thing you can say for Switzer: He took two very good
teams [at Oklahoma and in Dallas] and he didn't screw 'em up. A lot
of coaches would have. Would you like to see him have a better
relationship with Troy? Sure. Would you like to see him discipline
some players? Sure. Would you like to see him get in at six in the
morning and stay until eight at night? Sure. But I will say this: He
has really done so much better this year [curtailing his nightlife].

"And let me tell you, this team could have crucified him after
that fourth-and-one deal. But they all stood by him. They could
have quit on him the next week, but they didn't. The one thing I'd
hate to tell Troy is that the rest of the team is really starting to love
Switzer. You can just see it out on the practice field. It's amazing."

It was. Switzer said that week on his radio show that "ninety
percent" of the Cowboys would rather play for him than for any
other coach they've played for. That figure was low.

Yet a couple of days before the Green Bay game, a couple of
magazine writers noticed that Switzer didn't make it in for the start
of 10 A.M. meetings. They were stunned. A head coach coming in
that late before the biggest game of his professional career? One
said, "The lack of work ethic will eventually get this team." How
could I argue against that without looking like a Switzer apologist?
How could I begin to explain Switzer to a writer (or to a quarterback) set on evaluating him by conventional standards?

Jones says, "It will be much more difficult to criticize him if he
wins a Super Bowl. That's why this is so tremendously important
for him."

Before Sunday's NFC championship game at Texas Stadium, Jimmy
Johnson, working his last game for Fox, approached Jerry Jones on
the field and shook his hand. Previously when their paths had crossed,
they had engaged in rather childish shouting matches. This time, said
Jones, "There definitely was some closure there. It felt good."

A few minutes later, Lacewell left the shadows of his new "box"
to use a nearby Stadium Club restroom. Fox's pregame show set
was in the Stadium Club.

There, "as God would have it," says Lacewell, was Jimmy Johnson, using the urinal next to him. For a rare moment, Lacewell was

speechless. Johnson spoke first. "Lace," he said, "tell Barry I went down on the field to tell him good luck, but I couldn't find him."

As Johnson turned away, Lacewell said, "Hey, I'm glad you're back in coaching. You're a great coach."

Brett Favre, the NFL MVP, said something after Green Bay's ambush of San Francisco that defined the difference between his playoff approach and Aikman's. Favre said, "I kept waiting for something bad to happen. When it didn't, I said, 'Hey, we can play with these guys.'" At Texas Stadium, a house of horrors for Favre after five straight losses, he probably waited for something really bad to happen.

It finally did. Early in the fourth quarter, with Dallas up 31–27, Favre went gunslinging for Mark Ingram and, apparently, didn't see Larry Brown. Earlier, Favre and Robert Brooks had smoked Brown on a 73-yard touchdown pass. But no one ever seems to see Brown until he intercepts the pass. It's almost as if Brown is so inconspicuous that he actually becomes invisible for a couple of seconds, then materializes in front of the ball.

Two plays after Brown's interception, it was 38–27 Dallas. That's the way the game ended. Even without Charles Haley, who had returned from surgery but wasn't quite ready to play, the Cowboys had spelled Super Bowl correctly. The difference was simply this: Aikman (two touchdown passes and no interceptions) had outperformed and outexecuted Favre (three touchdown passes, two interceptions), who still wasn't in Aikman's league, especially in a playoff game.

Now, as often happened after Cowboy games, it got inexplicably nuts. Michael Irvin, originally a Switzer skeptic, shocked Fox's national audience by saying, "Don't nobody deserve it more than the head coach. He takes all the shit."

No doubt parents in living rooms everywhere were asked by little Michael lovers what that last word meant.

In the locker room, Irvin's rage continued to spill over on the media around his locker: "I'm sick of it. When is the man ever going to get any credit? Write it! Give the man some credit."

Player after player approached Switzer, embraced him, and whispered in his ear how much they loved the coach. Yet Aikman's point was, sure they love him. He lets them do whatever they want. The one kind of love Aikman hadn't seen from Switzer was tough love. Switzer wouldn't punish a player *because* he loved him.

But now Switzer, emotion lodging in his throat, told the media, "I really appreciate it . . . when . . . when players look you right in the eye and . . ." His eyes were blurring. "I mean, Troy gave me a game ball."

Aikman had taken the game's final snap and kneeled to kill the clock. With the ball under his arm, he had trotted toward the Cowboy sideline. The first person to extend a congratulatory hand had been the head coach. Almost reflexively, it appeared, Aikman had handed Switzer the ball. Aikman definitely had not meant for Switzer to take it as a peace offering. Aikman did not join his teammates in ordering the media to give the man some respect.

Anything but.

Aikman preceded Switzer on the interview stand in a room across from the locker room. When asked if this win had vindicated Switzer, Aikman said with irritation, "I wasn't aware we were supposed to do anything to vindicate him. I thought it was just a bunch of football players doing all we could to win games."

Then, for the first time in public, Aikman voluntarily mentioned the "self-imposed" problems the team had overcome. He said, "We overcame a great deal of things that could have been avoided." Of course, the journalists in Aikman's audience glanced at one another with curious looks. But before anyone could ask a follow-up question, Aikman said, "That's as far as I'll go." This was as close as Aikman would ever get to taunting. He was sending a cryptic little "in your face" to Switzer campers. Overcome more by pride than tears, Aikman was itching to tell the world that he and his teammates had pulled together and overcome the sick plotting of the coach and his henchmen.

As Aikman stepped down off the platform, he passed the approaching Switzer, who, in front of nearby reporters, said to Aikman, "Hey, thanks for the ball." Aikman mumbled a quick "Sure" and kept walking. No hug. No "I love you, man."

Back at his locker, Aikman told a smaller group of reporters, "Look, I don't want you guys to make too big a deal out of me giving him the football. There is still something left for this football team to achieve. I know that I'm not content, and I don't think this team is."

It was almost as if the "game ball" had been more of a cruel April Fool's joke. Aikman's comment ensured Switzer's ecstasy soon would blur with agony. Oh, how Switzer wanted Aikman to like and respect him. But Aikman wasn't going to give Switzer any credit—especially for supplying any Sooner Magic. Jimmy Johnson hates the word luck. Likewise Aikman believes a team creates "luck" with dedication and discipline.

To Aikman the only lucky one was Switzer, who was going along for the ride to his first Super Bowl.

18

RELIEF

A winner never whines.
          —*NFL coaching legend Paul Brown*

T he Buttes is one of those five-star Valley of the Sun resorts built into a hillside of scenic rock formation. From the street entrance, you wind up what seems like a mile of driveway until you reach the actual hotel. Or is it? As you pull into the lobby level, it looks more like some rustic one-story motel than a $285-a-night palace. But given a map and several days to explore, you discover The Buttes is a multilevel optical illusion of cavernous hallways and remote wings that makes Valley Ranch seem like a two-bedroom, one-bath house. The most-asked question at The Buttes: "Can you tell me how to get back to the lobby?" A typical answer: "Go to the end of this hall, take the elevator up one level, go left for what seems like half a mile, then make three rights and you'll see another set of elevators. Take one of those down two levels, walk through the pool area, then you'll see the stairs leading up to the lobby. It's easy."

From January 21 through January 28, the Dallas Cowboys took over The Buttes, which the Dallas-Fort Worth media began calling Fort Limo. Michael Irvin, Emmitt Smith, Nate Newton, and others had hired a fleet of limousines (eleven in all) from the Dallas company they trusted (First Impressions) to be driven to Phoenix for Super Bowl Week. The cost: $1,000 a day, per limo. (The problem: The Dallas drivers kept getting lost in Phoenix.) By midweek, The Buttes looked like a limo dealership. The Dallas Cowboys sure know how to do Super Bowl Week. Jerry Jones defended the "country club" atmosphere by saying, "If you've worked as hard as they have, with the ups and downs they've had, I think this is a reward." But Jones loved the publicity and allure that "Fort Limo" generated for Hollywood's Team.

On Monday, Nate Newton entertained reporters by saying, "The police came in and gave us a list of places not to go. I wrote 'em all down and went there, so I'm feeling pretty good today." Later, a more serious Newton defended "Fort Limo" by saying, "Hey, at least we're not out there drinking and driving. We're being responsible."

But naturally a predominant media theme that week was Cowboy arrogance. The Cowboys had gone from the despised but respected corporate arrogance of Tex Schramm's America's Team to the lovable, wholesome work-ethic Cowboys of Troy and Emmitt and Jimmy in 1992 to the hated chest-beating arrogance of Jerry Jones's potential '90s dynasty. *Arizona Republic* columnist David Casstevens wrote, "What other NFL owner would say, the week before the Super Bowl, that Arizona's 1 A.M. last call would conflict with the Cowboys' victory party? If the owner and some Cowboy players are determined to imbibe after the game and can't get drunk for free by 1 A.M., with a 4:30 P.M. kickoff, an argument could be made they don't deserve to be world champions. Victory party? Talk about presumptuous. How arrogant can you get?"

Indeed, Jones had voiced concern over the 1 A.M. law, because he knew from experience these bashes didn't get rolling until around midnight. Was he that confident it would *be* a victory party? He was. Casstevens concluded that around Jones's Cowboys was "an air of power and superiority, an unmistakable smell of money— money, money, money—as thick and cloying as spilled perfume."

If Casstevens had been around the Cowboys just a few weeks earlier, they would have just plain stunk. But now they were back— "back in our house, where we belong," said Irvin. Their Super Bowl opponent was basically the same Pittsburgh Steeler team they had dismantled in Pittsburgh to begin the 1994 season. If the Cowboys didn't make any silly mistakes, they figured this game would basically be a limo ride. So for many Cowboys, including the head coach and owner, this would be a work-hard, party-hard week.

Jerry and Gene Jones were given what The Buttes touted as "the world's largest suite." Switzer could have used it. He and Kathy turned his two-bedroom suite into a halfway house of family and friends sleeping on rollaway beds. Yes, he had come a long ways from that shack outside Crossett. Ain't football something? The NFL had even provided Switzer with his own twenty-four-hour limo for the week. Soon after the team arrived at the hotel, Switzer took one look around his suite and told Kathy, "We're at the Super Bowl!" On the suite stereo, he jacked up Marvin Gaye's "Let's Get It On" and he and Kathy spontaneously began doing a dance she describes as the "Arkansas Push." At that moment, through the open door walked Emmitt Smith, wondering what had gotten into his coach. Laughing, Kathy said, "Hey, let's get it on, Emmitt!" Emmitt just stood there, grinning and shaking his head.

The only man at The Buttes at least as happy as Switzer was Jones. He rented a bus that had been custom-designed to transport Whitney Houston on one of her tours, and each evening the Jones family and the Switzer family turned this Mercedes of a bus into the Arkansas Express and headed out to dinner. At the fanciest restaurants in Phoenix and Scottsdale, they were honored with the best tables and the most attentive service. Other diners gawked as if they were royalty. They laughed and told stories and toasted the night away, and several times that week Jerry Jones told this group he was happier than he ever had been. This was what he always yearned for with Jimmy Johnson. Now Switzer had become something Jerry Jones doesn't have many of: a trusted friend. No doubt, after enough *vino*, Switzer threw an arm around Jones and said, "I love you, motherfucker." Yes, they were having fun yet.

In a way, Troy Aikman tried to serve the Story of the Week as if it were the free breakfast eaten by the thousands of media people on hand for Tuesday's annual Super Bowl Media Day. But no one immediately partook. What happens at Media Day is that a plague of us media locusts descends on one team, breaks for the buffet breakfast, then descends on the other. First, for nearly an hour, the Steeler players and coaches fanned out to interview stations along one sideline and in the first few rows of the stands. Then came the Cowboy hour.

Naturally, Aikman attracted one of the largest audiences, maybe 100 to 150 reporters at a time. Right away, in answer to a question about how the season went, Aikman said, "This one has been a bigger emotional toll on myself and the team. This team has overcome a great deal more than the first two . . . This team overcame things internally it was a shame we had to deal with. They weren't necessary. In that sense I'm proud of this team for staying together."

Again, especially reporters from cities other than Dallas had to be mystified by these deep, dark unnecessary internal evils. But Aikman referred to them so routinely that perhaps most reporters thought these problems had been routinely reported in Dallas. They hadn't been. But that soon would change.

For journalists, Aikman has an admirable interview trait: He will not lie. He'll do a little polite sidestep occasionally, to protect teammates or coaches, but if you ask him what he thinks, he'll most likely tell you. Now, he no longer needed anyone to ask. It was as if he were daring somebody to write the truth.

The column by Jim Reeves broke in Thursday's edition of the *Fort Worth Star-Telegram*. Reeves wrote, "The Cowboys will attempt to win their third Super Bowl in four years Sunday with a coach and a quarterback who are barely speaking and an owner who is convinced that a victory against the Steelers is the panacea for that troubled relationship. He's dead wrong."

Reeves quoted Aikman as saying, "The idea that one game, one victory, would change the way I feel about this season—no, that's not going to happen."

Reeves wrote, "Aikman, on more than one occasion the past few weeks, has called this season 'the most difficult of my career' . . . The internal strife is at the root of the problem between Switzer and Aikman. Friends of the quarterback say the two haven't spoken more than a few words to each other since near midseason. That's when reports got back to Aikman that defensive line coach John Blake . . . complained to Switzer that Aikman regularly seemed to single out black players as targets for his occasional angry outbursts. The quarterback was furious and took pains to ask other players and coaches whether they had a problem with his approach."

Switzer's response to Reeves: "I respect him. If he wants to respect me is not important . . . I don't go around asking him."

He certainly didn't. That week, he and Aikman had found themselves on the same Buttes elevator and hadn't even nodded hello. As Aikman had vowed, they had not spoken since that Wednesday, December 6, practice after the Washington game.

On a 75-degree morning, the Reeves story hit The Buttes like a cold snap. It wasn't that the team was upset or torn over it, just surprised and confused, as if the players had awakened to a blanket of snow outside. That morning the Cowboys had one last mandatory interview session, in a spacious meeting room at the hotel. With the Super Bowl just three days away, players were hit with questions about racial problems on the team. *Huh?* Again, no doubt some of them had groused to Blake or Danny Bradley about Aikman's quick temper or his aloof attitude or even his "redneck" ways. But full-blown black-white problems? They certainly could have developed and surfaced if the team had lost to the Giants and Cardinals and collapsed in the playoffs, but as long as the team wins, black players are not going to go public with whatever problems they have with the franchise quarterback. What good would that do? Aikman had helped make many of them rich and famous. If any black player believed Aikman had used the n-word on Kevin Williams, that would have been another (bombshell) story. But the Williams incident had been resolved to everyone's satisfaction, except Aikman's.

The irony was that Aikman, through his voluntary "self-inflicted problems" comments to the media, had inflicted more problems on the team. The quarterback who despised distractions had helped create one—for his teammates and himself.

During that morning's interview session, Aikman clearly was not pleased he had to spend so much time answering questions about the two least favorite people in his professional life, Switzer and Blake. But, amid sighs, he did frame the *Star-Telegram* story in perfect perspective: "The players on this team know it has been discussed, it has been resolved and that is all that matters. There are a number of things being written about this week regarding my relationship with Barry. I don't think anybody pays any attention to it within our organization or locker room."

Really, they didn't.

So with minicams and microphones thrust in their faces, black star after star supported Aikman in tones of "Why are you asking me this question?" Even Irvin said, "I don't know what John Blake said . . . [but] I am as black as anybody you could ever see. I am as black as they come. And I know this man [Aikman] loves me."

Meanwhile, all the black stars continued to pledge their love for Switzer. Deion said, "Barry's a good man. He's not only a friend but a fishing partner."

The team seemed to be saying, "We love Barry, and we love the way Troy plays quarterback, so why don't we forget about this stuff and go kick Pittsburgh's ass?"

For the moment, though, the one guy getting his kicked was Switzer. Several hundred reporters fired questions at him for forty-five minutes. On Aikman he responded, "We are committed to winning. That's all that's important. I'm not going to drink RC Colas or double-date with him, but that's not important." Then, getting agitated, Switzer blamed his problems with Aikman on the media. "It's created because y'all ask [Aikman] all the time. Everybody keeps bringing it up. Rubs you raw. It's kind of like jock itch—you can't get rid of the thing."

Several reporters laughed at that analogy. But for Switzer, the sad truth was that *Aikman* kept bringing it up.

Probably backgrounded with information from PR man Dalrymple, who's from Pittsburgh, Switzer said, "I don't know that

Chuck Noll and Terry Bradshaw had a great relationship, but they won four Super Bowls together."

True. But did Bradshaw have no respect for Noll as a coach? Did Noll have confidants who led him to believe Bradshaw was racist or even gay? Was Bradshaw close to a Jimmy Johnson and a Norv Turner who wanted to see Noll fail? Did Noll suspect Bradshaw was out to get him fired?

No. Never in football history has there been a more complicated, bizarre, paranoia-wracked coach-quarterback relationship than the iceberg whose tip had been exposed by Jim Reeves.

Just when I thought the Cowboys' final Super Bowl Week media session could not get any stranger, Switzer was asked about a story that had just broken in the *Austin American-Statesman*. The NCAA, it said, had received information that several Cowboys had contacted recruits on Blake's behalf—and that Switzer had talked to recruits in Norman. Blake's program, it said, was already under NCAA scrutiny. Like father, like "son"?

"Déjà vu," Switzer told reporters. "Same problems I had twenty years ago. That tells me John is kicking their butt." Meaning, Blake already had made enough recruiting inroads in Texas that sources in or close to the Longhorn program in Austin had tipped the NCAA to these potential violations.

Sighing heavily, Switzer explained that, on the way to dinner with OU president David Boren the previous Saturday evening in Norman, he spontaneously stopped by to see Blake and bumped into a couple of recruits and their families, who wanted autographs and pictures. Switzer indicated he hadn't realized that *even this* could be an NCAA violation. His attitude was "Was I supposed to be rude to those people?"

Recruiting violations, limos, racism—Switzer no longer was having fun yet.

Drained, he left the media session, returned to his suite, and ranted and raved for a few minutes until he had gotten it out of his system. Wasn't his team a 14-point favorite in the Super Bowl? Wasn't this supposed to be a feel-good week?

Simultaneously, Aikman returned to his room, where he was consoled for the next hour or so by family and friends. Wasn't this the week every quarterback strived to experience? Wasn't he supposed to be basking?

That night on his KRLD radio show, Aikman took out his frustration by openly referring to Blake for the first time. Aikman: "I will say this: The gentleman who made those [racist] accusations, there's a reason he's no longer on the staff, which goes a lot deeper than he got hired on another job. I found out later . . . the individual who said that has no credibility."

Talk about vengeance. Those words from a former OU quarter-back-turned-superhero had the potential to hurt Blake's Oklahoma program worse than a minor NCAA violation. Imagine what some recruits (or their parents) thought if they heard that Troy Aikman hates John Blake for calling him a racist and that Troy says Blake has no credibility. Because Blake joined the recruiting battle so late, his first class was difficult to judge. He signed a few players Howard Schnellenberger probably wouldn't have; he missed on a few "difference makers." But several recruiting sources say Aikman's remarks probably damaged Blake to some degree.

When I spoke with Blake, he was stunned by the "bad guy" role he was playing at the Super Bowl. Again, nobody knew of Danny Bradley's involvement; Blake was taking the entire fall. In a way, I wished Switzer would step up and say, "Don't blame John Blake for this. I'm the head coach. Ultimately the responsibility was mine. Blame me." In a way, Switzer was hurting another of those who love him most.

But Blake certainly wasn't blaming Switzer. "The whole thing isn't fair," Blake said. "In many ways I was trying to help Troy by making Coach Switzer aware of some potential problems. But I know other assistants were jealous of my relationship with Coach Switzer and they helped turn Troy against me, and once he decides something, he's very stubborn. I can respect that. But the people around me who count know what I can do."

That evening back in my hotel room, I watched John Blake's picture flash again and again on ESPN. I had tried unsuccessfully to convince him of the axiom, "Any publicity is good publicity." After all, just a few weeks earlier, Blake had been a relatively unknown, unpublicized assistant coach. Now, soon after getting his dream job, John Blake was becoming known as Troy Aikman's arch-enemy. What a long, strange trip it had been for many involved with the 1995 Cowboys.

Kathy Switzer made sure her mother was invited to the Super Bowl. Kay Switzer's three children and so many of her old friends would be there, staying in a swanky resort and taking limos to incredible parties. Kay, somewhat surprisingly, agreed to come. Rather shockingly, she agreed to sleep on a rollaway in her ex-husband's suite—while girlfriend Becky Buwick shared Barry's room.

Yet Kay has gotten to know all of Switzer's long-term girlfriends. Becky and Barry have spent holidays with the Switzer children at Kay's house in Little Rock. Still, Kay would have preferred to sleep elsewhere, if she could have afforded it. But she doesn't have much money, she says. She lives alone.

What if she hadn't had the pride and guts to file for divorce in 1981? What if she had been "smart" enough to stay with Switzer, as he had wanted her to do? What if she had agreed to look the other way while he gallivanted? Would it have been worth it to be Mrs. Dallas Cowboy Coach? To sit next to Barry in first class on the team plane? Be the decorator-queen of his big new house? Constantly be around her kids, who want to be around the Cowboys? Be hoisted by Barry onto the Fox interview platform after the Green Bay victory, the way Jerry had lifted and swung wife Gene? From a distance, did the ex–Mrs. Switzer envy Mrs. Jones?

Occasionally. But it passes. "Oh, I did have a twinge of jealousy after the Green Bay game," says Kay Switzer. "But I'm okay. I still have my pride." For her, Super Bowl Week was a constant clash of happy and sad, belonging and not belonging. "When I got out to the Super Bowl, they all treated me like a queen. Barry was nice to me. And seeing all the [Arkansas and Oklahoma] alums and ex-players—everybody showed me so much love, as if I was part of it.

"And I'm not part of it."

The morning of the Super Bowl, Barry Switzer showed up as usual for the team chapel service. But for the first time, as various players prayed out loud, Switzer spoke up. Barry Switzer prayed to the group. Later, he said, "We were all totally nekked in our emotion, and I basically made a statement, a confession, about being blessed."

Blessed almost inexplicably with the Switzer Luck? No, that wasn't it. Switzer prayed, "Lord, thank you for these guys who have become my family."

Later, Switzer said, "I'm not a practicing Christian. You go through the agnostic principle when you're younger and you think you'll live forever. [Now] I certainly *hope* there is a God."

The day before the Super Bowl, NBC's PR people hyped an interview their Cris Collinsworth had done with Troy Aikman, to be aired during the pregame show. Troy Aikman, the flaks were saying, had been critical of Barry Switzer! For insiders a much more shocking story would have been: Aikman endorses Switzer! I had run into Leigh Steinberg on Friday, and he had indicated that this very well could be Aikman's last game as a Dallas Cowboy. That possibility had been reinforced by Dale Hansen, who told me he had talked with a couple of Cowboys close to Aikman (probably Mark Tuinei and Dale Hellestrae) who said Aikman would not play another season for Switzer.

In the interview, Collinsworth asked Aikman if Switzer is a good coach. Aikman paused significantly before saying, quite honestly, "I don't know."

Though it didn't register on Aikman's evaluation screen, Switzer did do something highly unusual and perhaps highly effective during Sunday's Super Bowl introductions. He stood at the end of the gauntlet of Cowboys and as the offensive players were introduced and came running by, low-fiving teammates, Switzer said to each of them, "I love you."

Nearly all of them would have given Switzer their Bud Light any day.

Several times during Super Bowl XXX, Switzer probably could have used a beer. He must have felt like the Cowboys were playing in Washington or Philadelphia.

Usually when the Cowboys visit Sun Devil Stadium to play the Arizona Cardinals, they turn it into Texas Stadium West. By game time, Cowboy fans from Southern California and all over the Southwest have acquired about half the 75,000 or so seats. The Cowboy blue usually drowns out the Cardinal red, turning the Arizona visit into a ninth Cowboy home game. But on Super Sunday, I scanned the throng at kickoff and realized I was sitting in the world's largest bumblebee nest: Eerily, at least two-thirds of the 76,347 were wearing Pittsburgh black and yellow-gold and screaming for the Steelers. Did that many more Steeler fans make the pilgrimage and outbid Dallas high-rollers for scalper's tickets? I seriously doubted it. But because so many of the seats are corporate-controlled and filled by people who are neither Cowboy nor Steeler fans, could it have been that the Cowboys' limo-riding superiority complex had turned many neutral observers into Pittsburgh fanatics? Very possibly.

Just as oddly, the game turned into a microcosm of the Cowboy season. Out they jumped to a 13–0 lead with 5:56 left in the first half. They even held the Steelers again and got the ball back with 4:56 left. Start the party? Just as it had appeared before the November 12 San Francisco game, this looked suspiciously like a Cowboy cakewalk—another Super Bowl blowout. But the Cowboys stalled, and suddenly the Steelers converted a third-and-20 and a third-and-14, and with 17 seconds left in the half, they cut the lead to 13–7.

Game on.

But midway through the third quarter, Steeler quarterback Neil

O'Donnell suddenly became possessed by the devil in Mr. Jones. How else can you explain what happened? Yes, the Cowboy pass rush was about to hit him like the running of the bulls, but O'Donnell has been pressured before. Was it brain-lock? A damp spot on the ball, causing it to slip and sail? O'Donnell flung a pass that didn't appear to come within 15 yards of a receiver. But it hit Larry Brown right where he stood, in lonesome zone coverage. It was as if Brown took a quick glance from side to side and thought, "Is he throwing to *me*?" Brown later said, "I got a little nervous while the ball was on its way because I knew nobody was around me and it was coming right to me, and I didn't want to look like a complete fool and drop it."

Because Brown didn't have to dive for the ball, he was in perfect position to run with it after he caught it. Forty-four yards later, the Cowboys had the ball at Pittsburgh's 18. Two plays later, it was 20–7, Dallas.

The Steelers shaved the lead to 20–10 with 11:20 left in the game, then immediately recovered an onside kick. You could just hear Cowboy fans saying, "That stupid Switzer . . ." And here came the Steelers, nine confident plays, 52 momentum-shifting yards, and it was 20–17. An Aikman sack halted the next Cowboy drive, and they punted with 4:15 left. On second-and-10 at their 36, it happened again.

This time, apparently, O'Donnell and his receivers miscommunicated on a route adjustment against a blitz. But ultimately, the responsibility is the quarterback's. O'Donnell mentally went to Disneyland again, whipping a pass into the flat that might have knocked the breath out of Larry Brown if he hadn't caught it. It was Brown who took off for Disneyland as the Super Bowl MVP. His 33-yard return set up a 6-yard Cowboy "march" to the clinching 27–17 touchdown.

Take away the two interceptions and Pittsburgh easily could have won. Super Bowl XXX's bottom line: O'Donnell threw two mystifyingly awful interceptions that set up Cowboy scoring drives of 18 and 6 yards, while Aikman made no mistakes. Aikman wasn't spectacular enough (15 of 23 for 209 yards and one touchdown) to win the MVP award, but the difference was that Dallas had Aikman and Pittsburgh didn't. O'Donnell's interceptions weren't great plays by Brown, but bad plays by O'Donnell. Who knows? Maybe he was so spooked by the lurking specter of Deion that, under fire, he instinctively threw away from No. 21 and forced panicky passes in Brown's direction.

In a fitting conclusion to the season, Brown had done less to win the honor than any MVP in Super Bowl history. Larry Brown had become an even lesser-known MVP than Cowboy linebacker Chuck

Howley, who was voted MVP in a losing cause in Super Bowl V. Larry Brown would talk by phone to President Clinton after the game. Larry Brown would become as much a media phenomenon as Downtown Julie Brown. Larry Brown would do Letterman. Larry Brown would sign a $2.5-million-a-year free-agent deal with the Oakland Raiders. Larry Brown. Life is strange.

Equally bizarre was this scene: NFL commissioner Paul Tagliabue, who had ripped Jerry Jones on that morning's *This Week with David Brinkley*, had to present the Vince Lombardi trophy to Jones in an internationally televised postgame ceremony. That morning, Tagliabue had reacted bitterly to a previous Jones comment that the NFL is like a commune "where people got out and worked and gained assets and position, then turned around and gave it back to everybody else who's not working. That's not America." Tagliabue told Brinkley, "Jerry Jones dishonors the agreement he made when he came into the NFL partnership. He takes what does not belong to him. The NFL is what we sell. It belongs to the thirty teams, not the Dallas Cowboys."

So did Jones gloat? Did he wear his Pepsi boots or take the trophy from Tagliabue and hand it to Phil Knight? No, this time Jones was smart enough to let his team's victory do his talking (and also to invite up onto the victory stand wife Gene, who had earned a moment in the spotlight). Jones commended the Steelers, then complimented his team not for its talent but for its mental toughness and character. Jones didn't say a word about lawsuits or ex-coaches. He knew the mounted silver football he shook for emphasis with his right hand—the third Lombardi that would go on display in his new mansion—roared like the F-16 fighters that had flown over before the game. Millions watching knew that Jerry Jones had proven he could fire Jimmy Johnson and win a Super Bowl with Barry Switzer. This was Jones's crowning moment.

Then it was Switzer's turn to speak, and for the second time that day, he was nekked with his emotions. He took the NBC microphone and said, "All that counts is family—my personal family and this one right here [the Cowboys]." Then he looked at a Jones, whose grin belied a wince. You could almost see Jones thinking, "My God, what is he going to say now?" Switzer said, "All I want to ask Jerry is, 'Are we having fun yet?'" Then Switzer, playing off the infamous "we gonna do it, baby" from his first Cowboy press conference, yelled, "We did it! We did it! We did it!

*   *   *

The tent that served as the postgame interview area was a mad scramble of media and mixed Cowboy emotions. At one interview station sat what appeared to be a terribly relieved Aikman, who wearily sidestepped any more Switzer questions.

Inadvertently, though, he complimented his coach. Aikman said, "Things have fallen into place for us—for what reason I'm not sure."

The Switzer Luck. As efficiently, imperturbably brilliant as Aikman again had been through a playoff drive, he surely couldn't have done it without some Switzer Luck. Even Aikman, as postseason great as he is, needed Detroit's collapse and San Francisco's collapse. He needed Brett Favre and Neil O'Donnell to make a star of Larry Brown. He needed Howard Schnellenberger to get fired and John Blake to get hired and get gone.

He also needed a coach who could keep lots of explosive egos from blowing up the team during December. This time, he needed a Barry Switzer instead of a Jimmy Johnson. When it was darkest, Johnson might have taken this team over the edge with him.

Though neither would admit it—particularly Aikman—he and Switzer actually made a great team.

For sure, Switzer needed Aikman more than the coach could bring himself to admit. At Oklahoma, Switzer was king. In Dallas, Aikman is franchise MVP. Not Switzer. Not Jones. Not Emmitt, Michael, or Deion. The individual most responsible for the three Lombardi trophies is No. 8.

In the NFL, quarterback is a more difficult position to play than running back. A quarterback makes so many more critical decisions than a running back that an Aikman carries a much greater responsibility to avoid losing. An Emmitt can contribute just as much to winning as an Aikman, but a team can overcome a bad game by a running back easier than it can an error-prone quarterback. As rare a competitor and a talent as Emmitt is, you can find more Emmitts than Aikmans.

Consider Aikman's production during each of his team's three-game runs to an NFL title: In 1992–1993, he was 61 of 89 for 795 yards and eight touchdowns, with no interceptions. In 1993–1994, he was 61 of 82 for 686 yards and five touchdowns, with three interceptions. In 1995–1996, he was 53 of 80 for 717 yards and four touchdowns, with one interception. That's 17 touchdown passes against only four interceptions in nine high-pressure games (including three Super Bowls).

That's why, over at his interview station, Jones was saying, "It is wonderful to be riding Troy Aikman's coattails."

*   *   *

A moment later, a telephone was taken up to Jones and Switzer. On it was an old buddy of theirs from Arkansas. Jones told him, "Mr. President, for Gene and I, this is the best one of all. [The team] dwelled on the positive when they could have pointed fingers. This is a lesson for us all."

Then it was Switzer's turn. He first thanked Bill Clinton "for the time you hunted me down" after a tough Cowboy loss. (During the 1994 season, Clinton reached Switzer by phone at the Melrose Hotel to console him. Switzer says, "I think Hillary was out of town and he just wanted to talk some football.")

From the Super Bowl, Switzer told Clinton, "We did it our way, and you're a winner, too—an ol' boy from Arkansas."

That became Switzer's theme of the night: *We did it our way, baby!* As Charles Haley told Switzer while hugging him as the game ended: "Coach, your way is the best and the most fun. Love works, and I thank you."

That had been Switzer's point from the moment he said "we gonna do it": Love works. Not belittling players or cutting backup running backs or throwing planned or unplanned fits. Not cracking "actor" whips or fining those who miss "rat-turd" curfews. Just love. Switzer didn't say "I'm gonna do it." He said *we* are. He wanted the players and assistants to get the credit for the actual Super Bowl victory. But he wanted vindication for the method.

This time, anyway, Switzer's way had worked.

A nice guy had finished first.

Over at his interview station, Emmitt Smith was saying with his usual childlike awe, "I've never had a chance to play for a coach like Barry Switzer. He allows his players to be themselves and to get close to him. It made me want to go out and work harder and play harder for him—not that I did not want to work hard for Jimmy. I had no choice. But coach Switzer made my life and my job easier and made me enjoy the game more. This year I felt like a kid all over again."

But the most vocal of many Cowboy "love" converts was one star who soon would need a little tough love. Michael Irvin was still tongue-lashing the media for bashing Switzer.

Remember what Jones said about how people around Switzer feel his vulnerability and just want to help him? You doubted that any Cowboy, hooked to a lie detector, would call Switzer a great coach. But he was *their* coach. They had returned his love and helped him break through and win a Super Bowl. Irvin said, "You have to give my boy [Switzer] his pops and his props [proper respect]. Because he deserves it. Imagine coming in and the only way you can back it up is by winning a championship."

Imagine how Aikman felt listening to the Michaels and Deions and Haleys—players whose talent he obviously admires—gush love for *Barry Switzer*. How could Aikman bring himself to celebrate a blow being struck for Switzer's way? Would Switzer's way slowly destroy what could be the Team of the Nineties? Would the lack of discipline eat away the foundation until Aikman no longer could overcome Switzer?

The Irvin interview, featuring his criticism of the media, was carried live from the interview tent by the Cowboy radio network. Dale Hansen interrupted to tell KVIL listeners, "Boy, I'm getting tired of this from Michael Irvin. He knows better. He was one of the critics of Barry Switzer during the season . . . I'm tired of hearing his lectures."

Moments later, Hansen apologized on KVIL. After the broadcast, he told *Dallas Morning News* media columnist Barry Horn, "If he [Irvin] is going to scream at people for criticizing Barry Switzer, he is also talking to Troy Aikman. Troy Aikman is far and away Barry Switzer's biggest critic. Do you think if Troy Aikman stood up for Switzer that Dale Hansen or Randy Galloway would be so critical of Switzer?"

Do other championship teams create such divine madness?

Back in the Switzer suite at The Buttes, they no longer needed Marvin Gaye or the stereo. The music sprang from the fingers of Greg Switzer, who's studying to be a concert pianist. On a hotel piano, Greg was indulging himself with an audience-participation number, Ray Charles's "What'd I Say." One after another, family members and friends tried to top each other with clever verses. Kathy Switzer brought down the house with:

> We're at the postgame party
> and we're having a blast.
> Sorry, Dale Hansen,
> this is your last.

During the week, it seemed that everyone around The Buttes had Super Bowl tickets. But everyone was looking for Cowboy Postgame Celebration tickets, said to be worth $1,000 and up on the scalper's market. The event, planned by Jerry Jones's daughter, Charlotte, was being staged on short notice in a giant heated tent pitched out on the desert ground a quarter of a mile from the hotel. Alcohol couldn't be served in a club or hotel past 1 A.M.? Fine, said the Joneses, and turned their bash into one big private party, with buses shuttling constantly from The Buttes' rear entrance down to the tent. Total cost of the party: about $250,000.

When I arrived around 11, I pitied those who had paid dearly for a party ticket. Switzer was at the entrance, well into his champagne, waving dozens of people past overwhelmed ticket-takers. About all you needed to say was "Hey, congratulations, Barry! I'm from Arkansas!" Or, "I'm from Oklahoma!" And Switzer would squint and say, "Hell, get in here." Inside were enough people to comfortably fill two giant tents, and most of them I'd never seen before. They formed a claustrophobic's nightmare of multiplying coats, ties, cocktail jewelry, evening gowns, plastic glasses, paper plates—*help!* Though I couldn't get near the stage at the far end of the tent, somebody said Reba McEntire and Toby Keith were up there performing. The music blasting through the speakers was too loud to be heard. Conversations could take place only by yelling in each other's ear.

Most Cowboy players stopped by the party, but for obvious reasons, didn't stay long. I was told Jerry Jones was up by the stage . . . and over by the gourmet pizza station . . . and over by one of several bars . . . and somewhere in the very middle of the crowd . . . and I figured Jones was so happy that he had morphed into nine or ten Jerrys so he could multiply his good time by nine or ten.

Switzer was hugging just about everyone in sight and yelling sweet everythings in their ears. He threw a hammerlock on me and yelled several sentences in my ear. I wish I could report that he told me he had decided to thumb his nose at his critics and quit. But I could not understand one word he said.

Moments later, Switzer saw Lacewell. Though Lacewell can celebrate with the best of 'em, he appeared quite sober. Switzer gave his old buddy the biggest, longest hug yet. Then Switzer yelled to the crowd around them, "They could blow up this entire fuckin' tent and we'd be the only two sumbitches left standing!"

Lacewell, who isn't much of a hugger, seemed a little embarrassed and didn't hug back very hard.

For Lacewell and many Cowboy officials—excepting Jones—the party password was "relief." There wasn't much joy. Just one long sigh. By vowing to win it all, then signing Deion, they had put themselves in something of a can't-win position. More important than winning was avoiding the firestorm of criticism that would have followed losing. For many in the organization, Switzer's "We did it!" was more of a "Thank God we did it." No freak injuries to the stars. No freakish bounces during the three postseason games. No mutiny. No "him or me" ultimatum from Aikman. The season's (and party's) theme could have been borrowed from a new movie, *Waiting to Exhale*.

This attitude infuriated Kathy Switzer. A few days later she said, "Here we had all our family and friends together. It was a beautiful, great experience. But this was so different than when I was in the locker room after Oklahoma won the national championship in '85. That was a much happier moment. There wasn't one flaw that night. But this was just relief. I mean, where was the champagne [in the locker room]? It's really sad.

"[Earlier in the week] I had said to Charlotte, 'It's too bad one team has to go home a loser.' And she said, 'Kathy, their [Pittsburgh's] high is just getting here. They can be satisfied with that. We've been here and won it.' I understand that. But for the Switzers, we were on Pittsburgh's page. We were just happy to be there. Then at the party, all I heard was 'Well, the monkey's off our back.' Dad was the happiest I had ever seen him, but I guess Dad's spoiled now, too. I guess this will change him the same way."

At the party, Kathy made a surprising request. She asked if I would go with her to talk to Dale Hansen. She never had talked to him, and she wanted to check him out and see what Troy's buddy was saying after her dad had coached the Cowboys to a championship. After Kathy promised not to punch Hansen in the nose, I took her over to where Hansen was holding court and eased into the conversation.

After a while it was just the three of us. Kathy wanted to know what Hansen thought Aikman would do next. All Hansen knew for sure was that Aikman had promised him and Randy Galloway that as soon as the season was over, he would do tell-all interviews for them about Switzer and his "Oklahoma Mafia."

Kathy listened for a while and said, "I still think Troy's going to go into Jerry and say, 'He goes or I go,' and Jerry's going to say, 'Barry, it's been great, but . . .'"

To Kathy's relief, Hansen disagreed. "Troy says he will not do that. But then you have several players telling me Troy won't play for Switzer again, and I don't think winning a Super Bowl will change that attitude."

As I listened, it struck me how shocked the surrounding celebrants would have been to hear the coach's daughter and the quarterback's buddy debate Aikman's future in Dallas. This crowd was ready for their Troy to win them three more Super Bowls. Same time, next year!

About that time Aikman briefly took the stage and made a few remarks, closing with "Have fun tonight and don't drink too much. I'm going to do that for you." That got a big laugh and ovation, though some were probably surprised such an all-American boy like Troy would say something like that. Once again, he was just being honest.

19

MASTERS OF THE UNIVERSE

If you tried to sell the story of Jones and Switzer as fiction, publishers wouldn't buy it. They'd say it's too unbelievable.

—Dale Hansen

A few days after the Super Bowl, Barry Switzer returned triumphant to Norman, Oklahoma. These people, he knew, would be happy for him. He made a grand entrance into that Saturday's University of Oklahoma basketball game. He gladly signed lots of autographs. During a time-out, he jumped alongside the cheerleaders and mock-cheered, exhorting the crowd. He had a ball. He basked.

He no longer felt the "negative haze" he had when the team returned to Dallas. He says, "We *had* finally won the thing, and nobody was content. It was like there was an empty feeling. It was like the only time you could enjoy it was for a few hours after it was over."

But even in Norman, Switzer was haunted by the prospect that, any day, Troy Aikman might walk in and tell Jerry Jones he wouldn't play another game for Barry Switzer. Would Jones actually fire the coach of the Super Bowl champions? Paranoia formed a negative haze over his better judgment. He and his confidants wrestled with his options. Should he quit? Not yet: He didn't want anyone thinking Aikman and Hansen and Galloway and the rest had run him out

of town. Should he, as Larry Lacewell suggested, apologize to Aikman? That way, if Aikman wouldn't accept his apology, Switzer
would know where he stood, once and for all.

No, said Switzer, he wasn't ready to go that far. A friend of
Switzer's said, "He will not kiss Troy's ass."

Soon, back in Dallas, Switzer sat down with Jones and asked
him the question: What if Aikman delivers an ultimatum? Without
hesitation, Jones told Switzer his Cowboy future was "non-nego-
tiable." Nothing Aikman could say would make Jones fire Switzer,
the coach was told. Jones talked in terms of a "ten-year"
Jones/Switzer plan.

Switzer supporters were jubilant. Still, Switzer wasn't sure he
could take more than one more year of the mental cruelty that was
coaching this team. One night over dinner and drinks Switzer told
friends he would coach just one more season. "I think I can talk Jerry
into letting Lacewell do it," Switzer said. Imagine: Larry Lacewell following Jimmy Johnson and Barry Switzer as head coach of the Dallas
Cowboys. His friends doubted Switzer would really quit. But who
would have thought Switzer ever would have been hired?

While Aikman was doing the Leno show, Switzer turned down Letterman and the ESPY Awards. Getting dressed up and made up isn't
Switzer's idea of celebration and recognition at his age. "I've done
all that," he says. "I'm not knocking the ESPYs and ESPN, but to
put on black tie and sit there in the audience with a big grin—that's
work. I'd rather stay here and do something constructive. I've been
to New York enough."

Several times during the season Becky Buwick reminded
Switzer to remember "you've always been a hero, and you're doing
the same job you always did before, no matter what the Dallas
media is saying. Don't read the papers. Negativity sells. Focus on
the team, not on the fantasy. Remember, 'My value comes from me,
not from the media.'" She says, "The thing that's hard with the
Cowboys is to say, 'Wait a minute, what's reality?'"

Very little is real, says Switzer, outside the white lines and the
confines of the coaches' offices. "I'm not sure being an actor isn't
the best trait you can have in this business. I've told Jerry this whole
business is phony. Hundreds of [NFL-related] TV shows . . . some
fat boy sitting there on TV repeating something some deep throat
told him. Everybody's on stage. The players, me, Jerry, everybody."

What was real to Switzer was going to the White House with his
team to see his buddy Bill Clinton.

But this time only eighteen Cowboys chose to make the victors' trip to Washington. After all, they were the first team to win three of four Super Bowls. Many of these players had done the White House after the first two championships. (Cynics cracked that some Cowboys were more interested in visiting the "white house" leased for sexual liaisons in Valley Ranch.)

What was real to Switzer was riding in the team's victory parade through downtown Dallas.

But this time only twenty-eight Cowboys showed up for the parade. Even first-year Cowboy Deion Sanders said he had prior commitments on the West Coast.

You couldn't miss Switzer, though, in one of the first convertibles. Of all the players, coaches, and officials, Switzer appeared to be having the best time as he steadily waved his appreciation to the wave of applause that followed the car. While most players looked a little bored, Switzer genuinely appeared to be getting a kick out of the fifteen-minute ride. "It was a blast," he said, as if talking about a Six Flags Over Texas ride. "I wanted to go around again."

Alongside Switzer in the convertible sat Larry Lacewell, with the amused look of a man watching himself in a dream.

The day before the parade Troy Aikman had surgery on his throwing elbow in Birmingham, Alabama. But he flew straight back to Dallas. "He knew," says Jones, "how much it would mean to our team and our fans to have him in the parade."

Aikman left the parade peeved at Switzer again, for an unlikely reason. A source close to Aikman says, "He couldn't believe Switzer—the head coach—didn't even ask him about his arm. Troy sounded like he was about fifteen years old. He kept saying, 'Can you believe it?'"

Well, yes. They hadn't spoken a word to each other for two months, and Switzer had spent the previous week thinking Aikman might try to get him fired.

But the good news for Switzer was that Aikman still cared enough to be upset. That surprised me. So did this: Aikman told Hansen he wanted to take a rain check on that bombshell interview he had promised to do. Was the Aikman-Switzer relationship about to undergo the same shocking transformation that Aikman vs. Johnson did? Would Switzer give up catching fish for tropical fish?

No.

All that winning had done was force a cease-fire. If Aikman had publicly blasted Switzer after winning a championship with him, Aikman would have come off to some fans as a crybaby. PR advantage: Switzer.

*   *   *

A week or so later I interviewed Jones in his oblong office, which
was originally designed by Tex Schramm. In the distance from the
door to his desk you almost could time players in the 40-yard dash.
We sat in front of Jones's desk and talked for four straight hours,
sustained by Diet Pepsi and a year's worth of meaty topics. Deep
into the interview, when I asked about Aikman vs. Switzer, Jones
began choosing his words as if each were a first-round draft choice.

"First, let me say, Barry is ideal for me. Ideal. But—and this may
surprise you—Troy does not have a Barry issue. Barry has a Troy
issue. It should not be Troy's burden to extend himself into issues with
Barry. It is not Barry's *burden*, but it is his business. There are philo-
sophical differences between the two, having to do with discipline and
structure, and Troy is righter than Barry, if there is a right and wrong
here. Barry and I already have addressed some of the discipline issues,
and I think Troy will see some changes. But I do not think there is any
personality problem between Troy and Barry. Troy and I are not close,
so maybe I don't know for sure. But I don't sense one."

Which led Jones into his "proprietary interest" speech. He sees
Aikman and Switzer as partners with whom he can build the tallest
monument in NFL history. But while the Jones family will be running
the Cowboys "for many years," he says, Aikman has only a "window
of opportunity" as a quarterback. In that time, said Jones, "Troy
could become the most successful player in the history of the game."

Meaning, he could win more Super Bowls than anybody ever.
Aikman had told me, "I know I'll never have a break-out year."
Meaning, he would never have record-setting yardage and
touchdown-pass numbers while sharing the offense with Emmitt
Smith. "But I know we could win a lot of Super Bowls."

Jones's message: Aikman should try to make the best of what is
still a great situation.

As a reporter, I was remiss. But I was hesitant to question Jones
more specifically about what I knew about the many incidents and
accusations involving the coach and the quarterback. Maybe I
hadn't yet done enough research. Or maybe I was still struggling to
believe they really happened.

A few weeks later Jones called and said he needed to talk. Obviously, *he* had done more research. I met him at his new home in
Highland Park, where artisans still climbed and kneeled, finishing
the hand-carving and detail-painting. It's not the mansion's size that
inspires awe, it's the intricate carving and painting of the walls, ceil-
ings, cabinets—seemingly every surface in the house. Though the

Joneses moved in at Christmas, the house remains under construction for the fourth year.

Jones eagerly showed me his latest acquisition, a Norman Rockwell painting for which he paid more than $1 million. *The Flip* was a *Saturday Evening Post* cover in 1950. Jones stood smiling and gazing at it for maybe a minute, which could have been his personal record for standing without speaking.

Jones also took me down to his favorite room, a subterranean den with a bar and walls lined with hand-carved family and Super Bowl crests. One wall opens by remote control to reveal a wide-screen TV. Jones flipped it on for a moment and—I swear—a tape of an old *Dallas* TV show episode was in the VCR.

Among the pictures on the walls were two taken at stadiums. One is Jones's wife, Gene, with Joe Namath; the other is Jerry, Gene, and Kevin Costner. Gene is looking at Costner, well, admiringly. "She got caught, didn't she?" Jones said with a big grin.

We wound up back at the dining room table. This time, if possible, I did most of the talking. I made Jones aware of all the hand-carved details of the Aikman-Switzer clashes. Jones concluded that his coach occasionally "went off half-cocked" and "made some bad judgments," based on information provided by those he trusted.

That said, Jones emphasized he was getting more comfortable with Switzer by the day. Winning the first Super Bowl changed Jimmy Johnson, said Jones. Not Switzer. "He hasn't changed a bit."

But: "I want Barry to use all the skills God gave him—to do everything in his power to improve this relationship. And I want Troy to be receptive. I want the assistant coaches to start telling Troy what Barry *does* in staff meetings. They've been hesitant, because they knew Troy wasn't receptive before. But I want them all to be man enough to do that now."

I told Jones he was in for even bigger problems with these two. "Oh," he said, "it will be a challenge."

What if Aikman walks in and says he just can't take it anymore?

"It will not come to that," Jones said.

If it does, say several sources close to Jones, the owner will find a way to talk Aikman out of it.

As Jones walked me out to my car, I couldn't help noticing the physical toll his seven seasons in Dallas have taken on him. The pouches under his eyes have deepened. He has gained some weight. After all, he doesn't even play golf. The Dallas Cowboys are his life.

But Jerry Jones loves his life.

For an unknown businessman, there is no faster route to fame—or infamy—than buying a sports franchise. Jones got famous even quicker than he got rich. Just because he owns a football team, Jones is now widely recognized on the streets of New York and Los Angeles. Similarly, Jones could have become a national laughing-stock if Jimmy Johnson's Cowboys hadn't soon started winning.

But the major difference between Jones and most sports owners is that he operates his team on a daily basis. His secrets to success? "You need to know enough [about football] to know what you don't know. You need to have the love and total [365-day] commitment [to running the franchise]. You need to use logic—just pure and simple logic. And you need some imagination, some creativity."

Most people get too distracted by everything that is *Jerry*! to realize he's smarter than his competition.

Though I often was struck by how lonely and unhappy Aikman and Switzer could be, those adjectives never applied to Jerry Jones. He has the three Lombardi trophies in his new castle. He has the beautiful wife, the adoring children, and the grandchildren. He has the reputation as one of the most powerful men in sports. He has his best buddy, Barry. He has more than both. He has it all.

Jerry, Barry, and Larry took a break from preparing for the NFL draft to saddle up Jones's jet and fly to Las Vegas for the Tyson-Bruno fight. Jones and Switzer attracted about as much attention as any of the ringside celebrities. You can only imagine how they strutted their stuff. A media friend says they now think they're "Masters of the Universe," borrowing from Tom Wolfe's *Bonfire of the Vanities*. For sure, Valley Ranch is one big bonfire of vanities. For years Cowboy players have gone down in the flames that are Cowboy fame. It will be interesting to see who gets burned during this dynasty.

Yet Jerry, Barry, and Larry returned safely from Vegas and again were in rare form on draft day, as ESPN contrasted shots of their "war room" against Jimmy Johnson's in Miami. About four minutes after the Cowboy brass had made their first pick—Kavicka Pittman of McNeese State—they were cued that they were about to be on live. Trying to keep from laughing, Jerry, Barry, and Larry went into Jimmy-style fist-pumping. It wasn't so much that they were mocking him, but playing the game the way Jimmy taught them. They were actors, and all the world was their stage.

Right on cue, an ESPN commentator said, "As you can see, the Cowboys are very excited about their pick."

About two months after the Super Bowl, Aikman and Switzer finally talked, in the coach's office. The conversation degenerated into a lot of *You said* and *No, I didn't*. There were exaggerations and denials on both sides. Aikman told me he suggested to Switzer that

I sit in with them next time, to verify what I had been told by each. Switzer told me Aikman did not suggest that.

I told both of them I'd be glad to sit between them. Each might learn something. Maybe they have, if they're reading this book.

From a distance, it appears Barry Switzer has it all. He has three children who love him. He has dozens of "sons"—ex-Sooners—who love him. He has many Dallas Cowboy stars who love him. He has an owner who's nuts about him. He has sex appeal and pied-piper charisma. He has wealth and fame. He has the Switzer Luck.

Can you believe it? He even has a Super Bowl ring.

Several rival coaches and general managers have scoffed that Jones basically gave Switzer that ring by merely hiring him. But that's not true. Switzer earned his ring by doing something many coaches in his position wouldn't have—by merely persevering. Any coach following Johnson would have had problems. Many eventually would have been overwhelmed. Handling the psyche of this football team is like handling nitroglycerin. At least Switzer didn't drop it. No matter what he did or didn't do as coach, at least he didn't buckle under some of the most extreme media and fan criticism a coach has experienced. Just as Switzer can't know the pressures of playing quarterback for the Cowboys, Aikman can't know the pressures of coaching them.

Switzer should be proud of his ring.

Yet his friends in Oklahoma say he has only one real friend in Dallas—Dale Boutwell, his old running buddy from Cotton Plant, Arkansas. Friends say Switzer still seems miserable at times, still drinks too much on occasion, still can be a dangerous influence on those he loves the most—such as his ex-players. One said, "You get around him, and you love him so much that it's almost like you want to please him and you start doing some of the stuff he does."

The wild stuff. The Frank Switzer stuff. You hope Barry Switzer won't always feel trapped in his past. You hope that, no matter how blessed he is, he won't always feel he's the bootlegger's boy.

In mid-April I spoke one last time to Aikman. He didn't sound as if he were the proud owner of three Super Bowl rings collected in just four years. He came across more like a tormented, disillusioned victim of the three-ring circus that is the Dallas Cowboys.

Aikman was reacting to the recent drug charges against Michael Irvin the way the fan in the street was—with surprise, dismay, and perhaps anger. Aikman remains one Cowboy—one of the few, probably—who actually believes pro athletes should be role models. It was as if Irvin and other Cowboys were tarnishing America's—and Aikman's—view of America's Team as the country's foremost role models.

"The shine is off the star," Aikman told me.

Several of his confidants were predicting Aikman's disenchantment would become a dangerous distraction for the quarterback during the 1996 season and, as he turned thirty on November 21, would drive him closer to retirement. They predicted that constant tarnished-star questions from the media would be so humiliating for Aikman that he would lose heart and focus. Aikman, they said, couldn't understand why Jerry Jones hadn't rebuked Irvin publicly or vowed to clean up some of the out-of-control behavior on the team.

Yet Jones never pretended to be in the business of saving souls or hiring role models. To anyone close to the team, the concept of the Dallas Cowboys being the country's most exemplary citizens has been laughable since Tom Landry's early days as coach. They're pro football players, for heaven's sake. At least Jones doesn't present them as anything more. From the start Jones has been about nothing more than winning bragging rights for himself and his customers. He's no angel. His coach is no angel. No more than four or five of his players—if that—would qualify as role models.

Aikman himself has some flaws (smokeless tobacco, foul language, beer drinking) a parent wouldn't want a child to emulate.

Yet in seven NFL seasons, Jones's teams have won one more Super Bowl than Landry's did in twenty-nine years. In the end, that's all that most fans truly care about or remember. What's more, Jones has provided America with its best real-life soap opera—with its most consistently entertaining team on and off the field.

Yet in the end trophies can't be won without an Aikman.

Near the end of our conversation, Aikman reflected on the two most trying years of his football life. He sighed and said that somehow he would make it work with Barry Switzer. For now, he has no other choice.

For now.

More than ever, the Cowboys are a team of nitro egos one jostle away from implosion. Only winning will keep this team from the sudden rubble of Aikman vs. the players who love Switzer. Yet even winning couldn't ultimately keep Jones and Jimmy Johnson from splitting like atoms.

Aikman-Switzer has the same volatile potential.

But in mid-April Troy Aikman said, "I'm worn out from all this—it has eaten me up for two years. I mean, it got so bad last year we had assistant coaches threatening to retire. But I don't know what to do about it. I guess it's just my problem. I guess I'll just have to live with it. I'll just keep doing things the same way I've always done them. I'll be just as competitive and committed to winning."

Somewhere, Jerry Jones was smiling.